Auguste Bébian: Paving the Way for Deaf Emancipation

Auguste Bébian: Paving the Way for Deaf Emancipation

Fabrice Bertin

Translated from the French
by Nicolas Carter and Chris Hinton

ISBN: 978-2-36616-102-1 ISSN: 2428-6362
Legal deposit: July 2023

French version published April 2019 (ISBN: 978-2-36616-066-6)
Publication Director: Murielle Mauguin

Distributed by
Gallaudet University Press
Washington, DC
gupress.gallaudet.edu

...

French original reread by Laurent Strumanne, INSEI (INSHEA)
Cover image: Anne-Laure Draisey, INSEI (INSHEA)

Works published in the collection "Recherches"

directed by Dimitri Afgoustidis

Explore these and other works at *www.inshea.fr*

Excellence corporelle et handicap
Boxe en France, capoeira au Brésil
Martial Meziani - 2015

Handicap et parentalité. Le principe du pangolin
Chantal Lavigne - 2015

Vivre avec des troubles psychiques et devenir adulte
Audrey Parron - 2016

Évolution de jeunes enfants avec autisme
Impact des modes et des durées du suivi
Chrystalla Yianni Coudurier - 2016

Réinventer l'école ?
Politiques, conceptions et pratiques dites inclusives
Greta Pelgrims and Jean-Michel Perez (eds.) - 2016

Transformer ses pratiques d'enseignement
pour scolariser des élèves avec autisme
Philippe Garnier - 2016

Sexualité et handicap mental
Lucie Nayak - 2017

Le développement de pratiques professionnelles inclusives
dans l'enseignement secondaire. Une étude au Québec
Geneviève Bergeron - 2018

The original French version of this book:
Auguste Bébian et les Sourds : le chemin de l'émancipation
Fabrice Bertin - 2019

La formation des pédagogues sourds
Véronique Geffroy - 2020

Inclusion is coming : Vulnérables et tourmentés dans *Game of Thrones*
Thierry Bourgoin - 2020

La vision des inclus. Ethnographie d'un dispositif
pour l'inclusion scolaire (Ulis)
Godefroy Lansade - 2021

Vulnérabilités en écho dans les métiers relationnels :
les savoirs professionnels interrogés
Matthieu Laville and Philippe Mazereau (eds.) - 2021

Altérité(s) et société inclusive
Isabelle Queval (ed.) - 2022

La scolarisation de l'enfant-voyageur en France
Problème pédagogique ou politique ?
Virginie Dufournet Coestier - 2022

Accompagnement inclusif pour des enfants
présentant un Trouble du spectre de l'autisme
Gaëtan Briet - 2023

Auguste Bébian: Paving the Way for Deaf Emancipation
Fabrice Bertin - 2023

By the same author

- *Les Sourds. Une minorité invisible* (Autrement, 2010)
- *Ferdinand Berthier ou le rêve d'une nation Sourde* (M. Companys, 2010)
- *Le théorème de la chaussette* (Eyes, 2016)

Contents

Portrait of Auguste Bébian
by Marie-Joseph-Charles Chassevent
Commissioned in 1879-80 by the INSMP
Oil on canvas, 200*140 cm
Ref. F/21/203 in the Arcade database of the French Ministry of Culture

Acknowledgements

The research work that culminated in this book has been, above all, a collective adventure. A true adventure in the sense that research into Auguste Bébian is a challenge, a leap into the unknown, so deeply hidden are the documents from which we can retrace his life. My heartfelt thanks are therefore due to the association "*Bébian, un autre monde*" and in particular to its president, Geneviève Pomet, who gave me the initial momentum. Across the ocean, our daily, rich and enthusiastic exchanges nourished my thinking. The sharp eye and dogged perseverance of Ninja – the cunningly inverted pseudonym of Janine Leclerc, a peerless detective despite her tender age of 68 (also cunningly inverted), were essential in negotiating the sometimes hazardous paths of the Bébian/Michaux family tree. Thank you, Ninja!

A warm thank you also to everyone whose path I crossed, briefly or more lastingly, in France, in Guadeloupe or elsewhere, who gave of their time and effort and helped point me in the right direction: Yves Bernard, Michelle Balle-Stinkwich, Lennart Anderson, Caroline Brizard, Dimitri Garnier, Gérard Lafleur, Julie Bernard Le Bec… the list is far from exhaustive.

Special thanks are due to Dimitri Afgoustidis, who directs the "Recherches" collection at INSHEA, for his attentiveness and encouragement; to Stéphane Gonzalez, president of the association Eyes Éditions for the considerable support he provided; and to the management team at the Institut National des Jeunes Sourds in Paris, for allowing me to access and reproduce previously unseen documents.

The title of this English-language version was the subject of long and intense reflection on how best to represent the part played by this unique figure who traced out the path to Deaf emancipation without being able to follow it, this man who forged the key to open a door he would never cross, the educator who took on the role of guide, leading the way to citizenship by devising tools to make visible, and draw people's gaze toward, the "gestures" naturally used by the Deaf. He was the first to demonstrate that these gestures constituted a complete linguistic system, a language in its own right, and not some kind of semaphore, and that as a consequence, bilingual education for Deaf children was the only possible way to guarantee autonomy, and – above all – that this language was the expression of a culture and an identity. With this in mind, I would like to extend my sincere thanks to Professor H-Dirksen L. Bauman of Gallaudet University, and to my colleagues and friends at the EHESS, Soline Vennetier and Andrea Benvenuto.

The active, constructive and patient reflection of the translators of this book, Nicolas Carter and Chris Hinton, must also be warmly saluted. They demonstrated great sensitivity to the political dimension as well as to the purely linguistic challenges. Thanks, lads!

Two quotations – one from the first Deaf professor, Ferdinand Berthier, the other from Claudius Forestier (1810-1891), a former INSMP student and later principal of the Lyon Institution for Deaf-Mutes[1] – ultimately set the tone for this whole endeavor: in his *Notice sur la vie et les ouvrages d'Auguste Bébian* (Ledoyen, 1839, p. 10), Berthier writes: "*Bébian was our master. It is to him that we owe the ability to share with our brothers in misfortune the thousand kinds of joy that touch our souls, or, to put it more simply, the ability to continue his presence among them.*" Forestier, in an address to the Paris Academy of Moral and Political Sciences, decrying the absurdity of the decisions taken in Milan in 1880 at the congress "for the improvement of the fate of the deaf-mute," also pays tribute to the "master" Bébian: "*Our great master Bébian underlined the superiority of sign language over artificial speech…*"

This book received a grant from the Tepsis Laboratory of Excellence (ANR-11-LABX-0067) as part of the "Investing for the Future" Program (*Programme Investissements d'Avenir*).

Finally, I would like to dedicate this book to Fred, for all the reasons he knows.

And my everlasting gratitude to that friend across time and frontiers: Auguste Bébian.

1. See pp. 139-140.

A capital question: **deaf/Deaf**

"Which one are you", Nancy Rourke, 2010

In this work, the author has chosen to follow common usage in linguistics and the social sciences: the term "deaf", spelt without a capital letter, refers to the entire non-hearing population, i.e. to the physiological and pathological aspect, whereas "Deaf" refers to linguistic and cultural membership of an anthropologically defined minority, as for any ethnic group; the capital letter in no way reflects a value judgment.

This distinction between "deaf" and "Deaf" was employed for the first time in 1972 by the linguist James Woodward from Gallaudet University (Washington D.C.) to clarify the object of his argument. It also reflects two different perceptions of the same subject: a person with little or no hearing, and a person who is culturally differentiated. It is not a mere typographical detail; as will be seen in the coming pages, these perceptions have been translated into actions across the centuries. If knowing what – or rather who – we are talking about is so fundamental, it is because the way we choose to name them contains the seeds of an answer: should we focus on something that is missing and seek to compensate for it,[1] or should we place deafness within the context of a certain universality and see it simply as a singular way of being in the world?

This terminology, in addition to identifying what precisely we are discussing, creates a degree of distantiation with regard to genetic determinism and the clinical dimension of deafness. Being Deaf is above all about being a speaker of sign language, as the sociologist Bernard Mottez reminds us: "*Hard-of-hearing is something that comes naturally. It's physical. Deaf is something you become. It's social. You learn it. You take it. You catch it. You catch it from your own: your peers, your elders, from Deaf adults.*"[2]

The categorization "Deaf" encompasses a more diverse and heterogeneous population than the term "deaf-mute",[3] (which usually refers to the congenitally profoundly deaf): a person affected by central deafness (recognized as being "hard of hearing") can identify as Deaf, since the physiological criterion is not relevant. For clarifying the difference between medical and social models of deafness, it is true that sign language is the product of what was originally a physiological trait (the total absence of hearing) and this linguistic system remains inherently associated with deaf people, for whom it is their first language. That being said, we should not allow the relationship between deafness and sign language to overshadow the linguistic facts: just as speaking French is not "reserved" to the French alone, audiometric criteria are by no means a pre-requisite for using sign language.

This spelling convention is, of course, anachronistic in as far as "Deaf issues" were not "a thing" in the 19th century, but we take

1. The notion of "missing" is of course relative, the sense of "completeness" being inevitably subjective.
2. Bernard Mottez, "Quelques aspects de la culture sourde", *Les sourds existent-ils ?*, texts collected and presented by Andrea Benvenuto, Paris, L'Harmattan, 2006, p. 151.
3. The term "deaf-mute" is now avoided, but it will feature widely in this book, when citing 19th-century and early 20th-century texts, as it was then in common usage.

the liberty of adopting it in order to underline this cultural reality that Auguste Bébian brought to light,[4] on the grounds that realities preexist their designation: such "deliberate anachronisms" are a part of History, though we generally try to avoid them.

4. François Buton, "L'éducation des sourds-muets au XIXe siècle. Description d'une activité sociale", *Le Mouvement social*, 2008/2 n° 223, p. 69.

Preamble
Writing a biography: choosing between myth and oblivion

1. A double-edged task

Writing about someone's life, whoever he or she may be, is a difficult task, a more or less inaccessible horizon in as much as it is an illusion to think one can grasp all of a person's multiple dimensions: for example, it is not always possible to understand how a private event might have affected a public action. To comprehend someone's existence or thoughts based on what posterity has retained, based on what that person has revealed at a given moment in time, in a specific context, whether by choice or strategy, is a challenge; and this is true whether they have written numerous works, as in the case of Garibaldi,[1] or just one, as in the case of Auguste Bébian.[2] Indeed, what can we truly know about someone's hopes, dreams, passions or discouragements? It is not so much a question of deconstructing a character's mythical nature, as one of peeling away the layers: the writing of a myth is a revealing process. Yet, as historian François Dosse so rightly says when he speaks of a "biographical wager":[3]

> *"Like history, a biography is first written in the present tense, but within a relationship of even greater involvement, inasmuch as the writer's empathy is always required."*

---

1. Jérôme Grévy, *Garibaldi*, Presses de Sciences Po, 2001.
2. *Notice sur la vie et les ouvrages de Auguste Bébian, ancien censeur de l'Institut royal des sourds-muets* (J. Ledoyen, 1839, Paris) by Ferdinand Berthier is the only biography of Bébian. The serial published between May 19 and June 14, 1911 in the Guadeloupean newspaper *Le Colonial*, recounting Auguste Bébian's life, implicitly refers to this.
3. François Dosse, *Le pari biographique*, Paris: La Découverte, 2005, p. 7.

As a historical genre, biography poses a certain number of problems for historians, while at the same time making it possible to put into perspective and grasp what motivates a given collective movement. The genesis of a "movement" comes into being through personal itineraries that are, *a posteriori*, masked by this collective facet… As summed up by historian Guillaume Piketty, using the case of the Resistance during the Second World War, which we tend to look upon as a monolithic ideology:[4]

> *"Before being a history of (re)groupings, the history of the Resistance is a matter of individual choices, of personal reactions. It forces one to remember the concepts of free will and choice, to which it adds a particular intensity. In the early stages at least, the decision to resist was always taken in isolation, against the majority, without any knowledge of what was to come."*

Biography writing is sometimes a balancing act: one should not so much reconstruct a person's history as consider it from a global perspective. For example, above and beyond his unusual pathway, the person "Auguste Bébian" reveals a certain dynamic, a specific phase in the construction of the history of Deaf people. This movement, this path of thought, then leads to concrete actions. Such an individual path raises questions relating to a given moment in time, during periods of serenity or on the contrary of adversity and doubt. Jean-François Sirinelli explains this in the introduction to his Dictionary of French Political Life in the 20th Century:[5]

---

4. Guillaume Piketty, "La biographie comme genre historique ? Étude de cas", *Vingtième siècle : Revue d'histoire*, n°63, July-September 1999, p. 124.
5. Jean-François Sirinelli (ed.), *Dictionnaire de la vie politique française au XXe siècle*, Paris, PUF, 1995, p. VI, Guillaume Piketty, *ibid*. See also René Pilorget, "La biographie comme genre historique", *Revue d'histoire diplomatique*, Jan.-June 1982, pp. 5-42 ; Philippe Levillain, "Les protagonistes : de la biographie", in René Rémond (ed.), *Pour une histoire politique*, Paris: le Seuil, 1988, pp. 121-159 and Pierre Centlivres, Daniel Fabre and Françoise Zonabend (eds.), *La fabrique du héros*, Paris: MSH, 1999.

"Although for a long time an implicit interdiction weighed upon the biographical approach, those times are fortunately over, for it is true that such an approach, far from being reductive, on the contrary allows for a wide sweep of the net; the political stakes of an era, the possible routes open to individual choice, and the parameters that weigh upon this choice can be implicitly understood."

As we shall see in the next section, biographical study has gradually found its epistemological place in the historical field. Independently of these methodological considerations, people have always written about other people's lives, with different objectives, from hagiography to simple narrative: to tell, to understand or to convince.

2. A study long disdained

In 1896, in *Revue historique*, which he had himself founded twenty years earlier, Gabriel Monod wrote:[6]

In history, we have become too accustomed to a desire for the brilliant, resounding and ephemeral manifestations of human activity, great events or great men, instead of focusing on the great and slow movements of institutions, of economic and social conditions."

This opinion sums up the consideration given to scholarly biographies. The 19th century, which saw history emerge as a field of research, was not conducive to the genre, perceived with contempt and synonymous with amateurism. At a time when history was establishing itself, biography was considered unworthy of sharing such progress: a lengthy eclipse began, lasting until the end of the 1980s![7] Historian Marc Ferro, co-director of the *Les Annales* review,

6. Gabriel Monod, *Revue historique*, n°7-8, 1896, p. 325 quoted by Anne Levallois, "Le retour de la biographie", *L'homme et la société*, n°146, Oct.-Dec. 2002.

7. In 1989 Marc Ferro, historian and co-director of *Annales*, published an article with an evocative title in *Magazine littéraire* : "La biographie, cette handicapée

was the first to demonstrate scholarly biography's "return to grace" when he published a voluminous study of Pétain in 1987.[8] The journal is symbolic, advocating a "new history," freed from events and great men and centered on the long view, on the history of mentalities. However, we must also underline Michel Foucault's initiative a decade earlier, in the 1970s, when he instigated a project to write "the lives of infamous men",[9] which took concrete form in 1978 with the creation of the collection entitled *Les vies parallèles*:[10] rather than writing about the lives of illustrious men, he wanted to shed light on those that remained in the shadows, lives strewn with pitfalls of all kinds.

The biography of Auguste Bébian was written in 1839, the year of his death, by Ferdinand Berthier.[11] The latter was not a historian in the strict sense of the word (we must remember that professional historians did not yet exist), but he was a recognized intellectual: at that time he was a member of the Historical Institute of France, a correspondent of the Geographical and Historical Institute of Brazil,[12] and the eldest of the teachers at the Royal Institute for Deaf-Mutes in Paris.[13] He had himself been first a student and then a friend of

---

de l'histoire" ("Biography as crippled history") (April 1989). He discusses two symposia that had just taken place: one on the Russian revolution of 1905, without referring to Tsar Nicolas II, and the other on the Vichy government that made no mention of Pétain!
Dosse, *Le pari biographique*, p. 111.

8. Marc Ferro, *Pétain*, Paris: Fayard, 1987.
9. Michel Foucault, "La vie des hommes infâmes" (The Lives of Infamous Men) in *Les cahiers du chemin,* n°29, 15 Jan. 1977, quoted in *Dits et écrits*, Gallimard, vol. III, 1994.
10. This is the title of a collection published in 1978 by Gallimard. Short-lived, this collection included just eight works, the first being on the subject of hermaphrodite Herculine Barbin, who committed suicide in 1868.
11. Ferdinand Berthier, *Notice sur la vie et les ouvrages d'Auguste Bébian, ancien censeur de l'Institut royal des Sourds-muets*, Paris: Ledoyen, 1839.
12. He listed this works on the cover of *Les sourds-muets avant et après l'abbé de l'Épée*, published in 1840.
13. In 1829, Ferdinand Berthier and Alphonse Lenoir, also Deaf, became full teachers at the INSMP out of a total number of six teachers and a teaching staff of twenty-six (sixteen men and ten women: teachers, but also aspirant

Bébian's: the biography is therefore a form of homage, and during this post-revolutionary period, it was customary to write history in such a way as to legitimize past events or actions.[14] Since the beginning of the century history had in fact been considered as an intellectual discipline in its own right,[15] but historians gradually become aware of the fundamental importance of original sources and of a certain quality of reflection when writing history:[16] Augustin Thierry (1795-1856) and Jules Michelet (1798-1874) are perhaps the most emblematic of the "romantic" historians who characterize this period. It is in the following manner that Augustin Thierry explained what led him to become a historian:[17]

> *"In 1817, motivated by the burning desire to contribute to the triumph of constitutional opinions, I set about searching in history books for*

---

teachers, tutors, *répétiteurs*, "deaf-mute" monitors (two men and two women), workshop foremen (tailor, cobbler...), drawing master and writing mistress). Yves Bernard, *Approche de la gestualité à l'institution des sourds-muets de Paris, XVIIIe-XIXe siècles*, doctoral thesis, Université Paris V, 1999, p. 483.

14. Christian Amalvi, *De l'art et la manière d'accommoder les héros de l'histoire de France*, Paris, Albin Michel, 1988; Jacques Guilhaumou, Patrick Garcia, Jacques Lévy and Marie-Flore Mattei, in collaboration with Marie-Hélène Lechien and Jean-Claude Pompougnac, *Révolutions, fin et suite. Les mutations du changement social et de ses représentations saisies à travers l'image de la Révolution française et les pratiques du bicentenaire, Annales historiques de la Révolution française*, 1992, vol. 287, n° 1, pp. 140-142; Y. Delaporte, *Les Sourds, c'est comme ça*, MSH, 2002. The myth surrounding Abbé de l'Épée's encounter with the deaf female twins, at the origin of the lessons he went on to develop *"is nothing more than a series of symbols: the darkness and the natural elements unleashed symbolize the state of confusion into which the Deaf were plunged, while the light glimpsed from the house where the twins live brings the promise of the shift from a state of wildness to one of culture."* Yves Delaporte, "L'abbé de l'Épée : de la légende au mythe", *Art pi !*, special edition, 2012.
15. France's national archives were created in 1808, which indicates a growing awareness; the École Nationale des Chartes was created in 1821 as an establishment for the teaching of history. Jean and Lucie Favier, *Archives nationales. Quinze siècles d'histoire,* Paris: Nathan, 1988; Lucie Favier, *La mémoire de l'État. Histoire des Archives nationales*, Paris: Fayard, 2004.
16. Philippe Poirrier, *Introduction à l'historiographie*, Paris, Belin, 2009.
17. Augustin Thierry, *Lettres sur l'histoire de France*, Paris, Just Tessier, fifth edition, 1836.

> *proofs and arguments that would support my political ideas.* [...] *Without ceasing to subordinate the facts to the use I wished to make of them, I observed them with curiosity, even when they proved nothing for the cause I hoped to serve* [...]."

As we can see, historiography, the writing of history, has a utilitarian function, and Berthier is no exception to the rule: his understanding of the events creates a feeling of rupture.[18] The writings of Louis-Émile Vauchelet[19] or Jules Ballet[20] subsequent to *Notice sur la vie et les ouvrages de Auguste Bébian*[21] are largely based on this first biography.[22] In fact, is it a biography or a hagiography?

The determination of the "historians" of those post-Revolutionary years to as far as possible legitimize the course of events, and to show that a certain intellectual and moral regeneration was inhe-

---

18. For example, Auguste Bébian's date of birth, which Berthier gives as August 4 in his book (*Notice*, p. 1) coincides with the date of the abolition of privileges. Is he establishing a parallel? The emphatic sentences *("there are men whose modest and laborious life, for a long time buried in the silence of office and study, wait only for an opportunity to come out into the open, to astonish those around them, and, taking up a useful specialty, to conquer by perseverance a reputation victorious over oblivion and ingratitude. He whose life and works I am about to sketch, monuments to a higher intellect and to a devotion tested by injustice and persecution, is one of the few benefactors of humanity who are entitled to the recognition of their contemporaries and of the future",* ibid.) along with those that show that there is a before and an after *("Before Bébian, our weak imagination,* taking fright at *the slightest difficulty...",* Notice, p. 11), do they not serve to highlight the exceptional nature of the character?
19. The newspaper *Le Colonial*, May 19- June 14, 1911.
20. Jules Ballet was registrar of mortgages in Pointe-à-Pitre and inspector for the bank of Guadeloupe: he was a student at the mutual school run by Bébian. Schankenbourg, Ch. (2011). in Danielle Bégot, *Guide de la recherche en histoire antillaise et guyanaise Guadeloupe, Martinique, Saint-Domingue, Guyane, XVII*[e]*-XX*[e] *siècles*, Paris: CTHS, 2011.
21. Berthier, Notice.
22. For example, Louis Vauchelet quotes extensively from Ferdinand Berthier's work (*Notice*) and repeats certain formulations to the letter (to explain Laurent Clerc's departure, he uses the same words as Berthier: *"forced by his shamefully modest salary,"* or he recounts the episode of the Duchess of Berry's visit in the same terms).

rent in the Revolution, is perceptible in Berthier's work. They all tended to emphasize the qualities and genius of their people[23] in their writings: the period was that of the foundation of the great "national stories". Bébian, says Berthier, is one "*of the small number of these benefactors of humanity*,"[24] a pantheon in which Abbé de l'Épée, "*an angel fallen from heaven*,"[25] "*the messiah of a people far too long in decline*,"[26] has the central role. Auguste Bébian is presented from an exceptional angle, to such an extent that nearly fifty years later, Benjamin Dubois, himself Deaf, who could not have known him, justifies the reproduction of articles or paragraphs in his *Journal des sourds et des sourds-muets* – writings previously published in the *Journal des sourds-muets et des aveugles* run by Bébian himself – by the fact that the latter had achieved a degree of relevance that remains unprecedented:[27]

> *"The pages we are reproducing here will show just how observant Bébian was. So far, we know of no hearing-speaker who has surpassed or even equaled him… what Bébian recorded in 1826 corroborates point for point their own remarks on the deaf-mutes of today."*

23. On several occasions Berthier mentions the deaf-mute nation, particularly prior to the establishment of the Second Empire (1852). At the opening of the 1856 banquet, he declares: "*A brief explanation, in passing, concerning the term Nation that we thought we could give ourselves, and which seemed to some to incorporate our very firm intention to reject the society of our speaking brothers. Far from it!* […]", Société centrale des sourds-muets de Paris. *Banquets des sourds-muets réunis pour fêter la naissance de l'abbé de l'Épée*, Paris: Hachette, vol. II. Florence Encrevé, *Les sourds dans la société française au XIX*e *siècle. Idée de progrès et langue des signes*, Grâne: Créaphis, 2012, p. 121.
24. Berthier, Notice, p. 1.
25. Ferdinand Berthier, *Les sourds-muets, avant et depuis l'abbé de l'Épée*, J. Ledoyen, 1840, p. 8.
26. Société centrale des sourds-muets de Paris, *Banquets…*, Paris: Hachette, t. III., 1864.
27. Benjamin Dubois, "Physiologie du sourd-muet, par Bébian", *L'abbé de l'Épée. Journal des sourds et des sourds-muets*, n°2, 1888, p. 28.

There is undoubtedly a mythical, legendary dimension to Berthier's *Notice*, which other sources can verify.[28] Without ignoring this, we should explain that the aim of our work is not "*to destroy the myths in order to reach the truth*," but to use them as an object of study to try to understand what they reveal.[29]

The historian Alain Corbin, who deliberately chose to make known a certain Louis-François Pinagot, a clog maker from Orne in Normandy who lived in the 19th century, and to retrace his life as far as possible, poses a fundamental problem for biographical history: the individuation of identity markers. Even though he considers Pinagot's life to be essentially stamped with the seal of "subsistence requirements," he examines an extremely rich array of social and cultural phenomena that apparently permeated his life course. He does not content himself with reconstructing affective relationships, forms of sociability, language, education, religion, and money. Convinced that the senses, and their perception by society, are historically dated, he also considers other dimensions such as the physical landscape, sound or smellscapes, the sense of the past or the construction of citizenship. The identification of all these identity markers also requires a considerable effort of disorientation by the historian: one must rethink the temporalities of village society at the end of the 18th century and the beginning of the 19th, i.e. the rhythm of existence and the spatio-temporal framework in which it evolves:[30]

> "[…] *To take just one example, consider the familiar stages of the French Revolution as it is taught today* […] *I doubt that this has anything*

28. For example, the documents preserved in the archives provide accurate details of the circumstances that led to Auguste Bébian's dismissal from his position as, on January 3, 1821. These circumstances, or even any account of them, do not appear in *Notice*.
    AMHCS, Bébian bundle, Pinart collection.
29. Grévy, *Garibaldi*, p 16.
30. Alain Corbin, *The life of an unknown: The rediscovered world of a clog maker in nineteenth-century France*, trans. A. Goldhammer, Columbia University Press, 2001, p. 128.

to do with the way in which Louis-François Pinagot thought about the late eighteenth century, to the extent that he thought in terms of periods at all."

The epistemology of biography has thus significantly evolved and is no longer centered solely on one individual: that is the central challenge of this book.

Preface
A central place in the history of the Deaf community

The year 1791[1] marks a key date in the history of the Deaf community: the official creation of France's National Institution for Deaf-Mutes in Paris (INSMP[2] – *L'institution Nationale des Sourds-Muets de Paris*), the world's first establishment for the education of deaf people. This official acceptance of responsibility followed on from the philanthropic initiative of Charles-Michel de l'Épée, known as Abbé de l'Épée, to bring poor children and adolescents

1. The decree of July 29 formalized the allocation of the former premises of the Célestins convent to the school run by Abbé de l'Épée (a decision made the previous year by the Paris authorities). The new Institution was to share the premises with Haüy Valentin's Institute for Blind Youth (created by decree on September 28). This highly conflictual cohabitation (Haüy was a revolutionary, Sicard was not) lasted just three years: on February 13, 1794, *"The Institution for the Deaf-Mutes of Paris is moving to the Saint-Magloire Seminary in the Rue du Faubourg Saint-Jacques."* François Buton, *L'administration des faveurs. L'État, les sourds et les aveugles (1789-1885)*, Rennes: PUR, 2009, p. 63 and AN, série F 17 1036, pièce n° 516, *Actes de la commune de Paris pendant la Révolution*, quoted by Florence Encrevé, *Les sourds dans la société française au XIXe siècle. Idée de progrès et langue des signes*, Paris: Créaphis, 2012, p. 78
2. The INSMP bears different names, depending on the period. Between its creation in 1791 by the Constituant Assembly, and 1804, the year when Napoleon I became Emperor of France, the official name was the *Institution nationale des Sourds-Muets*. The adjective *nationale* was changed to *impériale* under the Empire (1804-1816), before becoming *royale* during the Restoration and the July Monarchy. For a brief four-year period under the Second Republic (1848-1852) it then reverted to *nationale*. In 1852, with the accession of Louis-Napoléon Bonaparte, known as Napoléon III, the Institution once again became *impériale* for the duration of the Second Empire (1852-1870), not definitively recovering its initial form until 1870. At the end of the 1960s it was officially baptised the *Institut national des Jeunes Sourds* (National Institution of the Young Deaf). It was initially established – just over ten years before Auguste's arrival in Paris – on the site of the Célestins convent, near the Arsenal, together with the National Institution for the Young Blind, run by Valentin Haüy, but the cohabitation proved complicated, and lasted just three years. On February 13, 1794, the former premises of the seminary of the Oratorians of Saint-Magloire were reassigned to the INSMP.

together in his home during the second half of the 18th century, for the purposes of their education. To this end he used the gestural method; this was a breakthrough in pedagogical history; previously, only the acquisition of spoken language was believed to allow such an education.

But we must separate the history of Deaf people, as subjects, from the history of their education and the methods employed for that purpose; the two are often confused. In this respect, and as we will see later, it is important to highlight the trailblazing role of Auguste Bébian as a hearing person, *répétiteur* and then deputy principal at the INSMP, between 1816 and 1821, along with that of Ferdinand Berthier, the Institution's first deaf teacher, from 1829 to 1875. There is no doubt that this institutionalization made possible an awareness of identity and an emancipation of Deaf people. Indeed, the latter, brought together for the first time in the same place, could without interruption practice their natural idiom, sign language, which until then had only been used in a marginal and isolated manner: this was an essential condition, because a language necessarily requires speakers. This visibility, this spotlight on Deaf people, should not obscure the fact that they had existed long before, and independently of, this step forward, however important it may have been. This is the main problem facing researchers: the almost total absence of direct sources, i.e. sources from Deaf people themselves. Somewhat prosaically, the second difficulty relating to research on the history of Deaf people relates to the identification of deafness, which was not always recognized as a disability. Before the end of the early Middle Ages, traces left by Deaf people are relatively few and far between: gathering these scattered and diffuse sources is a fastidious task that sometimes comes down to sheer luck: one often finds references to Deaf people in the least expected places.[3] This is an interesting observation, as it reveals a range of judgments. The most important question relates to mute-

3. Aude de Saint-Loup, "Les Sourds-Muets au Moyen Âge. Mille ans de signes oubliés", in Alexis Karacostas (ed.), *Le pouvoir des signes : Sourds et citoyens*, INJS, 1989, p. 11.

ness, to the absence of vocal production rather than to imperfect hearing or absence of hearing: it focuses on one's capacity to think, to develop one's thoughts, on reasoning and intelligence in the absence of articulated language. Are "deaf-mutes" truly human? A once-divisive issue.

1. A fragmented history up until the 18th century

Prehistory has taught us nothing about deaf people, or at least nothing that we are able to interpret. Generally speaking, many questions remain regarding the everyday lives of people from that period, when written language did not yet exist. Inasmuch as their oral (unwritten) culture leaves no direct traces, deaf people are even more concerned by this lack of resources in that it stretches, in their case, over a far longer period of time: no trace left directly by a deaf person was discovered until the 18th century, 1779 to be more precise, in a book by Pierre Desloges.[4] It is generally accepted that prehistoric men and women used multichannel communication, both vocal and gestural, with the latter almost certainly coming first. Indeed, if we consider articulated language to have appeared between 250,000 and 100,000 years BCE, this is very late compared to "gesture reciprocity" which is estimated to have existed between 25 and 30 million years BCE.[5] Only written documents offer any certain proof of the existence of deaf people. The first written record was found in 3300 BCE in the East, in Ancient Mesopotamia. It is referred to as cuneiform, due to its "wedge-shaped" characters.[6] In the first writings available to us, Assyriologist Jean Bottéro, a specialist of Mesopotamian civilization, deciphered two cuneiform characters

4. In 1779, Pierre Desloges published his *Observations d'un sourd et muet, sur un cours élémentaire d'éducation des sourds et muets, publié en 1779 par M. l'abbé Deschamps, chapelain de l'église d'Orléans* (Paris: B. Morin, imprimeur-libraire, 1779).
5. Michael C. Corballis, "L'origine gestuelle du langage", *in* "Aux origines du langage" (dossier), *La Recherche*, n° 341, p. 35.
6. From the Latin *cuneus*: wedge.

designating deaf people ("*sukkuku*" and "*ashikku*"), thus proving that ancient Eastern civilizations had already identified and named the phenomenon of deafness and differentiated between deafness and muteness, though the two terms were often linked. The first signified "deaf", while the second meant "mute". This distinction is even more worthy of mention in that in the West, in chronologically much later civilizations – such as Ancient Greece and Rome – the relationship between deafness and muteness eluded any such discernment. Two of the greatest doctors of ancient times, Hippocrates (4th century BCE), and later Galen (2nd century CE), were both convinced of the existence of an anastomosis between the nerves of the tongue and those of the ears.[7] Similarly, the Greek (*kophon* or *alogos*) and Roman (*mutus*) terms used to designate deaf people indicate a confusion between deafness and muteness, which are necessarily related – a defect of the tongue leading to hearing problems, and *vice versa*. So while the deafness/muteness relationship is not systematic, it is important to note that the semantic field of all these terms in one way or another suggests an intellectual deficiency, as they are also synonyms for "idiots".[8] For example, *sukkuku* means deaf, but also someone whose mind is "clogged up, dazed, uneducated and stupid". The Greek terms *kophon* (used in the Greek version of the Gospels) and *alogos also mean "deprived of reason"*.

While these etymological indications provide us with information on how deaf people were viewed, we know next to nothing about their everyday lives. We know that the Persians and the Egyptians displayed a certain religious "solicitude" towards deaf people on account of the mystery that surrounded them, but to what extent?[9] The Nile Valley has left iconographic evidence of the social roles likely to have been played by certain "disabled persons."[10] The Talmud – a

7. In medicine, an anastomosis is a communication, a connection between two organs or nerves.
8. It would even appear that before applying to deaf people, the initial meaning of these terms had to do with stupidity.
9. Henri-Jacques Sticker, *Corps infirmes et sociétés,* Paris: Dunod, 1997, p. 47.
10. *Ibid.,* p. 48.

collection of rabbinic traditions which in Judaism is a complement to the Bible – states that deaf people and people with no spoken language should not be placed in the category of idiots and the irresponsible, because they can be educated. This might explain the traditional Jewish respect for deaf people. However, we do not know whether this prescription describes a reality or was instead intended to change people's behavior…

In classical Greece, in the city-states of Sparta and Athens, and in ancient Rome, babies born with a deformity were subjected to the "rite of exposure".[11] This involved taking the child outside the city walls and leaving it to die, in water, in a hole or, as was the case in Sparta, on a rock. While to our modern minds such an act is an extreme abomination, it was not seen as an execution by the ancient Greeks and Romans. It was a matter of returning to the gods that which was interpreted as being a sign of their anger: "*They were exposed because they made people afraid; they were both the sign and the cause of the gods' anger.*"[12] Yet due to the invisible nature of deafness, the vast majority of deaf children almost certainly did not meet such an end: "*The blind, the deaf and the non compos mentis were not placed in the same category as the malformed.*"[13] It was indeed the malformations – club feet, hare lips, extra fingers or toes – that scared people. As Fernand Fourgon so pertinently remarks: "*certain authors assert that the Spartans threw them into the chasms of Taygetos, that the Athenians executed them and that in Rome they were thrown into the Tiber. Yet as far as we are aware, no ancient text mentions such things*". That being so, even though they probably escaped this rite of exposure, the everyday lives and living conditions of deaf people in ancient times were almost certainly unenviable. Indeed, Erving Goffman points out that it was the Greeks who were the first to name signs of disgrace (defined according to their civilization) when they invented the term

11. Marie Delcourt, *Stérilité mystérieuse et naissance maléfique dans l'Antiquité classique*, Paris: Droz, 1937.
12. Sticker, *Corps infirmes*, p. 39.
13. *Ibid.*, p. 45.

"stigma", which refers to "bodily signs of physical disorder."[14] In this particular case, the stigma is not immediately recognizable; it is more likely to be revealed later on, when communication begins, for example. So it is the visible manifestations of deafness – the absence of voice, a strange voice or, when more fully developed, a gestural expression – which may potentially constitute the "stigma" and not the deafness itself.

Be it benevolent divine expression or curse, deafness is a subject of debate, as is the natural mode of communication, by means of gestures. Works on semiogenesis show that the iconization of a deaf person's experience is potentially an emerging sign language, as long as the signs are accepted.[15] As early as ancient times, certain philosophers accepted the linguistic aspect of deaf signs, albeit without taking things any further. Plato (427 BCE to 348 BCE) reports a dialogue between Socrates and Hermogenes, where the former says:

> *"Suppose that we had no voice or tongue, and wanted to communicate with one another, should we not, like the deaf and dumb, make signs with the hands and head and the rest of the body?"*

Which leads Hermogenes to reply:[16]

> *"I do not see that we could do anything else."*

These observations, these assertions, do not however lead to any valorization of gestural expression. While the latter is not ignored, it is merely perceived to be a preliminary step towards the acquisition of a language that can only be articulated. In his approach to sensibilia, Plato's disciple Aristotle adopts a completely different

14. Erving Goffman, *Stigma: Notes on the Management of Spoiled Identity*, NY: Touchstone, 1963, p. 11.
15. Ivani Fusellier-Souza, *Sémiogenèse des langues des signes. Études des Langues des signes primaire (LSP), pratiqués par des sourds brésiliens,* doctoral thesis defended at the Université de Paris VIII, 2004.
16. Plato, *Cratylis,* transl. Benjamin Jowett, New York: Scribner's Sons, 1871.

hypothesis: he recognizes the fundamental role that sensorial experience plays in the enrichment of knowledge:[17]

"There is no part of the intellect that does not first come from the senses."

This said, he categorically postulates the primacy of speech when it comes to intellectual development and the transmission of knowledge. For without vocal speech it is impossible to develop thought, because it is language that creates reasoning. Yet he goes on to add:[18]

"All people who are deaf from birth are mutes. They make sounds, but have no language".

In his opinion, deafness acquired after birth also prevents this development:[19]

"It is clear that if any given sense has disappeared, a certain kind of science will necessarily have disappeared with it, a science that is therefore impossible to acquire."

Aristotle's influence on Western thinking has been considerable and remains so: this unequivocal opinion persists, despite being very widely rejected by research and reality. A certain amount of caution is nevertheless required: the translation of Aristotle's writings from Greek into French would appear to be causing confusion.[20]

Because it was invisible, sensorial disabilities did not, in principle, lead to deaf people being physically eliminated at birth; but their

17. Aristotle, *Sense and Sensibilia*.
18. Aristotle, *History of Animals*.
19. Aristotle, *Posterior Analytics*.
20. According to Fernand Fourgon, there is an error, or approximation, in the translation from Greek into French of the term *logos,* literally "oral speech": an oral expression which can be both verbal and gestural!
Fernand Fourgon, "Historique de la pédagogie des sourds-muets", *Communiquer*, n° 37, 1978, p. 3.

gestural mode of communication did invalidate their humanity. It was through such communication that deafness took on a stigmatizing dimension. In his first publication, Auguste Bébian takes as his starting point this correlation between the development of intelligence and oral language to demonstrate that this causality is false:[21]

> *"People even believed – and this belief has not entirely disappeared – that speech was vital to the exercise of thought* [...]."

Rather than opposing Aristotle's argument head-on, he pushes it to the very limit:[22]

> *"But it is precisely because speech is not only the expression, but also the ordinary instrument of thought, that its imperfections have such unfortunate consequences, and have deservedly focused the attention of philosophers."*

These indecisions regarding the human or non-human status of deaf people are even more complex in that they have an individual variant: the deaf person's ability to adapt to his or her immediate entourage and to the outside world – the opposite being just as important to consider. While it is widespread and relatively common, gestural expression raises questions, as a potential language, as an equivalent of vocal speech, more even than a "strange" voice or an absence of voice. Given that one is directly related to the other, we might say that the problem lies in communication, in the relationship with others and with society, rather than in deafness itself.[23]

---

21. Auguste Bébian, *Essai sur les sourds-muets et sur le langage naturel, ou introduction à une classification naturelle des idées avec leurs signes propres*, Librairie L. Colas, 1817, p. 5.
22. *Ibid.*, p. 55.
23. This is also the conclusion reached by sociologist Bernard Mottez for whom "*deafness is a relationship*": it can only be defined bilaterally. There are only deaf people because there are people who can hear, and *vice versa*.
    Bernard Mottez, *Les sourds existent-ils ?*, texts presented and collected by Andrea Benvenuto, Paris: L'Harmattan, 2006, p. 144.

As a "civilization of gesture", nor were the Middle Ages particularly hostile towards the gestural mode of communication, in as much as, like ancient theatre, its function remained aesthetic or even practical – for trade for example.[24] This lengthy millennium was full of contrasts, having inherited ancient knowledge to which a few innovative ideas had been added. Its reputation as an obscurantist, intolerant and repressive period regarding deaf people, as in other areas,[25] seems undeserved, even though they were found to be "on the fringe of marginality":[26] research on this period is very embryonic, and without wishing to paint an idyllic picture, there are several indications that deaf people's participation in medieval society was certainly more effective than we have been led to think. Generally speaking, the Middle Ages have nothing to say on the matter of the disabled, but is this not a revealing silence? As Henri-Jacques Stiker says:[27]

> *"If the discourse is so scanty, it is perhaps because the disabled, the diminished, the invalid, spontaneously belonged to a world and a society that was accepted as varied, diverse, disparate.* [...] *Incongruous variety was the norm, and no-one was bothered with segregation, for it was most 'natural' for there to be malformations. It was more than mere tolerance: it was reality."*

As we pointed out at the beginning of this section, deaf people are mentioned in writings that group together the fringe elements of medieval society, among the Jews, homosexuals and prostitutes.[28] They were not systematically considered to be disabled. It is true that both physically and socially, deaf people were autonomous. They could work in the fields or in arts and crafts, for example.

24. Jean-Claude Schmitt, *La raison des gestes dans l'Occident médiéval,* Paris: Gallimard, 1990.
25. Régine Pernoud, *Pour en finir avec le Moyen Âge*, Paris: Gallimard, Folio, 1979.
26. Saint-Loup, *Sourds-Muets au Moyen Âge,* p. 14.
27. Sticker, *Corps infirmes*, p. 63.
28. Saint-Loup, *Sourds-Muets au Moyen Âge*, p. 11.

Because France was a rural country at that time, and work was essentially manual, deaf people fitted quite naturally into the social organization, as Michel Mollah points out:[29]

> *"Where did able-bodied poverty end? Where did infirmity begin? Byzantine legislation and morality made work the dividing line. Vagrancy and unemployment were political issues; physical or mental disabilities were moral issues."*

So there was a clear dividing line. To a lesser extent, religious congregations were another factor of social integration during this period. As early as the 9th century, some of them were entrusted with taking in and looking after deaf children. Strangely enough, these communities were governed by the monastic rule of Saint Benedict of Nursia,[30] and were obliged to observe silence: the spoken word was forbidden, so as not to interfere with divine meditation, and in order to meet the requirements of meditation, sign language dictionaries were introduced.[31] In 1953, Gérard Van Rijnberk counted 1300 signs, ordered in accordance with a syntax similar to French sign language (LSF).[32] To what extent was this of benefit to deaf people? It is impossible to say with any accuracy. A comparison of the sign language used by deaf people and that used by the monks shows many similarities, but without any his-

---

29. Michel Mollat, *Les pauvres au Moyen Âge*, Paris: Hachette, 1978, p. 30.
30. *"The first written dictionaries of signs date back to the 10th century, but such usage was vouched for in earlier periods. Furthermore, in the 33rd precept of the Rule of Saint Pachomius (4th century), translated by Saint Jerome (5th century) and which we find in chapter 38 of the Rule of Saint Benedict (6th century), there is a request to replace speech with a signum sonitu: a whistle or a knock on the table".* Saint-Loup, *op. cit.*, 1989, p. 19.
31. Dictionaries of gestural signs were created in Benedictine, and later on Trappist, abbeys governed by the rule of Saint Benedict. See René Poupardin, *Monuments de l'histoire des abbayes de Saint-Philibert*, Paris: Alphonse Picard et fils, 1905.
32. Gerard van Rijnberk, *Le langage par signes chez les moines*, Amsterdam, North-Holland Publishing Company, 1953.

torical evidence a reciprocal influence may only be assumed.[33] In the 17th century, we nevertheless find evidence of a deaf man, Étienne de Fay, who became a teacher for deaf children abandoned at Prémontrés Abbey in Amiens. Later on, in the 18th century, it was another priest, Charles-Michel de l'Épée, who was the first to create a school in France based on the gestural method, breaking with the oralist ideas of the time. Are these really mere coincidences? It is a question worth asking.

To illustrate this ambivalent and sometimes contradictory view, as early as 529 the Council of Orange authorized deaf people to request baptism by signs. At the same time, the Code of Justinian restricted their access to civil rights. This was the first legal status granted to deaf people and it is interesting to note that only people born deaf with no spoken language were totally deprived of civil rights: the criterion of speech was thus relevant to this exclusion. The other four "categories" (defined by the Justinian Code: deaf-mutism, natural deafness, acquired deafness and acquired muteness) were not so deprived, but saw their rights restricted. More than ever, "Helping deaf people to speak" (deaf people being the first category defined by the Code) thus became a necessity in order to escape an overly coercive categorization.

Socially, deaf people were therefore not forced to beg, nor were they ostracized from society like other disabled persons at that time. This does not mean that there were no deaf beggars, just that the phenomenon was apparently rare. Of one hundred and twenty deaf people recorded in the Middle Ages in the West, only four were beggars.[34] Social judgment of the latter was harsh. The 12th century bishop Guillaume de Mende reported on his discussions with deaf people for the purposes of preaching Christianity, demonstrating obvious irritation: "*There are many deaf people who refuse to hear the word of God, and a large number of mutes who do*

33. Aude de Saint-Loup, Yves Delaporte et Marc Renard, *Gestes des moines, regards des sourds,* Siloë, 1997. Here the monastic signs are those of the Burgundian monastry in La Pierre-qui-Vire.
34. Saint-Loup, *Sourds-Muets au Moyen Âge* p. 15.

not wish to speak, even though they are able to do so."[35] Whether or not the metaphor is employed here, he assimilates foreigners, mutes and deaf people, all of whom are in his eyes "imperfect". In both cases, deafness and muteness, he believed there was a conscious refusal to hear the word of God.

It would nevertheless appear that the clergy were more tolerant of deaf people than was the temporal authority that removed their civil rights. The linguistic function of signs was confirmed by Saint Jerome as early as the 5th century:[36]

> *"Through signs and everyday conversation,* [...] *through the eloquent gesture of the entire body, deaf people may understand the Gospel."*

The thinking of another "father of the Church", Saint Augustine, is very much along the same lines. His ideas strongly influenced the theology of the Middle Ages and well beyond, for we find elements of it in philosophical and theological reasoning such as Jansenism. In *De Magistro*, Saint Augustine puts into perspective the Aristotelian theory of an exclusive interdependency between articulated language and intellectual activity, considering the gestural expression of deaf people to be a means of communication that can be used to access the "inner master", i.e. God. Yet as Christianity spread, there were constant reminders of the superiority of speech over gestural communication, with appeals to God to provide justification: "*In the beginning was the Word and the Word was with God – and the Word was God,*" says the Gospel according to Saint John.[37] The Word is oral in nature, and of course vocal; even though it would appear to be written nowhere that the Word cannot be gestural! Generally speaking, the Bible is full of "*God said... and so it came to be,*" thus emphasizing the original creative power of speech. It was the Aristotelian current that prevailed at that time, remaining firmly anchored in collective representations. Eloquence and mastery of

35. *Ibid.*
36. *Ibid.*, p. 16.
37. John 1:1.

speech demonstrated the intelligence of the person with whom you were talking. These notions did not apply specifically to deaf people, but they clearly influenced their natural and privileged form of communication. The Middle Ages were a "civilization of gesture", in as much as the gesture was co-verbal! As Jean-Claude Schmitt says:[38]

> " [...] *People constantly call to mind the primacy of speech, of which gestures are merely the more or less docile and more or less necessary servants* [...]. *Gesture is of course ever present, but only as if snuggled against the shadow of the Spoken Word. While not ignoring gesture, but without being able to really specify its role, official culture cannot bring itself to give it the same importance as speech. This is in fact the logical result of a long tradition of spiritualizing speech and language, the consequence of which is to designate, by contrast, the heaviness of the body as being proper to sin."*

So at the end of the Middle Ages, the fact that voice alone made it possible to access thought and develop humanity, and that deaf-muteness was irreversible, seemed to be confirmed: the opinion of Aristotle and the philosophers, along with the doctors of ancient Greece – Hippocrates and later Galen, for whom deaf-muteness was caused by paralysis of the fifth pair of facial nerves (their writings on anatomy being authoritative during the mediaeval period) – created the idea of a static state. Yet the later dissociation, due to medical progress, between deafness and muteness made it possible to envisage speech education and voice training. In order to pursue the objective of humanization, the restoration of the vocal function became more than ever unavoidable: "giving [deaf people] a voice" and allowing them to achieve human status made a reassuring social normalization possible.[39] New perspectives opened up, and prejudices fell away, to make room for others...

---

38. Schmitt, *La raison des gestes*, p. 358.
39. In the Western world, because as we saw on p. 22, the two terms were not confused in the East.

2. Articulated speech as a criterion of humanity

As this idea of "demuting" grew, the history of Deaf people blended in with that of their education, focusing on learning vocal speech and on "curing" deafness. The case of the "deaf young man of Chartres", reported in 1703 to the French Academy of Science,[40] illustrates this obsession with hearing,[41] without which there could be no salvation, and shows how deafness was viewed at the start of the Enlightenment. At the end of the 17th century, around 1690, a certain Félibien, member of the Académie des Inscriptions, revealed "an unusual, possibly unprecedented event" to the scholars present. The commentary written later on by the philosopher Bernard Le Bouyer de Fontenelle fed the debate on the development of the human mind and the emergence of ideas: according to him, and to all Cartesians, all ideas are innate; whereas empiricists maintained that they came directly from the senses. The case of the "deaf young man of Chartres" was an opportunity to carry out an empirical test, to compare theory with practice. Published for the first time in 1703, and then republished 36 years later in *Histoire de l'Académie Royale des Sciences*, Fontenelle's text reported that in

> *"Chartres, a young man in his twenty-third year, the son of a craftsman, deaf and mute at birth, suddenly began to speak, to the astonishment of everyone in the town. When asked about the circumstances of such an apparently marvelous result, he replied that three months before he found his voice, he had heard the sound of bells, and had been extremely surprised by this new and unknown sensation. Then a sort of water came out of his left ear, and he was able to hear perfectly with both ears. He*

40. Académie des sciences, *Histoire de l'Académie Royale des Sciences… avec les mémoires de mathématique & de physique… tirez des registres de cette Académie*, Paris: J. Boudot, 1703, p. 18-19, V.

41. Fabrice Bertin, "In Chartres, the miraculous healing of a young deaf-mute man: Félix Merle", Charles Gardou, *Le handicap dans notre imaginaire culturel. Variations anthropologiques 3*, Toulouse, Érès, 2015.

spent three or four months listening, without saying anything, getting used to repeating the words he heard in a low voice, and improving the pronunciation and the ideas attached to the words. At long last he felt he could break the silence, and declared that he was able to speak, albeit imperfectly. Immediately, skilled theologians questioned him about his past state, their main questions revolving around God, the soul, the goodness or moral evil of actions. He did not appear to have pursued his thinking so far, although he was born of Catholic parents, attended Mass, and was instructed to make the sign of the cross and to kneel in the attitude of a man at prayer; he had never attached this to any intention, nor understood the intention which others attached to it. He did not have a clear notion of what death was, and never thought about it. He led a purely animal life, fully occupied with present and perceptible objects, and with the few ideas he received through his eyes. He did not even glean from the comparison of ideas all that it seems he might have gleaned from them. It is not that he did not naturally have a mind, but the mind of a man deprived of contact with others is so little exercised and cultivated that he only thinks when he is unavoidably forced to do so by external objects. The greatest value of ideas resides in their mutual exchange."

This last observation leaves one wondering: paradoxically, its relevance and accuracy did not lead to a more favorable view of gestural expression, which might compensate for defective oral communication; on the contrary, they argued for the learning of articulated speech.

A century earlier, at the beginning of the 16th century, the first official references (or at least, those that have reached us) to the education of deaf people at the Spanish court, by Pedro Ponce de León (1520-1584), tell us that "de-muting" was the preferred solution. Indeed, it was at that time that the first "pedagogy" for deaf children appeared in Spain. The fame of silent painters Juan Fernández Navarette (a pupil of Titian) and Pinturicchio (an Italian disciple of Sienese master Pietro Perugino), undoubtedly helped, in circles of power, to dispel prejudices against deaf people. Pinturicchio had become the painter of the Popes, and Navarette the painter of Philippe II, King of Spain, in 1568.[42] It was in this context of intellectual and artistic exaltation that Pedro Ponce de León, a Benedictine monk from the monastery of San Salvador in Oña, intervened. In or around 1542 he was asked to he was asked to help an influentail family influential family of the Spanish mobility, the Velasco family, who held the high office of Constable of Castile.[43] Pedro de Velasco, the third in the line of constables, had no descendants. His brother Juan, Marquis of Berlanga, had seven children: three who could hear (Iñigo, Inès and Isabel) and four who were deaf (Francisco, Pedro, Catalina and Bernardina). Ponce's task was to teach the four deaf children to speak, so as to preserve their property rights and keep the title of constable in the family should the sole hearing heir of male sex die – the girls being excluded from such a transmission. The title of constable logically reverted to Iñigo, in 1557.

To ensure this education, and probably inspired by the phonological methods of ancient times,[44] Ponce devised an articulation technique and with help from his contemporary Melchior de Yebra,[45]

---

42. Navarette took part in decorating the royal palace of the Escurial. This is not unrelated to the raised awareness of noble families with one or more deaf children.

    Yves Bernard, *Approche de la gestualité à l'Institution des Sourds-Muets de Paris aux XVIIIe et XIXe siècles*. Doctoral thesis in linguistics defended at the Université de Paris V, 1999, p. 20.

43. The position of Constable of Castile was created in 1382 by King John I of Castile to replace that of Alférez Mayor del Reino. The constable controlled the army in the king's absence. It was a lofty position, being made honorary and hereditary by King Henry IV of Castile in 1473: the Velasco family held the office until it ceased to exist in 1713.

44. More specifically, the phonetic method of Antonio de Nebrija, author of *Gramática castellana* in 1492.

45. Melchior de Yebra (1524-1586) was a Franciscan monk who confessed "*persons deprived of speech*" and dying people who no longer had the strength to talk. He confirmed that many people were able to make themselves understood, whence his interest in deaf people. When considering the manual alphabet, Yebra was inspired by the writings of Bonaventure de Bagnorea, a 13th century theologian. Bernard, *Approche de la gestualité*, p. 23.

    Harlan Lane, *When the Mind Hears*, New York: Random House, 1984.

also formalized the first manual alphabet. His method consisted in giving the tongue and lips a precise position prior to vocal production, with the larynx being likened to a musical instrument such as the flute, for example. His writings – if he produced any – have not reached us, and his experiment is known to us only indirectly, through the testimonies of his pupils.[46] This first documented attempt to teach speech to deaf people took place in a political context of reconquest and of the struggle against the Moors, based on the widespread dissemination of the Castilian language.

In 1585, Iñigo de Velasco in turn passed his title on to his own son, Juan Fernández, who had three children: Mariana, Bernardino (hearing, and a future constable) and Don Luís, either born deaf or becoming deaf at the age of two, according to testimonies.[47] The task of teaching Don Luís fell to the tutor Ramirez de Carrión.[48] To this end, he took inspiration from his predecessor, with the one difference that he moved directly onto learning to speak, with no gestural support. At that time, a certain Juan de Pablo-Bonet (1579-1633) was secretary to the incumbent constable, Don Bernardino de Velasco. In 1620, and under his own name, Bonet published what is known as the first book to deal with teaching speech to deaf people: *The reduction of letters to their primitive elements and the art of teaching mutes to speak.*[49] In his book he explained the method – perhaps that of the monk who had initiated it, Pedro Ponce – that is considered to be the basis of current oral methods. Don Luís' great uncle being himself a pupil of Ponce (Pedro de

46. Certain accounts suggest that he recorded his experiments in a manuscript. On this matter, see Harlan Lane, *When the Mind Hears*, New York: Knopf Doubleday, 2010, p. 87.
47. Don Luís (1610-c.1664) took on responsibilities as Marquis de Fresno, which implied a certain level of consideration. Yves Bernard, *Approche de la gestualité*, p. 20.
48. Ramirez de Carrión (1584-1660) was a sort of "professional" private tutor who also taught the hearing. Bernard, *Approche de la gestualité*, p. 21.
49. Juan de Pablo-Bonet, *Reducción de las letras y arte para enseñar a hablar a los mudos*, translated into French by Eugène Bassouls and Auguste Boyer; published in 1889 in the *Revue internationale d'enseignement des sourds-muets.*

Velasco), as Harlan Lane points out, it is possible that the tutor's manuscript was preserved by that family.[50] In any event, "*the method of teaching the deaf in Bonet's book is consistent with what is known of Ponce's method.*"[51] He recommended the use of signs proper to deaf people and of the manual alphabet codified by Pedro Ponce, for the purpose of learning articulation.

This first work on the subject of educating deaf people had a considerable impact in Europe, largely due to Kenelm Digby, nephew of the English ambassador to Spain. While visiting the Spanish court in 1623, in the wake of the future king of England, Charles I, he was introduced to the young Don Luís, a source of pride, and proof that it was possible to teach deaf people to speak. A well-known intellectual and a member of the king's inner circle, Digby wanted to prove the immortality of the soul, and published his thoughts in 1644. In his two books, *On the Nature of the Body* and *On the Nature and Operations of the Soul,* he writes about his encounter with "*the talking mute brother of the Constable of Castile*" and is filled with praise for Don Luís' ability to speak, read lips and enter into discourse. Back in Britain, following the restoration of the monarchy in 1660, Sir Kenelm Digby was one of the founding members of the Royal Society, alongside his friend, the grammarian and mathematician John Wallis.[52] Henceforth, Great Britain and its scientists were to show a keen interest in the education of deaf people: John Wallis (*De loquela*, 1653), the Scotsman John Delgarno (*Ars signorum,* 1661) and the physician John Buwler (*Chironomia, Chirologia,* 1644). The latter, despite having initiated the school project, was not "*involved in any of the work or debates*".[53] "*They each published their own methods, but without any consultation or comparison of results*":[54] "*What is precisely so surprising, with regard to Great Britain's image*

50. Lane, *When the Mind Hears*, p. 94.
51. Lane, *When the Mind Hears*, p. 93.
52. Sophie Dalle-Nazébi, *Chercheurs, Sourds et langues des signes. Le travail d'un objet et de repères linguistiques en France du XVIIe au XXIe siècle*, doctoral thesis, Université de Toulouse II-le Mirail, 2006, p. 72.
53. *Ibid.*, p. 76.
54. Aude de Saint-Loup, *Diogène*, n° 175, p. 50.

concerning deaf-mutes, is that there is no debate. It would seem that only Wallis receives any attention."[55] This abundance of ideas and experiments is evidence of a real awareness which did not remain confined to British shores, spreading in turn to the Netherlands and Switzerland, where Jean-Conrad Amman was making a name for himself.[56] Considered to be the father of "pure" oralism, Amman excluded all gesturality, signs and action language of any type, as well as any symbolic or arbitrary dactylology. Throughout the 17th century, then, European scholars wrestled with the issue of educating deaf people.[57] Whatever their nuances, all of these methods focused on learning to speak, and as far as their objectives were concerned there was no major difference between them. There were however minor variations in the means employed: for example, we might distinguish between the pragmatic thinking of English scholar John Wallis, and the more rigorously phonetic thinking of Jacob-Rodriguez Pereire.

John Wallis' priority was to ensure the development of deaf children, by whatever means possible. There are three letters that refer to his interest in them and to his tutorage.[58] Learning to talk is a central feature, but does not focus exclusively on articulation; vibrations and breath are taken into account. In his correspondence he states that as far as he is concerned, the objective of his teaching is that language be understood and that reading and writing are absolutely essential. In the second letter, written in 1698, Wallis declares that he does not consider reading out loud to be essential:[59]

55. Dalle-Nazébi, *Chercheurs*, p. 75.
56. Jean-Conrad Amman published *Surdus loquens* in 1692, and *Dissertatio de loquela* in 1700, in which he linked writing and speech-reading. His publications became the basis for the institutional education of deaf children in Germany, at the urging of Samuel Heinicke.
57. This preoccupation appeared later on in France, with Jacob-Rodriguez Pereire, in the 18th century.
58. The first was sent to Irish physician Robert Boyle, in 1661; the second to Thomas Beverly (a teacher of five deaf-mute children); the third was written in 1700 to Jean-Conrad Amman, a doctor and tutor working in Holland.
59. John Wallis, quoted by Auguste Bébian, *Nouvelle méthode pour apprendre à lire sans épeler*, 1817, p. 138-139 of the 1886 edition.

> *"I have tutored several other deaf-mutes, without even attempting to teach them to speak; I simply taught them to understand what people wrote to them, and to sufficiently express their thoughts in writing. After just a short time they had made a great deal of progress, and had acquired far more knowledge than one might expect from people in their situation; and they were in a position (if further cultivated) to acquire all other knowledge that can be transmitted by reading. However, this was just the second stage, the first being devoted to learning to speak."*

In France, the other trend was personified by Jacob Pereire, himself a disciple of the Swiss Jean-Conrad Amman. He expressed a certain conception of the education of deaf people, according to a sort of "secular tradition" that went back to the beginning of the 17th century, with the writings of Juan Pablo-Bonet. The justification for his teaching principles, based entirely on vocal speech, and excluding all gestures (for signifying purposes at least), was of a religious nature.

Jacob Pereire (1715-1780) was a Marrano Jew of Spanish origin whose family had settled in Portugal. In 1741 he emigrated to France with his mother and his brothers and sisters, arriving in Bordeaux, where Jews from the Iberian Peninsula who had been required to convert to Christianity had taken refuge. Pereire looked after one of his sisters who was deaf, and as soon as the family was settled in Bordeaux, he opened a small school. He "*set to work to teach speech to his first deaf pupil–his sister.*"[60] From 1745 onward, his reputation began to grow: he took charge of Azy d'Étavigny, the deaf son of a La Rochelle dignitary, who had previously been tutored by Étienne de Fay, a deaf monk from Prémontrés Abbey. De Fay, consigned to historical oblivion[61] and anonymously referred to as "*the old deaf-mute of Amiens*"[62] up until the end of the 19th century, is revelatory

60. Lane, *When the Mind Hears*, p. 75.

61. A fire destroyed any sources that might have made him known to posterity.

62. A civil servant at the French Ministry of the Interior in the 19th century, Théophile Denis, found his trace in 1887. He refers to him as "France's first teacher of deaf-mutes", Paris, *Revue française de l'éducation des sourds-muets*, n° 10, p. 217, 1896 ; n° 11, p. 242 and n° 6 and 7, 1894.

of history's silence concerning Deaf people. In any event, he must have been sufficiently well-known in his time for a local dignitary to have entrusted to him the education of his only his son.

Azy d'Étavigny was 18 when Pereire met him, finding him to be an *"intelligent young man, able to read, write and sign."*[63] There was an element of duplicity in the attitude of Jacob Pereire, and other tutors,[64] who claimed to teach speech without the use of gestures. Rousseau notes that:[65]

> *"Sire Pereyre, and those like him who teach the deaf not only to speak but also to know what they are saying, are of course obliged to first teach them another no less complicated language that will help them to hear this one."*

According to accounts provided by pupils, which give some idea of the procedures employed, Pereire worked first on demutization, using tactile sensations (of the neck in particular) and signs with phonetic or graphic equivalence that were always linked to articulation. Doubts nevertheless remain as to the effectiveness of this "learning process": in 1748, Azy d'Étavigny's father informed Pereire that less than a year after the end of his tutorship, his son's articulation had

---

63. Jean-Jacques Rousseau, *Lettres, mélanges et théâtre*, Paris: Baudoin frères, (s. d.), edition published by M. Toquet, vol. VI, p. 118. In total, Pereire *"managed the education of twelve deaf-mute boys or girls; but the two students he presented to the* Académie des Sciences *in 1751 had, before coming under his care, already obtained an initial degree of instruction. In Amiens, young d'Étavigny hade taken lessons with an old deaf-mute whose mind was, so they say, filled with wonderful knowledge; from this man he had learned, as from the age of seven or eight, to use signs to ask for the most necessary things in life."*
Joseph-Marie de Gérando, *Des sourds-muets de naissance*, Méquignon l'aîné, 1827, vol. I, p. 400.
64. Tutors from this period tried to keep their methods secret, so as to preserve a lucrative "business capital", in as much as it was a question of teaching the acquisition of speech to deaf people from the well-to-do social classes. Their exact methods are unknown.
65. Jean-Jacques Rousseau, *Essai sur l'origine des langues*, posthumous publication, 1781, Paris: Gallimard, Folio, 1990, p. 65.

become "highly defective and almost unintelligible."[66] In any event, the education of deaf people continued to be the objective, even if the means employed varied. It was an initiative by Charles-Michel de l'Épée (1712-1789) that would crystallize tensions. Beforehand, as certain sources attest, several educational centers for deaf people had existed, but they were not institutionalized.[67] As we have seen, religious communities had indeed been welcoming deaf people since the Middle Ages, and their discretion – or at least the discretion of the sources that have come down to us – is perhaps proof of a certain continuity of this practice, rather than of its discontinuance.

3. The pedagogical initiative of Abbé de l'Épée: mere parenthesis or lasting break?

It was with Charles-Michel de l'Épée, known as Abbé de l'Épée, that the question of the education of deaf children became controversial: his method called into question what had not until then been challenged. His initiative broke away from the only practices that existed at that time for the education of deaf children, starting with the question of which children were to be educated. Education was based on a system of tutorship, aimed at a well-off population able to pay for such services. In contrast, de l'Épée referred to himself as "*the free teacher of the deaf and mute.*"[68] His pedagogical innovation aside, the educational trend that he established was aimed at the working class and the poor: his initiative was philanthropic.

Charles-Michel de l'Épée was a contemporary of Jacob Pereire, born three years before him, in 1712. Born into a wealthy family – his father was an architect to King Louis XIV – in 1720 he went to Mazarine College where he took lessons with the Jansenist

66. Jean-René Presneau, *Signes et institution des sourds, XVIIIe-XIXe siècles*, Seyssel, Champ Vallon, 1998, p. 86.

67. Aude de Saint-Loup, *Diogène*, n° 175, 1996.

68. Maryse Bezagu-Deluy, *L'abbé de L'Épée. Instituteur gratuit des Sourds-Muets, 1712-1789*, Paris: Seghers, 1990.

philosopher Adrien Geffroy. This encounter was of considerable importance and had a major impact on the young man's life. The period was marked by a theological conflict between Jesuit casuists (who followed the theses developed by Luis de Molina more than a century earlier) and Jansenists (followers of Jansenius and his *Augustinus*) in deep disagreement on the subject of divine grace and human freedom, and hence of predestination.[69] Initially purely religious, this conflict became political. Royal power took up the cause of the Jesuits. To some extent these special circumstances perturbed the ecclesiastical career to which de l'Épée (who had adhered to the Jansenist theses) was destined. Indeed, this choice initially prevented him from entering the priesthood, but it revealed in him a social and pedagogical vocation that undoubtedly led him to take an interest in a minority.[70]

In this, the influence of his teacher, Adrien Geffroy, was undeniable. As de l'Épée writes:[71]

> "[…] *he had proved to me the indisputable principle that there is no more natural link between metaphysical ideas and articulated sounds, which strike our ears, than that which exists between those same ideas and the characters marked in writing that strike our eyes.* […] *He immediately came to the conclusion that it would be possible to teach deaf and mute people using characters marked in writing and always accompanied by sensory signs, just as one teaches other men using words and gestures which indicate their meaning.*"

---

69. For a more complete approach, see: Augustin Gazier, *Histoire générale du mouvement janséniste depuis ses origines jusqu'à nos jours*, Paris: Honoré Champion, 2 volumes, 1924; Jean-Pierre Chantin, *Le jansénisme*, Paris: CERF, 1996.
70. In 1713, in the middle of the conflict, the *Unigenitus* papal bull was signed by Pope Clement IX; the bull was written into national law by Louis XV in 1730. Approval of this bull was required by the spiritual and temporal authorities in order to access academic ranks leading to the priesthood. Due to his Jansenist convictions, de l'Épée refused to sign it.
71. Charles-Michel de l'Épée, *La véritable manière d'instruire les sourds et muets, confirmée par une longue expérience*, Paris: Nyon, 1784. Bezagu-Deluy, *L'abbé de L'Épée*, p. 54.

In 1736, with support from Monseigneur Bossuet, who was at that time in charge of the diocese and who looked favorably upon the Jansenist theses, Charles-Michel de l'Épée was nevertheless appointed curate (and not priest; he was in charge of people's "souls" but was not allowed to administer the sacraments) in the village of Feuges, near Troyes. He ran the parish for two years, not being ordained as a priest (which is a state and not just a function) until 1738. This did not prevent him from returning to Paris the following year to protest against the university's rallying to the *Unigenitus* papal bull, thus demonstrating his Jansenist convictions once again. This somewhat chaotic and eventful career, running against the mainstream doctrine, placed the young priest somewhat on the fringe, something that no doubt directed his future decisions.

Until 1760, the life of Charles-Michel de l'Épée, now anointed as an "abbot" (*abbé*), was uneventful.[72] An encounter with two deaf female twins was to dramatically change his destiny. The circumstances of this encounter remain unclear and are often recounted in the manner of a tale, with many different versions. The historical reality was confirmed by Abbé de l'Épée himself:[73]

> *"This is how I became a teacher of the Deaf and the Mute, unaware at that time that there had been others before me. Father Vanin, a highly respectable priest of the Christian Doctrine, had begun the education of twin sisters, deaf and mute from birth, using engravings. The charitable minister having died, the sisters found themselves bereft of help, as for quite a long period no-one was prepared to continue or recommence the work. So seeing that these two children would live and die in ignorance of their religion if I did not try to find a way of teaching it to them, I was moved with compassion, and I said that they could be brought to me, that I would do what I could."*

72. In the modern period, the term "abbot" began to be used for persons who had received the sacrament of priesthood. This term was normally used to designate the superior of an abbey.

73. Charles-Michel de l'Épée, *Institution des sourds-muets par la voie des signes méthodiques*, Paris: Nyon, 1776, p. 8.

It was as a result of this meeting, whether by chance or not, that he set up a class at his home in Rue des Moulins in Paris,[74] at the late age of 58. Living in relative ease due to his father's inheritance,[75] he welcomed deaf children into his home without asking for payment. The fact that Abbé de l'Épée had met the two sisters is by no means insignificant, on the contrary: he witnessed the possibility of communication between deaf people, through gesture.[76] His first contact with deafness was therefore not a confrontation with infirmity, but with communication, albeit of a different kind. This was an eminently decisive element in deepening the reflection of a man with an atypical personal background, for whom education was a constant preoccupation inherent in the Jansenist tradition:[77] *"Teaching, in all its forms, is an ordinary thing for Jansenist priests."*[78] In 1784, after two decades of teaching, he published *La véritable manière d'instruire les sourds et muets* (The true way of teaching the deaf and the mute), an essay in which he set out the rudiments of his method. De l'Épée made a major break, immediately confronting his predecessors and the competitors of his time by advocating learning by gesture: "methodical signs". These were an artificial creation, but not *ex-nihilo*, as the method was developed from the natural sign language of deaf people. So de l'Épée was not the "inventor" of sign language. He took considerable inspiration from it, in an attempt to bring it closer to the grammatical structure of the French language,

74. During the 17th century, the Jansenists' creation of Port Royal's "small schools", considered to be *"from many standpoints an exceptional pedagogical adventure"*, may have inspired Abbé de l'Épée. see: Frédéric Delforge, *Les petites écoles de Port Royal : 1637-1660*, Paris: Le Cerf, 1985, p. 355, quoted by Bezagu-Deluy, *L'abbé de L'Épée*, p. 49.
75. Bezagu-Deluy, *L'abbé de L'Épée*, p. 50.
76. However, we must not forget that he was not the first to have observed this communication, as pointed out by Plato and later on by Montaigne, thus demonstrating a certain longevity.
77. Abbé de l'Épée had dedicated himself to numerous educational tasks, in various parishes, long before becoming involved with that of deaf people. Bezagu-Deluy, *L'abbé de L'Épée*, p. 50.
78. Bezagu-Deluy, *L'abbé de L'Épée*, p. 95.

injecting artificial signs, some of which have survived.[79] But above and beyond its pedagogical ambition, the methodical sign method was also a way for him to maintain a certain intelligibility, or even a certain "control", over the signs used by Deaf people.[80] Between 1760, when the abbot gathered together a small number of deaf pupils to teach, and 1780, when his method was first published, a substantial lexicon was gradually compiled as his pupils progressed. Indeed, at the start of the experiment, the number of signs had to be limited, to allow the abbot to recognize them all. But as time went by, their evolution and number were such that communication escaped the teacher's comprehension, adversely affecting his objective of teaching his pupils to read and write.

The abbot's method was therefore a sort of signed French, the use of which was laborious, as it was necessary to visualize everything related to French grammar (gender, number, etc.):[81]

> *"The aim was to ensure that the syntax of the language used by the teacher was modeled on that of French: whence the appearance of a list of signs, such as certain prepositions, definite and indefinite articles, gender, and a time-aspect-mode system, modeled on those of French. In addition to these signs, the teacher provided the nature (adjective, noun, verb, etc.) of the elements by using gestures indicative of additional categories."*

The structure of sign language does not present a specific vocabulary for definite or indefinite articles, for example; it is not that they do not exist, but they are expressed differently. So whereas the French language needs to add the preposition à (to) to the verb *aller* (go) to signify movement ("go to…"), sign language, due to its spontaneous spatial expression, needs just one signifier – the à (to) is present in the sign, but has no signifier of its own.

79. For example, the [for] sign.
80. Christian Cuxac, *Le langage des sourds*, Paris: Payot, 1983, p. 26.
81. *Ibid.*

The linguistic logic introduced by de l'Épée – based on, but distorting, the "natural" gestural communication of deaf people – was therefore highly complex. The pupils must have found it quite hard to learn. The sign language resulting from this method was clearly considered as a tool for learning the French language and was not really recognized for its own sake.[82] Bébian criticizes this logic in his essay:[83]

> "[Methodical signs] *are to true sign language what college expressions and the jargon of the people are to the French language.*"

To build a name for himself and gain recognition, de l'Épée organized "public lessons" for four years, from 1771 to 1774. From then on, his initiative had an enormous impact, first nationally, and then abroad. Many people became interested in the work of the "free teacher of the deaf and mute" and the "French method" spread. Joseph II, Emperor of Austria, who came to Paris in 1777 to visit his sister Marie-Antoinette, visited the abbot's school in the Rue des Moulins. As a sign that the greats of this world were very interested in the abbot's work, Joseph II planned to create a similar school in Vienna. He later sent young Abbot Stork to train with de l'Épée. On 21 November 1778, official recognition was granted to the Abbé de l'Épée school, which was placed under royal protection.[84]

This recognition was a consecration of the supremacy of Abbé de l'Épée's enterprise, and due to its official nature, it increased the tensions between the supporters of the two approaches: one of them oral, the other gestural. The controversy began and became public with the publication in 1779 of Abbé Deschamps' *Cours élémentaire d'éducation des sourds et muets* (Elementary course on the education

82. For a more comprehensive linguistic analysis: Christian Cuxac, *La langue des signes : les voies de l'iconicité*, Paris: Ophrys, 2000.
83. Auguste Bébian, *Essai sur les sourds-muets et sur le langage naturel, ou introduction à une classification naturelle des idées avec leurs signes propres*, Librairie L. Colas, 1817, § 59.
84. Quoted by Bezagu-Deluy, *L'abbé de L'Épée*, p. 209.

of the deaf and mute), a veritable plea in favor of the oral method, accompanied by a cutting criticism of sign language. It was a man who had become deaf and whom we have already mentioned, Pierre Desloges, who responded to this attack, even though he had not himself been a pupil of Abbé de l'Épée. That same year, in the form of a reply, he published his *Observations d'un sourd et muet sur un cours élémentaire des sourds-muets* (Observations of a deaf mute on an elementary course for deaf mutes) – the elementary course in question being that of Abbé Deschamps. A work which Saboureux de Fontenay, a former pupil of Pereire's, an adept of oralism and himself deaf, took a step further:[85]

> *"He is indirectly attacking me, I who have declared war on the habit of conversing by means of gestural signs."*

The tone became decidedly offensive and aggressive; it was a question of "attacks" and "war".

While up to that point it had been intermediaries who had inflamed the debate, it was in person that de l'Épée engaged in a polemic with Samuel Heinicke, principal of the German institution in Leipzig. Heinicke's method, revealed after his death, was original in that it incremented the methods known and inspired by Juan Pablo-Bonet and Jean-Conrad Amman, tutors who focused exclusively on vocal speech, with a "third sense": Heinicke combined sight and touch with "taste" for vowels, in accordance with a "taste scale".[86]

> *"According to him, pure water placed on the tongue leads to the formation of the vowel A; a few drops of absinthe, the vowel E; very strong vinegar, the vowel I; sugar water, the vowel O; a few drops of olive oil, the vowel OU (the German U)."*

85. A letter by Saboureux de Fontenay, dated October 10, 1779, quoted by Michel Poizat, *La voix sourde, op. cit.*, p. 134.
86. Abbé Lorenzo Hervas y Panduro, *Historique de l'art d'apprendre aux sourds-muets la langue écrite et la langue parlée*, translated from the Spanish and annotated by André Valade-Gabel, Paris: Delagrave, 1875, p. 51, note M.

In 1781, Heinicke indirectly attacked Abbé de l'Épée through his disciple Abbé Stork, who had been sent to Paris on the orders of Joseph II of Austria. De l'Épée himself replied to Heinicke and there followed an exchange of correspondence that institutionalized a "conflict of methods": oralization and vocal speech versus gestural signifiers.[87] Submitted to the arbitration of an assembly of scholars in Zurich, de l'Épée and his method emerged victorious from the discussions, the assembly finding in favor of de l'Épée on January 15, 1783.[88] Following royal recognition, it was now a scientific body that was to consecrate him. Above and beyond the polemics and the preferred pedagogical options, it was a certain idea of education that became the subject of debate: should we strive at all costs to (re) establish vocal speech and only apprehend the individual in terms of his sensory deficiency, or should we consider gestural speaking without denigrating it and take deafness into account collectively? A fundamental question, still relevant today; the answer not only determines the nature of the education given to deaf people, but also reflects a certain humanist conception of personhood. Abbé de l'Épée substantiated this question at his death:[89]

> *"Abbé de l'Épée's work is recognized and often supported worldwide. Whether discussed, recommended or rejected, it is widely disseminated. The Abbé published articles, wrote letters to countless correspondents, often well-placed in the society of the time. He published books. He carried out numerous interventions."*

---

87. In 1784, de l'Épée published *La véritable manière d'instruire les sourds et muets confirmée par une longue expérience*, with, in the third part, his controversy with Samuel Heinicke which lasted until 1783. We must not forget that these quarrels on the subject of pedagogical methods must not be confused with the history of Deaf people *per se*. Samuel Heinicke's school and "oralist-oriented" method did not systematically exclude signs: furthermore, the establishment allowed the two methods to co-exist.
88. Quoted by Michel Poizat, *La voix sourde,* Paris: Métailié, 1996, p. 135.
89. Bezagu-Deluy, *L'abbé de L'Épée*, p. 237.

Partisans of the French Revolution, defending the oppressed, saw their own reflection in Abbé de l'Épée's commitment – paradoxically, given that he was an ecclesiastic whose work had been consecrated by royal recognition! In 1791 therefore, in the context of Condorcet's project on the general organization of public education, it was decided that his school would be nationalized.[90] Premises were allocated to the INSMP, with which the *Institution des aveugles* was associated, in the Célestine convent in Paris. Cohabitation proved difficult, and in 1794 the Institute was transferred to Rue Saint-Jacques, taking over the premises of the former seminary of Saint-Magloire.

At the end of the 18th century, the foundations of gestural education thus seemed to be firmly in place: Abbé de l'Épée's work enjoyed institutional and scientific backing and its pedagogical validity was recognized. Shortly after de l'Épée's death however, this nascent edifice faltered under the effect of a gradual shockwave that emerged in the aftermath of the Revolution. At the turn of the 18th and 19th centuries, concerns about deafness shifted significantly towards medicalization and "curing".

Unlike the previous, more humanistic century, the 19th century was characterized by a constant concern for health and hygiene. Abbé Sicard, who succeeded Abbé de l'Épée in 1790, first called on Jean-Marc Gaspard Itard, who practiced medicine at the Val-de-Grâce in Paris, in connection with the "discovery" of the "wild child", later named Victor, who had been captured in the Monts de Lacaune forest in Aveyron and had grown up alone, in contact with nature and wild animals.[91] Probably abandoned at an early age, the local authorities turned him over to the *Institut des sourds-muets* in Paris, to learn to speak. Although Itard had not yet graduated – he

90. Report by Nicolas de Condorcet (1743-1794) and then by Charles-Maurice de Talleyrand Périgord (1754-1838) to the French National Assembly on September 10, 11 and 19, 1791, setting out the bases of a public education run by the Nation.
91. Doctor Itard became known to the general public due to his *Mémoire* (1801) and his *Rapport sur Victor de l'Aveyron* (1806). The story of this child was the inspiration for François Truffaut's 1970 film *L'Enfant sauvage*.

would do so two years later – he contacted the institution, where he would become the first doctor to take up a position. The child was also a favorite subject of observation and analysis for the recently created *Société des Observateurs de l'Homme* (Society of Observers of Mankind).[92] As soon as Itard arrived, he found an immediate justification for teaching articulated speech ("demutization" was Itard's thing), putting forward two principles. The first was strongly influenced by the medical and hygienic ideology of the time, stipulating that since deafness was treatable, it was better to make it disappear than to set up a proper education. From the beginning of the 19th century, health and hygiene were the main concerns, and increasingly so over the years.[93] People were more than ever obsessed with the specter of the degeneration of the species, and hearing impairment – deafness was equated with disease, a disease that must be eradicated.[94] Gestural communication was seen as a symptom. Itard's second principle represented a more direct attack on sign language, which some people at the time believed to cause tuberculosis, due to the inactivity of the respiratory system. Rather than blaming the hygienic conditions of the establishment (unsanitary), or the poor quality of the food (spoiled, inadequate or simply scarce), it was the insufficient ventilation of the lungs, caused by gestural expression, that was held responsible for these diseases, as the air supposedly circulated less![95] It was in this context that Jean-Marc Gaspard Itard became the Institution's first health officer. Indeed, from 1800 onwards, in the historical context of the "puritanism" affecting European societies, the body of the deaf person, the very essence of their communication, was subjected to increasingly strict control. Although their bodies have always been

92. For more on this, see p. 84.

93. Georges Vigarello, *Le propre et le sale. L'hygiène du corps depuis le Moyen Âge*, Seuil, 1987.

94. A theory of degeneration took shape after 1850, influenced by Benedict Augustin Morel who laid the groundwork (*Traité des dégénérescences physiques, intellectuelles et morales de l'espèce humaine*, Paris: Jean-Baptiste Baillière, 1857).

95. Aude de Saint-Loup, "Histoires de malentendus, histoire des sourds", in *Diogène*, 1996, p. 80.

the object of much attention and care, the search for hygiene in the 19th century was accompanied by an increased medicalization of deafness.[96] This was therefore seen as justification for recruiting a health officer for the Paris Institution. Alongside this logic of care were concerns of an "educational" nature: In 1836, Jean-Baptiste Puybonnieux, a professor at the INSMP, was outraged that deaf students with some remaining hearing capacity were being accepted at the INSMP:[97]

> *"While their ears, which remained sharp and keen through the use of speech, gradually close, and children who, raised with intelligence through speech more often than not ended up with clear hearing, become completely deaf in our midst."*

This argument was taken up and amplified for educational purposes later on, in the 1850s, by one of the physicians who succeeded Itard, Alexandre Blanchet:[98] it was he who set up the first attempts at integrating children into ordinary schools. Didactic reasoning was added to arguments of a physiological nature: at a cognitive level, sign language was declared incompatible with the learning of speech, because it called for a different system of symbolization.

This virulent deprecation of sign language, which had not existed in this form at the time of Abbé de l'Épée, was initially reflected in a confusion with pantomime. But in 1800, sign language had been in existence for several decades and the older students were fluent in

96. As soon as the Institution de Paris was founded, health walks were organised when time permitted and the pupils were regularly taken to the baths for reasons of hygiene: bathtubs were installed before a real swimming pool was built in the Institution's own premises. This was one of the first swimming pools constructed in a teaching establishment.
97. Jean-Baptiste Puybonnieux, *L'Impartial*, 1843, pp. 71-72.
98. In line with the approach to deafness as a pathology, he developed a pedagogical project designed to have any pupil with some remaining hearing capacity educated at an external school.
Alexandre Blanchet was the INSMP's surgeon, while the senior physician was Menière, who defended the puils against any medical or pedagogical experimentation.

its practice. Abbé Sicard therefore had ample time to observe the obvious difference between the elaborate linguistic communication of the older students and the "pantomime" of the younger pupils, newcomers to the institution.[99] In his *Journal*, Bébian describes Sicard's ignorance, something that by no means interfered with the latter's self-congratulation:[100]

> *"Abbé Sicard (here I call upon the testimony of all the teachers who saw him close up, and particularly upon that of the deaf-mutes who left the school he directed), Abbé Sicard never knew the language of his pupils… Abbé de l'Épée often reproached him, I am told, for not paying enough attention to this essential part of the art, but it would appear that he did not heed this wise advice; and in his public exercises, he needed all of his mental dexterity to hide the embarrassment and awkwardness of his pantomime. He could only make himself understood by his pupils with the pen or the manual alphabet, and until they were sufficiently educated to make use of this means of communication, their intelligence was for him a closed book. This explains the error in which he remained immersed, ignoring the enlightenment of day-to-day experience.* […] *In a way, the deaf-mute's intelligence was thus viewed as the work of his master, and as a creation of art. This illusion was too flattering for it not to seduce the imagination of Abbé Sicard, who believed he found in it, all together, the confirmation of his favorite principle and the approval of his method* […] *But among all the admirers of his successes, it may be that Abbé Sicard never had a more sincere admirer than himself."*

As soon as Abbé de l'Épée died, the enterprise he had created was threatened from within. A solid oralist ideology found echo therein and gradually invaded the premises, personified by Jean-Marc Itard, whose appointment simply reflected the prevailing will. A sign of the times that were to come, this appointment symbolized medical science's hold over the education of deaf people: for example, the physician Nicolas Deleau published his thoughts in the

99. Cuxac, *Le langage des sourds*, p. 66.
100. *Journal des sourds-muets et des aveugles*, vol. II, 1827, § 24-26.

form of eloquently titled books: "*Dissertation on the perforation of the eardrum to reestablish hearing in several cases of deafness*";[101] "*Description of an instrument with which to reestablish hearing in several cases of deafness)*";[102] and "*Observations concerning two deaf-mutes who can hear and speak, serving to prove that many deaf people can benefit from the same blessing.*"[103]

All the more so as, upon the death of Abbé Sicard, who left the Institution in a deplorable state, both financially and materially, it was the board of governors that ran the establishment.[104] When he died in 1822, his position was given to another abbot, Abbé Gondelin,[105] something of a puppet, whom Sicard had "designated"; a designation ratified by the administrators of the Institution because it presented the advantage:[106]

> "*of removing Jean Massieu* [...] *who had the drawback of being a deaf-mute himself, but above all of enjoying considerable popularity*

101. Nicolas Deleau, *Mémoire sur la perforation du tympan pratiquée pour rétablir l'ouïe dans plusieurs cas de surdité*, Paris: Crevot, 1822.
102. Nicolas Deleau, *Description d'un instrument pour rétablir l'ouïe dans plusieurs cas de surdité*, Paris: Impr. De Fain, 1823.
103. Nicolas Deleau, *Observations faites sur deux sourdes-muettes qui entendent et qui parlent, pour servir de preuves que beaucoup de Sourds peuvent jouir du même bienfait*, Paris: Denis, 1823.
104. *"As from 1812, Sicard ceased pontificating from his podium* [...]*; he was prey to intriguers, his intellectual faculties were dormant. The de facto leadership fell to Paulmier, a partisan of speech for the deaf, and to Abbé Salvan: 'a glorious reign ended in confusion'."* René Bernard, "Les cours normaux pour la formation des maîtres de sourds-muets", in *Bulletin d'audiophonologie*, vol. 11, n° 2, 1980, p. 25 quoted by Jean-René Presneau, *op. cit.*, 1998, p. 157.
105. A former teacher at the Bordeaux Institution (where Sicard was the principal), he held this position for just three months, during the summer of 1822, before resigning due to his demands concerning salary and authority being refused. From 1823 to 1827 he was replaced by Abbé Périer, former director of the Rodez establishment. Périer was equally incompetent and "*has proven to be a disastrous choice*": he was incompetent both as a teacher and as a principal (François Buton., *op. cit.*, 2009, p. 124) and the position was finally taken by a third abbot, Borel, for the next four years, from 1827 to 1831, before a layman, Désiré Ordinaire, was appointed (p. 44).
106. Session of March 16, 1822, INJS; quoted by François Buton, *ibid.*, p. 124.

among the pupils and the deaf-mute répétiteurs, for having been, with Bébian [...], the person really in charge of teaching at the Institution during the 1810s".

Bébian laconically notes that the position "was offered to the habit rather than to the talent".[107] It was the chairman of the board of governors, Baron Joseph-Marie de Gérando,[108] assisted by Itard, the Institute's physician, and by Paulmier,[109] the oldest of INSMP's

107. *Journal des sourds-muets et des aveugles*, vol. II, 1827, § 8.

108. *"The family name is Degerando and not Gérando. Up until the July Monarchy, Gérando signed all his papers Degerando. The particle, used later on, was taken up by the general biographies of the 19th century and by the catalogue of the Bibliothèque nationale de France, and we will follow this usage."* Jean-Luc Chappey, Carole Christen and Igor Moullier (eds.), *Joseph-Marie de Gérando (1772-1842). Connaître et réformer la société*, Rennes: PUR, 2014, p. 11.
Joseph-Marie de Gérando (1772-1841) (General Secretary of the Ministry of the Interior, State Councillor and French peer) was President of the INSMP's board of governors from 1829 (he had been nominated in 1814) to 1841, the year in which a major central administration reform set up a consultative committee to replace this board, a sign that the State was taking over. The board of governors, created in 1800 (decree dated *18 Fructidor An VIII*), was omnipresent in the Institute's affairs, including matters of pedagogy, in a context of indifference by the central administration (François Buton, "*Ce qu'administrer veut dire. Gérando et l'éducation des sourds-muets (1814-1841)*", in Chappey, Christen and Moullier (eds.), *op. cit.*, p. 143.
According to Bébian, *"the board of governors is a sort of fictitious and abstract entity that may only be grasped in terms of its acts, something that people would often not dare to admit... It is the blind god that presides over the Institution's destinies; it is a sort of domestic fatum, obedient to an occult force, to a sort of fatality that drives it to the ruin of this establishment".* Auguste Bébian, *Examen critique de la nouvelle organisation de l'enseignement dans l'Institution royale des sourds-muets de Paris*, Paris: Treuttel and Wurtz, 1834, p. 14.

109. The same person with whom Bébian had had a fierce altercation in 1821, leading to his dismissal. Louis Paulmier influenced Sicard during the last years of his life. On the cover of his book written in 1820 (Louis-Pierre Paulmier, *Le Sourd-Muet civilisé*, Paris, imprimerie d'ange-clo, 1820 (reprinted by Fox, 2010)), Paulmier introduces himself as a *"pupil for 20 years and collaborator of M. l'abbé Sicard"* and in the introduction to the reprinted edition of this work, the publisher notes that he *"blindly applied Sicard's method, with its methodical, artificial and excessively complicated signs..."*. He is unanimously described as ignorant and conceited. In a scathing letter to the ministry's divisional director,

teachers, who was the real leader. In 1828, Jean Itard asked the Académie de Médecine to give its opinion on the articulation lessons that he had been wishing to set up since the beginning of the century, in the prevailing social context of prudishness and a desire to control the body. In order to proceed with "demutization", gymnastics was introduced into the curriculum, in line with the "method" devised by Colonel Amoros.[110] This militaristic method

---

Noailles writes that, like Sicard, Paulmier was endowed with *"the disastrous habit of seeing the instruction of deaf-mutes as an opportunity to perform in public"*, that he was *"barely sufficiently educated to write French correctly"*, that his pupils were the least well-educated in the establishment, and that he *"shone"* only when it came to obtaining *"testimonials of high regard"*. Liasse Paulmier, fonds Pinart, quoted by François Buton, *op. cit.*, 2009, p. 200- 201. A former artilleryman, he joined the INSMP on October 26, 1801 (5 Brumaire de l'An XIII) and retired in 1829. A teacher, he regularly acted as an interpreter for courts in the Paris region. Yves Bernard reports that his interpreting skills were decried: *"...during his trial, another deaf-mute complained about the interpreter, Paulmier, a former teacher at the same institution – a disciple of Sicard, he only knew the 'methodical' signs – and unsuccessfully asked for Berthier's help"*; the latter *"saw in Paulmier nothing more than an honorable old man who was not very enlightened or well-educated"*. This opinion requires qualification: Paulmier showed a passionate interest in many university-level courses. See the excellent work by Bernard Variot, "*Approche de quelques aspects de la vie sociale des sourds-muets et de leur instruction au milieu du XIX*[e] *siècle, vus au travers de L'Impartial, journal de l'enseignement des sourds-muets, 1856-1859*", a thesis for the CAPINJS, ENSP, 1980, quoted by Yves Bernard, *Approche de la gestualité à l'institution des sourds-muets de Paris, XVIII-XIX*[es] *siècles*, doctoral thesis, Université Paris V, 1999, p. 390-91. This lack of competence was found in Abbé Sicard, appointed curator of the deaf person François Duval, but who, during the latter's trial in 1800, proved to be totally unable to communicate with him (not in sign language, which the accused had not mastered, but using gestural communication in the broad sense; it was Jean Massieu, a répétiteur at that time, who acted as interpreter (which gives an idea of Sicard's knowledge of visual thought). J. B. J. Breton, *Procès de François Duval. Sourd et Muet de naissance, sous la curatelle de Sicard*, Paris, 1800; reprinted by Fox, 2010).

110. The Spanish colonel Amorós (1770-1848) is considered to be the man who introduced gymnastics into France in the 1830s. Well-established in France, he obtained permission from the Ministry of War to open a gymnastics institute on the Plain of Grenelle. A great admirer of the Greeks, Amorós considered gymnastics "to be the reasoned science of our movements and their relationship with our senses, our intelligence, our feelings, our morals

was based on singing – thus requiring the use of the voice – and was designed to "purify" the mind and thus impose a certain "purity" and a certain morality... Deaf pupils were hence ascribed dubious impulses, onanistic tendencies and thoughts deemed "dirty" at that time, some people likening their behavior to that of animals. The hygiene (cleanliness) of the premises went hand in glove with a desire for mental hygiene.[111] In 1829, the INSMP issued a second memorandum, which provided for the *gradual elimination* of the use of sign language as the pupil advanced in age, so as not to be detrimental to articulation. A few years later, following the next memorandum, Bébian conducted *a critical examination of the new teaching organization at the Royal Institution for Deaf-Mutes in Paris* (his opinion was published in detail under this title in 1834),[112] criticizing the incompetence of the board of governors and the Institution's principal.

By the mid-19th century, "*the beacon had gone out*," in the words of Alphonse Esquiros,[113] and at the end of that same century sign

---

and the development of all our faculties". See *Manuel d'éducation physique, gymnastique et morale*, Paris: Roret, 1830 (reprinted in 1838 and 1848).

111. Georges Vigarello, *Histoire des pratiques de santé. Le sain et le malsain depuis le Moyen Âge*, Paris: Seuil, 1993.

112. This book is made up of 67 paragraphs: it offers a detailed examination and critique of the third *Circulaire*, published by the Paris Institution in 1832. There are four *Circulaires*, a term borrowed from the administrative world, the origin of which was linked to the the voluminous work (1200 pages) by Baron de Gérando: *De l'éducation des sourds-muets de naissance*. The first Circulaire dates back to 1827, the second was published in 1829, the third (the one to which Bébian reacted) in 1832 and the fourth and last in 1836. These formal, "official", texts impose the idea of the Paris Institution's superiority over the other French establishments, by invoking the memory of Abbé de l'Épée: yet most of the time it is simply a question of the INSMP's convictions and pedagocical essays, judged by the administrators of that same school! Works and exposés from all over the world (India, Mexico) are reproduced and commented on. The fourth *Circulaire* is the longest: 480 pages! ("Only" 250 for the third and even fewer for the remaining two).

113. Alphonse Esquiros, *Paris, ou Les sciences, les institutions, et les mœurs au XIXe siècle*, Paris: Comptoir des Imprimeurs Unis, 1847, t. 2, p. 443. The members of the supervisory board were *"honorable men, but who knew nothing about the education of deaf-mutes"* (*ibid.*, p. 445).

language was effectively banned at a congress held in Milan in September 1880. This ban was ultimately just a logical part of the process that had begun the day after Abbé de l'Épée's death. As if to prove that this decision was far from unanimous, at an assembly of physician-otologists meeting on the same day in Milan, the INSMP's assistant physician, Édouard Fournié, defended sign language for the instruction of young deaf people.[114]

Would it not be more accurate to consider Abbé de l'Épée's work as an unfinished pedagogical experiment, a parenthesis that was never closed, rather than as the beginning of a "golden century", the 19th century, which ended with the Milan congress? Far more than de l'Épée's official successor, Abbé Sicard, it was Auguste Bébian who, through his ideas and achievements, picked up the torch that Abbé de l'Épée had lit.

---

114. "De l'instruction physiologique du sourd-muet" (On the physiological instruction of the deaf-mute), an extract of the minutes of the sessions and of the International Otology Congress' essays, read or filed, 6-9 September 1880, quoted by F. Légent, "Approche de la pédagogie institutionnelle des sourds-muets jusqu'en 1900", Médic@, 2005 and Fabrice Bertin, *Les Sourds. Une minorité invisible,* Paris: Autrement, 2010, p. 166-169.

Chapter 1
Itinerary of a man in the shadows

Retracing the life of Auguste Bébian is an arduous yet fascinating task: the contrast between this character who is so essential to the history of the Deaf community, and our ignorance of him, is startling. Broadly speaking, of this story – or more precisely of the education of Deaf people – posterity has retained only the name and person of Charles-Michel de l'Épée, known as Abbé de l'Épée. A central figure in this education, as we have already seen, his "good deeds" are steeped in exaggeration and approximation.[1] One persistent and widespread notion even designates him as the founder of sign language! In fact, "all" he did was give legitimacy to the means of communication used by deaf people, the one that is most natural to them. This convergence is undoubtedly important, but does it not overstate this initiative? Without wishing to minimize the considerable role that Abbé de l'Épée played, and the paradigm shift he initiated, it nevertheless creates a problem: the history of the Deaf community is overly identified with his person. But to what extent should the history of a people or a cultural minority be confused with that of its colonizers and missionaries? If this abbot was indeed a precursor, it was only his first deaf pupils that made him so. The latter were essential protagonists, yet remain totally unknown to us.

Auguste Bébian (1789-1839), on the other hand, was the decisive spark that lit a fire that would later light up the path for Deaf people, albeit without Bébian himself. Such discretion was probably his most typical characteristic. Furthermore, these pages are a continuation of this: first of all a guide, before becoming the subject of

1. For more on Charles-Michel de l'Épée, see p. 45.
Many cities have named streets after Abbé de l'Épée, in recognition of his work: Paris, Marseille, Rouen, Poitiers, Clermont-Ferrand, Bordeaux, Reims and even Brussels, beyond the French frontier: *Priester de L'Épéestraat* (Abbé de l'Épée street in Dutch) is the street in which the Institute for the Deaf is located. It is so named in reference to *"the inventor of French sign language"* (a false claim, but one that reveals the power attributed to the Abbé).

this study, his presence is a pretext for considering the situation of Deaf people at the beginning of the 19th century. Indeed, he revealed and discussed inconsistencies while remaining outside the limelight. What is known about him is inversely proportional to the momentum, reflection and actions that subsequently led to the emancipation of deaf people, to their awareness of themselves as speakers of a language in their own right. Contributing to the reconstruction of a facet of this "forgotten" past is not only of interest in relation to the history of the Deaf community, but also to the history of the world as a whole, of which it is an integral part. Above and beyond Bébian as a person, his interaction with the Deaf world reveals questions and concerns, and underlines objections and fundamental inconsistencies that remain largely current. The friendship that developed very early in his life between him and Laurent Clerc, the emblematic deaf teacher of the National Institution for Deaf-Mutes in Paris, was decisive not only for the Deaf community,[2] but also for the study of sign language, as Anne T. Quartararo points out.[3] Having to ensure that "deaf-mutes" participated fully in the society which was theirs but from which they were excluded due to their lack of instruction, of accessible education, suffices to explain the meaning behind a fight that Auguste Bébian pursued in several forms. He never ceased to remind people that they were not dealing with foreigners, but with fellow citizens:[4]

---

2. "*One of the most important forces in the development of signing society in Paris and elsewhere as our current century progressed was, however, a hearing man, a true martyr for the cause of the deaf and, I am proud to say, my student and friend. In the declining years of Abbé Sicard, Roch-Ambroise Bébian rose like the sun partially dispelling the clouds. For the deaf, he holds a place next to Abbé de l'Épée*" recollects Laurent Clerc under the pen of Harlan Lane. (Harlan Lane, *When the Mind Hears*, New York: Knopf Doubleday, 2010, p. 117);

   Ferdinand Berthier, *Notice sur la vie et les ouvrages de Auguste Bébian, ancien censeur de l'institut royal des sourds-muets*, J. Ledoyen, 1839, p. 6.
3. Anne T. Quartararo, *Deaf Identity and Social Images in Nineteenth-Century France*, Washington: Gallaudet University Press, 2002, p. 50.
4. Auguste Bébian, "De l'enseignement des sourds-muets", *Journal de l'instruction publique*, 1828, p. 75.

"[...] one only needs to have lived with them for a few days to be convinced that, while like us they experience sensations of pleasure and pain, like us they also react in relation to their sensations. Their minds contain the seeds of the same faculties; the same feelings stir their souls... They differ from other men only in being deprived of one sense. And if education shows them in the full exercise of intelligence, it is because the teacher has received them from nature's hands, endowed with all the intellectual faculties."

The only biography of Bébian that we possess was written by Ferdinand Berthier,[5] who constantly describes Bébian as a profoundly benevolent man, a victim of this same benevolence, a "*character trait that honors this worthy teacher far too much for us to ignore it,*" and which he illustrates with this anecdote:[6]

"One day, he reproached one of them (his children) for having called him simply his master, and this in such a cordial tone, that it must, one can well imagine, have increased the energy and vivacity of [the child's] *feelings for him. Until then, the unfortunate deaf-mutes, victims of a prejudice based on the opinion of a famous teacher,[7] had been treated almost like savages, exposed without protection to the ill-treatment and profanities of the supervisors and even the servants. Bébian made all the employees feel that they were there for the pupils and not that the pupils were there for them* [...].

In the same vein, Ferdinand Berthier mentions the intervention of the first principal of the INSMP, on behalf of a young deaf person who was expelled from the institution on the basis of a false report. He wanted to show that this character trait was inherent to him, a constitutive part of his person and long before he took up his po-

5. Berthier, *Notice*. Inspiring the shorter and later biography, written by Louis Vauchelet in *Le Colonial* in 1911.
6. *Ibid.*, p. 21.
7. How could one not consider Abbé Sicard's opinion?

sition at the Institution. Hence this episode, dating back more than ten years before he joined the establishment, so in 1808 or 1809:[8]

> "[…] *all the beautiful books that he kept carefully under lock and key became prey to the flames; they searched in vain for the new Omar*[9] […] *Long after Bébian had left the college, one of his former comrades repented and confessed a wrongdoing that he still bewails to this day. He was one of his rivals, the most unfortunate of all in the scholastic struggle, because he was the one whose talent most closely resembled* [Bébian's]. *Not only did Bébian remain friends with him, he even fully trusted him later on."*

Notice sur la vie et les ouvrages de Auguste Bébian, his only existing biography, is far more a work of praise for Bébian than a history book; it simply describes him as a *"tireless champion of a holy cause"*. Ferdinand Berthier can unquestionably be defined as the craftsman and guardian of the memory of the man who was the first principal of the National Institution for Deaf-Mutes, even if it meant embellishing facts or distorting reality. This can be seen in the detailed and commented reading of Berthier's writings by the Institution's board of governors:[10] although these objections seek to incriminate Bébian, and do not make it possible to establish the facts, they add a certain nuance to Berthier's interpretation.[11] Overall, the board criticized him for always:

> *"...blaming the administration for Bébian's misfortunes and holding it responsible for this crime. The notes that precede have demonstrated*

8. Berthier, *Notice*, p. 6.
9. A reference to the caliph who ordered the burning of the Alexandria library in the 7th century. This thesis is nowadays disputed.
10. Minutes of the session of March 2, 1840. AMHCS, Bébian bundle, Pinart collection, (Annex 7).
11. The minutes cover ten pages, divided into two columns. The left-hand column contains quotes from the *Notice sur la vie et les ouvrages de Bébian* by Ferdinand Berthier; in the right-hand column, the quotes are refuted point by point.

the true cause: the disorder, the debts, the failure to meet commitments, the abuse of subscriptions, etc.
Now, can anyone be surprised thereafter by the temerity of someone who dares to present Bébian as a second Abbé de l'Épée and then to blame the misfortunes on the administration and the government? Indeed one would not conceive of this blindness if one were not aware that pride and ambition obscure reason and are capable of conflating everything and of daring anything."

Berthier's personal ambitions are clearly alluded to, and according to the board of governors, even explain his remarks – remarks which might also be construed as instrumentalizing Bébian. But to what extent does Bébian's mythical dimension carry a message? And what is the content of this message?

The aim of this study is not to deconstruct the myth but to grasp it as clearly as possible, to try to understand what it teaches us not only about a figure who played such a key part in Deaf emancipation, but beyond that, what it reveals about this particular world and contemporary problems. So we must first examine the contours and challenges of the biographical exercise and identify Auguste Bébian's place in Deaf historiography.

In many ways his path was entirely atypical. Along with his itinerary, his geographical and socio-cultural origins mean that on many levels he stands out as a unique character. This is why we believe that as far as possible it is essential to shed light on this fertile ground. We hypothesize that the environment and the framework of Bébian's childhood in Guadeloupe, followed by those of his adolescence in France, were closely linked to the new approach that he would later develop in relation to the issue of deaf people. His presence in France left its mark, as is clear from the way in which he was, and still is, remembered. This will be the subject of the first part of this book. This immersive encounter with a world that was unfamiliar to him, but whose substance he so intimately grasped, manifested itself in many ways, around one key idea: access to education and, beyond that, to citizenship. In this respect, two issues emerge: first of all the early stages of learning to read and the acquisition of the French language with a view to becoming autonomous; and secondly drawing, essential for someone learning to speak a gestural language that has no written form. We will examine these questions in the second part of the book.[12]

Through Auguste Bébian and his journey, we address essential anthropological and pedagogical questions, while at the same time revealing the keys to understanding a decisive period in the history of the Deaf community.

1. From one continent to the other

Although born on the western shores of the Atlantic Ocean, it was on the opposite shore that Auguste Bébian fulfilled most of his destiny, in the world of the Deaf community, which had no obvious connection to his original environment.[13] He was a young teenager when he arrived in Paris in 1802, but had spent his childhood on an island in the Lesser Antilles, in Guadeloupe to be precise, on a colonial plantation, known locally as a "*habitation*", with parents who divorced when he was between four and six years old.[14] His exact date of birth is not known to us and this approximation to some extent reflects the uncertainty that surrounds the entire life of this unusual figure. Just a

12. He points out that "[…] *the specific purpose of teaching deaf-mutes is that of teaching them the language of their country*" (*Journal de l'instruction des sourds-muets et des aveugles*, 1826, n° 4, p. 60).
13. Although this spelling convention is anachronistic given that there was not yet any deaf issue in the 19th century; we take the liberty of so doing in order to underline this cultural reality highlighted by Auguste Bébian. François Buton, "L'éducation des sourds-muets au XIXe siècle. Description d'une activité sociale", *Le Mouvement social*, 2008/2, n° 223, p. 69.
14. A *habitation* was an autonomous farming unit based on a servile labor force. Frédéric Régent (*Esclavage, métissage, liberté. La Révolution française en Guadeloupe, 1789-1802*, Paris: Grasset, 2004, pp. 74 & 93) offers a typical example of this which is not necessarily generalizable, it being proportional to the size of the property, thus justifying a highly codified organization: the organogram of the social organization of sugar plantations at the end of the 18th century is indicative of the repressive and hierarchical system upon which it is based. The difficulties encountered in locating Bergopzoom would seem to suggest a *habitation* of small size but also of relative importance: the cultivation of coffee required a much smaller labor force than that needed for sugarcane. *Idem.*, pp. 87 and 89.

few isolated instances offer us glimpses of a brief but intense existence; an existence that guided the Deaf community onto the road toward emancipation… The early years of this man who would later be called upon to play such a great role are nevertheless shrouded in enigma: did he experience something during those years that might explain his later commitment? How did he gain access to a quality education that allowed him to go to one of the best schools in the capital? Is our difficulty in grasping Bébian simply evidence of his discreet and modest character?

This mystery undoubtedly contributes to the legend and lends credence to the idea of "an unjust neglect", denounced by Ferdinand Berthier.[15] Indeed, the character of Auguste Bébian alone symbolizes the ambivalence of the Deaf world, reduced to a question of ears and hearing for some, while others lay claim to a singular culture and even a nation. Furthermore, at the very beginning of the 19th century, when the young Auguste discovered this other world, could one even speak of a "world"? The mark that he left there was sufficiently consequential for a Deaf person who had not known him in person to say of him, fifty years after his death, that *"in a short time* [he became] *a veritable deaf-mute with a total mastery of sign language."*[16] Other Deaf people, such as Joachim Ligot[17] or

15. Berthier, *Notice,* p. 44. Ferdinand Berthier laments this oversight on several occasions. In the very first lines of his book, the only one about Auguste Bébian, he declares his desire to rehabilitate *"a reputation that has overcome neglect and ingratitude".* (*Ibid.*, p. 5).
16. Benjamin Dubois, "Physiologie du sourd-muet, par Bébian", *L'abbé de l'Épée. Journal des sourds et des sourds-muets,* n° 2, 1888, p. 28.
Benjamin Dubois (1820-?) was himself deaf, and a former student of Valade at the INSMP. A deaf-speaker – he became deaf at the age of four – he set up a school for deaf-speakers in 1837, with ministerial authorization, and directed it with the help of his hearing sisters and parents.
In 1855, the school's grant holders were transferred to the national Institution, into two "special classes for teaching through speech", run by Dubois himself. He was permanent secretary of the former Universal Society of Deaf-Mutes, founded in Paris in 1838, and publication director of the review *L'abbé de l'Épée. Journal des sourds et des sourds-muets*, published in 1888-1889.
17. Joachim-Marie Ligot (1841-1899) could not have known Auguste Bébian directly, as he was born after Bébian died. *"Upon his arrival at the Paris Insti-*

Claudius Forestier[18] referred to him long after his death: the memory of Auguste Bébian remained alive. It is indeed significant that his only biographer was a Deaf man, Ferdinand Berthier (1803-1886), who had been his student and then his friend, an illustrious Deaf man decorated ten years later with the Legion of Honor by the President of France. The latter was a continuation of the former, creating an ocean-wide intercultural Deaf-Hearing tandem; this tandem is captured in the beautiful Creole word *lyannaj*.[19]

1.1 The Bergopzoom mystery…

The village of Morne-à-l'Eau, where Auguste came into the world in 1789 or 1791,[20] is a town in Guadeloupe,[21] a small colony located

tution, he was considered to be a backward child. It was thanks to his teacher, Ferdinand Berthier, that he was able to reveal his talents. He was a student-monitor in Berthier's class from 1856 to 1859, and took holy orders, becoming a Brother of Saint Gabrie, though he was to leave the order later on. A teacher in Rouen from 1872 to around 1877, he left teaching for health reasons" and regularly contributed to silent journals such as *L'abbé de l'Épée. Journal des sourds et des sourds-muets* and the *Gazette des sourds-muets*. He is regularly mentioned in the list of deaf elites educated in sign language, drawn up in 1879 by the French minister of the Interior, as Ernest Dusuzeau confirmed in 1912, during the Third International Congress of Deaf-Mutes in Paris: "[…] *Mr. Berthier succeeded in bringing light to the brain of young Ligot who later became one of the best writers. How did Mr. Berthier achieve such brilliant success?… By using sign language."* "La Méthode orale et la Méthode des signes," pp. 66-69 of the minutes of the Third International Congress of Deaf-Mutes. Nathalie Lachance, *Territoire, transmission et culture sourde,* Laval: Presses de l'université de Laval, 2007, p. 271.

18. Claudius Forestier (1810-1891), a Deaf person, was a student and then teacher at the INSMP. In 1840 he became principal of the Institution des Sourds-Muets de Lyon (an institution initially created in Saint-Étienne in 1815 by another Deaf person, David Comberry, and then transferred to Lyon in 1824).
19. *Lyannaj* means linkage, connection, but also unity in adversity.
20. On the mysteries surrounding this date of birth, see Annex 2.
21. Guadeloupe had been a French colony since 1635: discovered by Christopher Columbus, the island was abandoned and later colonized by the Compagnie des îles d'Amérique (which replaced the Compagnie de l'Isle de Saint-Christophe). On the verge of bankruptcy, the latter sold its islands to its governors. Guadeloupe was thus sold to Sieur de Boisseret, who in turn sold part of it to his brother-in-law Charles Houël in 1648. In 1664, the

in the Lesser Antilles,[22] approximately 600 km from the shores of South America and 10,000 km from Europe. It is to be found west of the island of Grande-Terre, one of the two main geographical parts of Guadeloupe, separated by the "Rivière Salée" sound, and is bordered by the Grand-Cul-de-Sac marine mangrove. The two main islands (Grande-Terre to the east and Guadeloupe proper to the west) nevertheless form only one part of this colony made up of the islands of Saintes (to the southwest), Marie-Galante (to the southeast) and Desirade (at the eastern end of Grande Terre).

The municipality of Morne-à-l'Eau, officially created in 1827 by order of Charles X, King of France, stretches between the mangrove, the large fish pools and the cane plain: it is a vast and disparate zone. It was successively named "Case aux Lamantins" (a place favored by manatees for reproduction), "Vieux-bourg", "Grippon" (from the name of a vast plain), then "Bordeaux-Bourg", before being officially named "Morne-à-l'Eau" (the etymology refers to a water source that flows along the "morne Grippon" – Grippon hill). The municipality's development really began with the construction of

---

Compagnie des Indes Occidentales, founded by Colbert, compensated the governors and re-established royal authority over the West Indian colonies. From 1654 onwards, the Dutch, who had come from Brazil, introduced the cultivation of sugarcane and the production of sugar, using enslaved Africans: from this moment on, the island became part of the slave system, which was based on slavery, the triangular trade, and the plantation economy (sugarcane for the most part). Historian Frédéric Régent (*Esclavage, métissage, liberté*, p. 21) estimates the slave trade practiced by European states (Portugal, Netherlands, Denmark, France, Great Britain, etc.) to have involved between 11 and 12 million people between the 16th and 19th centuries: this was undoubtedly "the largest deportation of human beings of all time", according to Olivier Petré-Grenouilleau (*Les traites négrières, essai d'histoire globale*, Paris: Gallimard, 2004, p. 10). From a legal standpoint, the Code Noir, established by King Louis the 15th in 1685, and which governed the life of the enslaved people, considered "slaves to be furniture" (Article 44).

22. Doubtless a word derived from Portuguese ("ante-ilhas", the "fore-islands"), the Antilles form an archipelago subdivided into the "Greater Antilles", made up of four of the largest islands Cuba, Hispaniola (modern Haiti and Dominican Republic), Puerto Rico and Jamaica; the "Lesser Antilles" form an archipelago in the shape of an arc that runs from Puerto Rico to South America.

the Canal des Rotours, named after the baron who financed the construction in order to drain the marshy area and connect it to the sea. The canal facilitated exports to the port of Pointe-à-Pitre, and made it possible to transport the many valuable products of this fertile region (sugar and rum) in barges via the "Salt River".

The map of the districts of Guadeloupe at the end of the 18th century shows its location:[23]

23. Régent, *Esclavage, métissage, liberté*, p. 73.

Figure n°1: Districts of Guadeloupe 1789-1793

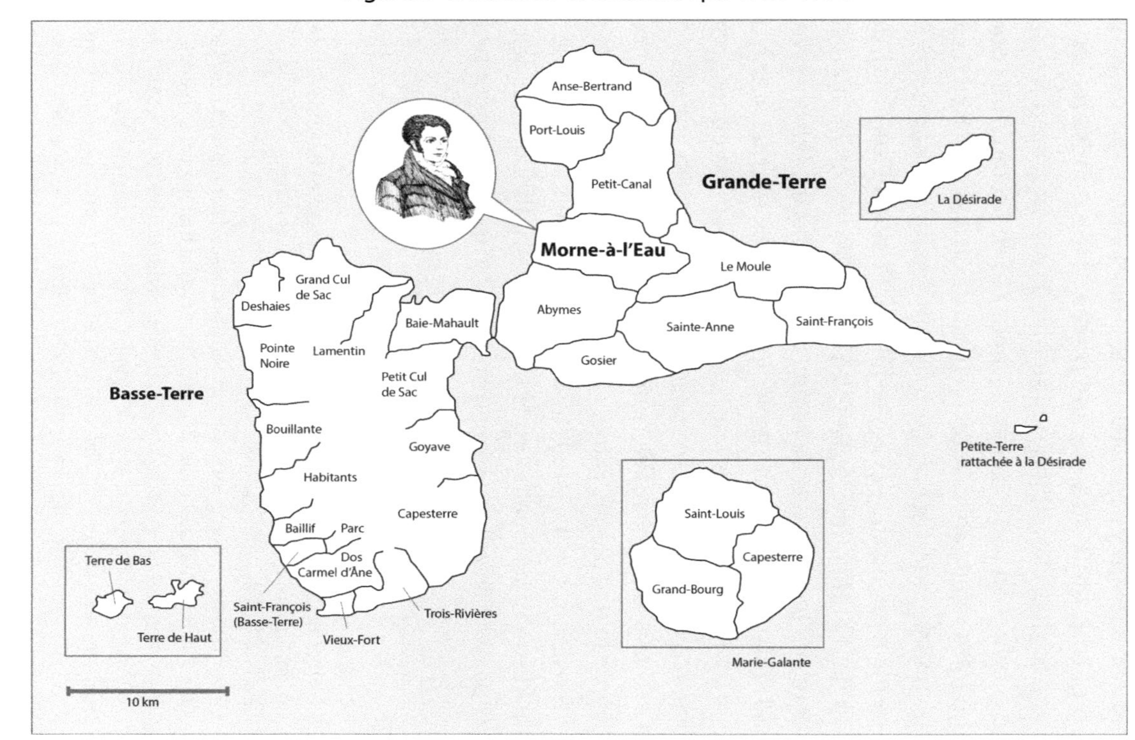

Ancestry/socio-cultural milieu

The Bergopzoom *habitation*, where Bébian was born, was located in a sparsely populated area.[24] The inhabited space was made up of crop-growing areas and places where goods and services were traded. Everything on the island was organized according to production and exports, in theory to the colonizing country, though a significant part of the production was exported through the underground economy, to North America in particular. Even the main towns, such as Basse-Terre or Pointe-à-Pitre, in full development at that time, *"exist solely for the benefit of the inhabitants for whom they serve as shops and as a warehouse. This is where one will find the merchants, artisans, judges, clerks, notaries, prosecutors and government officials who control and direct. There are no nobles, bourgeois, persons of independent means, or great minds. Every town is a factory for sugar, coffee, cotton, indigo, and for those who produce them."*[25] In his account, Father Labat[26] mentions just one usable road in Guadeloupe in the late 17th and early 18th centuries,[27] connecting the districts of Houelbourg and Bananiers: although Guadeloupe proper was already developed (its development had begun around

24. We know the name from the verification of affidavit (enquête de notoriété) concerning Joseph Bébian in 1828 (Annex 4).
25. According to Saint-Domingue intendant Malouet, quoted by Anne Pérotin-Dumon, *La ville aux îles, la ville dans l'île, Basse-Terre et Pointe-à-Pitre, 1650-1820*, Paris: Karthala, 1999, p. 493.
26. The district of Houelbourg corresponds to the modern-day industrial zone of Jarry, in Baie-Mahault (near Pointe-à-Pitre) while the "hamlet of banana trees" is located between Capesterre and Trois-Rivières. Jean-Pierre Sainton (ed.), *Histoire et Civilisation de la Caraïbe*, vol. II, Paris: Karthala, 2012, p. 49.
27. Father Labat (1663-1738) lived in the Caribbean for eleven years, from 1694 to 1705, recording what he saw and describing what he experienced. He lived in Martinique but made frequent short trips to Guadeloupe, and carried out missions on the islands to the north (Saint-Christophe and Saint-Domingue) and south (Saint Lucia and Barbados, for example). Even though they date back to before the period that interests us here, his accounts nevertheless give us an idea of the islands at that time. Sainton (ed.), *Histoire et Civilisation de la Caraïbe*, p. 43.

1654[28] with the cultivation of sugarcane and the production of sugar; the growing of coffee would come only later, also around Basse-Terre, in 1727-1728).[29] At that time the sugar factories were powered by water mills (with buckets) (the animal mill was only used when there was a water shortage). Grande-Terre's boom came later, at the beginning of the 18th century when windmill and cistern technologies were mastered. A land register of Grande-Terre, produced in 1732,[30] shows a very large number of *habitations* – only the Grands Fonds[31] were not occupied at the time.

---

28. Guy Lasserre, *La Guadeloupe. Étude géographique*, doctoral thesis, Bordeaux, 1961, pp. 327-340. Personal communication from Gérard Lafleur.
29. Belatedly introduced into Guadeloupe in 1727-1728, a few years after Martinique, the growing of coffee, like that of cocoa (which had been cultivated since the end of the 17th century), is said to be secondary to that of sugarcane, which was the majority crop at the time (previously, at the beginning of colonization, cotton and indigo were grown but their production was declining: cotton production was increasingly rare and indigo had practically disappeared, with the exception of Marie-Galante.) The breakthrough of coffee "as an export product would appear to be linked to the collapse of cocoa" following the earthquake of 1727 and a poor economic climate for sugar. Sainton (ed.), *Histoire et Civilisation de la Caraïbe*, p. 135.
   Initially produced for domestic consumption, coffee required less labor and was grown on sloping or smaller surfaces (for example, one of the surfaces recorded for these coffee plantations was about six squares, which was relatively small (one square being equivalent to 0.9448 hectares, or 9448m²). Historian Gérard Lafleur establishes the average surface area at 10.93 squares and the average number of enslaved people per coffee plantation at twenty-four: Gérard Lafleur, "La culture du café en Guadeloupe, de son introduction à sa quasi-disparition", *BSHG (Bulletin de la Société d'Histoire de la Guadeloupe)*, n°145, 2006, pp. 59-120). In 1833 however, a coffee plantation in Gosier was comprised of 138 squares: coffee plantations only really began to boom at the end of the 18th century, after the English occupation.
30. Personal communication from Gérard Lafleur.
31. The "grands fonds" (great depths) refer to a geographical area made up of the sometimes steep hills (the "mornes"), which create often very deep "fonds", in which ponds are often formed from rain runoff, creating a specific type of landscape, typical of one part of Grande-Terre. The area is extensive: it starts on the outskirts of Pointe-à-Pitre and extends to the municipalities of Abymes, Gosier, Sainte-Anne, Morne-à-l'Eau and Moule. This type of landscape contrasts with the flatter and less rugged landscapes in the western part of Grande-Terre.

The drawings by Guadeloupean draftsman Joseph Coussin (1773-1836) give us an idea of what the landscape and rural habitat might have been at the end of the 18th century and beginning of the 19th, i.e. at the time when Auguste Bébian was born and growing up:[32]

Figure n° 2: Mangrove and hill landscapes around Pointe-à-Pitre, circa 1805

Pencil drawing by Joseph Coussin, early 19th century, cited by Anne Pérotin-Dumon, *La ville aux Îles, la ville dans l'ile*, Paris: Karthala, 2000, p. 415

32. He was also a notary. Danielle Bégot (ed.), *Guide de la recherche en histoire antillaise et guyanaise : Guadeloupe, Martinique, Guyane, Saint Domingue, XVIIe-XXe siècles*, Paris: CTHS, 2011, vol. I, p. 307.

Figure n° 3: Rural and urban dwelling in Guadeloupe in the early 19th century: stone house with dormer windows and bull's-eye

House in the Grippon district, in Morne-à-l'Eau, where Auguste Bébian was born and raised. Charcoal drawing by Joseph Coussin, circa 1805, cited by Anne Pérotin-Dumon, *La ville aux Iles, la ville dans l'île,* Paris: Karthala, 2000, p. 415

The difficulties encountered in locating the Bergopzoom *habitation* mean we cannot confirm its activity: was it devoted exclusively to coffee growing? Generally speaking, sugar was the main crop, with sugarcane plantations covering a large portion of the cropland, "*with the exception of Gosier and Morne-à-l'Eau, part of whose territory belonged to Grands-Fonds, a region given over to secondary crops (coffee and cotton).*"[33] To this end, slavery existed on the island throughout the 18th century, known as the century of 'slavery triumphant'."[34] The sugar economy was very much the driving force behind this slave trade system. The farming structures, known as "*habitations*",[35]

33. Régent, *Esclavage, métissage, liberté*, p. 74.
34. Sainton (ed.), *Histoire et Civilisation de la Caraïbe*, p. 28.
In 1654 the Dutch set up the "plantation system" with a servile labor force; this model lasted until the first quarter of the 19th century.
35. In the 19th century, this word referred to the property, land and buildings (master's house and slaves' huts), the farm and the livestock, whereas in the 18th century the term was of a more general nature. Lasserre, *La Guadeloupe*, p. 340.

made sugar production possible: they were a vast whole, made up of land, livestock and crops, with housing and farm buildings in the center. As we have said, the inhabitant-owner reigned as an almost absolute master over these highly structured domains.

At the end of the Ancien Régime, the region of Petit-Canal and Morne-à-l'Eau, where the Bergopzoom dwelling was located, was widely cultivated (as was the whole of Grande-Terre): sugarcane on the lowlands and coffee on the hills.[36] The 1796 census shows Joseph Bébian as the inhabitant-owner of Bergopzoom, a farm with twenty-five enslaved people (twenty-one men and four women, along with twelve adolescents and four children; he and his son were the only whites) and declares his main activity to be coffee production,[37] referred to as a *caféière* (coffee plantation).[38] This *habitation* was probably not particularly large; it did not leave a historical trace to the same extent as others.[39] Was it a small *habitation* devoted

---

36. Mountain or big hill.
37. The "*nominative states of the citizens of all ages and all sexes, existing in the municipality of Morne a l'Eau, on the First of Vendémiaire, Year V of the French Republic, one and indivisible*" were subjected to a census in 1796 and 1797 on the order of Victor Hugues, appointed commissioner of the Republic in Guadeloupe in 1793, who wanted to know the state of the population and of the *habitations*. All the municipalities in Guadeloupe were covered. The 1796 census concerned Morne-à-l'Eau and mentions Bergopzoom as a "*particular coffee plantation*". "*États nominatifs des citoyens de tout âge et de tout sexe, existans dans la commune du Morne a Leau, au Premier vendémiaire de l'an V de la République française, une et indivisible.*" ANOM DPPC G1 501, n° 1 (ADG 5 J 228). The adjective "particular" signified that the owner was present, as opposed to the "national *habitation*" which denoted confiscation (due to it belonging to people who had emigrated, or who were absent and suspected of being royalists).
38. However "secondary" it may have been (as Gérard Lafleur demonstrates, this hierarchy is highly relative), this crop is not of a second order and does not imply lesser wealth. On the contrary: "*Up until the Second World War, coffee continued to be Guadeloupe's principal secondary crop grown by inhabitants who, while they certainly did not have the skills and resources of the sugar growers, to some extent possessed possibilities greater than those of other growers of secondary crops*". Lafleur, *La culture du café en Guadeloupe*, pp. 59-120.
39. Such as the Saintrac *habitation*, birthplace of Auguste's uncle, Jean-Jacques (born in 1769, died in 1813, fifteen years after his sister Félicité, Auguste's mother). Located in Petit-Canal, it had a surface area of 192 squares (*Hypothèques,*

entirely to coffee or did it also produce other subsistence crops and foods such corn and a few chickens, as Labat noted during his visit to the "*côte-sous-le-vent*" (west of the island of Guadeloupe)?[40] On Baillif (a Basse-Terre island) Gabriel Debien notes a *habitation* where a coffee plantation and sugar factory were located.[41]

The young Auguste thus grew up in a very rural and isolated environment, and one can only wonder about the education he received. Most of the population was certainly illiterate at the time, but he undoubtedly benefited from a solid instruction which, later on, when he became an adult, would allow him to follow the teachings of the naturalist Lamarck, win the Greek version of the open competition, and then begin his prolific career. This surely indicates that he belonged to a wealthy social class. Of his life then, we know nothing; he appears twice in the Republican census of 1796, where it is mentioned that he lived with his mother in Moule or with his father in Morne-à-l'Eau.[42]

---

transcriptions des actes de mutation, acte 71, vol. 19; research carried out by Madame Bégot).

40. Sainton (ed.), *Histoire et Civilisation de la Caraïbe*, p. 48.

41. Gabriel Debien, "La caféière et la sucrerie Bologne au Baillif (1787)", *BSHG* (*Bulletin de la Société d'histoire de la Guadeloupe)*, n° 3-4, 1965, pp. 11-21.
It is nevertheless important to consider the particular character of the "leeward coast", the west coast of the island of Basse-Terre. In the 18th century, it was a separate economic and social entity. The Bologne *habitation* was located on the heights of Baillif, growing both sugarcane and coffee, a model that can be found around Basse-Terre (modern-day Saint-Claude and Goubeyre, Baillif). The same owners grew sugarcane and produced sugar on the lower lands and had coffee plantations on the heights, which allowed them to make full use of slave labor, as the heavy work was done at different times for each crop. Personal communication from Gérard Lafleur.

42. The Nominal Roll of 1796 (ANOM: DPPC, G1,501, n°1 and ADG 5J228) lists a certain Bébian in the Morne-à-l'Eau municipality, living with his son and a person of the female sex ("anonymous?" "Aunorine?": the writing is unclear) and a "Michaux Bébian" in the neighboring municipality of Moule, "40 years old, owner, with Bébian son, 6 years old and Mirabelle, 4 years old". GHC (*Généalogie et histoire de la Caraïbe*) n° 240, October 2010, p. 6496. This census undoubtedly took place in 1795, when Auguste's parents were already divorced.
These censuses of Year IV and Year V show a profound change in the population: during the period between the abolition of slavery in June 1794 and its

An extremely troubled historical context

In 1802, young Auguste was sent to Paris to study. He was a young teenager, somewhere between 11 and 13 years old. Is this date a coincidence, or did it have to do with the reintroduction of slavery[43] as ordered that very same year by Napoleon, and which was accompanied by unrest and bloodshed?[44] Was his departure linked to his father's activities, "*sent in 1801 by General Lacrosse to the Spanish colonies of Porto Rico and Cuba with a mission order to legalize the Guadeloupean corsairs and inspect the consuls' accounts*"?[45] Did some level of collusion with the repressive powers that be lead to this departure? Was Joseph Bébian protecting his son from possible repression or was he simply ensuring his future and facilitating his rise in society?

---

de facto reintroduction in 1802, this population, which at the time stood at just over 100,000 (109,922 to be precise), was divided into 9% white, 13% "red" (mixed race or indigenous American, the category was somewhat vague; the term "slave" had disappeared), and 78% black (the term "negro" had also been replaced). Pérotin-Dumon, *La ville aux îles*, p. 278.

43. Slavery had been abolished by the Convention eight years earlier, on February 2, 1794 (16 Pluviose Year II). In fact, apart from Guadeloupe, this abolition only concerned the islands of Guyana, Saint-Domingue and two years later, Saint Lucia, when France took control of that colony; Martinique was not concerned, being under British control, and the Mascarene Islands refused to receive the representatives of the Directory in January 1796 (Petré-Grenouilleau, *Les traites négrières*, p. 233).
44. The period 1794-1802 was a very troubled time: Jacques Adelaïde-Merlande, *Delgrès ou la Guadeloupe en 1802*, Paris: Éditions Karthala, 1986 and <*http://www.lameca.org/dossiers/1802/sommaire.htm*>
45. GHC (*Généalogie et histoire de la Caraïbe*), n° 240 (October 2010), p. 6496.

So it was in this context that in 1802 in Basse-Terre or Pointe-à-Pitre,[46] Auguste (de) Bébian[47] boarded a ship to France. Did he disembark in Le Havre or Bordeaux? How did he travel to Paris to meet up with Abbé Sicard,[48] who had already been in charge of the INSMP for twelve years, who baptized him[49] and became his

46. The foundation of the city of Pointe-à-Pitre was decreed in 1763 by Governor Bourlamaque. For commercial reasons, a wetland site was chosen. Pérotin-Dumon, *La ville aux îles*, p. 320.
At the time when Auguste Bébian boarded a ship to France, there were three major ports in Guadeloupe: Basse-Terre, where the administrative authorities were located and which dealt with large numbers of passengers and with the export of coffee; Pointe-à-Pitre, a commercial town which was very much involved in the import and export of trade goods from Grande-Terre and part of Guadeloupe proper; and finally Le Moule which was a port for the exportation of sugar. However, not being protected from the swell, the latter was dethroned by Pointe-à-Pitre, which took on considerable importance during the English occupation (from 1759 to 1763, during the Seven Years' War) at the initiative of the occupiers and which continued to develop after its restitution to France by the Treaty of Paris (Personal communication from Gérard Lafleur). Young Auguste could only therefore have boarded ship in Basse-Terre or Pointe-à-Pitre.
47. The particle appears on his marriage certificate (December 9, 1822) as well as on his death certificate (February 24, 1839), but not on the register of the imperial university which records his prize (1809), nor on the verification of affidavit signed by the judicial authorities of Pointe-à-Pitre (October 6, 1828), or on the death certificate of his son, Honoré (August 21, 1836).
48. Officially appointed "head teacher" on April 6, 1790, at the age of 48. Alexis Karacostas, *L'institution nationale des sourds-muets de 1790 à 1800, histoire d'un corps à corps*, medical thesis, Université Paris V, Paris, 1981, p. 32.
A journey by stagecoach was the most likely: depending on the point of departure, it took between 55 and 80 hours to reach the capital, a time that would be considerably reduced by the end of the century with the introduction of the railroad. Jean & Françoise Fourastie, *Voyages et voyageurs d'autrefois*, Paris: Denoël, s. d.
49. "*He was presented to the baptismal fonts by the famous teacher*" writes Berthier (*Notice*, p. 6). To date, no certificate of baptism has ever been found.
Such a late baptism is surprising when we know that "*with the exception of Indigenous Americans, baptism was an act that concerned all persons (at birth) in Martinique up until the 19th century*". Vincent Cousseau, *Prendre nom aux Antilles. Individu et appartenances XVIIe-XIXe siècles*, CTHS, 2012, p. 181.

sponsor,[50] though he did not provide him with accommodation at the Institution? In 1888, Benjamin Dubois noted:[51]

> *"Admitted to the Jauffret Institution, he followed courses at Charlemagne high school, which benefited from the reflected prestige of his successes at the* concours généraux. *On days off and during school vacations, Bébian could always be found at the Institution des Sourds-Muets, among the students, in the classrooms, in the workshops. During recess, he joined in all of their games. In a short time he thus became a veritable deaf-mute with a thorough grasp of sign language."*[52]

50. Roch-Ambroise Sicard's father, Jean Cucurron, was consul in Fousseret, approximately 60 km from Toulouse, where Jean-Raymond de Bébian, Joseph's father and Auguste's grandfather, was a municipal magistrate. They were both municipal council members (to use modern terminology), and were approximately the same age (Abbé Sicard was born on September 17, 1742. Auguste's father was born around 1712, and Jean-Raymond de Bébian in 1708). Could they have met? Did consul Cucurron intercede with municipal magistrate Bébian when his son came to study in Toulouse (at the college run by the Fathers of Christian Doctrine)? The hypothesis merits verification.
51. Dubois, *Physiologie*, p. 28.
52. This is almost certainly an error, as the Institution Jauffret was created in 1837 by Anatole Jauffret, nephew of Jean-Baptiste Clair Jauffret (1766-1824) who was a teacher at the INSMP from 1795 to 1810 (see next footnote). In 1800, he also wrote an essay *"On a new and easy way to teach people who were born deaf to articulate"*. The essay was published in the *Midi, one of two newspapers created by* the *Société des Observateurs de l'Homme.* Jean-Luc Chappey, *La Société des observateurs de l'homme (1799-1804). Des anthropologues au temps de Bonaparte*, Paris: Société des études robespierristes, 2002, p. 132; Sophie Dalle-Nazébi, *Chercheurs, Sourds et langues des signes. Le travail d'un objet et de repères linguistiques en France du XVIIe au XXIe siècle*, doctoral thesis, université Toulouse II-Le Mirail, 2006, p. 111. The Institution Jauffret had been renamed by the time Benjamin Dubois was writing, at the end of the 19th century (Victor Hugo sent his children to the Institution and Jean Jaurès was also a frequent visitor) that there was perhaps a desire to associate Bébian with this reputation. On another note, the Institution sent its boarders to Lycée Charlemagne, where Auguste Bébian had gone to school.

Eight years later, Jean-Baptiste Clair Jauffret was appointed "*principal of the imperial school for deaf-mutes in Saint Petersburg*"[53] and it was at this moment that Auguste joined the Institution:[54]

> "*When he left the college, for three years he came to live near his sponsor and soon became aware of his vocation as a teacher of deaf-mutes.*"

2. A Parisian adolescent thrust into the Deaf world: a gaining of awareness

2.1 Abbé Sicard: militant Catholicism and instrumentalization of the INSMP

It was thus as a teenager that Auguste joined his sponsor in 1802: he was 13 (or 11, depending on the date of birth used). Abbé Sicard was 67,[55] and had accumulated numerous titles and honors:

53. Jean-Baptiste Clair Jauffret left Paris in 1810, the year in which Russian Empress Maria Feodorovna appointed him director of the newly created Saint Petersburg Institute, which he managed until his death in 1824. He left no written works or correspondence. Bogdanov-Berezovski, *La situation des sourds-muets en Russie,* printed text, 1901. (Translated into French, 2011 by Mme Bouchard). Berthier, *Notice*, p. 6.
54. Was this for a defined period? The formulation suggests so.
    Ibid.
55. Officially appointed as the immediate successor to Abbé de l'Épée, Roch-Ambroise de Cucurron (later known as Sicard: he gave up his paternal name, Cucurron, after being mocked – it does have a comical ring in French – and took the name of his mother, Françoise Sicard) was a key character in Auguste's life in Paris during these years of intellectual schooling. Approximately four months passed between the death of Abbé de l'Épée (December 23, 1789) and Sicard's appointment (April 6, 1790), during which period an abbot chosen by de l'Épée to succeed him, Masse, covered the interim, thus ensuring the continuity of the pedagogical initiative (Fabrice Bertin, "Un personnage-clé mais méconnu: l'abbé Masse", *Le journal d'information de Saint-Jacques*, n° 40, September 2012, p. 14)

eminent grammarian,[56] teacher at the *École normale* since 1795[57] and member of the *Institut de France* since its creation in 1802, and of several academies and other learned societies.[58] A member of the church, former student of the college run by the highly religious brotherhood of the Fathers of the Christian Doctrine of Saint-Rome in Toulouse, he made the INSMP a preferred observation post for the *Société des Observateurs de l'Homme* which he set up in 1800, as his paper *Mémoire sur les avantages qui peuvent résulter pour l'avancement de la science de l'homme, de l'observation des sourds-muets de naissance* [On the potential benefits for the advancement of human science of observing those born deaf-mute] testifies.[59]

56. The year after Bébian's arrival in Paris, in 1803, Abbé Sicard published a voluminous *Course of instruction for people born deaf, to be used to teach deaf-mutes, and which may be of use to those who hear and speak* (Paris: Le Clere; London: Charles Prosper, 1803), a work that was recognized outside of the INSMP but which Berthier described as being of no pedagogical use. Several years later, in 1840, Ferdinand Berthier explicitly considered Bébian, unlike Sicard, to be a continuation of Abbé de l'Épée. *"If it is a matter of dictating a tree, three signs are required. [...] A man was needed who was able to grasp and cultivate the entire thinking of Abbé de l'Épée. We now have such a man. Having devoted his entire youth in silence to the study of the language of the deaf and mute, Mr. Bébian rid teaching of all this intellectual baggage which served only to slow its progress, and restored it to this simplicity, to this truth, from which Abbé de l'Épée did not deviate for a single moment."* Ferdinand Berthier, *Les sourds-muets avant et après l'abbé de l'Épée*, J. Ledoyen, 1840, p. 40.
57. In 1797 he published a "childhood manual": *Manuel de l'enfance, contenant des éléments de lecture et des dialogues instructifs et moraux : dédié aux mères et à toutes les personnes chargées de la petite enfance* (Paris: Le Clere, 1797).
58. The same year his *Cours d'instruction...* was published, he was admitted to the Académie Française as a replacement for the Cardinal de Bernis, who had died in 1794 and who was a *"member of the Royal Academy in Madrid and of several other literary Societies"* as he wrote on the cover of this work.
59. Sicard's most famous deaf student, Jean Massieu (although it was in fact another abbot, Saint-Sernin, who had been responsible for a large part of his training, Sicard took all the credit, as Marc Renard notes in Ferdinand Berthier, *L'abbé Sicard*, 1873, p. 204 (reprinted by Fox)), wrote the story of his childhood *"to supplement the views of Citizen Jauffret who had asked him to do this. It was on 30 Messidor Year VI that this piece was written. It is even more accurate in that Massieu, in addressing Citizen Jauffret, was talking to one of his old friends"*, Urbain R. T. Le Bouvyer-Desmortiers, *Mémoire ou Considérations sur les sourds-muets*

This learned society was created, in a timely manner, following the discovery of the wild child of Aveyron. It was initiated by Sicard, along with Louis-François Jauffret, brother of Jean-Baptiste Clair Jauffret[60] who housed Auguste Bébian upon his arrival in Paris.[61]

> *"It is undoubtedly from the conversations between these individuals with links to the INSMP that the project to create a learned society was born. To avoid the difficulties that R. A. Sicard's Institute was facing at that time, it is probable that they hatched the idea of appropriating the discovery of the wild child of Aveyron, believing they could gain numerous benefits from it. Still too marked by his political past, Abbé Sicard called upon L. F. Jauffret to make this request to the administrators of the hospice of Saint-Affrique."*

The framework and the influence of the *Société des Observateurs de l'Homme*, created in the premises of the INSMP, on the education and ideas of Auguste Bébian undoubtedly affected his pathway in one direction or the other. To what extent was this learned society at the service of the education of the nascent deaf, and what might be the link? Historian Jean-Luc Chappey, author of a very comprehensive work of research on the society,[62] considers its creation to be a "*coup de force*", its members consisting mainly of fervent Catholics who thus found refuge from the Constituent Assembly, which was cracking down on the resistance, of which Sicard was a member:[63] this was the context in which Pierre Bonnefous (? -1805) became an assistant-teacher in 1792, with Dominique Ricard (1741-1803)

---

de naissance, 1800, Paris, 2e ed. 1829, p. 252 (quoted by Chappey, *La Société des observateurs de l'homme*. p. 49).

60. He was also the author of an article "On a new and easy way to teach people who were born deaf to articulate", published in the *Midi, one of the Société's two newspapers* (the other being *Le Nord*).

61. Chappey, *La Société des observateurs de l'homme*, p. 31.

62. *Idem*.

63. Ferdinand Berthier, *L'abbé Sicard, célèbre instituteur des sourds-muets, successeur immédiat de l'abbé de l'Épée. Précis historique sur sa vie, ses travaux et ses succès,* Paris: C. Douniol, 1873.

being appointed teacher that same year and editor of the *Journal de la Religion et du culte catholique;* Pierre Laromiguière (1756-1837) benefited from this network (from time to time he acted as teaching assistant) before being appointed professor of philosophy at the Sorbonne. The Institution thus became a refuge, a hideout, even more so after Sicard's political problems: as a monarchist and refractory, Sicard, who was imprisoned for a while, narrowly escaped the executions of September 1792 and was condemned to exile in 1797 by the Directory.[64] It was not until 1800 that he was pardoned by Napoleon. During this troubled period, it was Jean Massieu, his star pupil at the Institution of Bordeaux, and later *répétiteur* at the INSMP, who faithfully assisted him.[65] This learned society, or rather its creation in this city, demonstrates a certain conception of education for deaf people, pushed into the background.

The INSMP was the lynchpin of this network and the locus of diverse and multiple observations, such as the case of Tchong-A-Sam, a trader captured by the corsairs. The Institute was thus central to the emergence of this learned society and Auguste Bébian could not have failed to be influenced by its works, if only to dissociate himself from them: housed by Jean-Baptiste Jauffret and Sicard's godson, two eminent members of this society, he arrived in France at its height and could not have been unaware of its orientations. Although Auguste Bébian did not actually live at the INSMP, at least at first, as we have seen above, his visits were frequent.

64. François Buton, *L'administration des faveurs. L'État, les sourds et les aveugles (1789-1885)*, Rennes: Presses universitaires de Rennes, 2009, p. 62.

65. It was he who pleaded the cause of the *"father of the deaf"* to the authorities who imprisoned Sicard following his arrest *"on August 31, 1792 for having refused to swear the oath on the civil constitution of the clergy"*. He was arrested again in October 1793 (Vendemiaire Year II), suspected of maintaining a correspondence with counterrevolutionaries in exile: the record of Sicard's interrogation is reproduced in Karacostas, *L'institution nationale des sourds-muets*, Annex H; quoted by Buton, *L'administration des faveurs*, p. 62.

2.2 Facing the fact of audiocentrism: Bébian, the first bilingual and bicultural hearing person

Sicard's aim in educating deaf students differed significantly from that of Abbé de l'Épée, as can be seen in a letter that the abbot sent to Sicard in 1786:[66]

> *"What our aim should be, Sir, regarding deaf-mutes, is to make them understand and not to make them write, in other words, themselves compose. Your children, like those of Mr. Guyot, should already know several hundred words, and it would appear that they are very wide of that mark. You drum things into your students' heads, whereas* [Guyot] *expands and develops the ideas of his* [students]. *You force upon them, and yourself take on, an utterly useless task in order to teach them a science that we never teach to our disciples, and that they only learn through daily use. None of the students you have seen in my home have learned it any other way and our youngest are following the same process. But by wanting to force your students, from the outset, to know what they should learn through lengthy practice alone, you risk discouraging them, and that is one of the most feared inconveniences in the education of deaf-mutes… Remember that it is only by keeping them entertained that you will be able to teach them…"*

Abbé Sicard nevertheless demonstrated his willingness to follow in the founder's footsteps: *"I have found the glass* […] *it is up to you to make the glasses"*, says Abbé de l'Épée.[67] In practice, he significantly improved the methodical sign technique, which had little to do with the sign language practiced by deaf people of the time, and which had rapidly become unusable due to its complexity. For the young

66. Letter dated December 20, 1786, quoted by Berthier, *L'abbé Sicard*, p. 211.
67. Roch-Ambroise Sicard, *Mémoire sur l'art d'instruire les Sourds et Muets de naissance*, Paris: Le Clère, 1790, p. 8.

Auguste, a speaker of "natural" sign language, it was unquestionably an aberration that had to be remedied. As he himself explained:[68]

> *"What will it be like if, to a complication that is already too great, the teacher adds an analysis of grammatical forms that the deaf-mute will not know until much later on... Let us suppose that the teacher wants to dictate the following words to deaf-mutes: "regarder en haut avec un extrême plaisir" ("look up with extreme pleasure") (plate 3.A.f. 13). A single sign would suffice to convey these six words. One can hardly expect the deaf-mute to break down this sign by himself – it being for him the expression of a single idea – and to disentangle its elements. It is therefore up to the teacher to direct him.*
> *Let us see how these same words would be dictated in Abbé Sicard's school, and how many signs this explanation would require:*
> *1°) "Regarder" would require three signs: 1° - the sign for a radical (I will ignore the "double see", which was supposed to explain this word); 2° - the sign for the indefinite mode; 3° - the sign for the present.*
> *2°) "En", complex sign for the preposition which expresses the indeterminate relation of the contents to the container; in class, this sign is made by drawing in the air a horizontal circle, into which one plunges the finger in various places.*
> *3°) "Haut", one sign.*
> *4°) "Avec", one sign.*
> *5°) "Un", two signs: 1° - the sign for the indefinite article; 2° - the sign for the masculine gender.*
> *6°) "Extrême". This word, which is an adjective in the superlative form, and which could be translated by two or three different words, would require at least three signs in the school system.*
> *7°) "Plaisir", three signs: the sign for the radical, sign for the adjective, which becomes the noun.*
> *There you have it, thirteen or fourteen signs to express an idea that a deaf-mute can convey by a single gesture."*

---

68. Auguste Bébian, *Mimographie ou Essai d'écriture mimique, propre à régulariser le langage des sourds-muets*, Paris: Louis Colas, 1825, pp. 27-28.

It is a highly complex procedure: Christian Cuxac was one of the first to ponder this in the 1980s:[69]

"One might wonder what the children understood from the signs the teacher gave them, from their readings in French and even from their own written texts. Massieu and Clerc, his two students, apparently learned more French in spite of Sicard than thanks to him."

On a day-to-day basis, instruction was dispensed by Jean Massieu[70] – who had made it possible for Sicard to be chosen to run the INSMP, thus allowing him to avoid execution in 1792 – and a number of other teachers (deaf and hearing),[71] and yet Sicard de-

69. Christian Cuxac, *Le langage des sourds,* Paris: Payot, 1983, p. 71.
70. Sicard's star pupil; his autobiography puts the latter's pedagogical "success", and his consideration for deaf people, firmly into perspective. Born around 1772 in Semens, near Cadillac, in the Gironde, Massieu had two brothers and three sisters, all deaf like himself. It is therefore highly probable that he was already using some form of sign language before he arrived at the Institution. While he played a significant role in Sicard's career, he was only a *répétiteur*, never obtaining the title of teacher, his "master" holding him in low esteem. More generally, prior to their education, Sicard compared a deaf person to a kind of walking machine whose organization was inferior to that of animals. In his *Course of instruction for people born deaf (1799),* Sicard theorizes about his student's blank "slate" (or mind), a clean slate that must be "filled" with learning, and "humanized," (Sicard, *Cours d'Instruction d'un sourd-muet de naissance*, Paris: Le Clère, 1799, p. 5.) He believed there was a "deaf-mute" spirit, which from the very outset determined and justified a state of inferiority. Indeed, Sicard had no great ambitions for his students and the external representation of his various functions took up most of his time: unlike Auguste Bébian, he was more frequently taken up with intellectual questions than with pedagogical pragmatism. In this sense, his ideas differed little from the "oralist" pedagogues (those who equated education with "demutization" and the learning of vocal speech). Moreover, in his opinion, *"speech constitutes the irreducible distinctive feature between animal and man, the only one susceptible to progress"* (Roch-Ambroise Sicard, "Art de la parole", *Séances des Écoles Normale recueillies par les sténographes*, Paris: Imprimerie du cercle social, 1800 (an VIII), pp. 115-116, quoted by Chappey, *La Société des observateurs de l'homme*, p. 36).
71. These were former students at the school: Jean Massieu, previously mentioned, who in 1790 became the first deaf person with a teaching position (albeit without having the status; the incumbent teacher was probably unable to

nied them the ability to work at a higher level of abstraction, as we have already seen. The transformation that Bébian represents in the consideration given to the deaf pupils – *"showered with humiliation and mockery..."* treated like *"dogs and monkeys"* –[72] becomes even clearer when one considers that for Sicard this obstacle to abstraction was a justification for teaching the Catechism:[73]

> *"It was constantly necessary to simultaneously overcome two difficulties: those which present mysteries to which no tangible idea leads and which consequently lie so far beyond human conception that no known thing can take us there. That of a foreign language which had to be brought closer to that of nature, for beings who can only with difficulty learn the secret of our inventions. It was necessary to strip the language of all the luxury with which civilization had weighed it down, to only use simple sentences and to sacrifice everything to clarity. It was important to write only what the Deaf-Mute had understood."*

For Bébian, on the other hand, religion and its teaching were not prerequisites.[74] Furthermore, at first sight it does not appear that he himself was destined to become a teacher: according to Ferdinand Berthier, there was a certain consternation behind his

---

communicate), his colleague Laurent Clerc, and a little later Ferdinand Berthier and Claudius Forestier, all of whom came from the Paris Institute.

72. Berthier, *Notice*, p. 24.

73. Roch-Ambroise Sicard, *Catéchisme ou Instruction chrétienne à l'usage des sourds-muets*, Paris: INSMP, 1792, pp. VI-VII.

74. *"If the deaf-mute is of a favorable disposition, and if the teacher is perspicacious, if the attention of the former matches the care of the latter, then in the space of approximately one year, and I speak from experience, one might make far more progress than was expected, and lay solid foundations for a more extensive education, compared to religion or other forms of knowledge that may be acquired through reading."*
Auguste Bébian, *Essai sur les sourds-muets et sur le langage naturel, ou introduction à une classification naturelle des idées avec leurs signes propres*, Paris: J.-G. Dentu, 1817, p. 147.

commitment.[75] Auguste Bébian confirms this,[76] and recounts two episodes that led him to teaching, one of which demonstrates the virulence of his factual observations:

> *"Many years ago, I was sitting in on a lesson at the Institute for the Deaf and Mute; I was not yet involved in this kind of teaching; I did not even think I would ever have to do that; but I had already made a thorough study of the language of the deaf and mute. The teacher who was giving the lesson wanted to give it the air of a minor lecture, and produce a demonstration, in my presence, of one of the fundamental points of the lesson: the distinction between the words SORTE* [sort] *and ESPÈCE* [species].
> *I had no difficulty in realizing that the procedure was basically a misconception pompously dressed up in ambitious forms. I made my thoughts known to the teacher by expressing a timid doubt. I, who could not and did not wish to follow him into the clouds, asked him if I might ask the students one little question – With pleasure, he replied, I will pass it on to them if you wish – I preferred to take the chalk and write this simple question on the slate:*
> *Is Clerc a species?*
> *As we have seen, Clerc is one of the Institution's most distinguished alumni. They all answered: Yes, Clerc is a species. I had anticipated this answer. The teacher, stunned, began to make distinction after distinction. As I did not seem convinced of the strength of his reasoning, he became furious, the last resort of people who are in the wrong, and asked me if I was trying to challenge received wisdom. You can imagine how this remark must have surprised me, I who at that time had not even thought about teaching deaf-mutes, because until then I had simply believed, like the public in general, that such instruction left little to be desired.*

75. Berthier, *Notice*, pp. 9-10.
76. Auguste Bébian, *Journal de l'instruction des sourds-muets et des aveugles*, 1827, vol. 2, p. 52; he explains: *"Some of his disciples maintained a sort of cult fanaticism regarding his method."*

> *I had merely and humbly pointed out an error in passing, and I quickly withdrew in order to end the discussion. But, and I have often had proof of it, this man never forgot the event. The Holy Inquisition would more easily have forgiven a Jew or a Muslim."*

From this long quotation, necessary to an understanding of Bébian's commitment but also of the resentment towards him, two things seem to us to be especially revealing of a conflict in the making:

• A teacher's absolute refusal to question himself, and the personal, quasi-religious, turn this takes *("he became furious* [...] *and asked me if I was trying to challenge received wisdom*).[77] An attitude tinged with religion that recalls that of Clerc (which Berthier describes below);

• The spotlight on the fact that the methodical signs in use at the time were not effective.[78]

The incomprehension was highlighted; a second example illustrates the semantic confusion:

> *"Among a series of nouns that one of the répétiteurs had asked one deaf-mute to dictate to another student, were the words roasted chestnuts. From the signs that had been given, I noticed that the student who had dictated the words understood them no better than the student who wrote them down. To be certain of this, I had roasted chestnuts brought in, and I asked them to write the name on the board. They answered that they did not know it, and were very surprised when I told them that*

77. The phrase used in French, "*élever autel contre autel*" (literally, "raising alter against alter"), is more explicitly religious.

78. Berthier writes: "*The term* methodical *calls for some explanation. Without touching upon the accuracy of this epithet, I would simply point out that my first teacher made the serious mistake, in my view, of seeking to subject the language of signs to the conventional laws of language rather than to the natural course of thought; this is, moreover, the only mistake that can be leveled against this genius who had no models and no rivals. Today everyone agrees that a sort of anatomical spelling-out of words by means of gestures does not offer an exact and complete meaning any more than would the literal translation of an author, whose style and genius would be overlooked.*" (*op. cit.*, 1839, pp. 7-8).

they had just written it themselves without understanding it. Where could such a singular and easily foreseen surprise come from? This is the explanation: the répétiteur had represented the word roasted as he would have done to express roasted veal; he had put the chestnuts on the spit, confusing the specific sign with the generic sign…"

Ferdinand Berthier highlights the emancipatory role taken on by Bébian. The latter's commitment marked a dividing line: there was a before Bébian and an after:[79]

"[…] *Clerc feared laying himself open to an accusation of heresy, of sacrilege, simply by trying to place an innocently bold hand on the holy ark; his veneration for the tradition of the methodical signs of the abbots of the Sword and for Sicard was so religious, so deep, that Bébian, convinced of the powerlessness of his efforts, had decided to take care of it himself* […] *Before Bébian, our weak imagination, frightened by the slightest difficulty, rejected with horror the little books for children that fell into our hands; we wrote without knowing what we were saying.*[80] *We could hardly draw a line correctly; our memory bristled with sentences taken here and there; willy nilly, we composed centos*[81] *with neither head nor tail, just like parrots which, perched at the windows, repeat the words of passers-by without understanding them. So as far as our education was concerned, he had to make a fresh start, so to speak. But this is not the place to discuss the curious developments that this subject involves; they will find a better place in the Memoirs of a deaf-mute."*[82]

Auguste Bébian spoke his mind, acted in a straightforward manner, and his actions were feared. Ferdinand Berthier relates that, despite all the precautions taken to keep him away, Bébian introduced himself to the Duchess of Berry, who was visiting the

79. Berthier, *Notice*, pp. 7 and 11.
80. Emphasized in the original.
81. A literary work made up of elements from other works, rearranged to form a different text.
82. Berthier, *Notice*, pp. 11-12. Unfortunately, this project never saw the light of day.

INSMP accompanied by the governors (the Duke of Levis and Mathieu de Montmorency). Daughter-in-law of Charles X, the future king of France, she asked to see the students who, through the intermediary of their teacher, gave her books. And Bébian did not hesitate to object:[83]

> *"Impossible! They are naked, in no state to present themselves before Your Royal Highness, and even unable, for the last 4 months, to go out for a walk, due to a lack of clothing… "*

According to Ferdinand Berthier, it was the creation of such waves that led to his dismissal:[84]

> *"They wanted nothing better than to get rid of him. They simply lacked a reason. Where might one be found?"*

Objectively speaking, we will probably never know what really happened during this episode to make the board of governors uncomfortable, or what caused the altercation between Bébian and Paulmier later on, in 1821; the fact remains that pedagogical inconsistencies were highlighted, that an internal jealousy was exacerbated by the easy-going relationship that Bébian had with his pupils and which caused him so many problems.[85] Sicard trusted him to the point of considering him for a position as assistant. In a letter he wrote to Baron de Gérando in 1820,[86] he explains that he had thought of giving this position to Mr. Pissin, but that he had changed his mind because Bébian, he says, *"would inevitably be*

---

83. Berthier, *Notice*, p. 23.
84. *Ibid.*, p. 22.
    For the board of governors: *"Bébian's comments are pure invention. But we sought to hide the reason for his dismissal…"*
85. See Annex 7.
86. Letter dated October 20, 1820.
    AMHCS, Pinart collection, Bébian bundle, INJS.

under my new assistant. Which would be contrary to my intentions".[87] Auguste Bébian, who had been appointed répétiteur on August 20, 1817, was promoted to the position of deputy principal of the INSMP less than two years later, on April 30, 1819: a position created for him, but a position whose scope was unclear.[88] The following year, Abbé Sicard noted that: *"the administration not yet having determined the remit of his position, this has always been a meaningless title."*[89]

3. "A nice face": a silhouette with unclear contours

This same Louis-Émile Vauchelet, who met Auguste Bébian in Guadeloupe, possibly in Basse-Terre and certainly in 1835, remembered a man who was *"tall, with a nice face":*[90]

87. Letter dated September 20, 1820.
AMHCS, Pinart collection, Bébian bundle, INJS.

88. A report signed by the head of the second division sent to *"His Excellency, Secretary of State at the Ministry of the Interior"* mentions *"a position of* répétiteur (that) *has become vacant following the resignation of Mr. Pissin, appointed by Your Excellency on July 28, 1816* [...]. *Abbé Sicard, director of the Institution for deaf-mutes, has put forward Mr. Bébian (Roch-Ambroise, Auguste) to replace Mr. Pissin."* AMHCS, Report dated August 20, 1817.

89. Letter dated September 20, 1820. *op. cit.*
According to Harlan Lane (*When the Mind Hears*, p. 117), Sicard created this position to avoid the departure of Auguste Bébian: for Bébian's father, the position occupied at that time was unworthy and he wanted him to return to Guadeloupe. A letter from Abbé Sicard confirms this intention: *"When I expressed to you, a few months ago, the desire that Mr. Bébian should have a suitable title with which he could be honored in our institution, the title of third* répétiteur *being insufficient to flatter the ambition of his father who is constantly harassing him to once again take up, and never leave, a career in medicine"* and *"it is important that he now receive the title that you deem suitable, in order to flatter the father's self-esteem* [...]" Berthier, *L'abbé Sicard*, Appendix VII, p. 114.

90. Louis-Émile Vauchelet was born in Basse-Terre in 1830 (dying in 1913); Auguste Bébian having returned to Guadeloupe in late 1834, they may well have met in 1835, as it would seem that Bébian was living in Pointe-à-Pitre.

"I think I already told you in one of my previous letters[91] *that I was a child when I met Bébian in Basse-Terre. He had been referred to my father, then a notary, so that he might take an interest in him; which he did; and, while waiting for Bébian to reach his goal, my father asked him to give my sisters a few French lessons, and that lasted just 2 or 3 months. In spite of my young age, I remember that he was tall, with a nice face. Could I have guessed that one day I would be the humble writer of the biography of this good man, this unforgettable teacher?"*

His account is important inasmuch as we only have one representation of Auguste Bébian today: a large full-length oil on canvas painting currently held at the National Institute for Young Deaf People (INJS) in Paris.[92] However, he mentions the existence of a "black pencil drawing".[93] Was this drawing made during his lifetime? Did Charles Chassevent use it as a model for his painting?

---

91. Extract from a letter to Léon Belmont, managing editor of the *Le colonial* weekly newspaper which published a short biography of Bébian, spread over five successive issues, from May 17 to June 14, 1911 (n° 1 to n° 5).
92. Full-length portrait of Bébian, oil on canvas, 200*140 cm, 1879/1880, painted by Charles Chassevent.
93. The catalogue of the universal museum of deaf-mutes reveals that this drawing was still there in 1947: *Notice sur l'Institution nationale des Sourds-Muets de Paris des origines jusqu'à nos jours (1760-1896) suivie du catalogue du musée universel des sourds-muets*, Paris: Typographie de l'institution nationale, 1896; reprinted 1947.
This museum, created at the initiative of Théophile Denis in 1891, was comprised of two sections and included 2026 different works, from medallions to paintings: an artistic section (statues, painters, architects, photographers, etc.) and a historical section, subdivided into five parts (views and plans, overall and in detail, of buildings; portraits of the founders, directors, professors and benefactors; portraits of different people (writers, philosophers, doctors, politicians, etc.; portraits of distinguished deaf people, and various objects (medals, stamps, illustrated works, curiosities.) (*Musée universel des sourds-muets*. Summary catalogue written by Mr. Théophile Denis, honorary office manager at the Ministry of the Interior, curator of the museum, first edition, 1896). The full-length portrait of Auguste Bébian and the black pencil drawing are listed as numbers 703-704 in the "Portraits of Founders, Principals, Teachers and Benefactors" division.

The file for the procurement of the painting by the Fonds national d'art contemporain (FNAC) gives the artist as Marie Joseph Charles Chassevent[94] and not Marie-Auguste Chassevent as indicated on the plaque below the painting currently exhibited at the INJS.[95]

This portrait was painted in 1879-1880, forty years or more after Bébian's death. It was therefore based on other portraits,[96] sketches, and even engravings – there were excellent deaf engravers in the Institution's workshop and Berthier himself was a very experienced engraver.[97] Was it commissioned to complete the historical gallery created at the INSMP in 1875, containing "*some objects of art and some manuscripts*" in preparation for the museum's inauguration in 1891?[98] Auguste Bébian was indeed the Institution's first principal of studies (1819-1821).[99] It is compelling that at a time when the

94. Sainton (ed.), *Histoire et Civilisation de la Caraïbe*, p. 48. Marie Joseph Charles Chassevent was a painter born in Paris in the 19th century (no date given) and a student of painter Léon Cogniet (1794-1880) (coincidentally or not, Frédéric Peyson, one of Bébian's deaf students, whom Bébian took in when he left the INSMP in 1827, had also been Cogniet's student) and of Narcisse Virgilio Diaz (1807-1876). He made his debut at the Salon in 1851 and participated in the *Salon de Blanc et Noir* in 1886. His painting *Young Nymph with Cupids* received an award on May 9, 1927. *Dictionnaire des peintres sculpteurs dessinateurs et graveurs Bénézit*, p. 689.
95. The French Ministry of Culture's database lists this painting under the number F/21/203 and indicates the creation of a "full-length portrait of Bébiau (sic)", commissioned by the INSMP in 1879-1880 (and billed at 1200 gold francs, which in today's terms is approximately 4600 euros (<*www.insee.fr*> conversion into 1901 currency, the gold franc or germinal franc being a generally stable currency). See *D'or et d'argent. La monnaie en France du Moyen Âge à nos jours*. Conférences held by Jean Favier, Guy Antonnetti, Jean Tulard, Alain Plessis, Jean-Charles Asselain, Comité pour l'histoire économique et financière de la France, 2005).
96. Is this perhaps the "black pencil drawing", museum item n° 704? See note n° 93.
97. Personal communication from Yves Bernard.
98. Théophile Denis, *Musée universel des sourds-muets. Catalogue sommaire*, Paris: Typographie des sourds-muets, première édition, 1896, p. 81.
99. The position remained vacant for 38 years! It was then filled almost without interruption: Léon Vaïsse (December 23, 1859-1866) ; Rémi Valade (October 23, 1866-August 16, 1875) ; André Valade-Gabel (May 10,1877-December 31, 1885) ; Augustin Dubranle (January 1, 1896-April 22, 1898) and Jules André (May 12, 1898 to March 31, 1910).

Milan congress was banning the teaching of sign language, the spotlight was place on a teacher who was constantly promoting the fullest possible use of such teaching.[100] Might it be that the aim of this painting was to imply the posthumous approval of Bébian for the establishment's oralist turn, and to take advantage of his reputation?[101] This would fit in well with the museum's desire to put the INSMP forward as a "model."[102] In this portrait, the similarity between Bébian's pose and that of Louis-Philippe, King of the French (and not King of France) is perfectly obvious. Louis-Philippe's hand resting on the 1830 Charter is symbolic,[103] the intention being to mark the desire to break away from previous investitures.[104] Was this not also true for Bébian?

His face is painted in a juvenile fashion, despite the fact that in 1826 (maybe later) he was 37 years old! But it was common practice to idealize facial features at the time: Jacques-Louis David's portrait

---

100. p. 63.

101. The intervention by Édouard Fournié, INSMP's assistant chief physician at the Congress of Laryngology in Milan on September 6, 1880 shows that these orientations in favor of the eviction of the sign language were the preserve of the few and were far from being unanimous. Fabrice Bertin, *Les Sourds. Une minorité invisible,* Paris: Autrement, 2010, p. 166.
    In general, the representativeness of the voters at the congress "*for the improvement of the lot of deaf-mutes*" is questionable: "*Forty-six of the active members were officers and teachers in the two schools of Milan and three more came from the Pereire school in Paris; 49 votes in all with a constituency of three schools and 200 deaf pupils. The stronghold of signing, the United States, then had 51 schools, 400 teachers and over 6,000 pupils: it was represented by 5 votes. All but the Americans voted for a resolution exalting the dominant oral language and disbarring the minority language whatever the nation.*" Harlan Lane, "A Chronology of the Oppression of Sign Language in France and the United States", in *Recent Perspectives on American Sign Language*, New York: Psychology Press, 1989.

102. Denis, *Musée universel des sourds-muets*, p. 81.

103. Whether in the official portraits painted by François Xavier Winterhalter in 1839 (oil on canvas, 260×190 cm) or the portrait by François Gérard in 1834 (oil on canvas, 222×156 cm) (Musée national du château de Versailles).

104. For example, *Le sacre de Charles X (May 29, 1825),* painted by this same François Gérard (oil on canvas, 514×972 cm, Musée national du château de Versailles).

of Bonaparte crossing the Alps at the Grand-Saint-Bernard pass is a case in point.[105]

In modern times, just one painting of Bébian was done at the end of the 20th century, by Bernard Truffaut, a Deaf person and an amateur historian with a relatively productive research activity.[106]

While simply shown as soft and curly in the painting by Charles Chassevent at the end of the nineteenth century, the frizzy hair in this particular portrait indicates the stereotypical image of a man of mixed race. Marc Renard, who among other things re-edited *Mimographie*, a work published in 1825, agrees:[107]

> *"No biographer wonders about any racism towards Bébian… He was a Creole from Guadeloupe* […]"

Figure n° 4: Painting by Bernard Truffaut
in *Les cahiers de l'histoire des Sourds,* Orléans, n°3, 1990
(Yves Bernard, *L'esprit des Sourds, op. cit.*)

105. Jacques-Louis David, *Bonaparte franchissant les Alpes au col du Grand Saint-Bernard*, (oil on canvas, 259×222 cm) (Musée national du château de Malmaison).
106. This led to the publication of *Cahiers de l'Histoire des Sourds*, between 1990 and 1996.
107. Marc Renard, *Écrire les signes*, Les-Essarts-le-Roi: Fox, 2004, 2014, p. 54.

Can this racism be characterized? The research conducted for this book suggests that much of Auguste's maternal ancestry came from Basse-Terre or the archipelago of Saintes, where the population was largely multiracial but where there were also more whites than elsewhere in Guadeloupe, although there was a relatively large number of enslaved people there.[108] Furthermore, in the Morne-à-l'Eau census of 1796, owner-resident Joseph Bébian (and his son), was one of only two "Whites" out of a total of thirty-nine people living on the farm, despite the fact that the "Red" column allowed for the mention of people of mixed race. The question thus remains unresolved…

While it is difficult for us to know what Auguste Bébian really looked like, the same is not true of his thinking, which we can grasp through his numerous writings. Auguste Bébian's principal publications were eight in number.[109] Not all of them were initially intended to be published in book form; for example, *Éloge de l'abbé de l'Épée* was initially a speech given as part of a competition organized by the *Société royale académique des sciences de Paris*. They were not all books in the strict sense of the word: the *Journal des sourds-muets et des aveugles*, for example, was intended to encourage debate.[110]

As we will see later on, his writings have their own style, one that is highly visual, even poetic.[111]

---

108. Jean-Luc Bonniol's thesis (*Terre-de-Haut des Saintes. Contraintes insulaires et particularisme ethnique dans la Caraïbe*, Paris: Éditions Caribéennes, 1980) reveals a multiracial population. However, official figures concerning the composition of the population of Saintes and Désirade in 1814 show that whites represented 30.58%, free people of color 5%, and enslaved people 64.41% (figures based on research by G. Lafleur, in *Bulletin de la Société d'Histoire de la Guadeloupe*, n° 172, p. 68, 2005). By way of comparison, the populations at the same date in Guadeloupe proper and in Grande-Terre were respectively 11.67%, 7.80% and 80.51% (census conducted in 1814 during the English occupation). As F. Régent's research demonstrates, this was a complex issue, "*La fabrication des Blancs dans les colonies françaises*", in S. Laurent, T. Leclère, *De quelle couleur sont les Blancs?* Paris: La Découverte, 2013, pp. 67-75.

109. Annex 10, p. 339.

110. "*The conflicting opinions on the fundamental principles of the method and the diversity of the systems to which the teachers gave themselves up, had decided Mr. Bébian to stimulate free discussion on this interesting subject by creating a journal for deaf-mutes and the blind*," Berthier, *Notice*, p. 17.

111. p. 151.

Chapter 2
From deaf to Deaf

1. A parallel world?

As we have seen, the Deaf world at the end of the 18th century and during the first third of the 19th century was the environment in which Bébian grew up. It was not the only one, but multiple connections link him to this particular environment: we use the term "world" to signify that there was a distinct system of values, of a "cultural" nature we would say today. It was Ferdinand Berthier who gave tangible form to this, in particular through the creation of banquets celebrating Abbé de l'Épée, "the Deaf nation's birth certificate",[1] but fifty years after Auguste Bébian's death, Joachim Ligot, a former student of Ferdinand Berthier and himself deaf, recalled the essential influence of Bébian:[2]

> *"The vast knowledge that he* [Ferdinand Berthier] *was able to acquire and his range of learning did as much honor to his prodigious aptitudes as to the competence of his illustrious teacher, Bébian, who can never be too highly praised. It may be truly said of these men: like teacher, like student."*

1.1 The dynamism...

Unfortunately we know very little of the Deaf world at this time: there are just a few descriptive and analytical clues provided by the direct or indirect accounts of Marie Marois,[3] Saboureux de

1. Bernard Mottez, *Les Sourds existent-ils ?* Paris: L'Harmattan, 2006, p. 340.
2. Joachim Ligot, "Essai sur l'éloge de Ferdinand Berthier", *L'abbé de l'Épée. Journal des sourds et des sourds-muets,* n° 4, 1888, p. 50.
3. Marie Marois de Magnitot (1748-1829), a deaf orphan, was placed into Jacob Pereire's care at the age of seven, by Comte Saint Florentin, a minister under Louis XV, along with another deaf child of the same age, Marie Leurat. Jean-René Presneau, *Signes et Institution des sourds*, Seyssel: Champ Vallon, 1998, p. 88.

Fontenay,[4] Azy d'Étavigny[5] and Jean Massieu,[6] who were all students of various teachers during this period (Jacob Pereire, Abbé de l'Épée, Abbé Sicard and Étienne de Fay)[7] and above all of Pierre Desloges,[8] artisan bookbinder. Desloges was a strong supporter of sign language, a language "*so desperately neglected, and essentially spoken only by the deaf and mute,*"[9] and he defended Abbé de l'Épée though he had not been one of his students. His work, the first by a deaf person, was written in reaction to a publication that same year of "*Elementary course for the education of deaf-mutes*"[10] by another teacher, Abbé Deschamps, chaplain of Orleans cathedral. This Elementary course was a full-scale attack on the methodical signs method, to which Pierre Desloges put forward a counter-argument, providing in passing a valuable description of deaf people at the end of the 18th century. This work must be considered with caution however, because while it offers an abundance of information on the Deaf community of the time, it was perhaps amended by the publisher. Indeed, the text is preceded by a "warning":[11]

---

4. Saboureux de Fontenay (1737- ?) was entrusted to Pereire by the Duke of Chaulnes, his godfather, in 1750. Presneau, *Signes*, p. 88.
5. Azy d'Étavigny (1728 - ?) was the son of the Manager of the Cinq Grosses Fermes de La Rochelle (the authority for the collection of royal taxes). In 1746 his father asked Pereire to take care of his education.
 Presneau, *Signes*, p. 83.
6. Roch-Ambroise Sicard, *Album d'un sourd-muet. Notice sur l'enfance de Massieu,* Lons-le-Saulnier: Imprimerie de Courret, 1851.
7. See p. 37.
8. Pierre Desloges, *Observations d'un sourd et muet, sur un cours élémentaire d'éducation des sourds et muets*, published in 1779 by Abbé Deschamps, chaplain of Orleans cathedral, Paris: B. Morin, printer-bookseller, 1779.
9. *Ibid.*, p. 79.
10. Étienne-François Deschamps, *"Cours élémentaire d'éducation des sourds-muets, suivi d'une dissertation sur la parole"*, Paris: Debure, 1779.
11. Desloges, *Observations*, p. 4-6. Desloges' book was edited by Abbé Copineau, a great linguist of the time and a friend of Abbé de l'Épée; Copineau, like Sicard, campaigned for the "nouvèle ortografe" (new spelling), which explains the differences from standard spelling in this text, which must not be taken to be mistakes by Desloges. Personal communication from Yves Bernard.

> *"The short piece of writing presented to the public was indeed composed by a young deaf and mute man whom I met at the home of Abbé de l'Épée. This young man is not a student of that famous teacher; but having written this work to defend Abbé de l'Épée's method, he felt it necessary to pay tribute to him; he even wished to encourage him to revise his work and thus make it publishable. The lofty occupations of this virtuous clergyman, and perhaps to an even greater extent his modesty, did not allow him to bother with such a thing. The author turned to me, and it was with great pleasure that I took it upon myself to do him this small favor."*

Pierre Desloges' work is evidence of a dynamic of exchange among Deaf people in Paris, independently of the school recently created by Abbé de l'Épée at his own home in Rue des Moulins: in these troubled times of the Revolution, they knew each other, met together and discussed a range of subjects:[12]

> *"Our ideas are developing and expanding, through the opportunities given to us to see and observe new and interesting objects* [...]. *There is not a single event in Paris, in France or in the four quarters of the world that does not become a subject of our discussions. We express ourselves on all matters with as much order, precision and celerity as if we enjoyed the faculty of speaking and hearing."*

At the end of the day, there are relatively few traces that allow us to glimpse the Deaf world at the beginning of the 19th century. *La presse silencieuse* (the silent press), abundant thereafter, did not really reach its heights until the end of the century, though certain newspapers chronologically closer to the period that interests us made their appearance at the end of the 1830s.[13] They were part

12. Desloges, *Observations*, pp. 13 and 15.
13. The *Bulletin de la société universelle*, managed by Benjamin Dubois (the "Société centrale des Sourds-Muets" founded in 1838 by Ferdinand Berthier, became the "Société universelle" in 1867) appeared for the first time in January 1870 and *La Défense des sourds-muets* by Joseph Turcan in Aix-les-bains was created

of a "tradition" inaugurated by Auguste Bébian in 1826 when he created the *Journal des Sourds-Muets et des Aveugles*, the publication of which ceased the following year.[14] It was only thirteen years later, in 1839, that another newspaper picked up the baton: *L'Ami des Sourds-Muets, a newspaper for the parents and teachers of deaf-mutes, useful for anyone concerned with education*, a newspaper that aimed to "*popularize methods of teaching and submit them to the most severe philosophical scrutiny.*"[15] In turn, five years later, this press institution gave way to another newspaper "*of the same kind, to be published by Mr. Morel,*"[16] which appeared the following year with the name *Annales de l'éducation des sourds-muets et des aveugles,* running for six years, from 1844 to 1850.[17] Two other newspapers, not directly related to the previous one, were published a few years later to bolster this editorial mass: the *Benefactor of the deaf-mute*

---

in 1894. Between 1870 and 1900, fifteen newspapers came into being, with varying lifetimes (between a few months and a few years; Henri Gaillard's *Le Journal des Sourds-Muets* ran for twelve years, from 1894 to 1906).
Bernard Truffaut, "La presse silencieuse avant 1900", *Cahiers de l'Histoire des Sourds,* n° 4.1 et 5.1, Orléans: association Étienne de Fay, 1990 (summary table: Annex 7).

14. Le *Journal des Sourds-Muets et des Aveugles,* created by Bébian in 1826 (running until 1827) adopted a pedagogical tone and only lasted for eight issues: the first was published in August 1826 and the last in October 1827. It was intended to appear every month, but only the first five issues ran on this basis; the sixth did not appear until March 1827 (instead of January) with the final two issues coming out five and eight months later (the newspaper's summary and prospectus are set out in Annex 9).
15. *L'Ami des Sourds-Muets. Journal de leurs parents et de leurs instituteurs, utiles à toutes les personnes qui s'occupent d'éducation*, n° 1, Nov.-Dec. 1838, p. 2. This newspaper was created in Nancy in 1838 by Joseph Piroux, a hearing person, principal of the town's deaf-mute institute and former INSMP student; it was published every two months over a five-year period (from Nov.-Dec. 1838 to July-Aug. 1843).
16. *L'Ami des Sourds-Muets,* July-Aug. 1843, p. 129.
Édouard Morel was the nephew of Baron de Gérando, President of the INSMP's board of governors.
17. Joseph Piroux nevertheless agreed that there was a "divergence of opinions." *Ibid.*, p. 2.

and the blind[18] and finally the *Impartial.*[19] Abbé Sicard's publications offer no clue to what was really happening in the Deaf community, inasmuch as, aside from the institution he directed, he was in no way involved with it. Auguste Bébian describes his arrival at the Institution as follows:[20]

> *"When I came to the Royal Institution, I found in this school, or more specifically in the classes, a system of rudimentary, obscure and arbitrary signs, partly natural, partly conventional. Through this hybrid, crude, ignoble and incomplete language, the most picturesque, the most elegant expression appeared dull, flat or bizarre; the most vivid, the most graceful image came across as cold and trivial* [...] *I revealed to the deaf-mutes the richness, energy, elegance and flexibility of mime language, and with this powerful instrument, supported by the philosophical study of the language, there no longer remained any obstacle capable of stopping the deaf-mutes – no author, poet or prose writer that one could not bring within their reach."*

1.2 ... of a large yet invisible population

If one wishes to consider the situation of deaf people, one must also consider their number: awareness is progressive, an emerging issue at the time!

---

18. This newspaper was filled with valuable information about deaf people, through their lives in institutions in France. It was founded in 1854 by Abbé Darras, almoner at the Saint-Médard-les-Soissons institution (Aisne), and was only published for a period of two years. The number of "schools for deaf-mutes" was constantly rising, from less than half a dozen in 1789, to twenty in 1827, thirty-nine in 1844 and forty-seven in 1858 (reaching seventy in the 1880s). François Buton, "L'éducation des sourds-muets au XIXe siècle. Description d'une activité sociale", *Le Mouvement social,* 2008/2, n° 223.
19. *L'Impartial. Journal de l'enseignement des Sourds-Muets was a newspaper created in 1856 by* Jean-Baptiste Puybonnieux, librarian and archivist at the Institution impériale des Sourds-Muets de Paris (for the Institution's name changes, see p. 20) and Hector Volquin, teacher in charge of the special articulation course at the Institution. It was only published for a period of three years (1856-1859).
20. Auguste Bébian, *Examen critique de la nouvelle organisation de l'enseignement dans l'Institution royale des sourds-muets de Paris*, Paris: Treuttel & Wurtz, 1834, p. 35.

At the end of the 18th century, the parliamentarian Jean-Baptiste Massieu (unrelated to Jean), who headed the Committee of Public Instruction, relied on the estimate of 4,000 deaf people in France when he put forward to the Convention the idea of creating some ten Institutions in the country:[21] the figure turned out to be far lower than the reality! Indeed, the second census, carried out by the government a little more than thirty years later, in 1828, took the figure to 12,000, with the objective for Institution principals to "develop the activity of education" in line with the numbers.[22] A few years later, in 1831, Auguste Bébian estimated the deaf population in France to be between 18,000 and 20,000,[23] a figure he raised to 22,000 in 1834.[24] This is a credible number if one takes the official statistics established later by the Baron de Watteville, inspector general first class of charitable establishments, who, in his 1861 report, based on a census carried out ten years earlier, put forward an initial figure of 29,433.[25] This number was revised downwards to 21,576, taking into account the case of people who had become

21. François Buton, *L'administration des faveurs. L'État, les sourds et les aveugles (1789-1885)*, Rennes: Presses univ. de Rennes, 2009, p. 64.

22. *Ibid.*, p. 136.
This count took place in the same way as those carried out in Prussia, which organized no fewer than three counts between 1825 and 1828!
In the first issue of his newspaper written in 1826, Auguste Bébian writes: "In Europe alone there are more than 80,000 deaf-mutes." Auguste Bébian, *Journal de l'instruction des sourds-muets et des aveugles*, 1826, n° 1, p. 5.

23. "According to counts done in various regions, we estimate the number of Deaf-Mutes at one in every 1,800 or 2,000 inhabitants ... With no exaggeration, we may therefore consider the number of Deaf-Mutes in France to lie somewhere between 18 and 20,000 [...]"
Auguste Bébian, *Éducation des sourds-muets mise à la portée des institutions primaires et de tous les parents; Méthode naturelle pour apprendre les langues sans traduction,* Prospectus d'édition, Paris: Imprimerie de Béthune, 1831.

24. Bébian, *Examen critique*, p. 3.
He estimated the cost of educating a single student to be "10,000 francs" and challenged the notion that [such an education] would be possible for "[all of] France's 22,000 deaf-mutes".

25. Baron A. de Watteville, *Statistique des établissements de bienfaisance*, Paris: Imprimerie royale, 1861 quoted by Bernard Variot, *Approche de quelques aspects de la vie sociale des sourds-muets et de leur instruction au milieu du XIXᵉ siècle, vus*

deaf at a later stage: Bébian's 1834 estimates had therefore been realistic. These data were taken up in Ferdinand Berthier's campaign statement during his run for parliament in 1848,[26] as well as in the newspaper *L'Ami des Sourds-Muets*.[27] Bébian put forward these figures because he wished to show the reality of a scattered population, and wanted a systematic and free education for all deaf people within the public education system – for which a ministerial portfolio was created in 1828.[28] During the early 1800s, between 1813 and 1814 to be more precise, the INSMP took in eighty-eight students (fifty-nine boys and twenty-nine girls).[29] This was a closed universe, almost a prison, reminiscent perhaps of the hierarchical and supervised organization of the *habitations* in Guadeloupe, whose operation relied on the work of enslaved people.[30] Not that outside of this establishment the Deaf world did not exist; on the contrary, the work of Pierre Desloges demonstrates a certain vitality

---

au travers de L'Impartial, *journal de l'enseignement des sourds-muets, 1856-1859*, thesis to obtain the CAPINJS, ENSP, 1980, p. 158.

26. "[…] *as a proxy for my 22,000 brothers in France* […], *I believe I have acquired the right to intervene in the country's affairs, both as a fully-fledged republican and as a voice for the 22,000 deaf-mutes in France*" he wrote in his campaign statement in 1848. *La gazette des sourds-muets,* quoted by Yves Delaporte, "Berthier se présente à la députation", *Aux origines du mouvement Sourd*, Louhans, 1999; Buton, *L'administration des faveurs*, pp. 213-214.
27. In its July-August 1839 issue, *L'Ami des Sourds-Muets* published a "statistical table of Deaf-Mutes in every country of the world", showing the figure of 22,000 "deaf-mutes" in France (only 931 of whom were receiving an education, spread over 34 schools) out of a total population of 34 million. *L'Ami des Sourds-Muets*, July-Aug. 1839, p. 147.
28. Created by an order dated January 4, 1828, the ministry of public instruction lasted, under a series of slightly varying names, until June 1932, when it was replaced by the ministry of national education. Source : <http://data.bnf.fr/11989279/france_ministere_de_l_instruction_publique/>
29. Archives nationales, series F15 1944. In 1813, eighty-nine students (sixty-four of whom had scholarships) and eighty-eight the following year (sixty-three having scholarships). Anne T., Quartararo, *Deaf identity and social images in nineteenth-century France, Washington, Gallaudet University Press, 2008*, pp. 51-52.
30. One must nevertheless be careful not to generalize: some of the research on these habitations is still in its early stages. On the notion of habitation, see note 14, p. 70.

and real social participation.[31] That these went almost unnoticed, that traces of this community in the making are almost non-existent, gives pause for thought when it comes to our perception of this reality – or more accurately our non-perception: this is precisely what Auguste Bébian emphasized. When he arrived in Paris at the beginning of the 19th century, a small but dynamic group of Deaf people was already in place:[32] the capital contained 200 Deaf people for a population of 550,000 inhabitants.[33] A fertile ground thus pre-dated his arrival: if his meeting with the Deaf community was an event that made history, it is because a conjunction of factors occurred between this latent situation of deaf people and Bébian himself, who followed an entirely original path.

2. A period of transition

Bébian's arrival in France also coincided with the moment when Abbé de l'Épée's philanthropic initiative found an echo in the concern for "benevolence" so characteristic of the post-revolutionary period: the allocation of premises to the National Institution for Deaf-Mutes in Paris (INSMP) gave tangible form to this recognition.[34] This legitimization was nevertheless accompanied by two major evolutions: the creation of a scrutinizing body within the INSMP and the appointment of a doctor within the Institution's walls. Administrative reform and pedagogical planning, in contrast to a nascent Deaf

31. Desloges, *Observations*.
32. Although this was not an activist group, and it is anachronistic to talk about "the Deaf issue". Buton, *L'éducation des sourds-muets*, p. 69.
33. Estimates by Alfred Fierro (*Histoire et dictionnaire de Paris*, Paris: Robert Laffont, 1996, 1580, p. 278) and Ferdinand Berthier, who, in his campaign statement for the 1848 elections, writes: "*The capital contains approximately 200 free deaf-mutes*", i.e. 0.03%.
In 1880 France's population stood at 27 million, spread over a territory of 528,000 km² and was steadily rising: from 27 million in 1800, it rose to 29 million in 1815 and 35.4 million in 1846. Jean Claude Caron, *La France de 1815 à 1848*, Paris: Armand Colin, 2002, p. 35. Deaf people represent about 0.08% of this population.
34. See p. 27.

community that was gaining in self-awareness, structuring itself and asserting itself as a linguistic and cultural minority.

2.1 A "fictitious person" at the head of the National Institution for Deaf-Mutes in Paris

Institutional recognition undoubtedly made it possible to perpetuate what was initially an individual undertaking, but because it involved public money, it also demanded accountability. Which is why the State, whether under the Directory, the Consulate, the Empire or the Restoration, endeavored to exercise control, while to some extent groping around, because not only was this a turbulent period, the operation was also new; this control was exercised through a board of governors, attached to the principal.[35] The board, totally in line with the conceptions of the Ideologists, such as Cabanis or Destutt de Tracy,[36] was made up of doctors or "*honorable men who nevertheless knew nothing about the instruction of deaf-mutes.*"[37] The center of the decision-making power thus shifted. According to Bébian, it was furthermore "*the most serious cause of (the INSMP's) decline,* [...] *born from the constant pretension manifested by the*

35. The board was created in Year VIII (fall of 1800) by the Consulate, being replaced in February 1841 by an advisory committee, subordinated to the principal, who was directly appointed by the Minister of the Interior. The royal ordonnance of 1841 marked a real taking in hand by the central administration of the Institutions for the Deaf and the Blind, until then more or less run by this board of governors.
   Buton, *L'administration des faveurs*, pp. 119 and 147-149.
36. The "society of ideologists", founded in 1795 by this same Destutt de Tracy, a senator at the time, was a philosophical movement with the objective of rationalizing everything, of basing education on reason.
   "*Successor to the tail-end of the Enlightenment (Condorcet, Lavoisier, Sieyès), this revolutionary school, drawing inspiration from Condillac* [...], *philosophically speaking, nothing remains of it; politically, a great deal, because they constituted the backbone of State institutions*", writes philosopher Robert Damien ("Les Idéologues", *Médium* 2/2007, n° 11, p. 154).
37. Presneau, *Signes*, p. 159.

former board of governors to administer the institution alone and to direct the teaching alone".[38] Indeed, the principal of the INSMP, Sicard, effectively turned more and more to relations outside of teaching, which led to the second major change of the period. Until then medical involvement had been occasional, with the intervention of a health officer, Poulard, whose role was limited to medical inspections, care, and protection against epidemics.[39] At the end of the 18th century a certificate of deafness was also required for the admission of scholarship students.[40]

The INSMP being located "*two hundred meters from the Val-de-Grâce military hospital*" and from a civilian hospital created by Cochin, the parish priest of the church of Saint-Jacques du Haut-Pas, there was no need to have an in-house physician. Sicard's motivation was personal: "Victor", the wild child of Aveyron, was entrusted to him and he himself decided to call upon Jean-Marc Gaspard Itard, Larrey's assistant at the Val-de-Grâce hospital.[41] On the recommendation of Sicard and the board of governors, as well as at Itard's own request, in December 1800 he was appointed to the position of chief physician of the INSMP by the Consulate government.[42] This appointment

38. Alphonse Esquiros, *Paris, ou les sciences, les institutions et les mœurs au XIXe siècle*, 2 volumes, Paris: Comptoir des imprimeurs unis, 1847, p. 445.
    Alphonse Esquiros (1812-1876) wrote many essays (more than twenty, including for example *Histoire des Montagnards*, Paris: V. Lecou, 1847, 2 vol. and *Les Paysans*, Paris: Librairie de la Bibliothèque démocratique, 1872), along with several poems and novels. He was also a politician elected as a member of parliament on several occasions as from 1850.
39. Generally speaking, recourse to physicians was exceptional in towns, and even more so in the country. Robert Vial, *La chronologie de l'histoire de la médecine*, Paris: J.-P. Gisserot 1995, p. 49.
40. Other certificates were required in addition to this one, certificates of civism and indigence in particular. Bernard, *Esprit des Sourds*, p. 412.
    Poulard practiced at that time at the Salpêtrière and Bicêtre hospices, whose role was somewhat similar to that of the INSMP: caring for the indigent.
41. See p. 56.
42. A letter from Itard, dated 11 Vendemiaire Year IX (October 3, 1800), asked "*the Citizens governing the Institution to bring him justice, as he had for three years voluntarily carried out his duties in the establishment as a physician and surgeon, at the invitation of the Économe*". Itard asked that he be given the position that

was a sign of the increased medicalization of the institution, and of the trust placed in science when it came to remedial action. It was in opposition to this pathological and medicalizing conception, which took on tangible form within the walls of the institute through Itard's appointment, and in favor of the implementation of a true education, that Bébian made his voice heard:[43]

> *"Do the fleeting sensations that the ear perceives exert such a great influence on intelligence? And do ideas of sounds occupy such a considerable place in comprehension? On its own, the sense of hearing is far from having such high importance,* [...] *touch compensates* [...]. *How can we rouse this intelligence from its lethargic sleep? How can we revive these faculties which seem extinguished in inertia?"*

This did not stop him from devoting considerable space in his *Journal des sourds-muets et des aveugles* to auricular medicine and to the correspondence between Itard and Deleau.[44]

---

had just been created, with the corresponding salary. Quoted by Bernard, *Esprit des Sourds*, p. 412.

43. Bébian, *Journal*, Aug. 1826, pp. 9-10, 13.
A hundred fifty-five years later, in 1981, psychoanalyst Françoise Dolto described this same motivation and explained: "*What drove me to care for hearing-impaired children was that I was distraught by the non-recognition of such intelligence.*"

44. Bébian, *Journal*, 1826, pp. 6, 76-81, 96, 131-134, 164-166.
Nicolas Deleau was a physician with the hospices of Paris which, at the end of 1825, included seven boys and six girls who were "deaf-mutes," three of the boys being deemed "idiots" or insane and destined for the Hospice of the Incurables. René Bernard, "Les dossiers des boursiers d'antan à l'Institut des sourds-muets de Paris", *Bulletin d'information, Société centrale d'Éducation et d'Assistance pour les sourds-muets en France*, 1974, n° 35-36, pp. 119-123, n° 37-38, pp. 139-144, 1975, n° 39, pp. 92-97.
The report sent to the Académie de Médecine in 1827, containing a "Table of the various types of deafness cured by catheterization of the Eustachian tube" is evidence of his experiments. Bernard, *Esprit des Sourds,* p. 449.

2.2 Them, the hearing-speaking, and us, the deaf-mutes: the emergence of an identity

As we have seen, Ferdinand Berthier (1803-1886), a student and later on friend of Auguste Bébian, mentioned the important role that Bébian played, particularly in critically distancing himself from the method implemented by Abbé de l'Épée and taken up by his successor. This distancing undoubtedly led to an awareness of an anthropological nature. Jean Massieu[45] and Laurent Clerc[46] are

---

45. Jean Massieu (1772-1846) is one of the emblematic figures of Deaf culture: the *Notice sur l'enfance de Massieu, sourd-muet,* published in 1808, in Abbé Sicard's *Théorie des signes pour l'instruction des sourds-muets* (Paris: Imprimerie de l'Institution des sourds-muets, 1808, vol. II, p. 626) provides us with a relatively full description. He came from Semens, near Bordeaux in the Gironde region. He was born into a poor family of winegrowers, the fifth of six deaf siblings (three boys and three girls) - something that puts Sicard's pedagogical successes very much into perspective, as one can legitimately assume that Massieu had some sort of language when he arrived at the Bordeaux Institute in 1785, at the age of thirteen). Five years later, in 1790, he was appointed répétiteur at the Royal Institution for Deaf-Mutes in Paris at the same time as his mentor Abbé Sicard, appointed principal of that establishment the same year (see p. 20). For the first time in history, a deaf person became a teacher. Jean Massieu was referred to "*by imitating the movement of a hand lifting up hair draped over the shoulders*" (Louis-Pierre Paulmier, Le Sourd-Muet civilisé, Paris: De l'imprimerie d'Ange Clo, 1820., p. 34). Nowadays, we remember his passion for books and watches; he showed them to everyone: his sign name was "*He who takes a watch out of his pocket*".
46. Laurent Clerc (1785-1869), from Balme-les-Grottes en Isère came to the INS-MPP in 1797, at the age of twelve, and became *a répétiteur* eight years later. He became deaf at an early age, after a fall, and the accident left him with a scar on his cheek, a distinctive mark that gave him his sign name (Paulmier, *Le Sourd-Muet civilisé*, p. 34).
   In 1815, during a demonstration of Sicard's method in London, from June 2 onwards, he met a young American pastor of his own age, Thomas Hopkins Gallaudet (1787-1851) (Laurent Clerc was just two years his senior). Gallaudet, employed by the father of a young deaf girl (Alice Cogswell) to provide her with an education, had come to Europe in search of a method for educating deaf children. On March 9 of the following year, 1816, he was invited to the INSMP by Sicard, and suggested that Leclerc accompany him to New York in May. The latter accepted, "*impelled by his shamefully modest salary*" (Ferdinand Berthier, *Notice sur la vie et les ouvrages de Auguste Bébian, ancien censeur des*

emblematic of a generation that succeeded in being appointed to teaching positions (the latter became a *répétiteur* as early as 1790, Laurent Clerc later, in 1805); they had an "attitude of submission and boundless admiration" towards their "benefactors".[47] A veneration, or at least a respect, which was not really shared, as Sicard rightly points out in the introduction to his *Cours d'instruction d'un Sourd-Muet de naissance.*[48] He begins his book with the following observation:[49]

> *"Indeed, what is a deaf-mute from birth, considered in himself, and before any education has begun to connect him, in any way, to that great family to which, through his external form, he belongs? In society he is a perfectly null being, a living automaton, a statue, such as Charles Bonnet and later on Condillac present it; a statue whose senses must necessarily be opened, and directed, one after the other, to compensate for the one sense of which he is unfortunately deprived. Limited to physical movements alone, before tearing open the envelope under which his reason remains buried, he does not even have that assured instinct which directs animals that rely on this alone as a guide."*

A conception taken up by the eldest of INSMP's teachers and one of Sicard's close collaborators, Louis-Pierre Paulmier, who validated the idea that before being educated, "deaf-mutes" were completely

---

études de l'Institut royal des sourds-muets de Paris. Paris: Ledoyen, 1839, p. 13), which Bébian put at 500 francs a year (*Journal de l'Instruction des Sourds-Muets*, 1826, p. 357; the annual salary of a teacher was between 1800 and 2500 francs, which was comfortable, and "*equal to the pay of a deputy head clerk at the ministry of the interior*", says François Buton (*L'administration des faveurs*, p. 200)).

47. Yves Delaporte, Armand Pelletier, *Moi, Armand, né sourd et muet*, Plon: Terre humaine, 2002, p. 280.
48. This is in fact a summary of a private lesson given by Abbé Sicard to his favorite student Jean Massieu, thanks to whom he was able to obtain the position of head teacher at the INSMP.
49. Sicard, *Cours d'instruction d'un sourd-muet de naissance, et qui peut être utile à l'éducation de ceux qui entendent et qui parlent*, Paris: Le Clère, 1803.

uncultivated.[50] This conception was the exact opposite of the reality described by Pierre Desloges twenty-four years earlier, in 1779:[51]

> *"It would be a grave error to view us in some way as automata doomed to vegetate in the world* [...]."

Whether on purpose or not, Sicard's definition of "Deaf-Mutes from birth" utterly ignores this argument. As "head teacher", Abbé Sicard's influence over the teaching staff, particularly with regard to the way the students were judged, was of course considerable.[52] To this highly belittling perception may be added a coded and repressive organization within the very walls of the INSMP at the start of the 19th century. Although it was introduced after Bébian's time at the Institution (twenty or so years later), the regulation dated November 3, 1841 offers us a glimpse of this repression.[53] It sets out the duties of the visiting-room supervisor and gives us an idea of the living conditions of students at that time... The justification for the visiting-room was that students' contact with the outside world, families included, had to be kept to a *minimum* in order to

50. As he writes in his book Le Sourd-Muet civilisé: "*With his chisel, the sculptor works on the stone, finally managing to torment a block of marble to somehow move the matter; the teacher awakens the soul, develops understanding, allows a deaf person to speak, lets thought spring from his almost lifeless brain* [...]". Paulmier, *Le Sourd-Muet civilisé*. For a biography of Louis-Pierre Paulmier, see note n°104,p. 60.
51. Desloges, *Observations*, p. 15.
    In a relatively explicit fashion, Bébian also attacked this conception: "Some teachers, wanting no doubt to increase the luster and importance of the art to which they had devoted their talents, had no scruples about depicting deaf-mutes as some sort of living automata, walking statues, with no feelings to warm them and no spark of reason to enlighten them; veritable machines in human form, sensitive to physical impressions alone, and in whom the teacher's talent must create both a soul and a heart, and moral and intellectual faculties." *Journal des sourds-muets et des aveugles*, 1826, n° 1, p. 7.
52. Ferdinand Berthier reports that one of the Institution's employees referred to students as dogs and monkeys. (Berthier, *Notice*, p. 24).
53. Document reproduced in the newspaper *Coup d'œil* n° 41, 1984.
    Was it a case of simply ratifying existing practices? Or of tightening up the prevailing rules of conduct?

'civilize' them.[54] They thus lived cut off from the world and, even worse, the supervisor acted as an interpreter and had to report everything that was said to the principal. As for the clothes, although during the Duchess of Berry's visit to the INSMP in the 1820s[55] Bébian emphasized the nudity of his pupils, provoking the fury and exasperation of the governors, over the course of the century the uniform was to add the final touch to this drastic organization.[56] In a letter dated October 3, 1859, the principal of the INSMP explained to the minister why clothing was fundamental to the purposes of a civilizing mission, in order to subjugate students to the Institution. At the time when Bébian was a *répétiteur* at the INSMP, and later deputy principal (*censeur*), i.e. between 1817 and 1821, it was still a case of dealing with the most urgent matters, dressing the students in order to preserve morality or protect them from the cold, but the tone was set. Other reports mention the filthiness of the dormitories, the unbearable smell of the latrines, the lack of water, the unreliable heating, and the lice or ringworm that infested the students' hair and scalps.[57] The minutes of the May 26, 1826 session of the board of governors of the INSMP are interesting for our

---

54. The aim was to protect the students from the negative influence of outside contacts. There were fears about trouble-making and rebelliousness. For a long time the day students were kept separate from the boarders, at a residence near the Observatory. They were the poorest students and did not receive sufficient vocational training. Personal communication from Yves Bernard.
55. The episode is recounted by Ferdinand Berthier in *Notice* (p. 23): "*The Duchess of Berry, accompanied by the Duke de Levis and Mathieu de Montmorency, one of the most longstanding governors of the school, came to visit the house in 1819 or 1820, when Bébian, who had been purposely moved away, suddenly reappeared. He gave the princess some of the students' works. Madame asked to see them. Impossible! replied the honorable teacher, they are naked, in no state to present themselves before Your Royal Highness, and even unable, for the last 4 months, to go out for a walk, due to a lack of clothing. Two days later, there was a lively argument, following which he found himself obliged to resign his position and leave the establishment.*"
   This was not the real reason for his dismissal (see Annex 7); did Berthier not know the reason?
56. Document reproduced in *Coup d'œil* n° 44, 1986.
57. Document reproduced in *Coup d'œil* n° 45, 1986.

research in that they illustrate the living conditions and hygiene of the young "deaf-mute female students".[58] Most important of all, perhaps, these minutes show the predominance of the institution's first health officer, Jean-Marc Gaspard Itard, whom we quoted above, less than ten years after the Institution was created: medicalization was rampant. The introduction of gymnastics the following year, in 1827, was designed to help with the process of learning to speak: it was the first break with the system set up by Abbé de l'Épée.[59] To some extent, this organization is reminiscent of the panopticon developed in the 18th century by the Bentham brothers, Jeremy and Samuel, later highlighted by Michel Foucault and applied to places other than the prison world (hospitals, factories, schools…).[60]

While strictly speaking this did not concern Bébian, the girls being completely separated from the boys, to the point of having to use separate staircases to avoid all contact, and of having to live in rooms walled in or darkened by blinds, he nevertheless painted a terrifying picture of the situation.[61] This military organization would continue to develop, as in 1834:[62]

> *"The students were divided into companies and platoons, led by corporals and sergeants, proudly wearing yellow woolen braid on their sleeves, and marching to the beat of the drum. This imitation of the military regime of the colleges of the empire would be in bad taste everywhere today; but in an institution for deaf mutes! Good Lord!"*

Auguste Bébian set in motion a considerable degree of emancipation of deaf people, who from objects become subjects, building on a growing awareness of themselves as a linguistic and cultural minority. It was a student and friend of Bébian's, the deaf teacher

58. *Ibid.*
59. Didier Séguillon, *Une histoire à corps et à cri*, Exhibition catalogue, INJS, 1994.
60. Michel Foucault, *Discipline and punish,* 1977, Pantheon Books.
61. It was a question of "white flows", i.e. vaginal secretions and "*of licentious habits in which several of our female deaf-mutes would appear to have indulged…"*
62. Bébian, *Examen critique*, p. 26.

Ferdinand Berthier, who best symbolized this radical evolution. The "vertical hierarchy", Hearing/Deaf, based on the audiological criterion, was replaced by a horizontal, egalitarian relationship, through the linguistic modality of communication. The dividing line was no longer between the normal and the abnormal, but between those who spoke and those who signed. This essential awareness of identity, which distinguished "them", the hearing-speakers, from "us", the Deaf-Mutes,[63] was undoubtedly one of Bébian's indirect contributions. The spark of this emancipation lay in his solid knowledge of sign language,[64] the ease with which he communicated with the students, his close relationship with them;[65] his pedagogical successes clearly triggered a growing animosity toward a teacher capable of using the language of his students. As we saw with regard to the fierce criticism of Paulmier's teaching, in his *Journal des sourds-muets et des aveugles,*[66] Bébian recounts two observations that led him into teaching, one of which illustrates the virulent reaction that his comments aroused.[67]

Paulmier, after all, was a disciple of Sicard and an ardent supporter of methodical signs.[68]

The confusion is obvious, as the earlier example of "roasted chestnuts" (p. 102) also shows. This practice is called "signed French", and consists in replacing a word by a sign. More generally, an ut-

---

63. Deaf-mutes, some of whom used their voices: the paradox is only apparent, as the claim is essentially of an anthropological order.
64. "*His instinct allowed him to see in what way the signs used were wrong, defective, strange, arbitrary; and he never ceased to push for a complete reform* [...]" Berthier, *Notice,* p. 7.
65. "*On days off and during school vacations, Bébian could always be found at the Institution des Sourds-Muets, among the students, in the classrooms, in the workshops. During recess, he joined in all of their games. In a short time he thus became a veritable deaf-mute with a thorough grasp of mime language,*" wrote Benjamin Dubois in 1888 (Benjamin Dubois, "Physiologie du sourd-muet, par Bébian", *L'abbé de l'Épée. Journal des sourds et des sourds-muets,* n° 2, 1888, p. 28).
66. Bébian, *Journal,* 1827, vol. 2, p. 52; he explains: "*Some of his disciples maintained a sort of cult fanaticism regarding his method.*"
67. Quoted on p. 93.
68. The principle behind methodical signs is explained on p. 51.

terance made by signing is based on the syntax of French and not that of sign language, which presupposes a prior acquisition of the concepts of the written language in order to grasp its meaning. While the adjective attached to chestnuts or to veal is a common word in French, it is expressed differently in sign language. Physiologically, it is possible to simultaneously speak and sign (the two communication channels used are different), but cognitively it is not!

According to Ferdinand Berthier, there were frequent mistakes, even by Abbé de l'Épée:[69]

> *"As we have seen, Abbé de l'Épée's system (and bear in mind that he only used it in the classroom) consisted entirely in making the sign fit the word rather than the idea. The same system was also used by Abbé Sicard and his disciples, with the exception of Mr. Bébian."*

Auguste Bébian also observed that:[70]

> *"There are very few people who have a clear idea of the language of deaf-mutes. Some think it simply consists in using fingers to successively represent the letters that make words and sentences; others recognize a real language, but one that goes no further than representing tangible objects* […] *step by step, the sign follows the thought, like a shadow that takes on all its forms."*

Bébian himself had acquired a detailed understanding of sign language, which he illustrated using the example of the sign for peach:[71]

---

69. Ferdinand Berthier, *Les sourds-muets avant et après l'abbé de l'Épée*, Paris: J. Ledoyen publisher, 1840, p. 48.
This text was initially a speech given on May 26, 1840 to the Société des sciences morales, lettres et arts de Seine-et-Oise, winning the gold medal.
70. Auguste Bébian, *Essai sur les sourds-muets et sur le langage naturel ou introduction à une classification naturelle des idées avec leurs signes propres.* Paris: J.-G. Dentu, 1817, pp. 60 and 65.
71. *Ibid.*, p. 113.

> *"The idea of a peach is made up of the idea of its shape, its taste, its smell, its color, and even the tree on which it grows. All these circumstances, providing so many signs, will form a very good description that would convey the isolated idea of a peach; but its length would hamper the thought process. One must therefore choose from among these signs; and from the moment that there is choice, mistakes can be made. It is true that such a choice is not arbitrary, and that preference is given to the signs that best characterize the object. But there is no such predicament for signs relating to understanding."*

There is no doubt that through this linguistic awareness, Auguste Bébian initiated an anthropological and cultural emancipation of identity that would manifest itself a few decades later outside the walls of the Institution, like a baby whose umbilical cord is cut, freeing it from its mother. This emancipation was perceptible a few years after his departure, as we will see below. In spite of (or because of?) his deep understanding of the natural language of deaf people and his intense pedagogical thinking, Auguste Bébian was dismissed on January 3, 1821.[72] He had only been deputy principal at the INSMP for two years, and prior to that a *répétiteur* and then a teacher for just three years. And yet in November 1830, nine years after he had left the school, the deaf teachers – profiting from the insurrection that led to the overthrow of Charles X – showed no hesitation in petitioning the new king, Louis-Philippe I, just 3 months into his

72. We know all about the circumstances from Abbé Sicard's letter and Itard's medical report (p. 138).
    Bébian's letter to the INSMP's governors suggests that this dismissal was something of a relief for him, given the vague nature of his appointment as deputy principal two years earlier (a letter dated October 20, 1820 from Abbé Sicard to Baron de Gérando attests to this: "[…] *the governors not yet having determined the remit of the position* […]"), and Bébian himself talks about resignation. This letter is not dated, but it can be estimated to have been written between January 3 (date of his dismissal) and January 14, 1821 (there is a dated annotation by Sicard in the margin); it deplores the lack of defined duties, which had led him on several occasions to offer his resignation.

reign, for Bébian's return.[73] "The Deaf-Mute go to the King" was the headline in *La Sentinelle du peuple*, citing an earlier report in *Le Moniteur*.[74] A deputation led by Ferdinand Berthier and Alphonse Lenoir (they were the only incumbent teachers, both tenured only since the previous year) was thus taken to see the king by his aide-de-camp.[75] This must be seen as the first glimmer of independence: the school's management was not aware of the initiative. It is revealing that it was motivated by the removal of the man who was once in charge of teaching at the Institution. Did relations with Deaf people continue after his departure? It would seem so. The *Examen critique de la nouvelle organisation de l'enseignement dans l'institution royale des sourds-muets de Paris*, which Bébian published in 1834, shows that he remained very much aware of what was going on at the school.[76]

---

73. On July 27-29, 1830, following the Parisian uprising later referred to as the Revolution of the "Three Glorious Days", the government was overthrown and the king of France, Charles X, abdicated. The Restoration came to an end and Louis-Philippe I was appointed King of the French: Alphonse Lenoir, Deaf, appointed teacher the year before, the same year as Ferdinand Berthier, recounts the participation of Deaf people "*in the defense of the barricades*". Alphonse Lenoir, *Faits divers, pensées diverses et quelques réponses de sourds-muets*, 2nd edition, Paris, 1850, p. 40.
74. *La Sentinelle du peuple*, edition of November 14, 1830. Delaporte, Pelletier, Moi, Armand, p. 284.
75. Berthier, *Notice*, p. 30.
76. For example, on page 38 he comments on Article 7 of the Circular, which provides the reminder that "*the signs referred to as methodical, (that is to say the purely arbitrary and conventional mimic language) are definitively banned from the Royal Institute's teaching system*". Yet, Bébian objects, "*since the teaching reform brought about by my students, there has no longer been any question of methodical signs*"... This clearly shows that the board of governors had little awareness of classroom realities.
   Yves Bernard mentions an undated letter that Bébian himself wrote to the principal of the Institution, which describes the moral disengagement of the Institute's deaf teachers: "*If I have received*," writes Bébian, "*some of my former students who are now teachers, (Ferdinand Berthier and Alphonse Lenoir, tenured in 1829), who came to me as much through kindness & gratitude as by the need to receive, for their teaching, advice that they cannot find in your institution, this is due to my continued affection for them, & my consent in this regard was solely in*

A written document was thus presented to the new king of the French during this audience; it adroitly appealed to the king's emotions by referring to his "ancestor" thereby logically leading on to their request:[77]

> *"Sire,*
> *While we are unable to add our voices to the triumphant songs that celebrate the regeneration of France, our hearts respond with euphoria; our hearts have leapt with enthusiasm at the awakening of freedom and at the accession of a citizen-king proclaimed by the wishes of an entire people whom he has saved from anarchy."*

The stage was set: the assurance that Deaf people fully adhered to Louis-Philippe's accession (can we not see in this a degree of strategic flattery?), the evocation of liberty and the regeneration of the country. Abbé de l'Épée was compared to Auguste Bébian,[78] the subject of the audience, and if the founding abbot had been able, they said, against all odds, to introduce a dedicated education, it was thanks to the protection of the king's own father, the Duke of Penthièvre:[79]

---

the interest of their education & I even dare to say in the interest of your institution whose glory depends to a large extent on the level of education of these young men." Yves Bernard, *Approche de la gestualité à l'institution des sourds-muets de Paris XVIII-XIX*[es] *siècles*, doctoral thesis, Université Paris V, 1999, p. 487. Moreover, Théophile Denis reports that Frédéric Peyson, the future painter, was housed by Bébian after leaving the INSMP (Théophile Denis, *Frédéric Peyson, peintre sourd-muet. Notice biographique*, Paris: Imprimerie Bélanger, 1890). Their relationship was long-lasting, as it was this same Peyson who was chosen as a witness to the birth of Honoré Bébian (Ferdinand Berthier, "Lettre au rédacteur de L'Univers", *L'Ami des Sourds-Muets*, second year 1839-1840, p. 143.

77. Berthier, *Notice*, p. 30.
78. *Ibid*.
79. The comment is designed to place the king in a continuity: it is not the historical truth. The father of Louis-Philippe I, Louis Jean-Marie de Bourbon, Duke of Penthièvre (1725-1793), grandson of Louis XIV (of the "bastard" line), did indeed grant "*a pension of 800* [French] *pounds*" to the Count of Solar, a young unknown deaf-mute, taken in by Abbé De l'Épée in 1774, but he does not seem to have played any major role in de l'Épée's establishment. Revue d'études historiques,

"When Abbé de l'Épée, persecuted for his religious opinions, found himself obliged to create a new art in order to nourish his love of the good, his school, which foreign scholars and sovereigns hastened to visit, had just one protector in France, your honorable grandfather, the Duke of Penthièvre. The deaf and mute hope to find, in the heir to this prince's virtues, the same compassion for their misfortune, the same benevolence for the men who devote themselves to their education. Among these, there is one, the most distinguished of all, who has pushed back the boundaries of this charitable art, in which he has no equal [...] *It is thanks to his lessons that we are able to express our feelings to Your Majesty. Mr. Bébian directed the studies of our institution for several years..."*

They received a warm welcome and Louis-Philippe replied:[80]

"I am old enough to remember not only Abbé Sicard, whom I have seen since the Restoration, but also Abbé de l'Épée, whom I saw teaching his deaf-mute pupils in the little garden of the Palais Royal. I was very young at the time, I was only four or five [...] *Regarding the recommendation they are making on Mr. Bébian's behalf, I shall give it my especial attention; I will be delighted to reward the care he has shown to deaf-mutes; the reasons for exclusion that have just been stated no longer exist today. I have no doubt that Mr. Bébian has made good patriots of the deaf-mutes, men of use to the country, who can live with their families like other men and fulfill the same duties."*

Following this audience, the king invited Ferdinand Berthier and Alphonse Lenoir to dine with him, to enquire about Laurent Clerc and Jean Massieu whom he remembered. This gave Berthier

vol. 2, 1884, p. 107. Maryse Bezagu-Deluy, *L'Abbé de L'Épée. Instituteur gratuit des Sourds-Muets*, 1712-1789, pp. 192-222, Paris: Seghers, 1990; Yves Delaporte, "La construction d'un mythe," *Art pi!*, November 2012, p. 8.

80. Berthier, *Notice*, 1839, pp. 30-31.

the opportunity to insist once more upon the essential need for Bébian's return:[81]

> *"The institution was long affected by Clerc's departure for the United States; he was replaced as deputy principal by Bébian, with his unrivalled talents, who took things much further than his predecessors. But unfortunately we lost him* [...] *Yes, Sire, he made good patriots out of the deaf and mute, for his heart poured out into our own. Nephew of Dumolard and Barnave, his feelings are in line with such an honorable alliance.*[82] *His position has been abolished and leaves an immense void. We beg Your Majesty to return to the deaf and mute their most accomplished teacher and their most devoted friend. For him it will be justice; for us it will be an invaluable benefit."*

On December 14, 1830,[83] a month and a half after the teachers, it was the students who "flouted hierarchy" and addressed themselves

81. *Ibid.*, p. 32.
82. Canon Ballivet also mentions this ancestry: *"He left his widow, grand-daughter of Constituent Assembly member Barnave, in a precarious situation."* (Berthier, Notice, p. 62). Auguste Bébian was related by marriage to the revolutionary deputy.
83. A list of the leaders and participants can be drawn up from the Institution's handwritten manuscripts:
"Student Bezu, the future painter, distributed the petition; he was its author: expelled. Signatories to the petition: Haacke, Queille, Gremy, all of Rivière's students (one of the INSMP's four teachers, along with MM. Valade, Richard and Morel);
- Contremoulin, not very interested in staying; he prefers to join Bébian who is running his special day school in Mont-Parnasse: expelled;
- Imbert, who, as soon as he entered the classroom, moved swiftly toward Valade, rubbing his hands in a mocking manner, furrowing his brow, etc., etc.: expelled;
- Allibert, Itard's former and brilliant student, admits having pieced together another petition with Bezu, after a student had torn up the first; Forestier corrected it; Haacke revealed the content of the document: written on December 5, the petition stated that with Mr. Borel [the students] *did not work, that they wished to have Mr. Bébian."*
The petition itself has disappeared but leaflets offer some clues... *"Imbert caricatures the teacher, Valade, rubbing his hands as he moves toward the pupil, furrowing his brow then moving away while looking at him defiantly... In reality this is the logical and visual translation of the verbal sarcasm of hearing people... The anonymous letters are moving. They are addressed to Richard, as a pig's head,*

directly to the Minister of the Interior,[84] proving not only that the memory of Bébian had not faded with time, it had become stronger, for while the teachers had known him in person, the younger students probably had not. They denounced Abbé Borel "*who had almost no merit or talent*" and demanded the appointment of Bébian as principal of the school to replace him. These were not isolated events: sixty-one students signed this letter and "*the walls of Saint-Jacques were covered with inscriptions supporting Bébian*". The revolt was put down and the demand was not followed up. This was no doubt due to the ministry's determination not to give too much space to Deaf people, and to teachers in particular:[85] As François Buton points out, the Saint Jacques board of governors explicitly forbade him to have any kind of relationship with students, present or former.[86] Perhaps because of his reputation, but more likely due to the esteem in which he was held by the deaf teachers, the Institution's governors refused to reinstate Bébian, and were at pains to forbid any teacher or pupil from having the slightest relationship with him when in 1826 he decided to open a small school on the Boulevard du Montparnasse.

---

to Morel, Édouard as a donkey, and Octavie, spared from any animal references. Finally, to Borel, puffing away hard enough to set a windmill of words spinning. The sails of this windmill depict Valade, as a chicken, Rivière, as a bull, Morel, as a donkey, and finally Richard; all this accompanied by some highly explicit captions: 'man-machine', 'woman-machine', or simply 'machine'."

All of this concludes with the main demand: "*Long live Bébian! We want Mister Bébian, principal of the royal institute for deaf-mutes of Paris, we love him.*" Document reproduced in Annex 8, signed by Charles Ryan, who was awarded the "3rd class certificate of merit" on August 11, 1826 (Rivière's class). ("Distribution des prix de l'Institution royale de Paris, le 11 août 1826", Bébian, *Journal*, 1826, vol. 1, p. 50).

Bernard, *Approche de la gestualité*, p. 484.

84. Delaporte, Armand Pelletier, Moi, Armand, p. 285.

85. *Ibid.*, p. 286.

86. "*One can imagine the governors' fury when they learned that 'their' deaf-mute students and teachers had so symbolically flouted the Institution's regulations, which require prior authorization from the board of governors for any 'public' intervention by Institution members.*" Buton, *L'administration des faveurs*, pp. 142-143.

In the end, Auguste Bébian was not reinstated, but this event was a milestone and revealed the first institutional split between the principal and the speaking teachers on the one hand and the teachers, *répétiteurs* and Deaf students on the other. Ferdinand Berthier, whom we have already mentioned, represented the generation of Deaf people who dared to criticize and make demands, unlike Massieu and Clerc. On November 30, 1834 he organized the first banquet in homage to Abbé de l'Épée, "the birth of the Deaf nation".[87] The date and the person of Abbé de l'Épée were not chosen by chance: he was born on Thursday, November 24, 1712, and his reputation made it possible to diffuse the event beyond the walls of the Institution.[88] One has to appreciate Ferdinand Berthier's political skills... The newspapers of the time – *Le Temps, Le Moniteur universel, La Chronique de Paris, Le Courrier français, Le National, Le Journal des débats, La Gazette de France, La Quotidienne, Le Corsaire, Le Cabinet de lecture, La Tribune* and *L'Impartial* – all reported on the event, which did not go unnoticed.[89] This was part of a clearly stated objective to take the deaf issue beyond the walls of an establishment that had an educational vocation. At the second banquet in 1835, Berthier therefore proposed a toast to the press:[90]

> *"Ah, the press! It can certainly be said of them that 'they perform miracles!' They have given a voice to those who have for so long been mute. They have forced the great and the good, who have for so long*

87. Bernard Mottez, "Les banquets des sourds-muets et la naissance du mouvement Sourd", in *Le pouvoir des signes*, INJS exhibition catalogue, 1989. It would appear that it was Claudius Forestier (1810-1891), a student of Bébian and then répétiteur at the INSMP, who first had the idea: Nathalie Lachance, *Territoire, transmission et culture sourde*, Québec: Presses de l'université Laval, 2007, p. 267.
88. In 1789, as he lay dying, a Convention delegation promised Abbé de l'Épée that France would adopt his "children", and in 1791 a decree declared that "*the name de l'Épée... would be placed alongside those who were the most deserving of humanity and the motherland.*" Bezagu-Deluy, L'Abbé de L'Épée, p. 29.
89. Florence Encrevé, *Les sourds dans la société française au XIX*[e] *siècle. Idée de progrès et langue des signes*, Paris: Créaphis, 2012, p. 124.
90. *Banquets des sourds-muets réunis pour fêter les anniversaires de la naissance de l'abbé de l'Épée*, 1835, vol. 1, p. 29.

been deaf to this powerful voice, to finally lend a willing ear. [...]. *It is upon them that we shall call if any fools still try to hold us back and deny that an equal intelligence gives us equal rights as part of this great human family..."*

This was a key event inasmuch as the history of the Deaf community is not that of schools or of methods of education, even if we tend – even today – to put them in the same basket.[91] The *Comité des sourds-muets de Paris* had not been created for the sole purpose of organizing banquets. In 1836, Berthier remined everyone that:[92]

"The creation of this committee, just two years ago, had been made necessary by critical circumstances into which deaf-mutes found themselves plunged following active intrigues of which they were constantly on the receiving end, and by the need to combine their efforts so as to repel the attacks of certain men who exploited their infirmity in order to reap the rewards of their labor."

The objective of these banquets was very similar to the aim of those organized by Alexandre Ledru-Rollin in 1847[93] and to the vital

91. For example, the school run by a contemporary of Abbé de l'Épée, Samuel Heinicke (1727-1790; see p. 51), principal of the Leipzig Institute, is often placed in the "Sign-hostile" category and hence more or less ignored by history. Yet texts in Swedish describe the Leipzig school's centenary celebrations in 1878. Two Swedes, (one Deaf and one hearing) were present and wrote an account that shows the robustness of sign language in the school at that time. This is corroborated by Samuel Heinicke's second wife, Anna Catharina Elisabeth Heinicke (1757-1840), who became principal of the school after her husband's death in 1790.
Joachim Winkler, *Anna Catharina Elisabeth Heinicke (1757-1840): erste Direktorin einer deutschen Gehörlosenschule*, Hamburg, 2007.
92. Encrevé, *Les sourds dans la société française*, p. 123 and Annex 4.
93. Alexandre Ledru-Rollin was the guest of honor at the second banquet organized by the Comité des sourds-muets de Paris in 1835 to commemorate the anniversary of Abbé de l'Épée's birth. *Banquets des sourds-muets réunis pour fêter les anniversaires de la naissance de l'abbé de l'Épée*, 1835, vol. 1, p. 29.

role that they played in triggering the 1848 Revolution.[94] We might however wonder why Auguste Bébian left France on November 10, 1834 to return to Guadeloupe, i.e. just twenty days before this inaugural banquet in which he could have participated.[95] Did he disagree with Ferdinand Berthier and his initiative or had his overall personal situation become so untenable that he had to leave so quickly? Ferdinand Berthier reports significant financial difficulties and serious health problems in Rouen:[96]

> "[...] *Rouen's damp and unpredictable climate was affecting Bébian's health. He was in constant suffering and had endured more than one attack serious enough to worry his family and his adopted children* [...] *The position was untenable and Bébian was obliged to give it up. The unjust oblivion in which our wise teacher was languishing was weighing ever more heavily on him and his family. Their privation: they began to feel the anguish of financial embarrassment.*"

While the minister's letter to the prefect of the Lower Seine on March 19, 1834, which mentions Bébian "abandoning" his students[97] might make one think of a sudden departure from the city, it would appear that his departure from the country was forced:[98]

> *"He had just received what appeared to be an attractive offer; that of running a school abroad. He decided he would accept if he were unable to find a position in France. In 1833 he contacted Mr. Edmond Blanc, general secretary at the Ministry of Commerce and Public Works (who was responsible for the education of deaf-mutes), to ask him to give him the task, if only for one year, of teaching normal lessons* [...]. *In*

---

94. These banquets were introduced to counter King Louis-Philippe's censorship of all public meetings. Vincent Robert, *Le temps des banquets. Politique et symbolique d'une génération, 1818-1848*, Paris: Publications de la Sorbonne, 2010.
95. Berthier, *Notice*, p. 41.
96. *Ibid.*, pp. 38-39 and 44.
97. Letter from the minister to the Prefect of the Lower Seine on March 19, 1834 (series 3XP702, AD SM).
98. Berthier, *Notice*, pp. 39-40.

Paris he found nothing. His presence there awakened the slumbering intrigue that blocked the path of this honorable and talented man. He could not but fail, and he failed."

We will probably never know the truth… After Auguste Bébian's return to Guadeloupe, he and Ferdinand Berthier never corresponded, but Berthier's writing of *Notice sur la vie et les ouvrages d'Auguste Bébian* the year of Bébian's death, suggests a deep respect, whatever their relations may have been in other ways.[99]

3. Towards a Deaf geography?

As the map below shows, the construction of Deaf sociability did not cease at these dates or at France's borders.[100] While Abbé Sicard was certainly the official successor of Abbé de l'Épée, the considerable, even excessive importance that he attached to hearing for the development of intelligence clearly shows that he did not hold the same views as his predecessor.[101] The latter had raised the validity of gestural speech to the same level as that of vocal speech. To a greater extent than his sponsor, Auguste Bébian followed the path of de l'Épée: Ferdinand Berthier saw in him "[…] *the most ardent*

99. "*From then on, we heard nothing from him; we simply learned that during a long illness he had the misfortune to lose his son, and that this loss affected him so badly that it led him to the tomb,*" writes Ferdinand Berthier in *Notice* (p. 44). In a footnote, he adds: "*The first news to reach us came from a relative of a deaf-mute, a neighbor of our unfortunate friend*"; the relative was in Paris, the Deaf person in Pointe-à-Pitre! This goes to show the effectiveness of the Deaf "whispers" and also that Bébian continued to spend time with the Deaf community after leaving Paris.

100. In 1917, Louis Rémond (a Deaf (speaking) student at Saint-Jacques) mentioned in the *Gazette des Sourds-Muets* "*a deaf-mute named Deville, a lathe operator in Paris (who) married a deaf-mute in 1844. This was undoubtedly the first ever endogamous marriage: it represented 'a profound change in the deaf world'.*" Yves Delaporte, *Les Sourds, c'est comme ça*, Paris: MSH, 2002, pp. 156-157.

101. He was selected by competition in April 1790. Bernard, *Approche de la gestualité*, p, 198.

defender of Abbé de l'Épée's work…"[102] Furthermore, in his *Notes sur les écoles françaises des sourds-muets* (Notes on French schools for the deaf and mute), a Swedish author named Nordin, principal of a school for the deaf in Sweden, described Bébian as "Sicard's brilliant successor" (which officially he was not!), from whom he dissociated himself by clearly choosing sign language for teaching.[103] According to the text, this was a "total methodological revolution" that French and American schools were to follow. In the 1890s, while the resolutions of the Milan Congress were being brutally implemented in France, the Bébian method was being applied in the United States and "continues to be so" in 1901, writes Nordin in his book. To what extent? We lack details, but this indicates the considerable scope of this method. His testimony must be taken with caution, it is not entirely accurate, but it does show that outside France, Bébian's memory lingered on.

The map depicted here, taken from Franz Herman Czech's book and dated 1838, shows that at the beginning of the 19th century, a network, a Deaf geography, was developing.[104] As potential meeting places, schools were involved, creating a network, a territory, independent from the physical territory.

---

102. Berthier, *Notice*, p. 46.

103. Fredrik Nordin, *Anteckningar från franska döfstumskolor*, Stockholm: Tryckt hos C. W. Carlsson, 1903.

104. Franz Herrmann Czech, *Versinnlichte Denk- und Sprachlehre, mit Anwendung auf die Religions- und Sittenlehre und auf das Leben, mit 72 Kupfertafeln*. Wien, Mechitaristen Congregations-Buchhandlung, 1838.
Available online: <http://daten.digitale-sammlungen.de/~db/0001/bsb00013608/images/>

Figure n° 5: Overview map of Institutions
for the instruction of the Deaf and Blind,
and their teachers, including those that existed in 1837
along with suspended institutions and their teachers

UIBERSICHTS CHARTE

Sowohl der im Jahre 1837 bestandenen, als auch der vordem eingegangenen oder verlegten Anstalten zur Bildung der Taubstummen und Blinden, und ihrer Lehrer

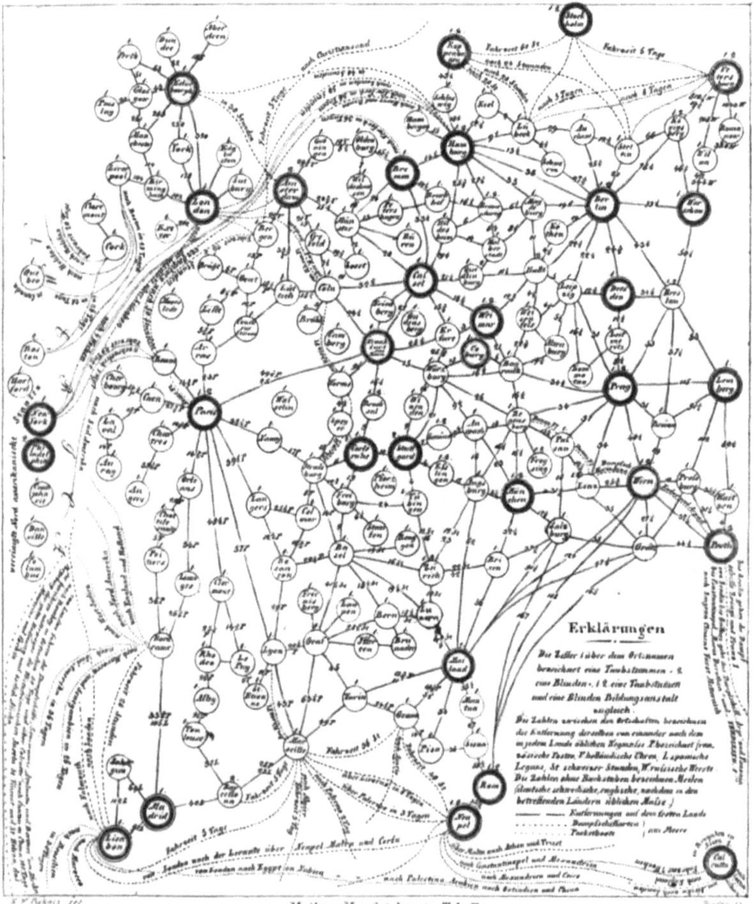

Meilen-Vergleichungs-Tabelle

	davon gehen auf 1 Grad des Aequators		davon gehen auf 1 Grad des Aequators		davon gehen auf 1 Grad des Aequators		davon gehen auf 1 Grad des Aequators
Eine Oesterreichische Meile	14,66	Eine Sächsische Meile	[illegible]	Eine geogr. od. deutsche Meile	15,00	Eine Englische Meile	69,[illegible]
" Polnische "	15,37	" Schwedische "	10,41	" Preussische "	14,[illegible]	" Französische Post	14,[illegible]
" Portugiesische Legua	18,00	" Schweizer Stunden	25,00	" Bayerische "	15,[illegible]	" Hannöversche Meile	13,00
" Russische Werst	104,33	" Spanische Legua	17,58	" Dänische "	14,77	" Niederländische Uhr	20,00

Chapter 3
Emergence of a new paradigm

Auguste Bébian brought more than just another way of thinking; he brought an entirely new paradigm, a profound change: thanks to him, the deaf became Deaf. This change in paradigm was not limited to teaching and pedagogy alone – it was of an anthropological nature. That said, it necessarily involved education and a consideration for deaf students who, as he always wrote, deserved to be taught by means of their own language. This language was a real linguistic system and not a tool to be gradually set aside, or a sign of intellectual inferiority as Joseph-Marie de Gérando (influential chairman of the INSMP's board of governors and a central figure throughout the early decades of the 19th century) believed,[1] a

1. Philosopher, anthropologist, Secretary General of the Ministry of the Interior, theorist of mutual and philanthropic learning, Joseph-Marie de Gérando (1772-1842) one of the great actors of the early decades of the 19th century (his surname was in fact Degerando, which is how he signed all his works through to the July monarchy. "*The particle came later: it was used by 19th century biographers and by the BNF catalogue, which is why we have chosen to use it here.*" Jean-Luc Chappey, Carole Christen and Igor Moullier (eds.), *Joseph-Marie de Gérando (1772-1842). Connaître et réformer la société,* Rennes: Presses universitaires de Rennes, 2014, p. 11). An active member of the *Société des Observateurs de l'Homme*, de Gérando "*found himself at the crossroads of several conceptual and intellectual horizons*" (*ibid.*, p. 21).

   He became a member of the INSMP's board of governors in 1814, under the imperial regime (this board had been created by the Consulate on July 26, 1800 (18 Thermidor Year VIII) and remained in that position until 1841 when the board was dissolved and replaced by a high supervisory council (decree of February 1841; this council governed all national charitable establishments and a specific consultative committee was set up for the INSMP). For a period of twelve years, from 1829 to 1841, Joseph-Marie de Gérando was president of the INSMP's board of governors, which ran the Institution to a far greater extent than the principal. François Buton, *L'administration des faveurs. L'État, les sourds et les aveugles (1789-1885),* Rennes: Presses universitaires de Rennes, 2009, pp. 120-122.

means of communication that needed to be "*rectified or improved.*"[2] However, the board of governors had become so important in the early 19th century, that until 1841 and the reform that gave the central administration its decision-making powers, it was the board that in fact ran the INSMP, over and above the incumbent principal.[3]

As we have seen, the initial groundwork for the education of deaf children was prepared by Abbé de l'Épée at the end of the 18th century. Bébian himself estimated that only 1,800-2,000 of them went to school or benefited from an education, out of a total population of between 18,000 and 20,000 – so a very small proportion.[4] Bébian's objective was "*to generalize education for deaf-mutes*", and as he says:[5]

---

2. Sophie Dalle-Nazébi, *op. cit.*, 2006, p. 171.
Joseph-Marie de Gérando writes: "*I have no doubt that while the way of thinking of those who are deaf-mutes from birth is generally far less developed than that of other persons of the same age, this must be attributed in part to the fact that they have no other signs than those of the language of action.*" Jean-Marie de Gérando, *Des signes et de l'Art de penser considérés dans leur rapport mutuel,* Paris: Goujon fils, 1799-1800, vol. 4, chap. 12, p. 345.
3. Buton, *L'administration des faveurs*, p. 147.
From the 1820s through to the reform of 1841, by royal decree of King Louis-Philippe on February 21, the boards of governors of the *Institutions nationales des Sourds et des Aveugles*, created by the Consulate in Year VIII (*ibid.*) can be considered as being in the hands of philanthropists and persons of importance, who were chosen to run these establishments.
4. As we saw on page 109, this was a relatively accurate assessment on his part, made on the basis of other estimates: "*According to the counts made in various regions, we estimate the number of Deaf-Mutes at one in 1,800 or 2,000 inhabitants. In Austria, where censuses would appear to be more accurate, they count one in 1,000; in the Tyrol one in 500; and the proportion is even higher in some areas of Switzerland, and even in our départements. So with no exaggeration, we can put the number of Deaf-Mutes in France at 18 or 20,000, at least nine-tenths of whom are deprived of any schooling and condemned to drag out their useless and dreary existence in a profound dulling of the mind.*" Auguste Bébian, *Éducation des sourds-muets mise à la portée des institutions primaires et de tous les parents; Méthode naturelle pour apprendre les langues sans traduction,* Prospectus d'édition, Paris: Imprimerie de Béthune, 1831.
5. *Idem.*

> *"If such an objective appears audacious, it is because we have insufficient confidence in the child's intelligence. The wonders that the latter is constantly achieving under our very eyes show just how active and powerful it is. Yet we pay no more attention to it than we do to the sunlight that shines down on us every day."*

Auguste Bébian's strictly pedagogical thinking, which was the concrete translation of this new paradigm, will be the subject of the second part of this book: it was both considerable and innovative. It considered matters essential to the autonomy of deaf people, subjects that are still debated today, a sign of their complexity. It was a question of how sign language should be written, something that Bébian felt to be vital in order for speakers of this gestural and three-dimensional language to be able to set their thoughts down on paper and also to take notes in their own language, without having to go via French, and to learn to read, a crucial means of social participation for deaf people. To make deafness heard as a linguistic and cultural singularity within a *de facto* universality, such was Bébian's concern and challenge. To this end, he demonstrated the pressing need to educate deaf people and showed no hesitation in setting up a newspaper, a modern initiative in 1826, and protesting against what was, in his eyes, the highly negative turn taken by the INSMP.

As from 1817 and his first publication, he never ceased explaining, arguing and demonstrating the linguistic value of sign language and, as can be clearly seen in his final publication, noting a certain disillusion.

1. An innovative mindset, breaking away from the ideas of the past

Bébian's dismissal in 1821 from the INSMP did not mean that he lost interest in teaching, far from it! Aside from his foundational book, *Essai sur les sourds-muets et sur le langage naturel ou introduction à une classification naturelle des idées avec leurs signes propres* (Essay on deaf-mutes and on natural language, or a natural classification of ideas with their own signs), most of his work came after 1825.[6] Ferdinand Berthier writes about this activity:[7]

> *"He devoted every moment of his time to meditating on ways to perfect an education that was taking up his every waking moment. Aside from his works lauded in the most flattering manner by our administration and by the development committee established in 1826, he worked on other books which would later fill the bookcases of deaf-mutes, the absence of which had very frequently, and still today, led to unanimous complaints from French and foreign teachers. He developed not a single thought, project or wish that did not have as its goal to improve the lot of the unfortunate persons to whom he had dedicated his life. He wished to make the education of all of France's deaf-mutes both easy and free, and he had no doubts that this project would succeed."*

There is no doubt that his dismissal was inevitable: he had had the opportunity to put forward certain ideas that fully represented a form of humanism, to accustom students to a certain consideration:[8]

> "[…] *the deaf-mutes could not forget and would never forget his efforts to kindle in them the dignity of man, a dignity that, since then, a civil servant, whose name for seemliness' sake we will not mention,*

---

6. Five of his eight works were published after 1825:
   - *Mimographie ou Essai d'écriture mimique, propre à régulariser le langage des sourds-muets* (1825).
   - *Manuel d'enseignement pratique des sourds-muets* (1827).
   - *Lecture instantanée. Nouvelle méthode pour apprendre à lire sans épeler* (1828).
   - *Examen critique de la nouvelle organisation de l'enseignement dans l'Institution royale des sourds-muets de Paris* (1834).

   The *Journal de l'instruction des sourds-muets et des aveugles* is also evidence of Bébian's fertile action in terms of confrontation and mutualization. (Annex 10).
7. Ferdinand Berthier, *Notice sur la vie et les ouvrages de Auguste Bébian, ancien censeur des études de l'Institut royal des sourds-muets de Paris*, Paris: chez Ledoyen, 1839, p. 24.
8. *Ibid.*, p. 30. The INSMP regulations, enacted in 1841, offer a glimpse of the consideration accorded to students (p. 116-117).

has showered with humiliating mockery, making a cruel game of the infirmity of these poor children, and calling them dogs and monkeys. [...] *One day he reproached one of them for having called him simply their master, doing so in such a cordial tone, that it must, one thinks, have increased the energy and vivacity of their feelings for him... Until then, the unfortunate deaf-mutes, victims of a prejudice based on the opinion of a famous teacher, were treated like half-brutes, exposed with no protection to the ill-treatment and profanity of the supervisors and even the servants... Bébian made all the employees feel that they were there for the students, and not the students for them, a very clear and palpable truth, and one that people would nevertheless seem to be quick to forget, even now."*

In 1883, Claude Forestier, principal of the Lyon Institution since 1840 and a former student at the INSMP from 1819 to 1826, before teaching there for thirteen years, put forward Bébian's arguments to demonstrate the irreplaceable efficiency of sign language. In his paper to the *Académie des sciences morales et politiques de Paris*, designed to demonstrate the absurdity of the decisions made at the Milan congress of 1880 "to improve the lot of deaf-mutes",[9] he recalled:[10]

"Our great master Bébian underlines this superiority of sign language over artificial speech in the following manner:
'When it is a question,' he says, 'of making the deaf and mute feel the small nuances that a happy expression or an ingenious turn give to thought, grammatical analysis is powerless, and all the finesse of style is lost and disappears in explanatory periphrases. But the richness, the flexibility of sign language makes visible to the eye all the energy and

9. On this congress, see page 63.

10. Claudius Forestier, *Parallèle entre l'instruction des sourds-muets par le langage des signes et leur enseignement par l'articulation artificielle suivi de quelques observations sur la méthode du célèbre Pereire et sur les résolutions qu'a votées contre l'enseignement par le langage des signes le congrès international tenu à Milan du 6 au 12 septembre 1880,* Dissertation addressed to the *Académie des sciences morales et politiques de Paris*, Lyon: Pitrat aîné, 1883, p. 22.

all the subtlety of that thought, all the refinement, all the elegance of these turns of phrase and expressions."'

While he believed sign language to be an essential part of pedagogy, it was not a miracle solution, which is why he emphasized visual abilities:[11]

> "[...] *each was to receive a varied, extensive instruction, appropriate to the position he was called upon to occupy in the world. To the study of languages, letters and sciences, his pupils had to add, according to their natural dispositions, the culture of the arts, drawing, sculpture, painting, and various kinds of printing."*

The request for the authorization of a lithography diploma in Rouen, in 1832, was a step in this direction.[12] At a time when education, instruction, was only in its infancy (the ministerial portfolio dedicated to public instruction was not created until 1824),[13] this concern was relatively modern and deserves to be highlighted.[14] But Auguste Bébian's commitment to the Deaf community was as polymorphous as it was intransigent: in the September 10, 1833 edition of *Le Constitutionnel*,[15] he wrote and signed a letter to the editor, following "*the*

---

11. Berthier, *Notice*, p. 27-28.
    Bébian's perspective, which aimed to optimize the visual potential of his students and not to focus on vocal speech, is perhaps what distinguishes him the most from other pedagogues of the past or of his time. He "*tried to show that purporting to make the faculty that they were lacking the cornerstone of their education, was to insult common sense and experience, to use violence against nature, and ultimately to behave in a tyrannical manner.*" (*ibid.*, p. 19.)
12. Letter from Bébian to the mayor of Rouen, ADSM, series 2T1.
13. From 1790 to 1824, it was merely a division of the Ministry of the Interior.
14. On this matter, an industrial education project was "*presented to Count Alexis de Noailles*", writes Berthier (*Notice*, p. 37).
15. *Le Constitutionnel*, created in 1815 during the Hundred Days (and which ceased to exist in 1914) was a center-left leaning daily newspaper with liberal and anti-clerical tendencies. It was one of the press institutions favored by "liberals" or "independents", one of the country's three major political forces (along with the dominant "ultras" and the "constitutionals" or "doctrinarians"). It had up to 17,000 registered subscribers (Jean Claude Caron, *La France de 1815 à 1848*,

excellent note on the education of deaf-mutes that you gave us (series on July 12 and August 3)"[16] in reaction to what he deemed to be an unfounded accusation; and if he took it upon himself to underline this inaccuracy, it was because *"it would be embarrassing for a deaf-mute to try to clear himself of an accusation of this nature. It is a very delicate situation, when one is reduced to having to make an apology in public, so I am not surprised that you received no complaints from deaf-mutes."*[17] This was a reference to the *"natural tendency towards*

Paris: Armand Colin, 2002, p. 12-13) and was initially run by journalists Antoine Jay and Evariste Moulin. The BNF list of digitized newspapers: <*http://www.bnf.fr/fr/collections_et_services/anx_pres/a.historiques_titres_de_presse.html)*>

16. Here Bébian makes a mistake concerning the dates: it was in fact the issues of July 16 (n° 197, p. 1-2) and August 26 (n° 238, p. 1-2).

17. The author of the note to which Auguste Bébian referred is unknown, but his knowledge shows that he was close to deaf people and was very much a supporter of sign language (this is no surprise: Bébian's friendship with journalist Armand Marrast (Yves Delaporte, *Moi Armand, né sourd et muet*, Paris: Plon, 2002, p. 278) or that of Ferdinand Berthier with writer Eugène de Monglave (Florence Encrevé, *op. cit.*, p. 142) suggest a close relationship with intellectual circles). Furthermore, his first article ends with a reproduction of a letter signed "*Berthier, deaf-mute teacher*," which was sent to the editor and which would seem to have been a motive for writing this column: "*During the latest case against deaf-mutes* (the trial of Emeux, in which Berthier was the interpreter)*, like me, you were outraged to see the public welcome, and the bar profess, the opinion of a number of teachers representing deaf-mutes, before they had received any instruction* [...] *You hired me to write a few lines about the intellectual and moral state of the uneducated deaf-mute. It is not for me to comment on such a vast and fine subject when it has already been so well and so fully covered in the* Journal des Sourds-Muets et des Aveugles *by Mr. Bébian who was once my master* [...] *and to whom I am pleased to pay homage for the little that I know*."

Published as a two-part series (the lower half of the first two pages of the newspaper), this article appeared in the issues dated July 16 (n° 197) and August 26, 1828 (n° 238): it was to these two articles that Bébian was reacting. A third article was planned, to "*record the history of the royal institute from his death* (that of Sicard) *to today*", but apparently it was not published. Its aim was to recount the history of the education of deaf people and underline both the absolute need for such education, and the genius of Abbé de l'Épée. After a reminder of Pedro Ponce's method, based on articulation and on lip-reading, along with other previous attempts at instruction, the author excoriated the Paris school for being "*overcome by this disastrous method of articulation, to the absolute detriment of methods that are more effective and of real utility*". A *egoism"* attributed to Deaf people, which Auguste Bébian refuted with an argument based on his own experience. A veritable actor of his time, his thinking and his involvement in contemporary debates went well beyond the scope of the Deaf world. His *Nouvelle méthode pour apprendre à lire sans épeler* (a new method for learning to read without spelling) is one example.[18] It was intended for hearing children[19] and, as was the case with deaf children, he used their intelligence to justify his reasoning. He was against letter-by-letter spelling, a common technique at that time for learning to read:[20]

> *"The routine of barbaric times still reigns in our schools, and from one end of France to the other, children's intelligence is tortured by this absurd spelling which turns the principles of reading into a kind of divinatory art, and all words into so many obscure logogriphs* [...] *Is it not a veritable riddle that you set before a child when, for example, in the syllables ache-a-ï-enne-é, he is supposed to discover the word* haine*?"*[21]

---

lengthy argument ensued in an attempt to show that speech was essentially acquired through imitation, that it was ridiculous to think that could be acquired by a Deaf person, and an analogy with sight was made to illustrate this aberration: *"Imagine a man whose organs of vision are as healthy as can be, cover his eyes with a blindfold, or else plunge him from childhood into total darkness; this man, who is not blind, will not see; it is not his visual organs that are missing, it is the opportunity to use them, it is light. It is exactly the same for a person who is deaf from birth, he is not mute, and yet he does not speak, because he has had no opportunity to use his vocal cords; never having heard sounds, he has never practiced repeating them. Well! It is of this exercise of the vocal organs, until now neglected, that the teacher wishes to remind him, when he is 10, 15 or even 20 years old. Deprived of hearing, he will not be able to imitate sounds, and yet it is a work of imitation that must be done."*

18. Auguste Bébian, *Lecture instantanée ou Nouvelle méthode pour apprendre à lire sans épeler*, Paris: Imprimerie de Crapelet, 1828.
19. *"This work had also been motivated by his mission to shape, using a new system, the intelligence of young hearing-speaking students, charitably admitted into a school."* Berthier, *Notice*, p. 28. The nature of this mission nevertheless remains uncertain: was it official? No existing document confirms this.
20. Bébian, *Lecture instantanée*, p. I.
21. Here Bébian is imitating the names of the letters H-A-I-N-E in French (spelling out *haine*, the word for hatred) – transl.

Canadian researcher Yannick Portebois has shown that spelling reform is not simply a matter of pedagogy or language policy; it is an "affair of state" in the sense that historians of pedagogy see the state as an omnipotent entity.[22] Auguste Bébian's reflection and publication on reading was part of this more global debate on spelling reform, of which "*the apotheosis* [...], *its consecration by the Ministry of Public Instruction, especially from 1833 onwards (the date of its creation) was an important starting point.*"[23] Indeed, while discussions on the matter reached their peak in the late 19th and early 20th centuries,[24] if Berthier is correct, their origin dated back to the first third of the 19th century:[25]

> *"In 1828, there was a lively discussion on spelling reform in several newspapers. Bébian sided with Volney, Andrieux, and Laromiguière who, like Voltaire, Montesquieu, Duclos, Dumarsais, Wauilly, etc., considered this reform to be necessary. In his opinion it was the only way to solve the ever so interesting problem of the general education of the people."*

Indeed, on this point Auguste Bébian had expressed his perplexity some ten years previously:[26]

> *"Should we be surprised, then, if we come across people, particularly in the country, who after having attended school for six years or more, end up leaving without knowing how to read?"*

---

22. Yannick Portebois, "La réforme de l'orthographe, une affaire d'État", in *Histoire, Épistémologie, Langage*, Tome 25, fascicule 1, 2003. Politiques linguistiques (2/2), p. 71-85.
23. *Ibid.*, p. 71.
24. Yannick Portebois has drawn up a list of more than a thousand articles, either for or against, appearing in newspapers and journals between 1889 and 1914 (Portebois, *ibid.*)
25. Berthier, *Notice*, p. 18.
26. Bébian, *Lecture instantanée*, p. II.

This "orthographic debate", in which Bébian was actively involved, can be found in several newspapers.[27] The *Précis de grammaire historique* gives 1833 as the pivotal year; the year in which, according to the authors, the state imposed an official spelling:[28]

> *"The spelling used was that of the Academy* [the Académie Française], *which thereby became the official state spelling, and would henceforth be required for access to employment. A language bureaucracy was thus created. It still exists."*

In 1835, these discussions led to the first major spelling reform, which coincided with the sixth edition of the Academy's dictionary.[29]

---

27. The published articles that we have managed to find appeared in *La Gazette de France* on October 14, 1828, *Le Constitutionnel* (letter from Bébian) on October 25, 1828, *Le Courrier français* on October 19 and November 4, 1828, *Le Journal des débats* on October 31, 1828, and *La Quotidienne* on October 13, and again on November 5 and 29, 1828. The *Appel aux Français collection* (Paris: Corréard, 1829) recounts these disputes and provides extracts from the various newspapers. The idea of the reform, applied to Lamartine's poem "Le Chant Du Sacre" – an ode glorifying Charles X – is given as an example:
    Original text:
    Son port majestueux sur la foule s'élève
    L'or fait étinceler le pommeau de son glaive...
    Text using the reformed spelling:
    Son por majèstueu sur la foule s'élève;
    L'or fèt étinselé le pomô de son glève...
28. Ferdinand Brunot and Charles Bruneau, *Précis de grammaire historique*, Paris: Masson, 1933.
29. Later followed by those of 1878 and 1990.
    The two main changes introduced by the 1835 reform were the shift from *oi* to *ai* (*françois/français*) and the systemization of the plural form of words ending in *-nt* to *-nts* instead of in *–ns* (e.g. from *enfans* to *enfants*). Use of the "&" sign to denote "et" also disappeared.
    This was a longstanding demand. A century earlier, Voltaire had campaigned in vain for his *–oi* to be changed to *–ai*. His book *Le siècle de Louis XIV* (De Francheville, 1751) was in fact entirely written with the *–ai* and posterity has incorrectly linked this reform to Voltaire.
    Jacques Chaurand, *Histoire de la langue française*, Paris: PUF, "Que sais-je ?", 1969, reprinted 1991, p. 104-105.

2. A major body of work…

Curiously, in Bébian's work, which comprises eight publications, there is not a single mention of Guadeloupe, the island where he was born, where he grew up and to which he returned in 1834 with wife and child, after having spent twenty-two years in France.[30]

2.1 … diverse…

The eight books he left to posterity are all very different. They are all well documented and well argued. The first, published in 1817, is clearly titled *Essai sur les sourds-muets et sur le langage naturel ou introduction à une classification naturelle des idées avec leurs signes propres* (Essay on deaf-mutes and on natural language) and may be described as foundational.[31] It defined the main lines of his thinking, and the future works that would provide answers to his main preoccupation: that of making deaf people fully autonomous. He believed that this could only be achieved through education and, within this framework, by them writing their own thoughts, in their natural language, without having to go via written French and hence require translation. It was for this reason that he announced that he intended to work on transcribing this language. Announced in 1817, his *Mimographie ou Essai d'écriture mimique, propre à régulariser le langage des sourds-muets* (Mimography or Essay on Mimic Writing, suitable for regularizing the language of deaf-mutes)[32] only appeared eight years later, two years before a huge *Manuel d'enseignement pratique des sourds-muets* (Manual for the Practical Instruction of Deaf-Mutes) in two volumes (the first for students and the second for teachers), which completed the writing of sign

30. His son Honoré was born in 1830. Frédéric Peyson, painter and former deaf student of Bébian, had been chosen as a witness for the city hall declaration.
31. Auguste Bébian, *Essai sur les sourds-muets et sur le langage naturel ou introduction à une classification naturelle des idées avec leurs signes propres*, Paris: J.-G. Dentu, 1817, XVI + 150 pages.
32. Auguste Bébian, *Mimographie ou Essai d'écriture mimique, propre à régulariser le langage des sourds-muets*, Paris: chez Louis Colas, 1825, 42 pages. [Reprinted in full by Marc Renard, *op. cit.*, 2004, 2014.]

language, which was only in its infancy, and which was designed to be a "simple" notation system.[33] But this manual, as complete as it was, was just a first step, as Auguste Bébian himself pointed out:[34]

> *"This was merely the first step towards the goal to which all my work aspires. This book was for teachers alone; the Deaf-Mute are generally too poor to find many teachers willing to devote themselves to such an arduous and thankless task of education; there are too many of them for the government to ever think of paying, for all concerned, the costs of an education* [...] *Thus elementary education, this beneficence to which all Deaf-Mutes seem to be entitled, as a sacred debt that society owes to the unfortunate, has until now been but a rare exception for the benefit of a chosen few. In order to extend it to all, it is necessary to reduce the processes to such a simplicity that they can become part of elementary school teaching. This is the wish that comes from all our hearts, when we consider the cruel condition of the Deaf-Mute in society; a wish that has until now remained sterile, a wish without hope, a wish that we are undertaking to fulfill."*

The number of deaf people was estimated at "*22,000 of which only a small number are in school*".[35] To this end, Auguste Bébian began to write a book entitled *Education of the deaf and mute accessible to primary institutions and all parents. A natural method for learning languages without translation*, intended to "popularize the instruction of deaf-mutes".[36] While (according to Ferdinand Berthier)

---

33. Auguste Bébian, *Manuel d'enseignement pratique des sourds-muets,* (Tome I : Modèles d'exercices (204 pages) ; Tome II : Explications (371 pages), Paris: Méquignon l'Aîné, 1827.
Volume I - Modèles d'exercices (vol. in-4): VI, 204 p. and XXXII plates numbered excluding text (just one plate numbered XV-XVI, one plate XIX bis, the latter incorrectly numbered XXIX) including one fold-up, some in period colors; Volume II - Explications (vol. in-8), 371 p.
34. Bébian, *Éducation des sourds-muets*, publishing prospectus, 1831.
35. *Le Constitutionnel*, n°253, issue of September 10, 1833.
36. The prospectus for this work (*Éducation des sourds-muets)* is available on the site of the Bibliothèque électronique de Lisieux (placed online in July 2000; <*http://*

the Minister of the Interior at the time, Mr. de Montalivet, wanted this book to be published, and had organized a subscription,[37] the manuscript remained unfinished.[38] This was clearly a shame: the illustrated plates allow us to suppose an operation similar to that of the *Manual*.

In chronological order, *Éloge de l'abbé de l'Épée, ou essai sur les avantages du système des signes. Discours qui a obtenu le prix proposé par la Société royale académique des sciences*, published in 1819,[39] was Bébian's second publication. It was initially a speech given in the context of a competitive exam.[40] It is a quite fascinating text,

---

www.bmlisieux.com/litterature/bibliogr/bebian.htm>) along with the illustrated plates of deliveries 1 to 3 (Annex 6; sixteen deliveries were announced).

37. Berthier, *Notice*, p. 26.

38. An 1831 edition was found in the Bibliothèque Nationale; the author is unnamed but the title leaves little doubt: *Éducation des sourds-muets mise à la portée des instituteurs primaires et de tous les parents* (the only difference is the word "*instituteurs*" in place of "*institutions*").
We can estimate that writing began in 1828 (it is referred to in *Lecture instantanée*… to be published "at the end of May") and the warehouses, printers and publishers were planned: In Paris, at the author's home, rue des Cannettes, n°13; Treuttel & Wurtz, booksellers, rue de Lille; Louis-Colas, rue Dauphine; Moutardier, rue Gilles-Cœur; Charles-Béchet, quai des Augustins.

39. Auguste Bébian, *Éloge de l'abbé de l'Épée, ou essai sur les avantages du système des signes. Discours qui a obtenu le prix proposé par la Société royale académique des sciences*, Paris: J.-G. Dentu, 1819, 56 pages.

40. In 1818, as a subject for a competitive exam (literature section), the *Société royale académique des sciences de Paris* proposed *"in verse or prose, a eulogy of the recently defunct Abbé de l'Épée, founder of the Institut royal des sourds-muets"*. The winner of the competition was chosen the following year, and the Royal Academic Society awarded the prize to Auguste Bébian, at that time deputy principal at the INSMP; Étienne-François Bazot, the society's general secretary, writer, and member of the *Athénée des arts* was awarded the second prize. We do not know his reasons for entering the competition, but his text is prefaced by Paulmier, which would seem to suggest a certain level of familiarity. J.-M. d'Alea, *Éloge de l'abbé de l'Épée*, Paris: Rosa, 1824.
In his forty-page preface, Louis-Pierre Paulmier shows no hesitation in taking credit for the successes of Jean Massieu, Laurent Clerc and Ferdinand Berthier. The latter remonstrated and demanded a denial… Abbé Sicard himself denounced a "[…] *répétiteur* (who) *boasts about making students feel the force, and almost the harmony, of Racine's verse. The truth is that in his classroom he was*

as under the cover of a eulogy, it analyzes and criticizes Abbé de l'Épée's pedagogical system. He pays sincere homage to the Abbot: "*We find nothing but superiority in Abbé de l'Épée's methods* [...]", writes Bébian from the very outset.[41] But what he revered most about de *l'Épée* were his moral qualities, because he believed that not only did the abbot not follow through on his intuitions, he was pedagogically mistaken in the reasoning that led him to implement the "methodical signs", a mistake that could have very serious consequences:[42]

> *"The numerous grammatical forms, the long use of which has enriched our languages, are foreign and sometimes quite contrary to the language of deaf-mutes* [...] *while it is true that in the immense work that he was courageous enough to undertake, the father of the deaf-mutes sometimes paid the price of human weakness, with certain imperfections that are an inevitable part of any new invention, is it not to be feared that the authority of such a great name will mean that the same mistakes will be perpetuated by those who want to follow him in a career which always requires such rigor, and where the slightest deviation has the gravest consequences, and can even cause one to completely miss the objective?"*

To avoid offending sensibilities, while putting forward his ideas, Bébian writes on two levels: he praises the moral value of the abbot's action, his proven disinterestedness, the way he did everything possible for his students, his modesty, his constancy and his unquestionable generosity; but at the same time he advocates vehemently for the "true" sign language and the potential of Deaf people, and implicitly criticizes methodical signs. He uses footnotes

never able to explain this author". (Abbé de L'Épée, *L'art d'enseigner à parler aux sourds-muets de naissance, augmenté de notes explicatives et d'un avant-propos, par M. l'abbé Sicard,... précédé de l'éloge historique de M. l'abbé de L'Épée, par M. Bébian*. Paris: J.-G. Dentu, 1820, p. IV).

41. Bébian, *Éloge* p. 23.

42. *Ibid.*, p. 53.

to articulate this exercise, presenting his key ideas as additional, accessory information, even taking on the guise of other writers (whom, let it be said, he himself had been able to convince) to offer quotations that were at first very general, or philosophical, and then increasingly specific and technical. In this way he systematically dismantled Abbé de l'Épée's educational system without appearing to do so:[43]

> *"Abbé de l'Épée, who on twenty occasions in his book emphasizes the need to instruct deaf mutes in their own language, sometimes distorts this language himself in order to make it fit the forms of the French language* [...] *These artificial, abstract signs give no indications to the mind, and consequently it must often be impossible for the deaf-mute to find in them the scattered members of thought. So what happens? The same students who have written very correctly everything that was dictated to them by means of these signs, often have trouble expressing the simplest thought by themselves."*

His indulgence toward Abbé de l'Épée was due to the fact that the latter was the inventor but, he repeats, a readjustment was required. No-one had truly been able or willing to follow de l'Épée's lead, and subtly, Bébian warned against *"this prejudice as absurd as it is humiliating for the human species,* (which) *represented the deaf-mute as a kind of automaton,"*[44] a notion that had indeed been defended some sixteen years earlier by Abbé Sicard, appointed as de l'Épée's official successor in 1790.[45] Which did not prevent this work

43. Bébian, *Essai sur les sourds-muets*, p. 55, note c.

44. *Ibid.*, p. 2.

45. *"Indeed, what is a deaf-mute from birth, considered in himself, and before any education has begun to connect him, in any way, to that great family to which, through his external form, he belongs? In society he is a perfectly null being, a living automaton, a statue, such as Charles Bonnet and later on Condillac present it* [...]", he writes.
Roch-Ambroise Sicard, *Cours d'instruction d'un sourd-muet de naissance, pour servir à l'éducation des sourds-muets, et qui peut être utile à ceux qui entendent et qui parlent,* Paris: Le Clere; London, Charles Prosper, 1803, p. 6.

from being chosen the following year by the same Abbé Sicard, to appear in the preface of the book written by de l'Épée himself, but republished by Sicard, *L'art d'enseigner à parler aux sourds-muets de naissance* (The art of teaching the deaf-mute from birth to speak).[46] Abbé Sicard added his own explanatory notes to this edition, as if to better establish his legitimacy. In a way, one might say that Bébian's speech in praise of Abbé de l'Épée was the continuation of his first work, published two years before: *Essai sur les sourds-muets et sur le langage naturel ou introduction à une classification naturelle des idées avec leurs signes propres*.[47]

Bébian's subsequent publications are exclusively pedagogical, but by no means of lesser importance. They show that he did not restrict himself to the theoretical aspect of teaching. They are: *Mimographie*, his *Manuel d'enseignement pratique* and the draft of a manual for the parents of deaf children along with a reading method, *Lecture instantanée ou nouvelle manière d'apprendre à lire sans épeler* (Instant reading: a new method for learning to read without spelling), which demonstrates his pedagogical commitment above and beyond deaf children.[48] The *Journal d'instruction des sourds-*

46. Abbé de L'Épée, *L'art d'enseigner*. This text is in fact the second part of de l'Épée's foundational work, *La véritable manière d'instruire les sourds et muets,* Paris: Nyon l'aîné, 1784 (reprinted by Fayard, 1984).
47. For example, this sentence from his *Essai*, which echoes another in the *Éloge*: *"In the mind, thought necessarily precedes any signs intended to express it; in itself the word bears no relation to the idea; it can neither generate the idea, nor convey it, but it serves to recall it when a previous convention has linked it to the idea that has previously been fully grasped* [...] *with the help of signs* [...] *(which) are taken from the very nature of the idea"* (Auguste Bébian, *op. cit.*, 1817, p. 23) and *"*[...] *in itself the word bears no relation to the idea, it cannot therefore generate it; but it serves to recall it, when a previous convention has linked it to the idea that has previously been fully grasped. By what means has this connection of words and ideas taken place in us? It is by natural signs, in other words all those movements of physiognomy and gesture, resulting from our organization, and through which is depicted outside us, all that happens inside"* (Bébian, Éloge, p. 19-20).
Bébian does not hide this; in a footnote he writes: *"In this speech, I saw no difficulty in reproducing various ideas that had already appeared in* Essai sur les sourds-muets, et sur le langage naturel, *this small book being out of print"* (p. 53, note a).
48. Bébian, *Lecture instantanée*.

muets et des aveugles, which was published for two short years and of which he was the editor, was also of an innovative nature, aimed at decompartmentalizing specialized teaching.[49]

His final work, *Examen critique de la nouvelle organisation de l'enseignement dans l'Institution royale des sourds-muets* (Critical appraisal of the new organization of teaching Royal Institution for Deaf-Mutes), published in 1834, was very much the culmination of his thinking and his career.[50] In this book, meticulously and item by item, he reacted to the *Third Circular* issued by INSMP's management in 1832. In a very direct manner he criticized every single incoherence, demonstrating in the process his vast knowledge of places and practices, even though he had not been practicing for over ten years. It was a masterpiece of irony: from the outset, he gave his opinion of the management – we have seen elsewhere its scope for decision-making:[51]

> *"Let us ignore the little scenes prepared in advance for the public sessions. Let us leave it to the Principal, wherever his imagination may take him, to explain a way of teaching to which he himself is almost as foreign as is the audience listening to him. And without stopping too long to admire them, let us also pass through these superb buildings, which, over the last few years, have cost more than 1,400,000 francs. This grand exterior luxury cannot hide the poor quality of the teaching. Finally, let us take a small number of deaf-mutes, former students at the school, now teachers, distinguished subjects who are not part of the present system, and who show what a well-managed education of deaf-mutes might resemble* [...]."

49. The reason for creating the journal for the instruction of deaf and blind students was an "absence of any shared space" (prospectus, Annex 10, p. 320-321).
50. Auguste Bébian, *Examen critique de la nouvelle organisation de l'enseignement dans l'Institution royale des sourds-muets de Paris*, Paris: Treuttel & Wurtz, 1834, IV + 67 pages.
51. *Idem.*, p. 2.

This book was published the same year as his return to Guadeloupe, but it had been written the year before, in 1833, during an illness that caused him to hastily leave his position in Rouen: despite this pathology, he expressed a wish to influence teaching, albeit in a manner other than through his physical presence.[52] This critical examination was not a simple statement of what was wrong, it was a full assessment based on fifteen years of observations and pedagogical experiments:[53]

> *"When I joined the Royal Institution, I found in this school, or more precisely in its classrooms, a system of crude and obscure signs, part natural, part conventional, and arbitrary. Through this mongrel, crude, ignoble, incomplete language, the most picturesque, the most elegant expression appeared dull, flat or bizarre; the most vivid, the most graceful image became cold and trivial. Thought lost all elevation, all depth, all finesse. It remained shapeless, colorless, lifeless. It was no more than a hideous, unrecognizable skeleton.*
> *All literature was thus a closed book to the poor deaf-mutes. One was happy when a translation into signs was merely nonsensical. Most of the time it was a never-ending mistranslation. So God knows what errors were stuffed into the minds of these poor children! Students of that time can still confirm this. The famous deaf-mute M…, that great improviser of answers to Abbé Sicard's public exercises, did not understand Berquin's* L'Ami des enfants. *I revealed to the deaf-mutes the richness, the energy, the elegance, the flexibility of sign language, and thanks to this powerful instrument, supported by the philosophical study of the language, there was no longer any obstacle capable*

52. In a footnote, he writes: "*This examination, sent to the minister on December 5 last, had been written in haste* (as can be very clearly seen) *during the early days of my convalescence, following a cruel and lengthy and illness, which had forced me for a certain time to give up my teaching activities. From this dissertation I cut out the sections which, referring specifically to the Paris Institution, would only be of minor interest to the teachers. While I can no longer play an active part in advancing the instruction of deaf-mutes, I wish at least to put a spanner in the wheels of this retrograde vehicle.*" Bébian, *Examen critique*, p. 9.
53. Bébian, *Examen critique*.

of holding back the deaf-mutes, no author, poet or prose writer who could not be brought within their reach."

2.2 ...and a metaphorical use of the written language

Without exception, in all of his publications Bébian's writing enabled people to see; just like sign language, the visual language *par excellence*. His writings are filled with metaphors to illustrate his point, to support his arguments. He writes to show that thought precedes language:[54]

---

54. Bébian, *Journal*, n° 1, p. 21.
This question of thought/language is an old one, but still ongoing. From a pedagogical standpoint, it is manifested in various practices.
The term "thought" in fact covers two distinct mental activities depending on whether it refers to any mental event, without differentiation, or to a "reflexive" thought, i.e. a thought capable of reflecting on itself, which requires a language, whether vocal or gestural (one cannot produce an image which constitutes an analysis of another image, whereas a sentence can take itself as an object!). A contemporary of Bébian's, the German philosopher Hegel (1770-1831) expressed it thus: "[...] *since what is ineffable is, in truth, only something obscure, fermenting, something which gains clarity only when it is able to put itself into words because in reality the ineffable is the obscure thought, the thought in a state of fermentation, and which becomes clear only when it finds the word. Accordingly, the word gives to thoughts their highest and truest existence.*" (Hegel, G.W.F. *Phenomenology of Spirit,* transl. A.V. Miller, Oxford: Oxford University Press, 1977, p. 60).
But the idea that thought can precede language, which would then be merely a means of communicating independent thoughts, presupposes that the world possesses a prior order that language can only copy, and this is precisely where Bébian expresses his disagreement and underlines the linguistic character proper to sign language: each language "cuts up" the world in a specific way through its lexicon but also (and above all?) through its grammar and syntax, which implies the linguistic recognition of sign language. The hypothesis formulated in the 1950s by linguists Sapir and Whorf – that it is essential to study a language and its structures in order to go back and act on its mental universes – reflects this view (Jean-François Dortier and Nicolas Journet (eds.), "L'hypothèse Sapir-Whorf", *Les clés du langage*, Auxerre: Sciences humaines, 2015, p. 33).
This morphological aspect did not escape Bébian, who writes (*Journal,* 1826, n° 1, p. 25): "*From this we perceive that the signs of the deaf-mute must be strung*

"Our abstract terms are to reasoning what algebraic signs are to calculus. They form types of formulae which lay down a multitude of ideas ever ready to escape us. But we can calculate without algebra: we calculated before algebra was invented. We can think without words. We had thoughts before we spoke."

Concerning vocal speech and the ideas conveyed by it, and hearing, which feeds thought but only exercises a "slight influence over intelligence", he writes:[55]

" [...] *It is like a canal, the waters of which make no contribution to the fertility of the land it crosses, but which is no less the source of its wealth and prosperity, by allowing produce to flow in from faraway countries."*

The theme of vocal speech recurs frequently in Bébian's work; his objective is to show how sign language is the obvious linguistic means for teaching young deaf people: "*The sign follows the thought, step by step, like a shadow which takes on all of its shapes*", he writes in his *Essai*,[56] it is the mother tongue of Deaf people.[57]

He believed speech to be an illusory artifice:[58]

---

together in an order very different to the construction of our own languages, and particularly to the construction of French, which obeys the reciprocal influence of words far more than the relationships between ideas, and follows less the workings of the mind than it does the rules of grammar."

Regarding vocabulary, the Breton language, for example, distinguishes between the color "green/blue" when observed in nature (*glaz*) – and the exact same color, but more artificial (*gwer-glaz*) – borrowing the French color *vert* (green), which becomes *gwer* in Breton.

55. Bébian, *Journal*, n° 1, p. 11.
56. Bébian, *Essai sur les sourds-muets*, p. 65.
57. "*The spoken language thus figures in this method as a second living language, such as German or English, that one teaches a child alongside his mother tongue; without the study of the one causing the other to be forgotten.*" Bébian, *Journal*, n° 1, p. 187.
58. Bébian, *Essai sur les sourds-muets*, p. 32 and pp. 111-112.
"*The invention of speech supposes the existence of a prior language,*" he says. And as an example, he writes: "*There is this language that preceded all others, in the*

> *"A man's face is like a faithful mirror that reflects everything that is taking place in his soul: in society, it is not without difficulty that we learn to cover this all too transparent looking glass with the veil of an imposter. [...] speech, which creates so many obstacles to communication between peoples, places still further hurdles to the workings of the mind, sometimes holding out a deceptive helping hand that leads the mind astray, like those pale fires that shine in the darkness of the night, lending their perfidious clarity to the hesitant traveler, coaxing him off the path and into the swamp from whose emanations they spring."*

In order for the deaf student's education to be effective, "*no cloud must veil his thinking*", says Bébian,[59] and "*to make him reach the same point as the other, he must walk faster and take a more direct route*" he writes with regard to learning to read, which he also compared to an ascension.[60] He emphasized children's intelligence, so that potential teachers or the children's own parents would not hesitate to instruct them, and he compared this faculty with the light of the sun.[61]

---

first age of man. It is that of the child who cannot yet jabber, and who, smiling to see his mother, stretches out his tiny loving arms and already expresses his love; it is that of the traveler in a country where he does not know the language, when he wants to ask for food to assuage his hunger, and a bed to lay his head. It is through such a language that all the fibers of your heart were touched by this old man, bent by the combined weight of age and poverty; only a sigh alerted you to the sound of his voice, shame having tied his tongue; you would be ashamed to count whatever you drop into his trembling hand; it is with emotion that he grasped the gift of your generosity, and his gesture of tenderness and his eyes raised to heaven expressed his gratitude far better than the most beautiful of speeches" (p. 97-98).

59. Bébian, *Journal*, n° 1, pp. 25-26. And this thought "*thus escapes through natural signs, like the spark that springs from the compression of air*". *Ibid.*, p. 318.
60. Bébian, *Journal*, n° 1, 1826, p. 85.
    And again he writes: "*Gradually yet imperceptibly the method will bind together all areas of teaching, and via a gentle slope will effortlessly lead to the heights of instruction*". (*ibid.*, p. 89).
61. Bébian, *Éducation des sourds-muets*.
    In the final issue of the *Journal*, in the practical teaching column, he writes: "*I hereby propose, if this project is favorably received, to publish a collection of 2 or 3 thousand figures corresponding to at least as many words, be they nouns, verbs,*

3. From one school to another in France…

3.1 Relations with the INSMP's board of governors

Auguste Bébian's relations with the board of governors were not inexistant and would even appear to have been relatively good, at least until 1830: this was the body that funded the realization of the *Manuel d'enseignement pratique des sourds-muets* in 1827.[62] Berthier justified the writing of the *Manuel* in the following terms:[63]

> *"After the death of Abbé Sicard* [in 1822]*, the teaching was left adrift in vagueness and uncertainty, buffeted this way and that by the most erroneous fancies, with no strong hand coming forward to take the*

---

adjectives, etc. I may even succeed in rendering visible a large number of notions which at first do not seem easily expressed by drawing. These figures, accompanied by a nomenclature in four languages, may, I think, also be of great use in teaching foreign languages to children who have all their senses. I have explained in detail in the Manual of Practical Teaching how, by means of drawn figures, one can very early on allow the student to study alone, and make the most of the time between lessons." (*Journal*, n° 8, vol. II, p. 100). See quote page 153.

62. Auguste Bébian, *Manuel d'enseignement pratique des sourds-muets,* Paris: Méquignon l'Aîné, 1827.
The project for this work, published in 1827, had been approved by the board of governors four years earlier. Following the title page of the manual, an extract from the minutes of the board meeting of July 14, 1823, encourages Bébian to finish his *Manuel*, still incomplete.
Moreover, the esteem of the chairman of the board of governors is clear, as this additional extract shows: "*With his* Essai sur les sourds-muets et sur le langage naturel*, published in 1817, Mr. Bébian had already demonstrated the in-depth study he had made of the theory of languages and of the methods employed for the instruction of deaf-mutes. He was soon to be appointed to the position of répétiteur* [and then to that of deputy principal at the Paris establishment], *where he proved his exceptional talent; and we show no hesitation in declaring that Abbé Sicard never found a collaborator that had better mastered his thinking, and who, in applying his method, so greatly improved certain details. His* Éloge de l'abbé de l'Épée *met with deserved success."* Extract from a report made to the Board of Governors by Baron de Gérando, quoted by Marc Renard, *Écrire les signes*, les Essarts-le-Roi: Fox, 2004, p. 46.

63. Ferdinand Berthier, *Histoire et statistique de l'éducation des sourds-muets*, 1836, quoted in Berthier, *op. cit.*, 1839, p. 15.

helm. Such a sorry state of affairs inevitably brought home to the administration of the Royal Institution in Paris the urgent need to endow the establishment in its charge with a work of reference that would provide a stable understanding of the principles of a simple and logical method. There was no teacher more experienced, more knowledgeable than Mr. Bébian to whom they could entrust the writing of such a work. His Manual for the Practical Instruction of Deaf-Mutes was adopted and published by the board of governors in 1827. The author stripped teaching of this academic obscurity, of these pretentious subtleties wrapped in a superficial philosophy; he brought it back to this truth, this simplicity which must be the hallmark of every method and which ensures its success. It is mainly a practical work which may be placed with confidence in the hands of a tutor, or of a father or mother whose resources are insufficient for attending lessons in our schools."

Ferdinand Berthier indicates the teaching role that Bébian played, as required by the board of governors, or at least with its approval:[64]

"Young women teachers had been recommended to him by the same governors who would have found it wrong for him to take charge of the Royal School in Paris. Among these ladies, we might mention Miss Morel, Mr. de Gérando's niece, who went to Bébian's house for five or six hours a day over a period of several months."

The board of governors confirmed this but put it differently:[65]

"The Board has recognized that in principle, not only is it essential to give the teachers of deaf-mutes a Practical Manual in which the method is fixed and described by a series of exercises; but that the writing and use of such a manual is the first step to be taken to prepare for the progress and improvement of this teaching, and even to prevent it

64. Berthier, *Notice*, p. 27.
65. Extract from the minutes of the INSMP's *Conseil de perfectionnement*, reproduced and quoted in Renard, *Écrire les signes*, pp. 45-46.

from degenerating and falling into confusion and disorder due to the arbitrariness and uncertainty which would undoubtedly be introduced. The Council has also recognized that the work written by Mr. Bébian, entitled Manuel de l'instituteur des sourds-muets (Manual for a teacher of deaf-mutes), is suitable for this purpose; that it meets the essential needs of instruction, and that it promises to become, through the attention that its author can still bring to its completion and revision, a truly standard model that will finally give the method a precise and stable form."

There was a radical change in tone following the publication of *Notice sur la vie et les ouvrages d'Auguste Bébian* by Ferdinand Berthier, and this can be seen in the deliberations written after the board of governors' meeting on March 2, 1840:[66]

"Mr. Bébian did not create a method; we have not adopted his ideas at the Royal Institution. It was in fact the excellent work of Mr. de Gérando that created the method. Bébian's fortune was squandered and not put to good use. Is this not therefore nothing more than an incomplete work for which the Minister paid 1500 francs at the board's request?"

Yet at least one-fifth[67] of the 1,200 page book, *De l'éducation des sourds-muets de naissance,* published in 1827 by Joseph-Marie de Gérando, chairman of the INSMP's board of governors, was not so much a method as a compilation of foreign experiences (Spain, Italy, Switzerland, Holland, Denmark, United States…), followed by pedagogical considerations and thoughts, perhaps inspired by other writings.[68]

66. Annex 7.
67. Buton, *L'administration des faveurs*, p. 134.
68. It seems likely, for example, that he took inspiration from the words that Laurent Clerc pronounced during the public examination of the students of the American Asylum in Hartford, Connecticut, in 1818, concerning the mother tongue, an essential prerequisite for the acquisition of the national language: *"You will notice, that the language of any people cannot be the mother tongue of the Deaf and Dumb, born amidst these people. Every spoken language is necessarily a learned language*

3.2 Experiments and teaching in Paris and Rouen

1830 would appear to have been a milestone in the history of Auguste Bébian's relations with the INSMP's board of governors, with the episodes of the student mutiny and the address to the King.[69] However, the quality of these relations seems to have deteriorated following the inauguration of the Special Institution for Deaf Mutes by Auguste Bébian on Boulevard Montparnasse in Paris in 1826, based on the day-school model.[70] This was a source of tension with

for these unfortunate Beings. The English language must be taught to the Deaf and Mute, as the Greek or Latin is taught, in the Colleges, to the young Americans, who attend the classes of this kind. [...] *and yet to teach the Greek and Latin in Colleges, the professors and pupils have, for a means of comparison, a language at hand, an acquired language, a mother tongue, which is the English language, in which they have learned to think,"* (Laurent Clerc, "*An address delivered by Clerc and read by Mr. Gallaudet at the examination of the pupils of the Connecticut Asylum, before the Governor and both Houses of the Legislature, May 20, 1818*").

It is however surprising that this work by De Gérando, which quite comprehensively collated the pedagogical procedures used at the time, did not take into account Auguste Bébian's thinking in *Essai sur le langage naturel des sourds-muets...*, published in 1817, i.e. ten years earlier: it is hard to imagine that he was unaware of it or did not have time to read it...

Baron de Gérando had a poor opinion of sign language, which, incidentally, he did not know: "[...] *mime language is so true, so ingenuous, so transparent (if we may be allowed this expression), that it will be easy for the teacher to discover this territory: it will be enough for him to encourage his pupil to express himself, and to observe him attentively, in order to fully grasp his thoughts"* (p. 142). Indeed, for Gérando, gestural expression was a way to engage with a deaf student's thinking and communicate with him in such a manner as to then replace the gestures, vectors of ideas, with the visual symbolism of the alphabet and French writing, even if, as he writes further down (p. 210) vocal speech was necessarily superior to writing.

69. See page 121 and the demands of this petition (Annex 8, page 329).

70. To be precise, this establishment was located at n° 24 *bis*, as we are told by Auguste Bébian who signed his works as "*former deputy principal of the Institution royale des sourds-muets de Paris, principal of a special institution for deaf-mutes*" and indicated in the prospectus of the *Journal* that it was on sale at the "offices of the journal" at this very address. Bébian appeared attached to this pedagogical orientation: "[...] *he seemed to want it, because at the Institut royal de Paris, it had been deemed impossible to obtain anything from the day students*", writes Ferdinand Berthier (*op. cit.*, 1839, p. 37).

the INSMP,[71] which had opened its own day school three years earlier.[72] There were two completely opposite conceptions of the day school: that of the INSMP, designed to protect the boarding school from all harmful influences, and that of the establishment founded by Bébian, designed to be open to the outside world, while at the same time preserving sign language, which was to be promoted. He was simply putting into practice what he had written a few years earlier:[73]

> *"This language is the principle of the fine arts; it is to this language that sculpture and painting owe their most beautiful effects. It is by knowing natural signs and their connection with feelings, that the artist brings canvas and marble to life."*

Bébian's day school was entirely focused on gestural expression, free of any arbitrary codification supposedly intended to support its development:[74]

> *"This difficulty would not exist in a new establishment. As the arriving students are new, free from prejudices and free from habits, the teacher*

---

71. These tensions can be detected in the board of governors' 1840 report (a refutation of Berthier's *Notice* published the year before). The board accused Bébian of "*forever poaching students from the Institution Royale and diverting young teachers from their duties. We were forced to deny him entry into the premises and to forbid any contact with him. Nor can Mr. Berthier have forgotten our criticisms or his suspension on that occasion.*"
72. In the annex, Yves Bernard reproduces the prospectus for the INSMP's Free School for Day Students (*op. cit.*, 1999, p. 190, Annex n° 3). He writes: "*This institutional structure admitted students who for the most part came from extremely disadvantaged backgrounds. The Paris institution prohibited contact between boarders and day students. This separation was for moral reasons, to avoid the day students being a bad influence on the boarders. The separation was however to pose a problem for parents, who demanded that their children be trained as lathe operators. It was therefore necessary to circumvent such institutional reluctance, given the vital need for a vocational apprenticeship. In 1828, Abbé Borel, principal of the establishment, was to opt for the reintegration of day students into the institution for lessons, but not for recreation and meals*", p. 388.
73. Bébian, *Essai sur les sourds-muets*, p. 98.
74. *Ibid.*, p. 60.

will be able to shape them as he so wishes. He will have no trouble teaching them to choose signs that are always correct, and this will please them all the more in that they have a direct relationship with the subject. Once in use, these signs will be passed on from one to the other just as crystal-clear water flows from a pure source."

Unfortunately it would appear that no program of this special day school has survived. We have only Ferdinand Berthier's pen to inform us of its content:[75]

"Each [student] *was to receive a varied, extensive instruction, appropriate to the position he was called upon to occupy in the world. To the study of languages, humanities and sciences, his students had to add, according to their natural dispositions, the culture of arts, drawing, sculpture, various types of engraving. For some it was a noble recreation, for others a useful occupation, an honorable way of living. Foreign students were to be taught in their mother tongue."*

It would seem that the Institution was short-lived:[76] according to Ferdinand Berthier, *"His meagre resources did not allow him to maintain it."*[77] Yves Bernard emphasizes Bébian's pioneering nature in relation to the program; the INSMP followed in his footsteps a few years later:[78]

"Bébian did no more than precede the future programs of the Paris Institution, which in 1831 were to become more cultural than the oc-

75. Berthier, *Notice*, p. 27.
76. No trace has been found, despite a probable existence of four to five years. In 1826 the *Journal's* prospectus mentioned the existence of this institution, and Yves Bernard mentions the expulsion from the INSMP of a student called Contremoulin, following the mutiny that same year, a student who *"was not particularly interested in staying; he preferred to join Bébian who was running his special Day School in Mont-Parnasse"* (Yves Bernard, *op. cit.*, 1999, p. 484): an administrative request for establishment, indirect witness statements, or a land register may have been destroyed in a fire at Paris city hall in 1871.
77. Berthier, *Notice*, p. 28.
78. Yves Bernard, *op. cit.*, 1999, p. 388.

cupational apprenticeships it had been offering since its foundation. In 1837, subjects similar to those of normal schools were developed, allowing some deaf people to become teachers."

Following this abortive attempt to set up a school in Paris, Auguste Bébian applied to Rouen, following the death of Abbé Huby who had until then been in charge of teaching Deaf students.[79]

"Death had just taken away from the deaf-mutes of Rouen the respectable Abbé Huby, a student of Abbé de l'Épée. These unfortunate people were deprived of all instruction. The mayor, responsible for choosing a teacher, believed he had to turn to the Minister of the Interior, who designated Bébian as the most capable man."

According to the board of governors, this version was inaccurate:[80]

"Here is the truth: the mayor of Rouen had announced the opening of a school for deaf-mutes. Bébian put himself forward as head. The mayor contacted the Minister for information. The Minister asked the board, which bore witness to the talent and remained silent concerning the morality.[81] *Bébian was admitted."*

---

79. Abbé Huby, chaplain at the Hôpital des Valides in Rouen, had been trained in Paris by Abbé de l'Épée, before opening a free school in his town. Alexandre Lesguilliez, *Lettres sur la ville de Rouen, ou Précis de son histoire topographique, ecclésiastique et politique*, Rouen: Periaux, 1826.
80. Session of the board of governors, March 2, 1840, Annex 8, pp. 306 to 316.
81. Mood swings, character disorders or management defects are recurrent recriminations in this report. They are confirmed in writing by other protagonists such as Jean-Jacques Valade-Gabel who worked at the INSMP four years later (Valade-Gabel (1801-1879) was a teacher from 1825 to 1838 before being appointed principal of the Bordeaux institution (in 1850 he returned to Paris to finish his career)). He remembered that "*In Paris, Bébian was the only one who deserved the title of teacher; unfortunately he had made himself insufferable… let us draw a veil over the circumstances that led to his being sent away from the institution…*". And further on: "*During this period, Bébian had allowed himself to commit such misconduct that he had to be removed from the Institution, and the teaching, left in the hands of unskilled tutors, was falling apart before everyone's eyes*", (Jean-Jacques Valade-Gabel, *Lettres, notes et rapports*, 1894, p. 400, 444-445).

Whatever the case may be, Bébian was preferred to Paulmier, he with whom he had had an altercation eleven years earlier, who had now been retired from the INSMP for three years, and who was also a candidate, although his reasons for applying are unknown.[82] So on September 5, 1832,[83] Bébian officially took office (his nomination had been approved by the prefect on June 30) and he took charge of a new institution for deaf-mutes in Rouen until March 1834, although we do not know the exact date of the suppression of his position, or why it took place.[84]

Bébian's request for a lithography patent confirms his interest in industrial education.[85] Ferdinand Berthier gives a detailed account of the operation of this Institution:[86]

> *"In the elementary class, he says, the pupils will receive primary instruction, essential to all; at the same time, they will prepare to learn an art or a profession, using all exercises likely to give precision and*

82. Buton, *L'administration des faveurs*, p. 200.
83. The November 8, 1832 issue of the *Journal de Rouen* recounts the decree issued by the Mayor of Rouen to appoint Bébian as principal of the municipal institution (Art. 2) with a salary of 1,500 francs and a housing allowance of 300 francs (Art. 3), with the proviso that he agree to take in lodgers. (As a point of reference, the annual salary of teachers at the INSMP was higher: from 1,800 to 2,500 francs per annum between 1824 and 1829. Buton, *L'administration des faveurs*, p. 200).
84. A letter dated March 19, 1834 from the minister to the prefect declared that *"Mr. Bébian has abandoned his students"*, without offering any explanation. This institution was located in rue Saint-Maur; Abbé Huby's school was in Rue des Prés, at the "Chat qui dort" (M. Dubois, *L'abbé Huby*, 1935, p. 14). It was therefore a new school, but one that would not last: he was *"forced to abandon, given the limited level of allocations he was able to obtain"*, writes archivist A.-G. Hallin (A.-G. Hallin, *Renseignements sur les aveugles et les Sourds-Muets présentés à l'Académie (5 mai 1837)*, p. 7). Following Bébian's departure, it was another abbot, Abbé Lefebvre, who took over in 1835.
85. ADSM, series 2T1.
   "In 1826, he again submitted to Count Alexis de Noailles a short paper on a system of industrial education." Berthier, *Notice*, p. 36-37.
86. *Ibid.*

swiftness to the eye, strength and dexterity to the hand; in a word, using all gymnastic means that might help educate the organs.
Students from this class, whose financial standing requires them to have a more extensive education, which might, through the quiet and solitary pleasures of study, compensate them for being deprived of certain social pleasures and offer them honorable livelihoods through the practice of the arts, will be admitted to the advanced class. All students who show a particular aptitude for one of the arts studied in this class, such as the various types of drawing and painting, the various types of engraving, lithography, the art of engineering, etc., will also be admitted to this class.
Students envisaging a manual occupation, who have no need for an extended instruction, which they would see as a luxury and a waste of precious time (to which the needs of day-to-day existence already lay claim) will go from the preparatory class to the workshops, where, without forgetting what they have already learned, they will complete the apprenticeship for the trade chosen for them in accordance with their parents' wishes, their own tastes, and their individual dispositions; in a word, what their future requires.
These workshops can also provide an occupation and a livelihood for students who have completed their instruction and who wish to remain at the institution."

Once again according to Berthier, the press reported the results with enthusiasm.[87] Bébian's precipitous departure would seem to

87. *"Over time, the newspapers had mentioned the extraordinary results obtained in Rouen by his students, who were still only eight in number. In the presence of the rector of the Academy, the assistants and a number of guests, Bébian put his young deaf-mutes through exercises which met with general approval. But what astonished these gentlemen most of all, was to see with what clarity of analysis and speed of conception one of them, eight or nine years old, and in the care of his new teacher for just six months, answered the questions that were put to him and which presupposed a relatively advanced knowledge of the subtleties of language. Two girls, a little older, also gave satisfactory answers."* Indeed, on June 12, 1833, the *Journal de Rouen* writes about this visit, which had lasted more than two hours and had aroused much enthusiasm.

have been due to his increasingly disabling illness,[88] possibly of rheumatic origin.[89]

4. … and in Guadeloupe

The decision to return to Guadeloupe would not appear to have been a direct result of his illness. It seems, rather, that it was forced upon him after a series of dashed hopes, as Berthier relates:[90]

> *"He was offered a position as principal of a foreign school. He had decided to accept if he could not find a job in France.* […] *They were living in increasingly straitened circumstances, and beginning to suffer the anguish of financial embarrassment. He had to bid adieu to Paris,*

88. Bébian himself writes that he had put together his *Examen critique de la nouvelle organisation de l'Institut de Paris,* published in 1834 but in all probability written at the end of the previous year, during " *the early days of my convalescence, following a cruel and lengthy illness, which had forced me for a certain time to give up my teaching activities*" (p. 9).
89. A rheumatic pathology would appear to be the most plausible hypothesis, given that the attacks were intensified by "*the humid and fickle climate of Rouen becoming deleterious to Bébian's health*." The hypothesis of a tropical disease, however, whether previous or of slow incubation, can be ruled out. Ferdinand Berthier, whom it seems was corresponding with Bébian (the latter's financial difficulties were well known to Berthier and he reports having taken administrative steps at Bébian's behest) mentions repeated and ever more acute attacks while in Rouen ("*He was constantly unwell, and had experienced more than one attack serious enough to alarm his family, as well as his adopted family* [of pupils]" and "[…]. *One day, lying utterly incapacitated in his bed, unable to sit up, having a little movement only in his right hand* […]"). Berthier, *Notice*, p. 39. Given the lack of details at our disposal, it is impossible to make an accurate medical diagnosis. Was it this illness that caused him to return to Guadeloupe, where the climate was more clement? Special thanks to Jérôme Laubreton, doctor at the Poitiers teaching hospital.
    Berthier says (*op. cit.*, 1839, p. 38) that it was Achille Maupin, former student at the INSMP and then *répétiteur*, who did the teaching. At the time when Berthier was writing these lines, Achille Maupin had become a teacher at the Institut des Sourds-Muets in Besançon, located in Rue de la Préfecture and once visited by Charles X, King of France.
90. Berthier, *Notice*, p. 44.

to the France he loved so well, more than just a country for Bébian, and to the deaf-mutes, his adopted children from whom he had hoped never to be separated."

Auguste Bébian set foot in his homeland at the end of 1834, after an apparently difficult crossing that had lasted between five and six weeks.[91] In all likelihood he disembarked in Basse-Terre, the island's capital and, at that time, an active port: did he stay there for a while?[92] Was this when he consulted Mr. Vauchelet and met his son Émile?[93] Details of the final four years of Bébian's life, spent in his country of origin, remain vague and we know very little about them.[94] According to Ferdinand Berthier, and even according to the newspaper *Le Bienfaiteur*, he opened a school,[95] but the items that remain in the archives do not allow us to confirm this.[96]

The very idea of a mutual school was a response to the issue of mass education that was raised during the post-revolutionary years: to allow the majority of people, in classes of sixty or more, to be educated at a minimum cost. The students were supervised by a single teacher who, like an orchestral conductor, coordinated activities in which the more advanced learners explained or reformulated ideas for the benefit of the less advanced. This system was described in the newspaper *Le Moniteur*:[97]

"Every student is always where he should be; the classes follow one another, holding hands rather than being separated. There is more, and

---

91. *"He informed us of his safe arrival after a relatively grueling crossing."* Berthier, *Notice*, p. 44.
92. Note n° 47, p. 81.
93. Unfortunately there is no nominative census for Basse-Terre during the 1830s.
94. He died on February 24, 1839.
95. Berthier referred to the opening of this school "*following requests by several families*". Berthier, *Notice*, p. 44.
96. The newspaper *Le Bienfaiteur* mentions this school in a chart published in 1853 (*Le Bienfaiteur des sourds-muets et des aveugles*, 1853, n° 4, p. 100).
97. *Le Moniteur*, 1818, quoted by Anne Querrien, *L'école mutuelle. Une pédagogie trop efficace ?* Paris: Le Seuil (Les Empêcheurs de penser en rond), 2005, p. 10-11.

in each class or subdivision students are always placed at the level of which they have so far shown themselves to be capable; in this way the unique advantage of individual instruction is preserved and reproduced in its entirety within a large mass. Each individual is as active or even more active than if he were alone [...] *by guiding others, they prove to themselves what they have learned, in other words they genuinely perform the exercise required for proper learning. In turn, students and répétiteurs transmit only what they have learned, indicating what they have themselves successfully attempted. The most difficult, the most delicate, the most overlooked portion of the role of the teacher – by which I mean the proper direction of the faculties – is in a way achieved all by itself by this very regular, progressive exercise, in which all of the children's attention is maintained; emulation and imitative empathy increase through a truer classification, which makes analogies more evident, and more gradual the ladder to be climbed."*

The governor of Guadeloupe's decree of February 16, 1838 ordered the mutual school in Basse-Terre to be transferred to Pointe-à-Pitre,[98] and apparently it was only in that year that Auguste Bébian was appointed as its principal.[99] What had he been doing until then?

98. ADG, cote 3 K 1/11.

99. For 1838, the *Annuaire de la Guadeloupe* noted the appointment of "Mr. Bébian, director of mutual education at Pointe-à-Pitre".

Chapter 4
Bébian, forerunner and emancipator: an anthropological view of deafness

1. Why educate Deaf people... and how?

This question – *Why educate Deaf people... and how?* – could, by itself, sum up much of Auguste Bébian's philosophy and struggle. From his first book, *Essay on the Deaf and Natural Language, or Introduction to a Natural Classification of Ideas with Their Proper Signs*, he never ceased from defending this idea and, in his view, the only way to administer such an education was, indisputably, through the *language of mime and gesture.*[1] *"The sign is the shadow of the idea"* was his *leitmotiv*, the guiding thread of his whole life's work.

On the need to educate Deaf people, he affirms in the very first issue of his *Journal de l'instruction des sourds-muets et des aveugles* (Journal for the instruction of the deaf and the blind), under "preliminary observations":[2]

> *"Education (as the word clearly indicates) develops, brings forth the seeds that we bear within us since birth; but it does not produce them, it does not create them. The skill of the most artful teacher will no more be able to make the light of thought shine in the brain that lacks intelligence than to arouse feeling in inert matter* [...] *The moral and intellectual faculties of the deaf mute are essentially no different*

1. At that time, the terms *langage mimique / langage des gestes* referred to sign language, and had none of the pejorative connotations that they might carry today. *"The sign follows the thought step by step, like a shadow that takes on all its different shapes."* Auguste Bébian, "Essay on the Deaf and Natural Language, or Introduction to a Natural Classification of Ideas with Their Proper Signs", in *The Deaf Experience: Classics in Language and Education*, Harlan L. Lane (ed.), trans. Franklin Philip, Harvard University Press, 1984, p. 154.
2. Auguste Bébian, *Journal de l'instruction des sourds-muets et des aveugles*, 1826, n° 1, pp. 8, 9 and 14.

than those of the child who hears and speaks; if his intelligence is less active and less developed, it is because it has been less exerted. The deaf have only the ideas that they have acquired by themselves; they have received little or nothing from others [...] *Instruction develops the intellectual faculties; but far less so than exercise and communication* [...]*"*[3]

The argument that runs through all his writings is that educating Deaf people is both necessary and possible, even when he touches on facts that, at first sight, seem unconnected. As when he reported on the trials of two deaf men, Filleron and Sauron, brought before the Assizes of the Seine and of Cantal accused of theft, and even of murder.[4] Not only is this education essential, he asserts; to conceive of it other than in sign language would be little short of heretical:[5]

"It is therefore a great error to believe that the deaf can only deploy their intellectual faculties through the assistance of our languages. They also have a language of their own, one that is independent from all methodical instruction."

---

3. Contrary to most of the pedagogues of his day, Bébian often stresses, in his writings, the importance of active learning, which brings him close to the approach adopted by Johann Heinrich Pestalozzi (1746-1827) or Maria Montessori (1870-1952) almost a hundred years later, an approach that can be summed up by the metaphor: *"Children are not vases to be filled; they are fountains that must be allowed to flow."*
4. Filleron was accused of stealing from the orphans' hospice in Paris; Pierre Sauron of murdering Étienne Petit, his girlfriend's father.
   On Filleron's trial, Bébian concludes: *"I offer up this case as yet further proof – as if further proof were required – of the need to educate every deaf person."* And on Sauron's: *"If I recount here the sorry tale of their downfall, it is better to emphasize the need to enlighten them* [...]*," Journal*, vol. II, pp. 54 and 85.
5. *Journal de l'instruction des sourds-muets et des aveugles*, n° 1, vol. I, p. 15.
   "[...] *the art created by his* [l'Épée's] *genius is far from having received the improvements that one was entitled to expect from the efforts of so many skillful teachers"*, Prospectus of the *Journal*, 1826.

1.1 Little Ernest, or the need for sign language

The idea of educating children directly in *natural* sign language, i.e. the linguistic system employed by Deaf people themselves, without any form of codification such as the "Methodical Signs" system (which, in Bébian's view, was at best not properly thought through, and at worst an error, as Ferdinand Berthier writes)[6] was totally innovative. Here, at the beginning of the 19th century, when childhood was coming into its own as a phase of life[7] and when the age of admission to the INSMP was set at around ten years,[8] he defended the idea of education from the earliest age:[9]

---

6. "*The term* methodical *calls for some explanation. Without touching upon the accuracy of this epithet, I would simply point out that my first teacher made the serious mistake, in my view, of seeking to subject the language of signs to the conventional laws of language rather than to the natural course of thought; this is, moreover, the only mistake that can be leveled against this genius who had no models and no rivals. Today everyone agrees that a sort of anatomical spelling-out of words by means of gestures does not offer an exact and complete meaning any more than would the literal translation of an author, whose style and genius would thus be overlooked.*" Berthier, *Notice*, pp. 7-8.
7. Jean-Noël Luc, *La petite enfance à l'école, XIXe- XXe siècles*, Paris: INRP, 1982.
8. The cut-off point between childhood and adulthood is fuzzy: the "child" in question may be 9 years old or 22. François Buton, *L'administration des faveurs. L'État, les sourds et les aveugles (1789-1885)*, Rennes: Presses universitaires de Rennes, 2009, p. 75 and note below.
9. *Journal de l'instruction des sourds-muets et des aveugles*, n° 6, vol. I, pp. 297-303. This is a relatively modern conception: under Abbé de l'Épée, for deaf students of all ages, from six years old up to the most full-grown adults (Claude-André Deseine, for example, was admitted when he was 33!), lessons lasted only four hours in winter and five in summer, on Tuesdays and Fridays. No age limit, in other words, nor precise duration, as this was a private philanthropic undertaking. To be admitted to the INSMP, however, pupils needed to have attained a sort of "age of reason"; their tenth year. Sicard confirms this rule in one of his memoirs: attempting to educate the deaf before their tenth year would be futile; the education of Jean Massieu, a previously unschooled deaf pupil, admitted to Bordeaux at the age of thirteen in 1785 and appointed as tutor in 1790, demonstrates that the pupil must possess outstanding capacities of attention and patience to sit through Abbé Sicard's Course of Instruction, as it meanders through a general grammar, retracing the pre-generative trees of the French language on the blank slate of the man of nature…

> "[...] *from the tenderest age, even indeed in the cradle, the child is capable of attention; why not seek, early on, to steer this faculty in a direction favorable to the development of intelligence? Are the unfortunate deaf not already sufficiently deprived of means of instruction, that we should condemn their minds to remain uncultivated during those years in which, as is widely accepted, we acquire the major part of our knowledge? We often forget how deeply rooted the habits of early childhood become, and how much influence they exert over our entire existence. Attention is the principle of all our intellectual faculties. What constitutes the difference between minds, if not the degree of attention that each of us is able to give to his own ideas? How important it is to exercise or properly direct this precious faculty, on which the strength of the intelligence depends, at an early stage!*"

To illustrate his argument, he cites the case of one of his pupils, "Little Ernest", in the "practical instruction" section (just as he announced in the publishing prospectus of the *Journal*[10]), while reminding the reader that if he had not done so earlier, it was so that each person could form their own opinion from the historical summary that he developed from one issue to the next:[11]

> "*I remind the reader, at this point, of my promise to accept any questions that are addressed to me on this matter, and to respond, in so far as it is possible for me do so, with facts.*
> *If I have yet to deal with practical procedures, it is not that I have forgotten; rather, I thought it pertinent to begin by seeking out the very principles of the art, and examining the various methods employed* [...] *By explaining these to the parents and to the teachers, we give them the ability to make a judicious choice, and offer them a yardstick for judging the procedures that we may ourselves propose.*"

10. "*We welcome any questions that may be addressed to us, whether by parents or by teachers.*" (Annex 9).
11. *Journal de l'instruction des sourds-muets et des aveugles*, n°6, vol. I, p. 216.

He describes his method, the progress of this pupil,[12] and insists on what he sees as the key point: that the *langage mimique* ("mime language" as Sign was sometimes still called), while not a magic wand, is the indispensable basis of his teaching:

> *"The most interesting thing about him is the rapid development of his mime language. As this language will be the main instrument of his instruction, we give it particular attention. Through this means we can already explain to our little Ernest everything that we could explain through speech to a child of the same age endowed with all his senses* [...] *His greatest pleasure is to converse, and he would spend the whole day doing so, if we always had the leisure to listen to him; but he wants us to understand him; he reads your thoughts in your eyes; if he sees hesitation, he loses patience and becomes angry; but he soon returns to his idea, and doubles his efforts to express it; and it is rare that he does not succeed, as he is dealing with people who are much accustomed to penetrating his mind. We then point out to him what was vague or flawed in his expressions* [...]"

A resolutely pioneering approach, particularly as regards the *language of mime*, hitherto seen as incomplete or transitional – the position adopted by Abbé Sicard and, above all, by Joseph de

12. *"The young pupil of whom I write works, at most, but one hour a day, and it is hard to capture his attention for more than half an hour at a stretch; but this short time well used from day to day produces, after a number of months, a considerable mass* [...] *This child who, as can easily be believed, had not even the rudiments of schooling, who knew not one letter, whose hand had never held a pen, has already learned more than two hundred words, not only nouns but also adjectives and verbs* [...] *Like all children, our little Ernest asks us about all he sees, about all that is said in his presence; and in return for our willingness to answer him, we have accustomed him to pay full attention to our explanations, which, as you may well imagine, are always given in mime language* [...] *In another paper, I will explain the procedures that we employed,"* he concludes, but unfortunately he never did. *Journal de l'instruction des sourds-muets et des aveugles*, n° 6, vol. I, pp. 299-303.

Gérando,[13] chairman of the influential board of governors of the INSMP. Gérando, the author of a monumental 1,200-page tome, *De l'éducation des sourds-muets de naissance*,[14] takes a radically different stance to that of Bébian, stemming from a certain conception of deaf people and their language,[15] and running contrary to the pre-evolutionist ideas of his time: speech is on the side of progress, as opposed to this limited "primitive" language that has no graphic representation. On the contrary, writes Bébian, speech is not superior to gesture, quite the reverse![16]

> *"[...] speech, which creates so many obstacles to communication between peoples, places still further hurdles to the workings of the mind, sometimes holding out a deceptive helping hand that leads the mind astray, like those pale fires that shine in the darkness of the night, lending their perfidious clarity to the hesitant traveler, coaxing him off the path and into the swamp from whose emanations they spring."*

A position that marginalizes him, as the sociologist Sophie Dalle-Nazébi observes:[17]

> *"In considering that thought cannot be reduced to words and that gestures are effective in the development of rational thinking, he*

---

13. On Joseph-Marie de Gérando, see note n° 108, page 61.
14. Joseph-Marie de Gérando, *De l'éducation des sourds-muets de naissance*, 2 vol., Paris: Méquignon l'Aîné père, 1827 [On the Education of Deaf-Mutes from Birth]. This work, a major landmark in early 19th century deaf historiography, is a summary of experiences from other countries (Germany, Switzerland, Holland, England, Denmark, Spain, Italy, USA) accounting for about a fifth of the volume, along with teaching recommendations. Buton, *L'administration des faveurs*, p. 134.
15. Sophie Dalle-Nazébi, *Chercheurs, Sourds et langues des signes. Le travail d'un objet et de repères linguistiques en France du XVIIe au XXIe siècle*, doctoral thesis, Université Toulouse II – Le Mirail, 2006, p. 147.
16. Auguste Bébian, *Essai sur les sourds-muets et sur le langage naturel ou introduction à une classification naturelle des idées avec leurs signes propres*, Paris: J.-G. Dentu, 1817, pp. 111-112.
17. Dalle-Nazébi, *Chercheurs*, p. 147.

does not sketch the same portrait of the deaf population as the vast majority of his contemporaries."

His thoughts on the transcription of signs, which he published in 1825 under the title *Mimographie,*[18] are an attempt to reply to this argument; they reflect his forerunner mindset. With Bébian, deafness leaves behind the framework of infirmity: "[…] *most of Bébian's actions center around linguistic questions*", writes Christian Cuxac, a linguist specializing in sign language.[19] It is, indeed, a central preoccupation, as we shall see later.

On a very different subject, but one that still relates to Bébian's characteristic modernity, his concern for girls' education is noteworthy, at a time when it had few champions. As he writes to the board of governors:[20]

"[…] *they, too, are much worthy of the Board's benevolent attention, these poor girls, delicate and timid, exposed to so many dangers when they leave the Institution; for they cannot and must not all enter the almshouse recently founded by a committee of charitable ladies.*
I have heard that at the Royal Institute there is a year-round need for seamstresses to patch the linen, while there are sixty young girls here who need to learn to sew."

18. Auguste Bébian, *Mimographie ou Essai d'écriture mimique, propre à régulariser le langage des sourds-muets.* Paris: Louis Colas, 1825. [Reprinted in full in: Marc Renard, *Écrire les signes*, Éditions du Fox, 2004.]
19. Christian Cuxac, "La Mimographie de Bébian : finalité et destin d'une écriture de la LSF", *Surdités* n° 5-6, Paris: Gestes, 2004.
20. Auguste Bébian, *Examen critique de la nouvelle organisation de l'enseignement dans l'Institution royale des sourds-muets de Paris.* [Critical appraisal of the new organization of teaching Royal Institution for Deaf-Mutes], Paris: Treuttel & Wurtz, 1834, p. 56.

1.2 The *Manual for the Practical Instruction of Deaf-Mutes*: cornerstone of a "balanced" bilingual education

But it is doubtless the *Manual for the Practical Instruction of Deaf-Mutes*[21] that offers the most comprehensive summary of Auguste Bébian's thinking, and perhaps best illustrates this modernity.

Published in 1827, ten years after his first book,[22] Bébian's hefty 575-page Manual fills two volumes. It is a fully-fledged bilingual education course, the like of which is hard to find today. Its main goal is to lay the foundations for Deaf education, and to enable students to learn French through the medium of sign language.[23] Ferdinand Berthier describes the context surrounding its publication:[24]

> *"After the death of Abbé Sicard* [in 1822], *the teaching was left adrift in vagueness and uncertainty, buffeted this way and that by the most erroneous fancies, with no strong hand coming forward to take the helm. Such a sorry state of affairs inevitably brought home to the ad-*

21. Auguste Bébian, *Manuel d'enseignement pratique des sourds-muets,* 2 vols., Paris: Méquignon l'Aîné, 1827.
22. Auguste Bébian, *Essai sur les sourds-muets et sur le langage naturel ou introduction à une classification naturelle des idées avec leurs signes propres,* [Essay on the Deaf and natural language, or Introduction to a natural classification of ideas with their proper signs], Paris: J.-G. Dentu, 1817.
23. *"It is therefore to the study of language that the teacher's primary efforts must turn. For that is the special purpose of the instruction of the deaf-mute; it is also that of this Manual* [...] *Our sole focus, in this Manual, has been the study of language, and even then only a part of that study, but the most difficult and most important part, which forms the basis of all deaf-mute instruction: the teaching of grammar."* Bébian, *Manuel*, pp. 13-14.
   In his *Examen critique...* he is still more forthright: *"Through the simple language of gestures, one can give the deaf-mute all the knowledge he needs, even before he has learned the written language. Through speech you can teach him nothing* [...] *Through the language of gestures, an educated deaf-mute can transmit his education to his brothers; your system robs him of that consolation."* (*op. cit.*, p. 52)
24. Ferdinand Berthier, *Notice sur la vie et les ouvrages de Auguste Bébian, ancien censeur des études de l'Institut royal des sourds-muets de Paris.* Paris: Ledoyen, 1839, pp. 15-16.

ministration of the Royal Institution in Paris the urgent need to endow the establishment in its charge with a work of reference that would provide a stable understanding of the principles of a simple and logical method. There was no teacher more experienced, more knowledgeable than Mr. Bébian to whom they could entrust the writing of such a work. His Manual for the Practical Instruction of Deaf-Mutes was adopted and published by the board of governors in 1827."

The *Manual* is probably the finest illustration of his attachment to Deaf education; its introduction insists elegantly on the importance of reading and writing, which he saw as primordial:[25]

"...they will no longer be deaf or mute to those who can read and write; reading will open up to them all the treasures of human knowledge that are locked away in books."

The first volume brings together the proposed exercises for the student; its 204 pages include a wealth of illustrative plates. This work is inseparable from the second volume, with its 371 pages, which provides copious explanations for each exercise and can be seen as the teacher's book. It is very much a bilingual education course: the teacher is obliged to know proper sign language and to use it to help the pupils learn French, by explaining the workings of French grammar. From this perspective, as he reminds us, sign language plays an indispensable role:

"In the Manual for Practical Instruction (adopted and published by the board of governance and development of the Royal Institution for Deaf-Mutes), *I endeavored to rid the method of all the niceties in which it had become ensconced by a false metaphysics* [...] *We find signs in every language to express ideas, and signs to express the relations that we grasp or establish between them. The first form the dictionary of the language, while the others are the object of grammar."*[26]

25. Bébian, *Manuel*, vol. II, p. 13.
26. Bébian, *Manuel*, vol. I, p. 15.

Direct education in sign language – without the medium of speech – is, for Bébian, the most effective way.[27] He raises essential points for learning: the link between language and thought, the need to educate Deaf people, and how to set about that task pedagogically. At the outset:

> *"This language* (of signs) *starts out raw, like the intelligence that employs it, and limited, like the narrow circle of knowledge that it depicts. But usage and reflection soon give it greater precision and regularity. Analogy enriches it with all the relations that the mind can perceive between things, between ideas, and even between the ways in which ideas are expressed."*[28]

Analogy and drawing are, indeed, the techniques he recommends teachers to use when beginning the process of instruction:

> *"There is not a single teacher that does not feel, every day, how valuable it would be for the education of the deaf to have a series of engraved figures, representing all the objects worth knowing. It is barely conceivable that no-one has yet produced such a collection, of which the utility – nay, the indispensable necessity – is universally acknowledged and proclaimed."*[29]

Drawing is also mentioned by Joseph-Marie de Gérando, author of *De l'éducation des sourds de naissance* and chairman of the INSMP's board of governors, as one of the "five principal means" necessary

27. " [...] *the result of a comparison between instruction by articulation and instruction by mime language would probably not have been favorable for the new system* [rotation] *rekindled from the fifteenth century*". Auguste Bébian, *Examen critique*, p. 39
28. *Journal de l'instruction des sourds-muets et des aveugles*, n° 1, vol. I, p. 14.
29. *Ibid.*, n° 8, vol. II, pp. 100-101.
Analogy is considered essential for concept formation. Jean-François Dortier and Nicolas Journet (eds.), "L'analogie au cœur de la pensée", *Les clés du langage*, Auxerre: Sciences humaines, 2015, pp. 70-73.

for instruction.[30] The central role of imagery in psychology and pedagogy no longer needs to be demonstrated, whether for hearing or deaf people,[31] but for the latter it is indispensable if we are to leverage their visual capabilities. For this reason, Bébian's *Manual* contains drawings of exceptional precision… and in color.[32] Five years later, the *Third Circular* recommends producing "*a series of tables* […] *which might summarize* […] *the most essential notions*" as well as a "*series of lithograph drawings designed to revise the objects of the course*";[33] but it seems this recommendation was never followed. Fifteen years later Alphonse Esquiros mentions "*seeking the lithograph drawings in vain*".[34] Two years after the Circular, in 1834, Auguste Bébian visited the Institution:

---

30. "*We are presented with five principal means: drawing, with its conversion into symbolic writing; the language of action, with its conversion into methodical signs, the manual alphabet or fingerspelling, and the labial alphabet, accompanied by artificial pronunciation*." De Gérando, *De l'éducation des Sourds-Muets,* vol.1, p. 278. In general, these means are found recurrently from one method to the next; the disagreements arise over the degree of importance assigned to each technique. Auguste Bébian is the only educator to contest this model, as he does not recognize the codification of the "language of action" into methodical signs.
31. Christian Metz, "Images et pédagogie", *Communications,* 15, 1970. pp. 162-168; Alain Lieury, "Mémoire des images et double codage", *L'année psychologique,* 1995, vol. 95, n° 4, pp. 661-673.
32. The first volume, intended for the pupil, contains thirty-two numbered plates in addition to the main text, one of which folds out.
    It would be interesting to know who produced these drawings: were they Deaf people, friends or former pupils of Auguste Bébian? By that time, it had been six years since Bébian left the INSMP, but his relations with the Deaf Frédéric Peyson (1807-1877), then working as a painter, who was his pupil between 1817 and 1821, who came to stay with Bébian on leaving the INSMP in 1827, and witnessed the birth of his son in 1830 (Ferdinand Berthier mentions him in the journal *L'ami des sourds-muets* dated 29 June 1840), show that his contacts with Deaf people continued. Théophile Denis, *Notice biographique*, Paris: Imprimerie Bélanger, 1890, pp. 4-5.
    The financial investment was probably significant: the INSMP's board of governors, which commissioned and approved the book, also financed it, at least in part.
33. *Troisième circulaire,* 1832, art. 21-22, p. 262.
34. Alphonse Esquiros, *Paris, ou les sciences, les institutions et les mœurs au XIXe siècle,* 2 tomes, Paris: Comptoir des imprimeurs unis, 1847, p. 258.

"On visiting the Royal Institution some time ago, I inquired as to how work was proceeding on these tables and lithograph drawings. No-one, it seemed, knew what I was referring to, so deep is the impression that the administration's decisions leave upon the Royal Institute! [...] *The official, with infinite consideration, was so kind as to lead me around all the classrooms. I was sorely disappointed: not a single table, not a single drawing! Not one engraving, not even a poor little reading book!"*[35]

He also decries the spread of "line drawing" to the detriment of "imitative drawing", which makes such analogies possible.[36] This technique – in combination with analogy – is for him, essential, as we saw earlier: the two techniques are foundational to the educational approach he recommends,[37] namely not to move directly to

35. Bébian, *Examen critique*, p. 47.

36. *"I do not know whether sufficient thought has been given to the relevance of line drawing, and to the advantages or drawbacks of this teaching method, be it well or poorly designed. I doubt that one could find two pupils in the entire Institution who understand why, to what end and by what principles the hand – in line drawing – must often trace the figures other than as they are seen; in a word, why must one draw a straight line in the line-drawing class when, for the same object, you would draw a curved line in the imitative-drawing class"* (*ibid.*) pp. 26-27.
Line drawing supplements imitative drawing: it was introduced into schools as early as 1815. Pointing the way towards geometry or industrial drawing, it aims to represent the outlines of objects. A distinction can be made between two types of line drawing: *sight* or *freehand line drawing* (without instruments), and *graphic line drawing* (with instruments). Pupils begin by drawing straight lines of particular lengths and rectilinear figures, and may then move on to applying these in drawings for carpentry, flooring or tiling. Line drawing gradually came to incorporate the notions of "graphic design": plan, cross-section and elevation views, projections and penetrations of solids, the use of shading...
Sources: *Cours élémentaire de dessin linéaire d'arpentage et d'architecture* by J.-B. Henry. Librairie élémentaire et classique, Fouraut & fils, 1873, (plate on drawing instruments); *Dessin des écoles primaires* (Cours élémentaire et moyen. 50 modèles muraux comprenant 50 exercices) by V. Cayasse & J. Larue, cited by the website *www.le-temps-des-instituteurs.fr*
Imitative drawing was not restored to its rightful place until 1865 (by parliamentary act, on June 21).

37. Bébian, *Manuel*, vol. II, p. 17. Five years after this was written, in 1832, the INSMP recommended that: *"mime language, based on analogy, shall continue, alongside the drawing and intuition of objects, to be the means of introduction to education*

writing, but to go towards "*the language of gestures,* […] *means of transition to written language*".[38] To begin the process of learning how to read and write, he gives the following instruction to the teacher:

> "*Place Plate II* (reproduced below) *in front of the pupil. Beforehand, you will have taken the trouble to bring together, on a nearby table, all the illustrated objects. The pupil will doubtless recognize the objects at first glance in the figures that represent them.*"

This plate, and the following one (Plate III, reproduced in Annex 5), are seen by Bébian as aids for preparatory exercises that seek to give pupils a foundation for independent learning; the actual lessons of the *Manual* begin later. There are three of these preparatory exercises: starting by identifying an object and designating it by a word or a sign, followed by "reading by gestures", and conversely:[39]

> "*The exercises upon which we have just dwelt will, in a few days, become familiar to the deaf-mute. In this way he will soon be able, alone and as much for amusement as for study, to peruse and learn the names of all the perceptible objects whose illustrations you can place in front of him.*"

---

for deaf-mutes, and to serve as preparation for the comprehension of the mother tongue. It will be called upon to represent things and actions so as to impose their names upon them. Its usage will be gradually restricted in the more senior classes, as pupils make progress in the study of the mother tongue. It will then be used solely as an accessory instrument of explanation, assessment and testing " (*Third Circular* of the INSMP, 1832, art. 6). Which, as Bébian writes, is contradictory, as it forces ALL pupils to renounce the language of gestures in all their communications, whether between them or with other people, and exchange only through writing, speech, or fingerspelling (Bébian, *Examen critique*, p. 7).

38. Bébian, *Manuel,* vol. 2, p. 19.

39. *Ibid.*, p. 29.

Figure 5: *Manual for the Practical Instruction of Deaf-Mutes* - Plate II

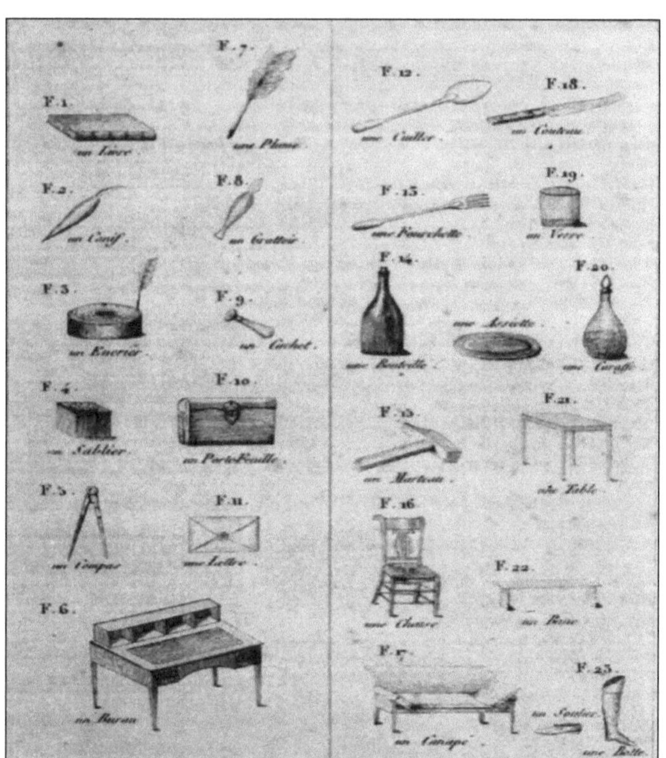

Why not go straight from drawings to the written word? The visual dimension is essential, he maintains, in order to consolidate the memory and respect visual thinking, which is why it is important to go through "the language of gestures":[40]

> *"There is no more direct and reliable way, nor any more powerful method, for initiating the deaf-mute into the secrets of our languages. The language of gestures can bend to all forms of thinking; it can express the most subtle nuances and the most sophisticated combinations."*

40. *Ibid.*, p. 19.

The basis of this method is set out in the preface to the second volume of the *Manual*, taking up twenty-six pages,[41] before the first lesson, which is devoted to the distinction between males and females, which the "*deaf-mute will* [...] *by observation* [...] *derive either from gestation or from breastfeeding*".[42] But while associating the written word with drawings or identifying genders pose no problem in themselves, assimilating syntax is a more delicate matter, and is not addressed until Lesson XXX (see below).

41. The preface details the various methods and processes of learning. Bébian stresses above all that the manual alphabet must not be confused with sign language. "*It is merely a sort of air-writing which, just like ordinary writing, can be used and understood only by those who know the language whose words are being traced. Fingerspelling must not be confused with the real language of gestures, which is independent from any articulated language; it is a natural pantomime, a living imitation of the things and actions that are the object of the conversation.*" (What the linguist Christian Cuxac calls "iconicity" or "saying by showing"; a key component of sign language, along with "saying without showing". Christian Cuxac, *Les voies de l'iconicité*, Paris: Ophrys, 2000. This dimension is essential: the linguist Marie-Anne Sallandre demonstrates that this iconicity is always present, even when it is "corrupted or degraded" (Marie-Anne Sallandre, *Compositionnalité des unités sémantiques en langues des signes. Perspectives typologique et développementale,* Dossier presented for the research supervision diploma (HDR), Université Paris VIII, 2014, p. 36). The transition from drawing and analogy to the "language of gestures" and subsequently to writing is the main theme of Bébian's argument: it finishes with translation exercises from word to gesture and vice versa, reiterating that the goal is autonomy: "*When the pupil has learned* [...] *sixty or so words* [...], *it is time to leave him somewhat to his own devices and teach him to study; that is, to do it alone* [...]."
42. In a footnote, Bébian mentions – and contests – the practice in force at the INSMP: "*At the Institution for the Deaf, the feminine is designated by the sign for weak, the masculine by the sign for strong, with no further explanation. The signs of Abbé de l'Épée are also used: the 'hat' sign for masculine and the 'bonnet' sign for feminine. When dictating, for example, 'Un banc, une table'* [a bench, a table], *we would add the 'hat' sign to the first sign and 'bonnet' to the other. I need hardly point out that such signs must impart false ideas; it is from the nature of things or from the demands of thinking that we should draw our means of instruction.*" *Manuel,* vol. II, p. 30.
"*In this case, the at times capricious law of the ear seems to have determined the highly conventional choice of gender. The same is true of the infinite number of nouns that bear no relation to male or female, and which, for want of a third gender in which they might have found a home, have been arbitrarily divided up into masculine and feminine.*" *Journal de l'instruction des sourds-muets et des aveugles*, n° 8, vol. II, p. 103.

The *Manual for the Practical Instruction of Deaf-Mutes* consists of a hundred thirty-one lessons in all, designed, as noted earlier, to teach the mastery of French by constantly placing two different grammatical constructions in parallel: nowadays we might call it "contrastive linguistics".[43] All the areas of grammar are addressed. To begin with, in addition to gender, it touches on "simple" notions such as plural formation,[44] the use of adjectives,[45] demonstrative adjectives,[46] numbers,[47] along with the conjunction "and",[48] before moving on to expressions of time

43. This is, of course, an anachronism. Unlike comparative linguistics, contrastive linguistics takes a synchronic rather than a diachronic perspective. Marie-Anne Paveau & Georges-Élia Sarfati, *Les grandes théories de la linguistique : De la grammaire comparée à la pragmatique*, Paris: A. Colin, 2003.
44. Lessons IV and V. The material for these lessons, with the aim of explaining plurals and putting them into practice, is Plate VII of the *Manual* (Annex 5).
45. Lessons VI, VII and VIII in vol. I; explanations in vol. II, pp. 39 to 43.
Two plates (reproduced in Annex 5 of the *Manual*), of which one is in color, illustrate the determining function of the adjective. This choice is justified on pedagogical grounds: "*We begin the study of adjectives by the colors, as this modification is external, and we can, in a sense, abstract it out, removing it from the subject so as to present it separately on paper, just as it is in language.*" (vol. II, p. 42).
46. Lesson X, "*Ce, cette, ces*" [This, these]. For this lesson there is no plate and no drawing, as *"it is not immediately clear by what rule we are guided in the choice of content of these first lessons; we appear to be advancing at random."* If the demonstrative adjectives are discussed before the definite articles (*le, la, les*), it is in order to *"present one difficulty at a time, and this difficulty should never be beyond the current development of the deaf pupil's intelligence."* Bébian, *Manuel*, vol. II, p. 46. They are not explained until lesson XLIV.
47. Lessons XI, XII and XIII. Bébian justifies the inclusion of the numbers at this point by the need to assimilate them in order to construct short phrases when learning about the representation of time in verbs: this is the gist of Lesson XV, on the *"application of the names of numbers to divisions of time* (reading the time)" and the following lesson, which covers "*the words today, yesterday and tomorrow.*"
48. Lesson XIV. This conjunction is presented here in connection with numbers (previous lessons), but the conjunctions "but" and "or" are not presented until much later (Lessons XCIV and XCV). He schematizes its usage thus:

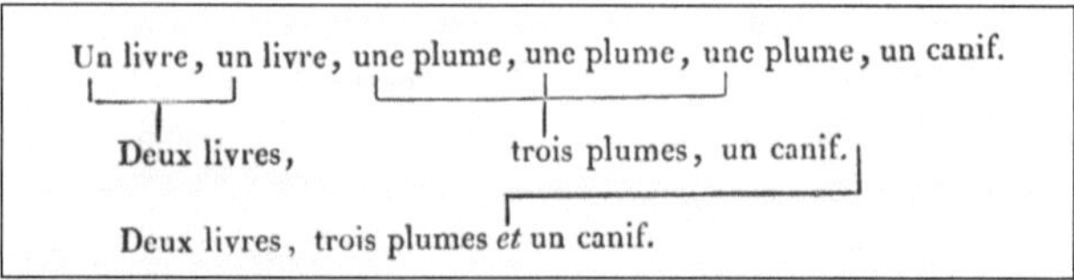

(Lessons XV and XVI), and personal pronouns (Lessons XIX, XX and XXI),[49] and thence to conjugation (Lesson XXII).[50]

Throughout the *Manual*, the specific structure of sign language is acknowledged. Bébian points out in Lesson XXX that:[51]

> *"In the language of gestures, the complement tends to precede the subject and the verb. The deaf-mute likes to show the purpose of the action before representing the action itself and the agent.*
> *He must therefore be taught to reverse his natural phrase order in order to conform to the French construction, as illustrated by the three examples in this table* (see Figure 6).
> *We recommend that the teacher should, as far as possible, enact the first examples of each rule. In any case, he should seek to represent them by some small piece of mime. Here, the example offers no difficulty: I strike this table."*

49. A plate is devoted to this subject (Annex 5).
50. He presents the root of a verb (for example, *dessin…*) and applies the conjugation depending on whether the action is past, present or future. He reminds us: "*The sign for the future is made up of the signs for* tomorrow, tomorrow, tomorrow, *etc. which we shorten by simply moving the hand forwards.*
The sign for the past *is made up of the signs for yesterday, yesterday, etc., which we also shorten into a single sign, by pointing the hand backwards over the shoulder."*
51. Bébian, *Manuel*, vol. 2, p. 85.

The plate accompanying this lesson schematizes the syntax of sign language:

Figure 6: *Manual for the Practical Instruction of Deaf-Mutes.* Lesson XXX: Complement of the Verb

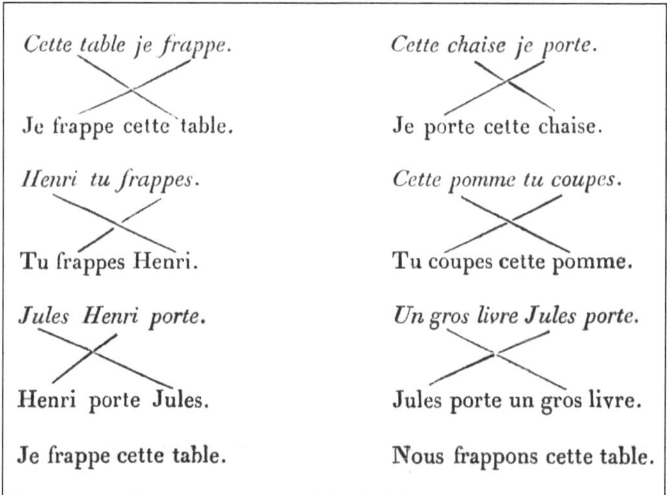

He also devotes particular care to the representation of time, this being totally different in French as compared to sign language. He reminds us that:[52]

> *"Deaf-mutes, in their own language, express habitual past action, or our imperfect tense, by adding to the root sign the signs corresponding to the words: past always, now finished* […] *The imperfect is one of the tenses that deaf-mutes had not understood. They were told that this tense expressed a double present and a double past, and the sign was in keeping with this definition."*

But the publication of the *Manual* was only one part of a journey that he had already sketched out in his *Journal* in 1827. Four years

52. *Ibid.*, p. 83.

later, in 1831, in the publishing proposal for an unpublished work, he again explains:[53]

"This was merely the first step towards the goal to which all my work aspires. This book was for teachers alone; and the Deaf-Mute[54] are generally too poor to find many teachers willing to devote themselves to such an arduous and thankless task of education [...] *Thus elementary education, this beneficence to which all Deaf-Mutes seem to be entitled, as a sacred debt that society owes to the unfortunate – has until now been but a rare exception for the benefit of a chosen few."*

His ambition goes further:

"A forthcoming public experiment will attest that the Deaf-Mute, equipped with the book that we are publishing, will benefit from going to school with other children. And he will not be the pupil that gives the master either the most trouble or the least satisfaction. There, amidst his young classmates, who will soon have learned his language, he will, under the discipline of a shared education, learn about social living, from which the Deaf-Mute remain too estranged in their special institutions, where they are as if sequestered from the rest of the world throughout their entire education."

Ferdinand Berthier attributes the non-publication of this work to a lack of money, and speaks of a missed opportunity:[55]

"The Minister of the Interior (Monsieur de Montalivet), *who appreciated the usefulness of this work, wished to support its publication by means of a subscription. It is a matter of regret that, for want of money, the*

53. Auguste Bébian, *Éducation des sourds-muets mise à la portée des institutions primaires et de tous les parents; Méthode naturelle pour apprendre les langues sans traduction,* publishing prospectus, Paris: Imprimerie de Béthune, 1831.
54. Intriguingly, Bébian uses lowercase sourds-muets in the *Manuel*, but uppercase *Sourds-Muets* in Éducation. The translation reflects the original typography in each case.
55. Berthier, *Notice*, p. 26.

work was not pursued beyond the first two deliveries. [...]. *That would have been a monument erected to France, to the 19th century, and to the author who first conceived the idea."*

Is this the work that Bébian mentions in 1834, and regrets not having been able to finalize?[56] At any rate, it no doubt foreshadows the criticisms expressed three years later in his *Examen critique de la nouvelle organisation de l'enseignement dans l'Institution royale des sourds-muets de Paris*,[57] but above all it reflects his often repeated wish to "*popularize the education of the deaf-mute*".[58]

2. From the light of the sun...

The creation of the *Journal de l'instruction des sourds-muets et des aveugles* by Auguste Bébian in 1826 was a daring and forward-looking initiative at a time when freedoms were being reined in. The historian Christophe Charle, author of a study on the French press from 1830 to 1939,[59] defends his choice of starting date in these terms:

"[...] *1830 is justified as the starting point relative to the French Revolution, as the revolution of July 1830 was sparked by the ordinances of Charles X, the most important of which suspended the freedom of the periodical press* [...]

56. "*Having undertaken this work, I was forced by adverse circumstances to interrupt it; I remain hopeful, however, that I will be able to complete it* [...]." Bébian, *Examen critique*. p. 62.
57. "*The Royal Institution was designed to perfect, simplify and propagate this method, so that all deaf-mutes might be restored to intellectual and moral life. Today, the Royal Institution seems to exist solely to extinguish hope and courage in the heart of all who seek to work for this endeavor.*" Bébian, *Examen critique*.
58. "*Nine years ago* (i.e. in 1825!), *I submitted a short article on this subject to Count Alexis de Noailles. As you can see, this idea has long preoccupied me. The more I think about it, the more I am convinced that this is the only way to enable all deaf-mutes to participate in the benefits of instruction.*" Bébian, *Examen critique*, p. 66.
59. Christophe Charle, *Le siècle de la presse (1830-1939)*, Paris: Seuil, 2004, pp. 10-11.

The second foundational event took place three years later, in 1833. The new regime adopted the Loi Guizot, which organized primary education for the first time and thus paved the way for the growth of an audience of new readers, beyond the traditional urban literate circles that formed the mainstay of the audience under the Revolution and the Restoration. And indeed, thirty years later, in the 1860s, the time necessary for the first social effects of an education law to be felt, the first 'popular' newspapers were founded [...]."[60]

This, however, was a pedagogical publication, not a general periodical. Moreover, it addressed a specialist field of education, and a recent one, since at the date of the first issue (August 1826) deaf education had been institutionalized for only 35 years.[61] In the prospectus announcing the publication of the journal,[62] Auguste Bébian set out his ambition:

"Since the example and the success of Abbé de l'Épée first aroused public interest in Deaf-Mutes, a large number of establishments have come into being, modeled on the institution of which he was the founder. But the art created by his genius is far from having received the improvements that one was entitled to expect from the efforts of so many skillful teachers. Even today, there is no full agreement on the true principles of this teaching. Each school has its own method, and often, in the same school, each teacher adopts and follows a different system.

60. The Deaf press played its part in this expansion, as the graph in Annex 6 shows.
61. The decrees of the Constituent Assembly date back to 1791 (p. 53).
62. Two slightly different versions of the prospectus have been found. The presentation text is identical, but the second seems to have been published several months later: it contains a *nota bene* in which Bébian mentions the suspension of the journal (without specifying for how long), "*though it has met its initial commitments to its subscribers* "; a suspension due probably to his workload, but "*as he has recently recruited two of his former pupils to assist him in his teaching duties, he can now reconcile that which he owes to the trust of the parents who have placed their children in his care with that which he owes to the wishes of his subscribers, most of whom have asked him for the continuation of this journal* [...] " (This second prospectus is reproduced in Annex 9).

We have lacked a common focal point, where all the scattered rays of the doctrine could come together, reflecting a brighter light on every branch of the teaching.
The Journal de l'instruction des Sourds-Muets offers teachers this meeting-place, where they can discuss their observations and the results of their work."

This exchange of opinions was also, probably, a way of consolidating an education free from religion, something Napoleon had sought to instate, but which still remained fragile:[63]

"Napoleon, despite reinstating the power of the priesthood, sought to protect secular education against any attack and created the University, to which he gave responsibility for National Education. From this moment (1815) *on, society was left at the mercy of two major currents of opinion* […]*, perpetually clashing without seeking common ground. Between the eclecticism of the University, which one illustrious priest called the "Vestibule of Hell", and the orthodoxy of Catholic teaching* […] *there could be no lasting peace."*

In 1830s France, the most visible constraint on the periodical press was the limited size of its potential readership. According to Charles Dupin, "*in 1820, newspapers counted one subscriber for every 338 people, but by 1826, they had only one subscriber for every 427 people.*"[64] Keeping a journal going, particularly one that focuses on a very specific theme, is a challenging task, both intellectually – Bébian edited the journal, and also wrote most of the articles – and financially,[65] even if the print run was no doubt relatively small

63. Daniel Stern (pen-name of Marie d'Agoult), cited by the website <*http:// www.le-temps-des-instituteurs.fr/histoire.html*>
64. Baron Charles Dupin, *Situation progressive des forces de la France depuis 1814*, Brussels: Lithographie royale de Jobard, 1827, p. 48, cited in Charle, *Le siècle de la presse*, p. 24.
65. For Bébian, subscriber satisfaction was clearly an important consideration.

compared to a daily newspaper.[66] The print run entailed production and distribution costs (proportional to the quantity): the subscription cost does not seem very high, moreover, compared to a daily newspaper[67]… It is impossible to establish the precise number of readers, but the potential audience was relatively limited, given the many constraints,[68] even if one includes the secondary readership or those who borrowed the journal from the *cabinets de lecture* reading rooms.

---

66. Auguste Bébian, publishing prospectus, *Journal de l'instruction des sourds-muets et des aveugles*, 1826, p. 2, Annex 9.
 He nonetheless mentions readers who are "foreign teachers" ("*He* [the editor] *will make every effort to prove worthy of the encouragements he has received, whether from the parents* of *deaf-mutes, or from French and foreign teachers)*", which suggests that the circulation was not as limited as it might seem.
 Fredrik Nordin's account lends credence to the idea of a network (see note 103, Ch. 2).
67. The price of the subscription to the journal was 24 francs for one year or twelve issues in Paris (about 92 euros at 2013 rates) and 26 francs in the overseas departments (about €100). The historian Gilles Feyel estimates at 80 francs a year (about €307) the cost of a subscription to a daily newspaper ("*which represents 421 hours' wages for a provincial worker*"). Gilles Feyel, *La presse en France des origines à 1944*, Paris: Ellipses, 1999, p. 67.
 The transport time, and thus the distribution time, was a significant obstacle: 18 hours from Paris to Le Havre, 20 for Lille, 40 for Nantes, 49 for Strasbourg, 55 for Lyon, 60 for Bordeaux and Brest, 80 for Toulouse…
 The production time was also considerable, due to the printing technology. Koenig's mechanical press, invented at the beginning of the 19th century, was not adopted by the major Parisian newspapers until the late 1820s. This made it possible to print 15,000 four-page copies in one run (real progress indeed, but soon to prove insufficient). Moreover, before the invention of stereotyping (also in 1820), the typesetting of a journal could not be transposed from one press to another for reproduction.
 Charle, *Le siècle de la presse*, p. 29.
68. In 1832, 53% of the population was illiterate and most of the people in France spoke regional dialects, or languages other than French, or were simply too poor. "*For the most part, the rural classes were practically excluded from the readership by these social and cultural obstacles, made worse by financial barriers. And yet these categories made up 80% of the French population!*" (Christophe Charle, *Histoire sociale de la France au XIXᵉ siècle*, Paris: Seuil, 1991, Ch. 1).

It appears, from the second prospectus, that five issues of the journal came out, from August to December 1826, before the publication was suspended for several months. The first issued is dated August 1826, but the following issues are undated. The sixth issue, which should, according to the journal's intended monthly periodicity,[69] be that of January 1827, contains a letter dated February 23, 1827, meaning that it was published at best in March, or even in April. Likewise the next issue, (which should have been February's) relates a distribution of prizes on August 14, 1827, and was therefore published in September at the earliest… The average rhythm of publication is closer to one issue every two months, with a total of eight issues spread out over seventeen months: the date of the final issue is not known with any accuracy. In his prospectus, Bébian reassures the readers:[70]

> *"He* (the editor) *has taken steps to ensure that there shall be no further interruptions to this publication."*

However, the journal was published for only two years, from 1826 to 1827, to the dismay of Ferdinand Berthier:[71]

> "[…] *And yet there had been talk of uniting it with the* Journal de l'instruction publique,[72] *because, the founder said, such a merger might*

69. "*He* [the editor] *had only wished to receive subscriptions for six issues*", writes Bébian in the *nota bene*.
70. "*This Journal, bringing out a 40- to 60-page issue every month…*" Auguste Bébian, publishing prospectus, *Journal de l'instruction des sourds-muets et des aveugles*, 1826, p. 2. Volume-wise, it lived up to its promises: Issue 7 is even 65 pages long (compared to an average of 55, see Annex 9).
71. Berthier, *Notice*, p. 18.
72. The *Journal de l'instruction publique* ([printed text] - 1827-1828 (I-VII) [?] - Paris: [s.n.?] - In-8. *http://catalogue.bnf.fr/ark:/12148/cb32797789x/ISBD),* in which Bébian published two articles in 1828, had been founded the previous year by a "society of educators and men of letters " and was published for only two years. It ceased publication in the same the year as the creation of the Ministry of Public Instruction (which did not become the Ministry of National Education until 1932).

widen the circle of too narrow a specialty, and succeed in attracting general attention, which could then be brought to bear upon the very particular object of the former publication."

It was perhaps with this aim of expanding the readership that Bébian, the journal's editor, recruited Pierre-Armand Dufau, a teacher of blind children. Reservations about the role of the board of governors probably guided his choice towards this person in particular.[73] For the editor, it was essential to bring deaf and blind people together, and was a widespread practice, notably in Germany, in the hope of enriching their respective educational experiences:[74]

"There has been much discussion, in Germany, of bringing the Deaf-Mute and the Blind together within the same institution, and this practice

---

Bébian's two contributions were: "De l'enseignement des sourds-muets" (*Journal de l'instruction publique*, 1828, 70-79(a)) (pages 74 to 79 reprise in full his article of August 1826 in the first issue of the *Journal de l'instruction des sourds-muets et des aveugles* entitled "Observations préliminaires") and "Opérations intellectuelles du sourd-muet" (*Journal de l'instruction publique,* 1828, pp. 242-255).

73. Who expressed his pleasure: "*As for myself, whom you have chosen henceforth to speak about one of the two classes for which your work is intended, I am honored by this choice* […]. "Bébian, *Journal de l'instruction*, n° 1, vol. I, p. 35.
Pierre-Armand Dufau, appointed to teach blind children in 1815, took over from Dr. Pignier as principal of the Institut des jeunes aveugles in 1840, with a view to re-establishing government control over the institutions for the Deaf and the Blind, an initiative made concrete by the ordinance of 1841, which set up a consultative committee in place of the board of governors and gave more power to the principals. Dufau did not hide his satisfaction: "*The institution had been managed* [until 1841] *by a board of governors consisting mainly of high-ranking civil servants, who, absorbed by their functions, had little time to devote to this administrative task; in practice, the entire burden rested on the principal, although the latter had no management responsibility* […] *Since 1841, the Institution has been administered by a managing principal, assisted by a consultative committee, which simply issues its opinion on the actions of the principal* […]. P.-A. Dufau, *Des Aveugles,* pp. 225-226, cited by Buton, *op. cit.*, p. 151. This appointment also corresponds to a political decision: "*Dufau presents himself as a liberal,*" *Ibid.*, p. 152.

74. Auguste Bébian, publishing prospectus, *Journal de l'instruction des sourds-muets et des aveugles*, 1826.

was even adopted in Paris for a while.[75] *The idea was no doubt inspired by charitable forethought, seeking to prepare some future consolation and means of communication for Deaf-Mutes who might come to lose their sight; a dreadful misfortune of which we have several examples. For this reason we thought we should include in this journal articles on the instruction of the blind and on the main establishments devoted to these unfortunates.* [...] *From this rapprochement between two kinds of teaching intended to relieve such cruel infirmities, there might perhaps emerge some beneficial indicators for improving one or the other affliction* [...]"

The prospectus – undated,[76] but the date can be estimated at 1826 – defines the content of this review, intended as a forum for the exchange of opinions and methods relating to the instruction of deaf people:[77]

"This Journal, bringing out a 40- to 60-page issue every month, contains: 1° The observations we have made during years of practice, or which have been communicated to us by parents or teachers, on the moral and intellectual condition of the Deaf-Mute prior to their instruction, on the development of their faculties, their ideas, their language and their education;

75. For three years, 1791 to 1794, i.e. from the date the INSMP was founded by decree of the Constituent Assembly (July 21 - September 28, 1791) to its installation at the site of the Saint-Magloire Seminary, Abbé de l'Épée's school for the Deaf and Valentin Haüy's school for the Blind existed side by side at the Convent of the Célestins. Buton, *L'administration des faveurs*, p. 29.
76. *"The first issue will be published in August"*, announces the *publishing prospectus*, p. 2, from which we can infer that it was written during the same calendar year, 1826.
77. The *Circulars* issued by the Chairman of the Board of Governors of the INSMP, Baron Degérando, beginning in the following year (from 1827 to 1836, p. 52) set themselves this precise goal of collecting information or questions about their Deaf pupils. *Première circulaire de l'Institut royal des sourds-muets, à toutes les institutions de sourds-muets d'Europe et d'Amérique*, Imprimerie royal, 1827, p. 4.

2° A comparative examination of the various methods hitherto employed for the instruction of deaf students, and an analysis of the French and foreign works dealing with this matter;
3° An historic record of all the Deaf-Mute schools of which we are aware, and the best-known teachers;
4° An exposé on the approaches that appear to be the simplest and most beneficial in the practice of teaching.
Finally, we shall overlook nothing that relates to this subject, and which touches upon the most interesting questions of philosophy, morals and even legislation.
We welcome any questions that may be addressed to us, whether by parents or by teachers. We shall present the differing opinions impartially; free discussion of the various approaches will determine the choice of the best method, which may be further enriched by all the benefits that the others have to offer."

With the exception of the observations "*communicated to us by parents or teachers, on the moral and intellectual condition of the Deaf-Mute prior to their instruction, on the development of their faculties, their ideas, their language and their education*", all of these themes were indeed addressed. The 6th issue is the only one to reproduce a "*letter from a mother on the education of her son*",[78] in many ways a progress report after eight years of schooling at the Institute.

78. Bébian had known this mother and her son, Gonzalve, for eight years (as he himself says on page 307): he recounts their arrival at the INSMP when "*I was still directing studies at the Royal Institution in Paris*". The child was seven or eight years old at the time, and the teacher initially advised the mother to take charge of her son's education herself "*being fearful of the consequences, for him, of a gathering of children whose primary education was generally so unlike the one he had received*" (out of a hundred children, he explains a in footnote, only "*a dozen*" paid for their keep; the others were admitted free of charge on presentation of a "certificate of indigence", and had been left to look after themselves before entering the INSMP at the late age of "*12, 14 and 16 years; all too often they manifest depraved habits* [...] *During the first years of their stay at the Institution, no effort is made to exert any moral influence upon them.*" *Journal de l'instruction des sourds-muets et des aveugles*, n° 6, vol. I, pp. 305-306.

The "Report on the Imperial Institute for the Deaf at Saint Petersburg"[79] or the one about the institutions in the United States[80] attest to communication between the different schools, which supports the notion of the network mentioned earlier. There is cause, however, to be doubtful about the goal of setting up a "meeting-place" for the teachers, "*where they can discuss their observations and the results of their work*" – the main motivation behind the creation of the journal – since most of the articles were written by Bébian himself.[81]

3. … to the extinguishing of the beacon[82]

Auguste Bébian's final publication, his *Examen critique* (*Critical appraisal of the new organization of teaching at the Royal Institution for Deaf-Mutes in Paris),* came out in 1834, a few months before his departure, but was written the year before, during his convalescence.[83] In it, he delivers a detailed critical analysis of the administrative and pedagogical changes at the INSMP.[84] It is a bitter but clear-sighted and cogently argued piece. He comments, at times ironically, on

---

79. *Ibid.*, n° 2, vol. I, p. 91.

80. *Ibid.*, n° 6, vol. I, p. 350.

81. A summary of the eight issues of the *Journal de l'instruction des sourds-muets et des aveugles can be found* in Annex 9.

82. "*The beacon has gone out,*" observed Alphonse Esquiros in 1847 (Esquiros, Paris, vol. 2, p. 443).

83. As we saw earlier, it was probably this same illness that forced him to leave Rouen: "*This appraisal, addressed to the minister* […] *in the first days of my convalescence, after a cruel and lengthy illness that has forced me to give up my teaching work for some time, and perhaps for a very long time,*" Bébian, *Examen critique*, p. 7.

84. The "official" formal texts of the new organization seek to impose the idea that the Paris Institution is superior to the other French establishments, by invoking the memory of Abbé de l'Épée, whereas in most cases they simply reflect the pedagogical experiments and convictions of the INSMP, as assessed by the administrators of the selfsame school!
The very term *Circular* echoes "*the overarching position that its directors want to see it* [the INSMP] *occupy* […], *the* Circulars *are just one example of the efforts by which the Institutions attempt to set themselves up as central public authorities in their respective fields of activity,*" Buton, *L'administration des faveurs*, p. 138.

the 3rd Circular of the INSMP,[85] starting out from the damning observation, which he repeats several times, that "*the Institution has no methods.*"[86] The observation that the institution was losing its way had already been made by Bébian in 1832, when the *Third Circular* was issued, but it was not until one year later that he wrote this reply, addressed (he claimed) to the minister, before making it public.

Désiré Ordinaire, appointed as principal in 1831,[87] and consequently placed in charge of implementing the program defined by the Circular, is, writes Bébian, "merely the agent" of the board of governors, in which all the real power resides.[88] Bébian no doubt recalled with resentment his erstwhile sudden removal and was keen

85. For example, he describes the introduction of the arithmometer as a "sort of plaything", that could never constitute "*an improvement, even if it were a game of Ludo, refined into a game of mythology, chronology or history. Moreover,* the arithmometer, *from which some benefit could surely have been derived, was no sooner adopted than it was abandoned, in keeping with the tradition of the Royal Institute. It shared the fate of almost all the administration's designs.*" Or, on the reintroduction of articulation and lip-reading lessons: "*Let us not forget that lessons must now be given by speech. What an ingenious idea, to appoint deaf-mute monitors to correct errors of articulation!* " Bébian, *Examen critique,* note 1, p. 29, p. 49.
86. *Ibid.*, p. 63.
87. Désiré Ordinaire was the scion of a well-to-do family, a doctor of medicine and professor of natural history at the faculty of sciences at Besançon, becoming Rector of the Academy of Besançon in 1821, and of Strasbourg three years later. His father was a lawyer at the parliament of Besançon, and later mayor of the town and chairman of the General Council of Doubs. His uncle was the naturalist Claude-Nicolas Ordinaire (1736-1808), known for his study of the volcanoes of Auvergne (*Histoire naturelles des volcans : comprenant les volcans sous-marins, ceux de boue, et autres phénomènes analogues*, Levrault frères, 1802) and for recording the local consequences of the 1789 Revolution (hand-written notes published in book form in 1989: *Le Puy-de-Dôme au soir de la Révolution*, Clermont-Ferrand: Presses Fac de droit, 1989). His brother Jean-Jacques (1770-1843) invented a system for teaching ancient languages (*Méthode pour l'enseignement des langues*, Paris, 1821) and subsequently became a member of the Conseil de perfectionnement of the INSMP in Paris, set up by his brother. His son Édouard kept up the family tradition of occupying positions of responsibility, becoming a parliamentary deputy under the Second Empire and later Prefect of Doubs.
88. Bébian, *Examen critique,* p. 61.

to avoid repeating the steps that led to his dismissal in 1821.[89] Article by article (the *Third Circular* has thirty articles, only two of which were actually applied),[90] Bébian picks the texts apart, examining them from every angle, displaying a solid knowledge of the INSMP in the process, even seven years after his dismissal; more detailed, indeed, than that of the articles' authors! On Article 25, for example (relating to educational walks in the grounds of the Institute, which no longer had the enjoyment of its garden, as it was rented out to a florist) or Article 7 (banning Abbé de l'Épee's "methodical signs" from the establishment, which, Bébian tells us, had fallen out of use more than ten years earlier and even then, "*the Principal would not be able to identify them, any more than could any of the administrators.*")[91] But what he denounces above all is the teaching methods: lip-reading and artificial articulation are advocated, whereas, he claims, half the

---

89. [...] "*Convinced that experience alone, and harsh experience at that, could enlighten the blind authors of such a plan, I kept my silence, being persuaded moreover that such a flawed system bore within it the germ of its own demise, and that time would be swift in serving justice upon it.*
A year has passed on this plan, and of the thirty articles in the decree, only two have survived. Who would believe that the decree was not dead and forgotten? And yet it is not so [...] *it is becoming urgent to signal this blindness; urgent and necessary, in order to prevent its consequences, not perhaps in the Royal Institution*, where my voice will not be heard, *but in the other institutions that persist in imitating the errors of the Grande École...*" Bébian, *Examen critique*, p. 9.
90. Articles 11 and 30. Article 11 relates to the organization of teaching ("*Each of the teachers of the Royal Institute shall, in turn, be tasked with receiving the newly arrived class of pupils. He shall lead them, without interruption, through to the last term of instruction.* Each teacher *shall thus dispense the full course of teaching for the same pupils. If, however, at some point, a pupil were identified as too weak to follow the same course as his classmates, he may, with the authorization of the principal, be returned to the previous course.*" Bébian points out that "*by 'each of the teachers', is meant 'except the deaf-mute ones'.*" Article 30 is purely formal ("*This deliberation document shall be addressed to the Secretary of State for the Department of Trade and Public Works, and transmitted by the principal of the Royal Institute to all the teachers*").
91. Bébian, Examen critique, pp. 38 and 49. The "transmission" system attributed a class to one teacher for a year, whereas the "rotation" system imposed the same teacher throughout a student's schooling, i.e. 6 or 7 years, depending on the period.

pupils have no aptitude for articulation and nine tenths will never be able to lip-read well enough to be educated by this method.[92] It amounts to a de facto prohibition of "mime language", and he is revolted by its blatant hypocrisy:[93]

> *"Thus when the Administration sought to forbid deaf-mutes from using mime language, either between themselves or with other people, it was careful not to extend this prohibition to the public exercises, as one might as well have closed the assembly room* [...] *What most pains the heart, is to see these poor guileless children coming onto a kind of stage to perform, for the amusement of the spectators, a few little exercises rehearsed several days in advance, and responding to supposedly improvised questions with answers prepared by their supervisors, and carefully learned by heart."*

He rails against the uselessness and "*futility of these pompous spectacles*". But it is Article 11 – ultimately the only one to be applied (Article 30 being purely formal) – that draws most of his fire: it proposes to replace the existing teaching organization, the "transmission" system, with a "rotation" system, which in effect excludes Deaf teachers, who cannot teach articulation![94] He decries this exclusion, pointing out that this is not the first attempt:[95]

> *"Away with it! Away with this vulgar common-sense method which, to teach deaf-mutes, employs their natural language, and supposes that it is appropriate for the teacher to be understood by his pupils.*

---

92. Article 8 of the Third Circular of the INSMP stipulates that "*pupils shall be taught articulation and the art of lip-reading by their respective teachers, assisted by the study supervisors and trainee teachers.*" Bébian, *Examen critique*, p. 35.
93. *Ibid.*, pp. 63-64.
94. *Ibid.*, p. 7.
95. Article 2 of the Second Circular three years earlier (1829) stipulated that "*the administration has appointed a deaf-mute tutor to assist the hearing-speaking teacher in each class,*" even if this was not followed through in practice, the Minister of the Interior "*ordered that existing entitlements be respected,*" Bébian tells us. *Ibid.*, p. 39.

And away with you, you deaf-mute teachers… how wrong we were to believe that you could instruct your brothers, and guide them along the path that you yourselves had traveled with success. In vain do you invoke your long-standing qualifications, your length of service. Why should this decree that tramples on the principles of reason respect the rights and titles of a few obscure – and deaf-mute – teachers?"

Not that, in Bébian's eyes, speech or articulation has no place; it is even necessary, and he defends its usefulness.[96] However, he writes:[97]

"Of the forty-five pupils in my class, when I was at the Royal Institution, three were deaf-mutes who were so fortunately endowed in this respect that, after returning to their families, it took them but a few months to learn to speak, and to speak far better than pupils who had been taking lessons in articulation at the Royal Institution for four years. To conclude, from these exceptional examples, that one can teach speech simultaneously to all the pupils of a populous institution, and even use speech as the principal medium of instruction, is excessively ignorant, and experience will soon confound such blind presumption."

He decries "*the continual and deplorable tendency of the board of governors to absorb everything into its own attributions,"*[98] which in his view was responsible for the decline of the Paris Institution: while France, with the establishment inherited from Abbé de l'Épée, was once at the forefront of the education of deaf children, this

96. "*Nobody in France today has, if I may say so myself, contributed more than I have to spreading the teaching of speech to deaf-mutes*" but "[…] *it is absurd, ridiculous, tyrannical, to seek to base the teaching of deaf-mutes on speech; to directly choose the faculty that they are lacking as the principal instrument of their instruction; a faculty that can artificially be restored to only half of them, and always incompletely.*" And he cites the Institution's founder, Abbé de l'Épée, to show that he shares his way of thinking: "*Teaching deaf-mutes to speak is not a task that demands great talent; it merely requires much patience on the part of the teacher, and also much patience and perseverance on the part of the pupil.*" *Ibid.*, p. 16.

97. *Ibid.*, p. 16.

98. *Ibid.*, p. 32.

was no longer the case, due – he writes frankly – to the arbitrary and incoherent decisions of the board of governors.[99] Likewise, he underlines the contradictions of the Circular: the prohibition of methodical signs, for example, although they were no longer in use by then. *"And with what should we substitute them? And how then do we guarantee the independence of the Rotation?"*[100]

This detailed examination leads him to conclude, provocatively, that one may as well dissolve the INSMP *"and redistribute the pupils into boarding schools for speaking children,"* as it is inevitable that Deaf pupils will communicate with each other in sign language, which the Circular precisely aims to eradicate.[101]

99. More than fifteen years after this warning signal, Abbot Darras of Soissons comes to the same conclusion: *"France lags far behind,"* he writes in 1853, in the journal of which he was the editor, *Le Bienfaiteur* (1853, p. 47).
100. *Ibid.,* p. 50. On the rotation system, see Note 91.
101. *Ibid.,* pp. 53-54.

Chapter 5
Bébian the pedagogue: a pioneering educational thinker

With Auguste Bébian, didactic observation and reflection took concrete form. For Bébian the pedagogue, the acquisition of reading and writing was of key importance for Deaf students, as we saw earlier, and though only 56% of the French population could read and write at that time,[1] he described it as a "vital necessity" for deaf people![2] And as a potential first step towards lip-reading:[3]

> *"To read on people's lips, they must know how to read on paper. When they can express their thoughts in writing, they will no longer be deaf or mute to those who can read and write; reading will open up to them all the treasures of human knowledge that are locked away in books."*

But how might the speakers of a visual language (in the sense that it is unwritten) "express their thoughts in writing" without going through French; for deaf people, a second language? Bébian sought, therefore, to begin by establishing a system of notation for sign language, not to institute a form of writing that could be used in place of French, but to enable what he saw as an essential process, as a stepping-stone towards initiation into the French language.

---

1. Bernard Variot, *Approche de quelques aspects de la vie sociale des sourds-muets et de leur instruction au milieu du* XIX*e siècle, vus au travers de* L'Impartial, *journal des sourds-muets (1856-1859)*, thesis for the CAPINJS qualification (to teach deaf children), 1980, p. 154.
2. *Ibid.*
3. Auguste Bébian, *Manuel d'enseignement pratique des sourds-muets*, vol. II, Paris: Méquignon l'Aîné, 1827, p. 13.

1. The writing of sign language

1.1 A foundational concept, reflecting a certain linguistic awareness…

Auguste Bébian's richest and most pioneering contribution, save perhaps for his *Manual for Practical Instruction*, was published in 1825 in the work entitled *Mimography: An Essay on the Writing of Sign in order to Standardize the Language of the Deaf.*[4] As the title suggests, the essay seeks to unify the "action language" used by Deaf people. This could be interpreted as an attempt to codify or "normalize" it, which might seem oddly in contradiction with Bébian's stated goal of ridding sign language of any intermediate coding system such as the "methodical signs" or, as we will see later, the spelling out of letters when learning to read. The sole purpose of this classification, however, as the subtitle of the work indicates, is to "standardize" – to regulate, but not to impose a rule or overarching norm dividing what is valid from what is not[5] – so that this "action language" can exist independently from the French language.[6] His focus on the linguistic dimension of the signs used by deaf people demonstrates precisely that he does not see them as a formal code. This is the

4. Auguste Bébian, *Mimographie ou Essai d'écriture mimique, propre à régulariser le langage des sourds-muets*, Paris: Louis Colas, 1825; reprinted in full by Marc Renard, *Écrire les Signes*, Les-Essarts-le-Roi: Éditions du Fox, 2004 and 2014.

5. Quite the contrary: "If *this sign is correct, if it is the faithful expression of the idea, it will be adopted in every school. If it is inexact, it will provoke discussion, which will enlighten people's minds and lead to a correction. The language will be perfected, will become fixed, and will be the same in every school* […]." Bébian, *Mimographie*, p. 11.

6. This, indeed, is the first benefit he ascribes to adopting *mimography*: the "*establishment of a regular and uniform system of signs that would bring fixity to this language hitherto left to the mercy of systems, whims and ignorance (the two other benefits concern the development of mime language – The formation of a mime-language vocabulary, as useful to the master as to the pupil: one would find the mime-signs to express ideas, the other the meaning of the words"* – and the keeping of records – "*A reliable way for the deaf-mute to retain knowledge acquired, and to develop it through study* ". Bébian, *Mimographie*, p. 43.

practical illustration of the argument developed eight years earlier in his first book, *Essay on the Deaf and Natural Language:*[7]

> "[...] *The thought necessarily precedes, in the mind, whichever signs are destined to express it; the word in itself bears no relation to the idea."*

This is also a response to the question of the intelligibility of signs, clearly formulated by Baron de Gérando two years later, and no doubt shared by many others; a question that casts doubt on their actual utility:[8]

> *"We are surprised to find that pupils, and even teachers, who belong to different schools, but schools founded on the use of the reduced pantomime, are quite unable to understand one another when they meet, because their systems of mime-signs bear no similarity: we are surprised to find that people who habitually frequent the deaf-mutes in our institutions, who often participate in their exercises, are nonetheless incapable, even after several years, to fix in their memory or perform any of these signs, so varied, rapid and fleeting is their execution* [...] *The utility of this system* [...] *depends on knowing just how helpful, in the education of the deaf-mute, the use of mime language really is, when taken to its highest degree of development; a grave, fundamental, question – currently controversial, as yet undecided, and which we shall put aside for later discussion."*

All of this lies behind Bébian's motivation to "*explore whether it might not be possible to depict gestures and commit them to paper, just as we commit speech,"*[9] for two essential reasons. Firstly, for purely pedagogical reasons, which reflect a constant concern with

7. Auguste Bébian, *Essai sur les sourds-muets et sur le langage naturel ou introduction à une classification naturelle des idées avec leurs signes propres*, Paris: J.-G. Dentu, 1817, p. 23.
8. Jean-Marie de Gérando, *De l'éducation des Sourds-Muets de naissance*, Paris: Méquignon-l'Ainé père, 1827, vol. II, pp. 265-266 and 269.
9. Auguste Bébian, *Examen critique de la nouvelle organisation de l'enseignement dans l'Institution royale des sourds-muets de Paris*, Paris: Treuttel & Wurtz, 1834, p. 29.

efficient learning, in which – as Bébian reminds us – autonomy is key. Starting out from the observation that "*the only dictionary of the deaf-mute is his teacher,*"[10] he draws the analogy with a hearing child studying Latin and who "*has only to open his dictionary in order to find, from the French word, the Latin word he needs*". Such a dictionary is essential for respecting the syntax of sign language, which has "*a construction which is peculiar to itself, or rather which is peculiar to the mind*":[11]

> *"From this we perceive that the signs of the deaf-mute must be strung together in an order very different from the construction of our own languages, and particularly from the construction of French, which obeys the reciprocal influence of words far more than the relationships between ideas, and follows less the workings of the mind than it does the rules of grammar."*

This comparison shows that he places the education of Deaf students on the same level as that of hearing students, and that his efforts strive towards this equality. For him, this writing of signs is essential, specifically because personal effort is more propitious for the acquisition of knowledge:[12]

> *"The mind is fortified; like the body, it grows in vigor only by exercising its strength. The progress that we make, the knowledge we acquire, is the product of our efforts; we come to look upon it as our property, as a more personal good, which further flatters our self-esteem, making it all the dearer to us."*

His argument also underlines the twofold advantage of this undertaking:

---

10. *Ibid.*, p. 39.
11. Auguste Bébian, *Journal de l'instruction des sourds-muets et des aveugles*, 1826, p. 25.
12. Bébian, *Examen critique*, p. 41.

> *"The teacher, meanwhile, no longer suffers the tedium of ceaselessly going back over the same words."*

The second driver of this motivation is more linguistic in nature, and stems from an observation: sign language has "become corrupted instead of being perfected." And this despite the fact that:[13]

> *"It is of primordial importance that, as a tool of thought, it should be fixed, "regularized"* [...] *it has sometimes been disfigured to the point of unintelligibility. This is what we saw happen when attempts were made to form signs based on the composition and etymology of French words."*[14]

In 1825 therefore, when this work was published, Bébian had been thinking for at least eight years about the best way to write a three-dimensional language in a two-dimensional medium. A difficult challenge, but a pre-condition, as he saw it, for the improvement of teaching techniques:[15]

> *"The education of the deaf-mute will not attain perfection until we have composed a mime-vocabulary sufficiently faithful to serve as a regulator for the language of gestures."*

With the publication of *Mimography*, Bébian demonstrates that this *sine qua non* condition is not utopian and that this form of writing is possible. He is well aware, however, that the task is still far from complete, and presents himself humbly as a mere initiator:[16]

---

13. *Ibid.*, pp. 45 and 47.
14. An allusion to methodical signs. He criticizes "*such a frivolous artifice*" as initialization: "*The correctness of signs has even sometimes counted for so little, that some have been retained whose value depends on the shape of the fingers indicating the initial letter of the word they are supposed to represent, such as* Vin, Tante, Oncle, Durant, Pendant, Jeu, *etc., acting as a reminder of the independence of sign language.*"
15. Bébian, *Examen critique*, p. 7.
16. *Ibid.*

> *"If it is felt that I have not entirely succeeded, I believe that I have at least done enough to establish definitively that the depiction of action language is not a chimerical undertaking. I have traced out the path; someone else – more gifted or with more support than I – will reach the goal."*

The November 25, 1825 issue of the national newspaper *Le Constitutionnel* hails *Mimography* as an "ingenious invention" and salutes the superiority of its author's talents: *"all the more honorable in that he has long been a stranger to the institution, and that, working in the background, he has always been less zealous to seek publicity than to make himself useful to the deaf-mute, all of whom are imbued with respect and gratitude toward him."*[17] Innovative as it was, this first notation of sign language in history was not destined for short- or medium-term posterity, but for a much longer timeframe: over a century later, it more or less directly influenced the American linguist William Stokoe.[18] However, as Christian Cuxac notes, *"the comparison between the two systems* [...] *ceases when it comes to their goals"*:[19]

> *"For Bébian, it was about transferring signs onto a stable medium by means of writing* [...] *The goal for Stokoe was altogether different: firstly because, being aware of Bébian's system, he knew that transcribing a sign language was – approximately and at least in part – possible."*

17. *Le Constitutionnel, Journal du commerce politique et littéraire*, n° 329, November 25, 1825, p. 3.
18. The American linguist William Stokoe was the first academic to publish, in the 20th century, an in-depth analysis that established the linguistic nature of American Sign Language (ASL). In *Sign Language Structure: An Outline of the Visual Communication Systems of the American Deaf*, New-York, University of Buffalo, 1960, he adopts the logic of structural linguistics to demonstrate that ASL is characterized by the phenomenon of double articulation and thus satisfies the definition of a structured linguistic system, a language in its own right.
19. Christian Cuxac, "La *Mimographie* de Bébian : finalité et destin d'une écriture de la LSF", *Surdités* n° 5-6, Paris: Gestes, 2004, p. 86.

As the linguist Brigitte Garcia also underlines,[20] "*Stokoe's initiative, some hundred thirty years later, emerged in a radically different epistemological context: modern linguistics had been founded.*" At the risk of sounding repetitive, it should be remembered that Bébian's objective is purely pedagogical and belongs within the educational framework that he advocates.[21] If he has recourse to linguistics, it is for this purpose, and from the angle of contrastive linguistics (an anachronistic term, as the field did not yet exist).[22] His aim is not to design a written communication system, but simply to transcribe signs, so that pupils can appropriate the written French language by relating it to their day-to-day language, and analyzing it themselves, with guidance from their teachers.[23] This notation only transcribes the sign, not the idea, but "*this improvement would be achieved by means of a few ideographic signs*".[24] Access to meaning is facilitated, to the detriment of an artificial and mechanical style of learning. The choice is best explained by Bébian himself:[25]

> *"An example will serve to convey my thoughts. Suppose the teacher wants to dictate these words to the deaf-mute: 'Look upwards with intense pleasure'* [...]. *This phrase could be rendered by a single sign. One can hardly*

---

20. Brigitte Garcia, *Sourds, surdité, langue(s) des signes et épistémologie des sciences du langage. Problématiques de la scripturisation et modélisation des bas niveaux en Langue des signes française* (LSF), Dossier presented for the research supervision diploma (HDR), Université Paris VIII, 2010, p. 52.
21. "*So we have, in very little time, reached the point towards which all the initial efforts of the teacher must strive* [...] *One must constantly place before* [the pupil], *and have him trace out with his hand, the words that we want to fix in his memory* [...] [Sign language] *will be the main instrument of his instruction.*" *Journal de l'instruction des sourds-muets et des aveugles*, vol. I, pp. 218-219.
22. Garcia, *Sourds, surdité*, p. 50.
23. " [...] *relations between ideas, made more palpable through the analogy of signs, may give rise to interesting and unexpected insights. I must point out that I in no way claim to have composed a writing system that immediately depicts ideas. A purely ideographic writing system* [...] *would not have served my goal, which is to enable deaf-mutes to apprehend the values of words by means of signs that are familiar to them.*" Bébian, *Examen critique*, pp. 9-10.
24. *Ibid.*, p. 10.
25. Bébian, *Mimographie*, pp. 27-29.

expect the deaf-mute himself to decompose this sign – which is, for him, the expression of a single idea – and untangle its elements… It is therefore up to the teacher to direct him […]. [The teacher] *wants the pupil to understand everything he reads and everything he writes. The surest way to bring him to this point is to make use of signs that are familiar to him, so that he can discover, in the very idea to be expressed, the reason for all the words that we employ to render that idea in our language.*
That is the principle; its application is not always easy. The various elements of an idea are sometimes so closely bound together in sign language that it is difficult to isolate them and assign the corresponding French word to each. To go no further than the above example, how are we to separate the gaze from its direction? How are we to show the expression of the organ, without showing the organ? Mimography could be of great utility here; without destroying the unity of the sign, it reveals distinctly all of its elements, which we must be able to recognize if we are to apply the words that will translate them."

While *Mimography* was the first attempt in history to write down a sign language, earlier attempts had been made to transcribe body movements, notably in 1700 by the choreographer Raoul Feuillet, who *"with the aim of making his compositions easier to memorize, had created a system for transcribing entire dances with complex movements, and it is not impossible that Bébian had heard about this."*[26] On the American continent, William Dunbar also reported, in 1804, on the use of sign language observed four years earlier among Native Americans to the west of the Mississippi, and their written description, which he sought to compare with Chinese writing.[27]

26. The publication of *Chorégraphie, ou l'art de décrire la danse par caractères, figures et signes démonstratifs* by Raoul-Auger Feuillet (1660-1710) had a considerable and long-lasting impact.
Cuxac, *Mimographie*, p. 85.

27. Letter from W. Dunbar to T. Jefferson, "On the Language of Signs among certain North American Indians", *American Philosophical Transactions*, Vol. VI, Part.1, 1804, cited in Sophie Dalle-Nazébi, *Chercheurs, Sourds et langues des signes. Le travail d'un objet et de repères linguistiques en France du XVIIe au XXIe siècle*, doctoral thesis, Université Toulouse II – Le Mirail, 2006, pp. 132-133.

The principle of *Mimography* is a simple one: to draw up a classification of gestures and organize a system rationally, since:[28]

> *"...it is known that the perfection of linguistic signs exerts great influence over the formation of ideas, and even over the development of intelligence; and it is not too presumptuous to claim that a regular system of signs based on nature would cut the task of the teacher – and the work of the pupils – in half."*

This determination to break things down and commit them to paper, to *"produce an itemized list wherein words and signs would be set out methodically in the order in which our ideas are generated,"*[29] reflects the concept according to which all human creations are either artificial or merely a rediscovery of what already exists in nature. This determination is found in other fields, such as chemistry: the first classification tests were being conducted at the same period.[30] But the most direct influence on Bébian probably came from the universal system for the notation of ideas devised and published in 1797[31] by Joseph de Maimieux,[32] a former major in the German Army and a friend of Sicard: in a foreword to de Maimieux' first book, the abbot evokes *"the universality of ideas."*[33]

---

28. Bébian, *Mimographie*, pp. 10-11.
29. Bébian, *Essai sur les sourds-muets*, p. 43.
30. In 1817, over half a century before the "periodic table of the elements", drawn up in 1869 by the Russian chemist Dmitri Mendeleyev, the German chemist Johann Döbereiner had succeeded in establishing a relationship between the atomic mass of certain elements and their properties. This led him to observe similarities between elements grouped into threes, which he called "triads": these early concepts were later developed by others (Chancourtois and Newlands, or Meyer).
31. Joseph de Maimieux, *Pasigraphie ou Premiers éléments du nouvel art-science, d'écrire et d'imprimer en une langue, de manière à être lu et entendu dans toute autre langue sans traduction*, Paris, 1797; he expounded upon this first work eleven years later in *Pasigraphie et pasilalie*, Paris, An VIII, and in *Carte générale pasigraphique* (1808).
32. De Maimieux was at that time President of the *Société des Observateurs de l'Homme*, founded in 1800.
33. *"This grand nomenclature is, for the practical metaphysicist, the most daring, the most stimulating and the most necessary undertaking, seeking as it does to shape*

1.2 …and a detailed analysis of sign language

In three plates, Bébian proposes a way of breaking down signs. The first focuses solely on movement:

Figure 1: Characters indicating movement (*Mimography*)

Caractères indicatifs du mouvement. P. I.

Mouvement — A Simples, B Courbes, C Circulaires, D Obliques.

De gauche à droite …… De gauche à droite et en arrière …… et en avant
De droite à gauche …… De droite à gauche et en arrière …… et en avant
De bas en haut …… De bas en haut et à droite …… et à gauche
De haut en bas …… De haut en bas et à gauche …… et à droite
En avant …… En avant et en bas …… et en haut
En arrière …… En arrière et en haut …… et en bas

Mouvements de contraction …… d'extension …… propres (a) (b)
Mouvements onduleux …… serpentans …… de progression &c. …… de tremblement

Accens modificatifs du mouvement.

Ces accens se placent sur les signes du mouvement pour indiquer s'il est lent, bref, léger ou foible. Successif; vif; prolongé; fort ou pénible; multiplié.

Accens imités des caractères du mouvement et se plaçant sur le Signe de l'organe, pour en indiquer:
le côté droit; la partie Supérieure; la partie antérieure;
le côté gauche; la partie Inférieure; la partie postérieure;

Signes de position, empruntés aux caractères du mouvement et qui se placent particulièrement devant le signe de la main gauche, quand il faut indiquer sa position relativement à la main droite.

plus haut — plus bas
plus en avant — plus en arrière.
devant — derrière.
plus en avant et plus haut.
plus en avant et plus bas.
plus en arrière et plus haut.
plus en arrière et plus bas.

(composé de … et de …) devant et plus bas.
(composé de … et de …) devant et plus haut.
(composé de … et de …) derrière, et plus bas.
(composé de … et de …) derrière et plus haut.

---

a clear, simple and easily remembered system out of the universality of ideas; in it, each expression defines the others, and all of them enrich the implicit definition of each one," cited by Yves Bernard, "La Mimographie de Bébian (1789-1839). Le signe est l'ombre de l'idée", *Liaisons, Bulletin du CNFEJS* (National training center for teachers of Deaf children), 7, 1995, pp. 39-40.

The distinguishing feature of this method is its use of "common" symbols, modeled on a circle: indicates movement from left to right, and from right to left; upward and  downward. To specify whether the movement is made forward or backward, the notation is completed by the symbols or respectively.

These symbols cover the direction of the movement and its start and end points, but its trajectory may be straight, curved, circular or even oblique (slanting). Bébian therefore adds a line to these half circles, and the end of the line indicates the type of trajectory: thus, a "straight" left-to-right movement on the level is noted but the same movement may be noted ,  or depending on whether it is curved, circular or oblique. For forward and backward movements, the initial line is again extended, either straight or oblique  . The notation is further enriched if the movement is accompanied by a contraction of the hand (closed fist), or even of the eyes or of the mouth:  ; or if extended rather then contracted. Bébian also identifies what he calls *"mouvements propres"* (separate movements) which simply designate "independence" of movement, i.e. where the movement described does not entail another: for example, an arm movement that does not imply a movement of the wrist (the greeting sign).

The lower part of this first figure, entirely given over to movement, details the accents added to the above symbols to signify amplitude, slowness or speed. As with the circle, the model used as a basis for his transcription, Bébian explains his source of inspiration: *"The accent for speed is like the wings of a bird, or the head of an arrow. The accent for slowness is borrowed from the shape of the horns of an ox. The one for shortness is well-known; it is a sign of prosody. I have inverted it to indicate the opposite modification..."*[34]

While this first plate describes movement in detail, the next breaks down the position of the hand into four columns: palm forward, back of hand, sideways or oblique:

Figure 2: Characters of the hand (*Mimography*)

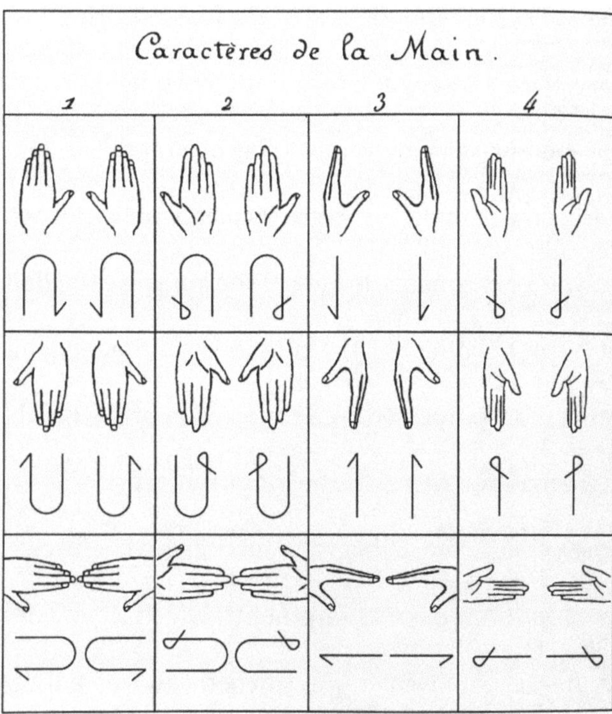

34. Bébian, *Mimographie*, (reprinted by Fox), p. 17.

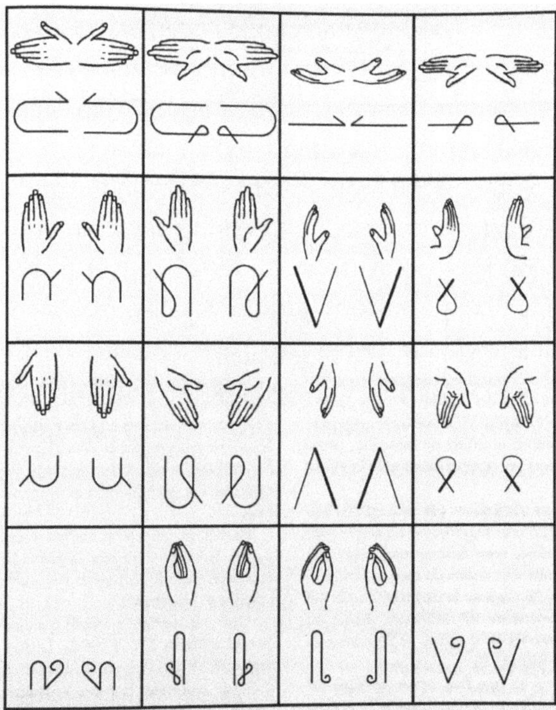

The rudimentary nature of this description, whereas Bébian recognizes the hand as the "*main instrument of mime language,*"[35] is a source of surprise for linguists:[36]

> *"Bébian's coverage of the hand is surprising in more ways than one: firstly, by the brevity of the text* [less than two pages] *devoted to characterizing this parameter. More surprising still are the illustrative plates: almost all the illustrations concern only the 'flat-hand' configuration and the various orientations it can take in space* [...] *It seems incredible that the 'royal' parameter of the linguists, the one that was the focus of attention for the American researchers, the easiest one to transcribe, because it refers to particularly stable forms, was neglected or under-evaluated to such an extent by Bébian."*

35. Bébian, *Mimographie*, (reprinted by Fox), p. 20.
36. Cuxac, *Mimographie*, p. 86.

By 1825, sign language had already been practiced collectively and intensively in the same place for more than half a century: this choice cannot therefore be justified by arguing that sign language was still only emerging… and modern linguistic research[37] on emerging or "primary" sign languages, based on linguistically isolated Deaf speakers (i.e. immersed in a hearing environment), whether adults or children, points to evidence of constituted structures and a plurality of hand configurations. It is probably not due to any lack of knowledge on Bébian's part, but rather, as the linguist Christian Cuxac suggests,[38] to a deliberate desire to distance himself from the system of methodical signs,[39] which, as we saw earlier, he held in low regard.[40] For Cuxac, this method, developed by Abbé de l'Épée, was introduced in or around 1780, some twenty years

37. Susan Goldin-Meadow, *The resilience of language: what gesture creation in deaf children can tell us about how all children learn language*. New York: NY Psychology Press, 2003; Ivani Fusellier-Souza, *Sémiogenèse des langues des signes. Étude de langues des signes primaires (ou émergentes) pratiquées par des sourds brésiliens*, doctoral thesis, Univ. Paris 8, 2004; Shun-Chiu Yau, *Création gestuelle et débuts du langage, création de langues gestuelles chez des sourds isolés*, Éditions langages croisés, Centre national de la recherche scientifique, 1992.

38. Cuxac, *Mimographie*, p. 88.

39. Abbé de l'Épée himself explains the process for constructing these methodical signs: "*We ask the deaf-mute to observe the joints of our fingers, our hands, wrist, elbow, etc., and we call them 'articles' or 'joining-words': we then write on the board that 'le, la, les, de, du, des,' link words together just as our articulations join together our bones (grammarians will forgive us if this definition does not accord with theirs); thence the movement of the right index finger extending and folding over several times to form a hook becomes the methodical sign that we give to any article. We express its gender by raising the hand to the hat for the masculine article 'le', and to the ear, reflecting the length of the hair of a person of the feminine sex, for the feminine article 'la'.*" Charles-Michel de l'Épée, *L'Art d'enseigner à parler aux sourds-muets de naissance*, Paris: J.-C. Dentu, 1820, pp. 16-17.

40. Bébian underlines the shortcomings of this system and its usage by default: "*Abbé de l'Épée must soon have realized the failings, or at least the insufficiency, of these signs, and it seems that he often corrected them with explanations or a sort of commentary in natural signs* […] *Why not go directly from the specific signs of thought to instituted language? This is no doubt what he would have done had he been more adept at the language of gestures, or even had he been better placed to appreciate its wealth and flexibility.*" *Journal de l'instruction des sourds-muets et des aveugles*, n° 3, vol. I, p. 153.

after he had started working with deaf students, and in addition to its pedagogical goals (to facilitate the acquisition of French by establishing similarities of structure with sign language), it sought to control the development of a language that was no longer "*a mere inventory of gestures grouped into a pantomime.*"[41]

The next three columns, to the right of this second plate, describe the "*characters for the various parts of the head and body,*"[42] twenty-six movements or positions are presented, such as the eyes (the gaze), the face (the nose, the ears), the torso or the legs (Figure 3), as well as the "physiognomic points", i.e. the facial expressions that accompany the signs. This precision demonstrates Bébian's detailed knowledge, as they are essential: they give nuance to utterances, coloring them with emotion, etc. (Figure 4). Thus, writes Bébian: "*We can, in this manner, write twenty-two physiognomic expressions, each of which is amenable to three nuances.*"[43] This may seem like a sizeable number, but it is in fact very small compared with modern descriptions:[44] the author himself recognizes that this is only a first draft, modestly inviting the reader to "*add some physiognomic points to those I have indicated,*" acknowledging, lucidly, that "*it can be done differently; it can be done much better.*"[45]

Joseph Piroux, a teacher at the INSMP before becoming principal of the school in Nancy, also decried this method: "*The principle of the methodical signs is therefore false, as these signs have destroyed the unity of the natural signs and of the language of action.*" (p. 237).

41. Christian Cuxac, *Le langage des sourds*, Paris: Payot, 1983, p. 25.
42. Where part of a limb is not used (for example, the upper part of the arm), a line across it indicates that it is not involved: "*Thus, to designate the forearm, we draw a line through the upper part of the character corresponding to the femoral section of the arm.*"
43. Bébian, *Examen critique*, p. 29.
44. Cuxac, *Mimographie*, p. 91.
45. Bébian, *Examen critique*, p. 12.
"*All the physiognomies in the world could not reflect all the movements of the soul. And of the facial expressions that appear the most significant, how many owe their clarity and energy only to their accompanying gesture? Mimography cannot lay claim to a precision that is denied to the living language that it depicts. We will believe that we have achieved our goal if we can indicate the physiognomic expressions necessary to clarity of thought.*"

Figures 3: Characters for the different parts of the head and body (*Mimography*)

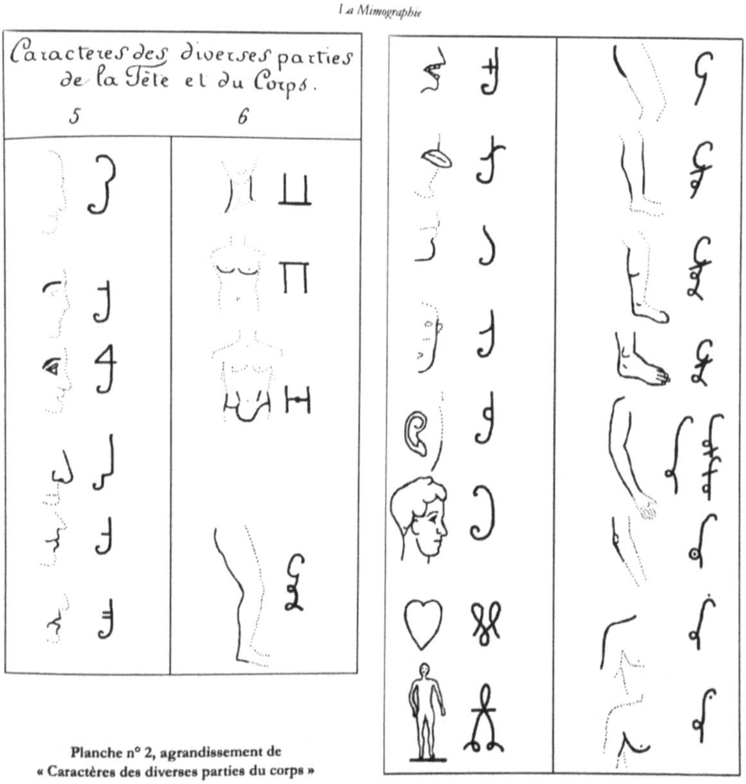

La Mimographie

Caracteres des diverses parties de la Tête et du Corps.

5 6

Planche n° 2, agrandissement de
« Caractères des diverses parties du corps »

A	Exclamation - Attention
B b	Non défini
C c	Gaieté - Tristesse
D d	Plaisir - Déplaisir Grand plaisir - Grand déplaisir Extrême plaisir - Extrême déplaisir
E e	Attirance - Répulsion
F	Compassion
G g	Modestie - Orgueil
H	Non défini
I i	Interrogation - Affirmation
J j	Non défini
K k	Non défini

A third and final table, divided into two parts (each with two columns) is devoted to examples of this notation, in particular to the "*play of the two organs whose movements are the most varied, and whose field is richest and the most vast: I refer to the eye and the hand*":

Figure 4: Use of mimography
(Plate III of *Mimographie*,
followed by an enlargement from *Écrire les signes*,
Fox, 2014, pp. 33 and 36)

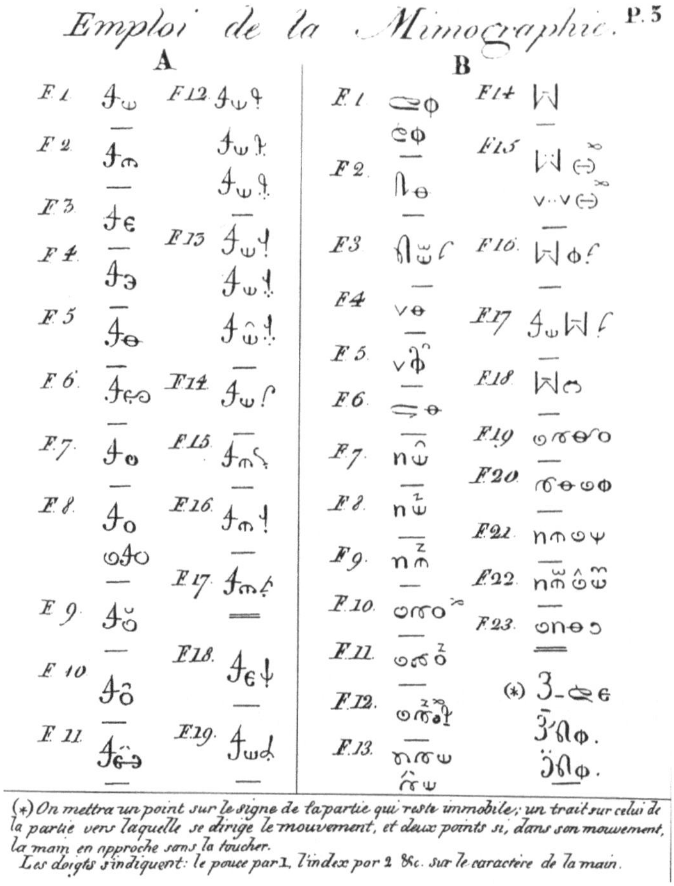

Emploi de la Mimographie. P. 3

A | B

F 1 … F 23

(*) On mettra un point sur le signe de la partie qui reste immobile; un trait sur celui de la partie vers laquelle se dirige le mouvement, et deux points si, dans son mouvement, la main en approche sans la toucher.
Les doigts s'indiquent: le pouce par 1, l'index par 2 &c. sur le caractère de la main.

Planche III - Emploi de la Mimographie - Partie A					
F1		Regarder en haut	F12		Regarder avec attention
F2		Regarder en bas			Regarder avec grande attention
F3		Regarder à droite			Regarder avec extrême attention
F4		Regarder à gauche	F13		Regarder en haut avec plaisir
F5		Regarder en avant			Regarder en haut avec extrême plaisir
F6		Regarder autour			Regarder en haut de façon prolongée avec extrême plaisir
F7		Fermer les yeux	F14		Regarder en haut avec respect
F8		Ouvrir les yeux Œil fermé puis ouvert	F15		Regarder en bas avec dédain
			F16		Regarder en bas avec plaisir
F9		Clignoter	F17		Regarder en bas avec compassion
F10		Ouvrir de grands yeux	F18		Regarder à droite gaiement
F11		Loucher	F19		Regarder en haut avec déplaisir

Thus, the notation ( ) (F1 in the table) designates the eye (first character), and the movement of the gaze looking upward. The same notation followed by , means "looking upward attentively", very attentively and extremely attentively.

Looking downward disdainfully is noted (example F15[46]), while looking downward with pleasure is written .

46. Describing, in succession, the eyes, their downward movement and the facial expression.

A notation without a facial expression implies a neutral physiognomy. For example, [notation symbol] (the eye closes). An accent over the movement, [notation symbol], indicates a blink, and if it is repeated, the character "z" is attached (Plate I): [notation symbol].

All the variations are therefore envisaged fairly precisely. Sometimes the character that modifies the movement is noted before the latter, if the accompanying gesture is to be produced before the actual signifier. This is the case with the sign for "give": [notation symbol] (closing of the hand, as seen from in front, followed by a forward curving movement and opening of the hand).

The purpose of this description is more pedagogical than linguistic,[47] which might account for some approximations and errors that are hard to explain coming from an advanced signer, as Bébian no doubt was.[48] But this system of notation was never to be applied, as Berthier deplores, laying the blame at the feet of the board of governors:[49]

> "[…] *this knowledgeable teacher had asked the administration to be allowed eight days to teach deaf-mutes how to mimograph signs; but the administration preferred to judge this work from a simple reading rather than on the basis of an experiment which, I have no doubt, would have proved conclusive."*

---

47. *"It was long proclaimed that the fundamental rule for the instruction of deaf-mutes is to* ***go from the idea to the word****; but when it came to its application, that principle was forgotten, and it was words that served as the pivot for all explanations; it was in words that we sought to find the signs that would be used to teach those words to the deaf."* Bébian, *Mimographie*, p. 35.
48. Christian Cuxac lists them in Cuxac, *Mimographie*, p. 89.
49. Berthier, *Notice*, p. 18.

The "expertise" of Baron de Gérando, and of Frederic Cuvier, chairman and member of the INSMP's board of governors, was effectively deemed authoritative. They concluded that the multifaceted nature of the signs was an obstacle to their use, a criticism that was reprised a quarter century later by another INSMP teacher, Rémi Valade, who was nonetheless a defender of sign language.[50] And so, it seems, mimography remained at the theoretical stage:

50. Y. L. Rémi Valade, *Études sur la Lexicologie et la Grammaire du Langage naturel des Signes,* Paris: Librairie philosophique de Ladrange, 1854. The key difference with Bébian's *Mimography* lies in Valade's approach, analyzing sign language through its "*correspondence with spoken languages, and necessarily through its description rather than its transcription,*" Yves Bernard, *Approche de la gestualité à l'institution des sourds-muets de Paris, au XVIII*e *et au XIX*e *siècle*, doctoral thesis, Univ. Paris V, 1999, p. 821. On this notation, see Bernard, *ibid.*, pp. 820-821. Valade's *"syrmography"* was never applied in practice and remained at the draft stage: its similarities to the *sign writing* introduced in the 20th century by Valerie Sutton is fortuitous, as she was unaware of Valade's system. This form of notation, created in 1854, is nonetheless independent of the French language, unlike the "*tachymimography*" notation proposed at the same period by Joseph Piroux. From 1828, the hearing Piroux (1803-1884) was principal of the Institution for Deaf-Mutes in Nancy, which he himself founded. Previously, from 1825 to 1827, he had trained at the Paris Institution, where he was a student teacher before himself joining the teaching staff. On returning to Nancy, where he founded his school, he recruited the deaf Claude Richardin, who became a teacher, having been a student of the deaf teachers Ferdinand Berthier and Alphonse Lenoir at the INSMP. (Quartararo, *Deaf identity*, p. 85.) In his first work (he published more than twenty in all, and edited the journal *L'ami des sourds-muets* for ten years), entitled *Théorie philosophique de l'enseignement des sourds-muets* (Paris: Hachette, 1831), initially a speech addressed to a learned society, he sets out the core of his "syllabic" or "Nancean" method, based on fingerspelling, drawing and signs, which would be published later, in 1846. In this book, *Méthode de dactylologie, de lecture et d'écriture* (Paris: Hachette, 1846), he explains why he is opposed to Abbé de l'Épée's methodical signs method and concludes, some twenty years after Bébian (whom, incidentally, he does not mention): "*The principle of the methodical signs is therefore false, as these signs have destroyed the unity of the natural signs and of the language of action,*" (p. 25) and consequently recommends using "natural" signs. In 1842 and 1843, in the journal he edited, *L'ami des sourds-muets,* he sets out his arguments: these articles, printed in the journal's education section, have been grouped together into a single volume by Marc Renard: Joseph Piroux, *Examen approfondi de l'ouvrage de l'abbé de l'Épée,* Les-Essarts-le-Roi: Fox, 2004.

this "*prototype* [...] *has no future in the medium term.*"[51] As we saw earlier, this analysis follows on from his criticisms of Abbé de l'Épée's "methodical signs" – made still more complex by his successor Abbé Sicard – but it is constructive criticism: his *Mimography* is intended as an alternative to the previously instated method, to enable Deaf pupils to effectively understand everything they read and write, as "*the conscientious teacher can never accept at face value that words learned* (dictated) *are understood,*" he states frankly.

Mimography is not designed to break free from the French language, but rather to explain "*the reason for all the words that we employ to render [an] idea in our language,*"[52] while conforming to the requirements of sign language. The most remarkable aspect of this initiative, aside from the linguistic awareness it displays, is the place it accords to a certain culture: that of orality, which makes a radical distinction between written and spoken modes of expression.[53]

For a complete biography, see: Joseph Turcan, "Notice biographique sur J. Piroux", *La défense des sourds-muets,* July 1885 and Anne T. Quartararo, *Deaf Identity and Social Images in Nineteenth-century France,* Washington: Gallaudet University Press, 2002, p. 83.

51. Cuxac, *Mimographie*, p. 91. According to this author, the teacher Ferdinand Berthier claims, "*somewhere in his writings,*" to have revised and perfected Bébian's system, and to have tested it out successfully with his own pupils. Aside from this brief allusion, there is no trace or report of the *mimography* characters being used in an educational setting.
52. Bébian, *Examen critique*, (reprinted by Marc Renard), p. 38.
53. Linguistic structures are not the only differences between spoken and written languages: whereas writing shuns repetition and strives to use varied vocabulary, speech makes use of repetition, among other techniques, to signal insistence or to check understanding. Punctuation – often presented as a set of marks designed to "replace" intonation – is quite incapable of conveying the richness of intonation, whether in its "grammatical" functions or its "expressive" functions. Finally, the situational difference is essential: in speech the interlocutor is close to, perhaps face-to-face with, the speaker, who sees the movement of their lips, captures their gestures and facial expressions, and decodes, consciously or otherwise, their intonation, etc.: communication is simultaneous. In writing, it is consecutive.

2. Reading, the gateway to independence

2.1 What is reading?

Instant Reading: a New Method for Learning to Read Without Spelling,[54] published in 1828, occupies a special place among Bébian's written works, all of which are about, or dedicated to, Deaf people and sign language. In this short volume (just twenty-eight pages) he explains his own method of reading. Once again, it is an indisputable testimony to Bébian's active engagement with the issues of his day. During the final years of the Restoration, and under the July Monarchy, numerous methods were devised for the teaching of France's schoolchildren. Education Historian Antoine Prost describes it as a phenomenon of considerable magnitude, seeing it even as a "veritable revolution."[55] By way of illustration, he cites the Peigné method,[56] which was certainly revolutionary in some respects,[57]

---

54. Auguste Bébian, *Lecture instantanée. Nouvelle méthode pour apprendre à lire sans épeler*, Paris: Crapelet, 1828.
55. Antoine Prost, *Histoire de l'enseignement en France, 1800-1967*, Paris: Colin, 1968, p. 119.
    One can identify "*596 reading methods designed by 404 authors of various origins* [...] *If, in addition to these 596 documents in various forms – manuals, books, wall tables, games, instruments of all sorts – we include certain alphabets and letter charts published in the* 19th *century, the number of reading methods probably exceeds the thousand mark.*" Christiane Juaneda-Albarède, *Cent ans de méthodes de lecture,* Paris: Albin Michel, 1998, pp. 7-8.
56. *Ibid.,* pp. 119-130.
57. The reading method developed by Michel-Auguste Peigné in 1831 (after working as a teacher and later as a proof-reader at the Royal Press, Peigné was engaged by the Ministry for Public Instruction in January 1831, staying there until 1838) proposes a major change relative to earlier strategies: children are quickly taught to read words and phrases that correspond to acquired "sounds" and "articulations". Not only does he abandon the reading of Latin – quite often still present in manuals in the first half of the century – and adopts the new naming system in which each letter is designated by its phonetic value instead of its name, he also insists on taking as his starting point the child's "prior knowledge". The revolutionary nature of this method is clear by comparison with the other methods published in the 19th century: it was reprinted until 1894, and the Minister of Public Instruction, Montalivet, who commissioned

but other methods were arguably more audacious, totally revisiting the pedagogy of reading.[58] One such was the "whole words" (*mots entiers*) method, a thoroughly innovative idea thought up at the end of the 18th century by Abbé de Radonvilliers and the grammarian Nicolas Adam,[59] which consisted in learning to read words in their entirety, and not analyzing the syllables until reading was fully acquired. This is where we would expect to find Auguste Bébian, who, in his *Manual for Practical Instruction,* recommends whole word recognition.[60] Does he see it as the only method valid for Deaf children? He makes his views clear:[61]

> *"What is reading? The word has two meanings, which we can bring together in a single definition. To read is to recognize the sounds or meanings of characters that we see before us. For the deaf-mute, sound does not exist; the first part of the definition does not apply to him. For him, to read is only to recognize the meanings of the words before his eyes; it is to understand them."*

---

its publication, had 25,000 copies sent out to municipal schools over three years. Juaneda-Albarède, *Cent ans*, p. 58; Christiane Juaneda-Albarède, "Les méthodes de lecture au XIXe siècle", *Actes de lecture n° 37*, Association française pour la lecture (1992).

58. Juaneda-Albarède, *Cent ans*, p. 7.

59. Abbé de Radonvilliers "*suggests the idea for this method*" in a page and a half of his treatise *De la manière d'apprendre les langues* (Paris: Saillant, 1768, pp. 247-248) [On the way to learn languages]; Nicolas Adam developed the idea a decade later in *La vraie manière d'apprendre une langue vivante ou morte par le moyen de la langue française* [The true way to learn a living or dead language through the medium of French]. This method, constructed from 1779 to 1787, was originally intended for tutorial-based education, but it indisputably influenced authors of 19th-century methods, such as Louis-François de Neufchâteau. Cited in Juaneda-Albarède, *Cent ans*, p. 20.

60. Auguste Bébian, *Manuel,* vol. II, p. 24.
"When your pupil has, in this manner, seen eight or ten names that you have written on the board, one on top of the other, close the book of illustrations and show him the first of these words, asking him to give you its sign. If he does so, move on to the next [...] *."*

61. Bébian, *Journal de l'instruction*, n° 3, p. 155.

This preoccupation with learning to read was clearly stated by the INSMP from its inception,[62] but Bébian saw sign language as crucial to that goal. At the end of his first book, *Essay on the Deaf and Natural Language*, published in 1817, he reproduces a letter on this topic from John Wallis, a founder member of the *Royal Society*,[63] and underlines that:[64]

> *"... by means of signs, by which the deaf-mute naturally express their thoughts, he soon succeeded in enabling them to understand what they were reading, and thus to acquire all the knowledge that can be transmitted by books."*

Once "*the deaf-mute*," he writes,[65] "*have acquired an understanding of the written language, reading opens up to them all the treasures of human knowledge: the language of gestures can bend to all forms of thinking; it can express the most subtle nuances and the most sophisticated combinations.*"[66]

In his preface to *Instant Reading,* he justifies his intervention by criticizing "*the routine of barbaric times* [that] *still reigns in our*

62. The *INSMP* school *prospectus* reminds parents that "*the essential aim of the education of Deaf-Mutes being to put them in communication with other men, we teach them to read and write,*" Paris: Imprimerie des Sourds-Muets, 1792, p. 1.
63. Dalle-Nazébi, *Chercheurs*, pp. 74-75.
64. Letter dated 30 September, 1698 (119 years before Bébian's text), in which Wallis claims that he taught a Deaf person to read without going through the phase of decoding syllables "*34 or 35 years ago*" (thus in 1650-55). It is one of two letters reproduced in the Annex; the first is that of "*W. Dunbar Esq., of the Mississippi territory, to T. Jefferson, President of the American Philosophical Society, on the language of signs among certain North American Indians,*" dated June 30, 1800. Bébian, *Essai sur les sourds-muets*, p. 44.
65. Bébian, *Journal de l'instruction*, n° 2, p. 65.
66. Bébian, *Manuel*, vol. I, pp. 8-9.
The writing of this "*language of gestures*" seeks to provide "*a lynchpin for the attention, an aid for memory, an instrument of analysis for reflection and demonstration; finally, relations between ideas, made more palpable through the analogy of signs, may give rise to interesting and unexpected insights,*" he writes in the preamble to his *Mimographie* (p. 13).

schools."[67] With particular reference to the INSMP, he goes on to denounce *"a simulacrum of teaching that fails even to satisfy the needs of the humblest artisan."*[68] In 1826, Bébian, joined twenty years later by a teacher from the INSMP, Jean-Baptiste Puybonnieux, presents reading as *"the goal and immediate object"*[69] of teaching. Though the mastery of reading (and writing) is unanimously recognized as fundamental, even indispensable, it is a difficult skill to learn, and opinions about how to impart it (and consequently on the teaching methods) diverge radically.[70]

2.2 An original method

Auguste Bébian's short treatise, entirely devoted to reading, is in principle intended for hearing children, but it surely echoes the educator's preoccupation with enabling Deaf children to join "ordinary" schools. The study of sounds features prominently, it is true, but it calls not only on auditory memory, but also on visual

---

67. Auguste Bébian, *Lecture instantanée – nouvelle méthode pour apprendre à lire sans épeler*, Paris: Crapelet, 1828, p. I.
68. He recounts that *"the well-known Deaf-Mute M..."* (probably Massieu), a former pupil then tutor of Sicard at the INSMP, did not understand *L'ami des enfans* (a series of novellas for children by Arnaud Berquin, a work recognized by the Académie Française in 1784, and sometimes seen as the beginnings of children's literature). Bébian, *Examen critique*, p. 36.
   This concords with the letter published in the *Journal...* : *"I have before me, as you know, two Deaf-Mutes raised at the Royal Institution; they hold reading in a kind of horror; that alone suffices to tell me that they do not understand"* whereas his son Gonzalve, home-schooled, but following the precepts set out by Bébian, "enjoys reading" (p. 316).
69. Jean-Baptiste Puybonnieux, *Mutisme et surdité, ou Influence de la surdité native sur les facultés physiques, intellectuelles et morales*, 1846, p. 258.
70. This debate is still very much alive. The Gillot report of 1998 states that 80% of Deaf people in France are illiterate: the question of the acquisition of written language is therefore unresolved!
   The methodology leading to this figure is open to challenge. Firstly because it is opaque: how did the evaluators proceed? On what basis? Were they bilingual? But also on the term "illiteracy": what and whom are we referring to? A Deaf person who is being assessed on their second language (the first being SIgn), or is this aspect overlooked? In this case, to what extent can we speak of "illiteracy" in the conventional sense?

and kinesthetic memory. In this respect, the method is similar to that advocated by Pierre Régimbeau,[71] one of the first manual authors to manifest a concern with visual perception (a focus he shares with the ophthalmologist Émile Javal).[72] Bébian defines his method in these terms:[73]

> *"The method will be at times analytic, at times synthetic, and always guided by analogy. Analogy, which governs the study of languages, presided over their formation and their development."*

Bébian's *Instant Reading* was reviewed in a contemporary journal.[74] The editor describes the method and concludes: *"After close examination, I believe I have grounds to declare that this method offers great benefits. The most ingenious thing about it is that it teaches children simultaneously the elements of two arts – reading and writing – that are generally taught to them consecutively."*[75]

---

71. Pierre Régimbeau, *Différents titres comportant tous le terme "syllabaire"*, first edition: 1866; last edition: 1951 cited in Juaneda-Albarède, *Cent ans,* p.100. The fact that Régimbeau's method was constantly in print for the best part of a century bears witness to it success!
72. Émile Javal, *Méthode Javal, la lecture enseignée par l'écriture*, Paris: Alcide, 1893 (first book) – 1894 (second book).
    Javal, an ophthalmologist, seen as the theorist of modern orthoptics, was very concerned with visual hygiene.
73. Bébian, *Journal de l'instruction*, n° 3, p. 89.
74. *Revue encyclopédique ou analyse raisonnée des œuvres les plus remarquables dans les sciences, les arts industriels, la littérature par des membres de l'Institut et autres hommes de lettres*, vol. XV, October 1828, p. 30.
75. The combination of reading and writing was not self-evident and was a matter of debate in the 19th century, as much as the topic of letter-naming and spelling. James Guillaume, in the *Dictionnaire d'instruction primaire*, edited by Fernand Buisson, relates that this combination first emerges in the method developed by Py-Poulain Delaunay, published by his son Pierre in 1741, who recommends: *"One essential thing I recommend to parents wishing to teach their children by this method is to place the pen in their hand as soon as they begin to read, and to have them write, however young they may be; this exercise will bring about extraordinary progress,"* but it seems, according to E. Mir, principal of the École Normale in Perpignan at the end of the 19th century, that as early as 1584, a document recommended combining the two learning processes (E. Mir,

"This is what the method consists of: the various letters, single or double, that come together to form sounds or syllables are presented successively in a series of tables. Each letter is, as it were, incorporated into the figure of an object chosen precisely so that it can more or less take its shape. For example, an orange is used for O, a snake for S. The author has the student draw each of these figures and teaches him its name, which always begins, as I have just explained, with the letter being learned. It is clear that in drawing the first figure the pupil learns to recognize the shape of the letter; now, the teacher, by having him pronounce the associated name, gradually makes him detach the initial from the rest of the word, O...range, S...nake, until he no longer hears anything but the sound of the vowel, or the sibilance of the consonant; the rest of the word being completed quietly. After repeating this exercise several times, 'we show him,' says Monsieur Bébian himself (p. 13), 'the letter A with a pointing-stick; he pronounces it. We teach him to prolong the sound until the stick leaves the letter and passes to one of the consonants he has studied, and which he pronounces in turn: A... R. By moving the stick several times, increasingly quickly, from one letter to the other, we eventually obtain AR in a single breath. We then move on to the combinations or, ir, oir, etc., which present no new difficulty'."

Méthode MIR, enseignement de la lecture par l'écriture, Paris: A. Pigoreau, 1891, cited in Juaneda-Albarède, *Cent ans*, p. 85.) It seems, moreover, that Montaigne learned to read and write simultaneously. Pierre Delaunay is, in fact, the heir to a tradition. "*It is François de Neufchâteau, however, that we have to thank for no longer reserving the process to tutor-based education, and expanding it in the direction of public education; an idea often expressed during the revolutionary period, where writing sessions corresponded to children's need for action, but which remained at the project stage,*" Juaneda-Albarède, *Cent ans*, p. 86. (Nicolas-Louis François de Neufchâteau (1750-1828) was Minister of the Interior from Year V to Year VII (1797-1799), senior civil servant and author of a *Méthode pratique de lecture* (practical reading method) published in 1799, which reflected his major preoccupation with developing mass literacy).

Bernard, *Approche de la gestualité*, p. 483.

Figure 5
Principles of the *New method for learning to read without spelling*

Figure 6
Extract from the *New method for learning to read without spelling*

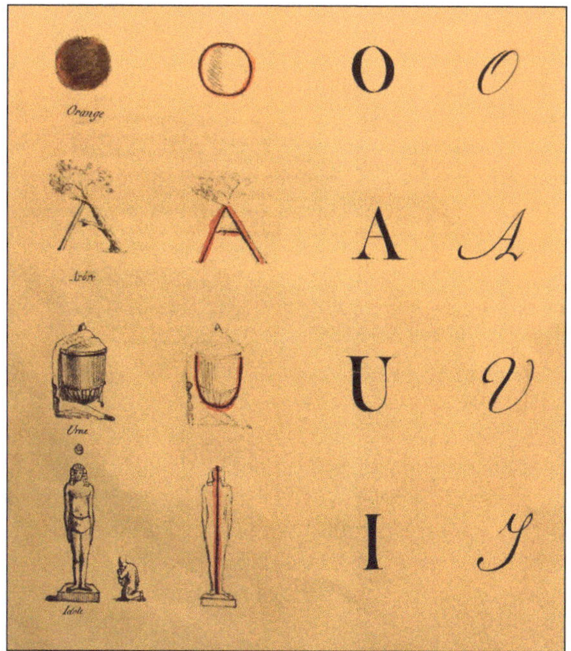

The figures in the plates, when correctly cut out, constitute a deck in which each card has the figure on one side and corresponding letters on the other. The study "of letters and syllables" is thus disguised as a game, an idea close to Bébian's heart,[76] and one that combines reading with writing, which was by no means self-evident.

Bébian is very insistent about the link between the two: writing, he tells us, is the art of painting speech.[77] Like Peigné, whose method was published three years later, he recommends starting with the known and progressing towards the unknown,[78] and linking children's language production to writing, before moving on to reading; an approach later advocated by other pedagogues.[79]

And like other methods that would follow (Régimbeau, by example), reading should be learned, for Bébian, without recourse to letter-naming;[80] it is therefore not a new idea in itself:[81]

76. Juaneda-Albarède, *Cent ans*, p. 33.

77. Bébian, *Lecture instantanée*, p. VI.

78. "*Every good method must progress from the known to the unknown*," *idem.*

79. For example Maurice Block, seen as one of the precursors of what is nowadays called the "global method". While it is true that this method starts out from a whole word, the word is analyzed in all its forms; Block's is therefore a mixed, synthetic-analytic method. Maurice Block, *Méthode Schüler. Enseignement simultané de la lecture et de l'écriture*, Paris: Hachette, 1880, cited in Juaneda-Albarède, *Cent ans*, p. 117.

80. Naming each individual letter (in French, at that time: / a, be, se, de, e, ɛf... /). Learning the letters presents no difficulty; the difficulty lies in assembling them to make syllables (spelling).
The old method of naming letters led to incomprehension. A "new" letter-naming system was therefore proposed, using the "values" or sounds of the letters, i.e. how they are usually pronounced when put together in syllables (/ a, bə, kə, də, ɛ, fə... /). The French word *sang* (blood), pronounced / sɑ̃ /, was often used as an example; spelled out under the "old" letter-naming rules, it yields / ɛs, a, ɛn, ʒe / whereas with the " new " method, it is / sə, ɑ̃ / (the syllable "–ang" is assimilated to a vowel), taking us as close as possible to the actual pronunciation of the word. The first to use this method were the pedagogues of Port-Royal in 1655.

81. Auguste Bébian, *Lecture instantanée. Nouvelle méthode pour apprendre à lire sans épeler*, Paris: Crapelet, 1828, pp. I-II.

"Is it not a veritable riddle that you set before a child when, for example, in the syllables ache-a-ï-enne-é, he is supposed to discover the word haine?[82]
I hear him painstakingly repeat esse-pé-ache-igrec-enne-ixe. *From this barbarous mixture of incoherent sounds, what new Oedipus could deduce the sphinx?"*

According to Bébian, this way of learning can be very rapid; this was no doubt, at least in part, what inspired his commitment to spelling reform. Stripping the French language of its complex spelling rules and initiating learners into a mainly phonetic system for reading and writing the language using the twenty-six letters of the alphabet was, for him, an indispensable measure.

Letter-naming is not the only topic of his foreword: Bébian also praises a work, *Statilègie*,[83] developed by Joseph-Bonaventure Bourrousse de Laffore,[84] and published the same year as the Manual. While he does not doubt the efficiency of the method – presented as "revolutionary", promising rapid learning success (in four, six or twelve days; fifteen at the most, at a rhythm of six hours a day)[85] – he regrets that the process is protected by an

82. Here Bébian is imitating the names of the letters H-A-I-N-E in French (spelling out haine, the word for hatred) – transl.

83. Bernard, *Approche de la gestualité*, p. 372.

84. De Laffore, a lawyer from Agen in southwest France, claimed, as early as 1827, to have developed a "revolutionary" reading method.

85. This ambition, and these promises, were never really put to the test: Bébian mentions a single experiment in Paris, *"which not everyone found conclusive"* (Bébian, *Lecture instantanée*, p. III).
The April 1828 issue of the *Journal de la langue française grammatical, didactique et littéraire* reflects on this method and contains a review by the editor, Marle l'Aîné, which concludes ironically: "Ah! So *you can teach* [children] *to read in 4 or 6 days? Could it be, perchance, that you have mistaken days for months, or for years, as – by asking poor teachers for 1,200,000 francs – you have clearly mistaken their wallets for the vaults of our millionaire bankers? Truly, Don Quixote could not have done better. Be advised, Monseigneur, Prince of the Methodists, that people today are no longer taken at their word, and that there remains only one way for you to prove that you are not a victim of your own imagination, namely to produce plenty of facts and to expose them to the light of day."*

inventor's patent, *"bringing the price to 1,200,000 francs for all of France's departments."*[86] Bébian's goal is humbler: *"to spare a few children's tears, be they rich or poor."*[87] He argues for the application of a "primitive method", a descriptor that evokes simplicity. His didactic approach was no doubt heavily influenced by the work of the writer Antoine Court de Gébelin and of Charles de Brosses, dubbed *"President de Brosses",*[88] where we find echoes of the "dual analogy" hypothesis, according to which letters, i.e. writing, were originally drawings of which a few bare outlines remain, associated by convention with an arbitrary phoneme.

But, as we saw earlier, the method proposed by Bébian draws on a wealth of diverse inspirations. All the more surprising, then, that the ideas of Joseph Jacotot,[89] as expressed in his *Enseignement universel, Langue maternelle* (Universal Teaching, Mother Tongue)

The Lafforian method was nonetheless authorized in 1829 by the then Minister of Public Instruction, Vatimesnil, on the strength of a report produced by a committee chaired by Francoeur. "*Did Laffore employ his talents as a lawyer to present his method in a favorable light* [...]? " wonders Christiane Juaneda-Albarède (*Cent ans*, p. 55). Although the method was contested and failed to gain unanimous support, it unquestionably inspired future explorations and improvements: it is based on the "*physiological laws of language*", particularly as regards the study of consonants.

86. More than 5 million euros in 2023 money. "*That is twenty-five times as much as the budget allocated to primary education in the entire kingdom. Such an exorbitant duty on an item, as it were, of basic necessity is tantamount to a prohibition* [...] " writes Bébian indignantly. Bébian, *Lecture instantanée*, p. III.
87. Bébian, *Lecture instantanée*, p. V.
88. Antoine Court de Gébelin, *Histoire naturelle de la Parole, ou grammaire universelle à l'usage des jeunes gens*, Paris, 1776.
89. While teaching rhetoric in Dijon, Jacotot had to seek refuge in the Netherlands for political reasons following the restoration of the Bourbons (his ideas were unacceptable to the new regime). In 1818, on being appointed lecturer in French literature (a subject in which he had no expertise) at the university of Leuven (although he knew no Dutch), he asked his students to learn the bilingual version of Fénelon's *Télémaque* (then in print) so that they could assimilate some notions of the French language.
    Jacques Rancière, *Le maître ignorant. Cinq leçons sur l'émancipation intellectuelle,* Paris: Fayard "10/18", 1987, pp. 7-8.

published five years earlier,[90] are not mentioned here, although they share the same ultimate aim as Bébian – emancipation[91] – and are based on two fundamental precepts. Firstly, the teacher, the master, does not know the object of study any more than the learners: a key condition to avoid the temptation of explaining, and thus preventing others from forging their own comprehension strategies. Secondly, we are dealing with equal intelligences: there is not, on one side, the repository of all knowledge and on the other, slow and ignorant learners. This principle of "equal intelligences" by itself sums up the revolutionary nature of this method: the role of the pedagogue, says Jacotot, is limited to guiding the learning process, sustaining it, but not directing it by issuing a raft of instructions that would undermine the learner's autonomy: knowing the field one is teaching can actually be an obstacle, as teachers tend to want to impose their own personal take on the object of study.[92]

This method proposes a complete overhaul of the pedagogy of reading, relying on almost totally autonomous learning. It was admittedly propagated more widely abroad (especially in England and Russia) than in France, where it never really gained leverage with the authorities of the July Monarchy.[93] The aim of the method was clearly to teach students to learn independently.

The sources that inspired Bébian, that nourished his thinking, whether directly or indirectly, were many and various. For example, although his method was based on sound, it was always associated with an image, just as it was in a method established during the previous century, the *Quadrille des enfants*.[94] It pinpoints a sound

---

90. Joseph Jacotot, *Enseignement universel, Langue maternelle,* Louvain: imprimerie H. de Pauw, 1823.
91. Rancière, *Le maître ignorant*.
92. *Ibid.*, pp. 121-175.
93. Christian Nique, *La Petite Doctrine pédagogique de la Monarchie de Juillet (1830-1840*), thesis, 1987, vol. 1, p. 46, cited in Juaneda-Albarède, *Cent ans*, p. 136.
94. The "Quadrille des enfants" (or, to give it its full title: "*Le quadrille des enfants, avec lequel, par le moyen de cent soixante figures et sans épeler, ils peuvent à l'âge de quatre ou cinq ans, et au-dessous, être mis en état de lire à l'ouverture de toutes sortes de livres en trois ou quatre mois, même plutôt, selon leurs dispositions*" [The

that is found not at the end of a word, but "*in the first syllable of the very name of the illustrated object.*" Memorization is facilitated by simultaneously studying the spelling and the drawing of the object, "*reduced to its essential outlines,*"[95] as can be seen on Plate 1.[96] But while he drew on a wide range of sources, it seems that Bébian also had a certain influence: in the above-mentioned methods – Régimbeau, Peigné, Block – we find a number of procedures already described by Bébian, such as taking words as a whole, breaking them down subsequently with a mixed analytic-synthetic approach that rules out no technique (auditory, graphic, or visual).

Auguste Bébian's ideas on reading, expressed in this short treatise, contain several innovative aspects, such as the use of color to teach reading. In addition to representing letters by drawings, the vowels are shown in red to distinguish them from the consonants, shown in blue:

Children's Quadrille, with which, by means of 160 figures and without spelling, they may by the age of 4 or 5, or even less, be made able to read on opening all kinds of books within 3 or 4 months, if not sooner, depending on their dispositions]) was established in 1744 by Abbé Berthaud. Juaneda-Albarède, *Cent ans*, p. 32.

95. Bébian, *Lecture instantanée*, p. VII.

96. Bébian, *Lecture instantanée*, plate 1.

Figures 7
Extract from the *New method for learning to read without spelling*

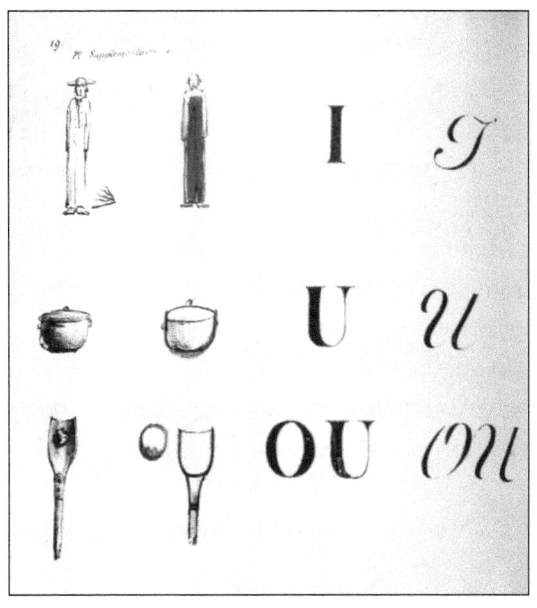

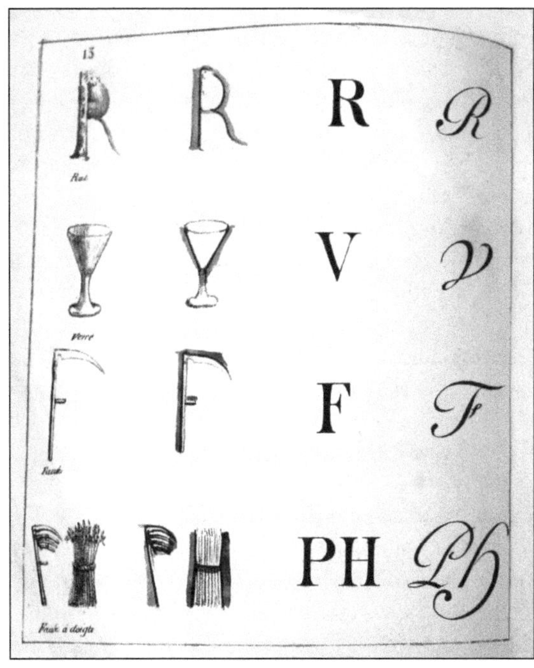

Before the second half of the 19th century, the use of color for reading methods was exceptional: Bébian was almost alone in using it, a few years after Edme-François Jomard, who was the true precursor.[97]

Curiously, Joseph Piroux – who published a reading method entitled *Méthode allant de l'écriture à la parole et de la parole à l'écriture* [Method going from writing to speech and from speech to writing] in 1834,[98] six years after Bébian – does not mention Bébian, although he must have known him.[99] Aside from the fact that Piroux recommends tying reading to vocal production (whereas for Bébian, as we saw, sign language is essential to this goal, "*tracing the gently-sloping path that leads, gradually but imperceptibly, to the summit of instruction*"),[100] their approaches have one thing very much in common: they were rarely used in the early part of the 19th century.

---

97. Edme-François Jomard, *Premiers tableaux*, 1815; *Nouveaux tableaux*, 1835. In 1815, Edme-François Jomard was part of the Interior Ministry committee entitled "*Société pour l'instruction élémentaire*" (with Baron de Gérando, Count de Lasteyrie, Abbé Gaultier and Count Delaborde) and drew up tables for use in mutual teaching, implemented at the height of the industrial revolution. These eighty tables were revised twenty years later, attaining an "*exceptional technical quality,*" with a strict double classification (phonetic and visual). They make use of color (red vowels, black consonants), an approach that became widespread mainly in the second half of the 19th century; its early use in Bébian's 1828 method is something of an outlier. Juaneda-Albarède, *Cent ans*, pp. 97-99.
98. Joseph Piroux, *Méthode allant de l'écriture à la parole et de la parole à l'écriture*, Nancy, 1834, (reprinted in 1860). It employs an original way of breaking down whole phrases. For example, the phrase "*Victor va à l'école*" [Victor goes to school] is presented in an engraving. It is broken down into words or syllables (*vic · tor · va · à · l'é · co · le*), and then into 'sounds' (*i · o · a · à · é · o · e*) and 'articulations' (*v · c · t · r · v · l · c · l*).
99. On July 1, 1825, Piroux became a student teacher at the INSMP, with a view to taking charge of the Institution he was tasked with setting up in Nancy (p. 237). Bébian had admittedly been dismissed four years earlier, but his presence was still felt at the INSMP, as we saw in Chapter 3. And surely Piroux's tachymimography (note 50) attests to a certain familiarity with Bébian's work?
100. Bébian, *Journal de l'instruction*, n° 3, p. 89.

Essential pedagogical questions

How do Deaf children learn to read? How do the users of a non-verbal (in the sense of being unwritten) language keep a trace of what is expressed? How do they access knowledge? These questions, which Auguste Bébian addressed head-on, remain largely unresolved to this day.[101] As Anne Vanbrugghe rightly summarizes, "*thinking about how to introduce reading and writing to deaf children calls for a decentering that is not always easy to imagine.*"[102] The introduction to reading is not limited to the question of deciphering, it also involves the question of meaning, and, if we are to enable full interaction with mainstream society, understanding must be linked to written production. As Christian Cuxac underlines:[103]

> "[…] *it is very clear that, contrary to what his title suggests, Bébian's method is aimed less at knowing how to read* (which may provide a way in to other people's thoughts, but is always marked by passivity) *than at knowing how to write: an act that takes thought, or the author's words, beyond the limits of the here and now of spoken discourse.*"

These topics and challenges go beyond the strict scope of teaching, which this educator addressed from a relatively unprecedented angle, at least as regards its goal: bringing autonomy – the central mission of education – within the reach of deaf people.

---

101. First-hand accounts of lived experience, write-ups of research actions, academic works… all converge on the same conclusion: that it is difficult for a deaf person to acquire reading and writing skills, as Anne Vanbrugghe reports (*Apprentissage de la lecture-écriture chez des élèves sourds dans la littérature scientifique francophone : élaboration d'une grille d'analyse au service de la complexité,* Master 2 thesis, Université de Paris-Nanterre, 2013). When it comes to solutions, however, there is much divergence.
102. Anne Vanbrugghe, *Apprentissage*, p. 7.
103. Cuxac, *Mimographie*, p. 82.

Conclusion

At the very least, Auguste Bébian opened up a space for reflection in a much-overlooked field: the education of Deaf people, previously seen as primitive and barely worthy of instruction. Beyond the purely pedagogical aspect, by championing the validity of a language, and of a culture, he enabled the Deaf community to take ownership of their own destiny. This is not to say that Deaf people were nonexistent; quite the contrary, as we have seen in these pages.

His advocacy of sign language, which he pursued to an unprecedented degree, deconstructed previous theories about language and thought, relativized the importance of any linguistic system, and offered respect and consideration to what had been looked down upon as mere gestures.[1] He was unquestionably the designer of a bilingual education system (sign language/French), a pedagogical approach that Deaf people have continued to call for and which still struggles to be implemented.[2] The term "bilingual" is of course anachronistic; I take the liberty of associating it with the cause upheld by this precursor, who ceaselessly advocated for signs to be seen as a language, by recognizing that they fulfilled the functions of any linguistic system:[3]

> *"Language is not only a means of communication between minds; it is, at the same time, the expression and the instrument of thought."*

---

1. As he writes in his *Journal*: *"One must therefore admit that we think – or at least can think – without recourse to any language. We think with ideas, bringing them together, comparing them to capture the relations between them* [...]." Auguste Bébian, *Journal de l'instruction des sourds-muets et des aveugles*, 1826, n° 1, p. 33.
2. In 2012, France's association for the parents of Deaf children (ANPES) counted 400 Deaf children with access to genuinely bilingual teaching (as opposed to French-based teaching interspersed with signs) out of 10,000 children in school, a mere 4%! <*https://secure.avaaz.org/fr/petition/ Charte_LSF_pour_les_enfants_sourds/?pv=106*>.
3. Bébian, *Journal de l'instruction*, n° 1, p. 18.

He repeats many variants of his *Leitmotiv*: *"The sign is the shadow of the idea."* And yet he sees the learning of French as primordial: a message he drives home on several occasions,[4] and one of the goals of his Mimography is to *"standardize gestures in order to produce a dictionary to better teach French."*

While Charles-Michel de l'Épée effectively brought about the institutionalization of Deaf education – a considerable achievement – it was every bit as essential to preserve the pedagogical orientation he had put in place. Auguste Bébian was fully committed to this goal; he even improved and enriched it, and above all shed light upon a gestural language that had remained in the shadows, misunderstood and disregarded. Aside from this didactic and anthropological disposition, which he shared with the *"genius of Abbé de l'Épée,"*[5] he displayed a degree of humility and considerable discretion, in stark contrast to the opportunism of some of his contemporaries, starting with Sicard. So much discretion, indeed, that we know very little about the man himself: he was quick to anger, some said, but was this perhaps due to the indignation that overcame him when he saw how Deaf people were treated?[6] The complaints made by the board of governors speak

4. *"It is the lot of the deaf-mute to submit to the law of the majority. He must learn the language of his country."* Bébian, *Journal de l'instruction*, n° 1, p. 33.
5. Bébian, *Journal de l'instruction*, n° 3, p. 139. His heartfelt admiration is evident from these lines: " [...] *his glory is the quiet and gentle glory of Saint Vincent de Paul; pure as the source from whence it emanates, it is of that rare kind that will flow unaltered across the ages, and will never have to stand the test of contradiction."*
6. *"Despite the value of the students trained by Bébian during his short time at the Institution, from 1817 to 1821, Berthier, Lenoir and Forestier were still répétiteurs in 1828. In 1829, two became teachers* (professeurs)*, but only after heated debate, as some of their hearing colleagues were categorically opposed. For Clerc, in 1816, regardless of his efforts and motivation, the title of supervisor* (maître) *was far from being assured,"* Yves Bernard, *Approche de la gestualité à l'institution des sourds-muets de Paris, au XVIIIe et au XIXe siècle*, doctoral thesis, Univ. Paris V, 1999, p. 564. In 1830, the pupils were still complaining about a supervisor who had not taught his class for two years, instead, he recruited the most educated students as tutors for his lessons, and treated them like dogs. Alexis Karacostas, "Fragments of Glottophagia: Ferdinand Berthier and the Birth of the Deaf Movement in France", *Looking Back: A reader on the History of the Deaf Communities and their Sign Languages*, International Studies on Sign Language and Communication of the

of his poor management, his lack of rigor, and his tendency to lose his composure.[7] But might it not simply be that Bébian's closeness to Deaf people caused him to feel strongly about an injustice and a discrimination that he saw as insufferable? Several examples point to how Deaf people were segregated: for the replacement of Abbé Sicard in 1822, Abbé Gondelin was appointed (on the recommendation of Sicard himself), not for his abilities, but because he offered:[8]

> *"...the advantage, in the eyes of the governors, of sidelining Jean Massieu, a 'model' student and later Sicard's deputy for more than thirty years, who doubtless presented the drawback of being deaf himself, but who above all enjoyed great authority with the pupils and the deaf tutors because it was he, with Bébian* [...] *who had exercised real responsibility for teaching at the Institution in the 1810s."*

Deaf, vol. 20, Signum Press, University of Hamburg, 1993, pp. 133-142. Berthier also testified on this subject, denouncing "*the poor quality of the food,* [...] *the brutality of the supervisors and the domestic staff,* [...] *the defective organization of teaching and constant changing of teachers (and it remained so for the first years of my stay at the establishment; nor was I the last to complain)...* " Ferdinand Berthier, *Sur l'opinion de feu le Docteur Itard, médecin en chef de l'Institution des sourds-muets de Paris, relative aux facultés intellectuelles et aux qualités morales des sourds-muets, réfutation présentée aux Académies de Médecine et de Sciences morale et politique*, Paris, 1852, p. 56.

7. Refutation of Ferdinand Berthier's book in Annex 8.
   Jean-Jacques Valade-Gabel, who became a teacher at the INSMP four years after Bébian's dismissal, noted in 1894: " *Bébian was, in Paris, the only one who deserved the title of teacher; unfortunately he had made himself insufferable* [...] *let us draw a veil over the circumstances that led to his being sent away from the institution* [...]." And further on: " *During this period Bébian had allowed himself to commit such misconduct that he had to be removed from the Institution, and the teaching, left in the hands of unskilled tutors, was falling apart before everyone's eyes*" (Jean-Jacques Valade-Gabel, "Lettres, notes et rapports", 1894, pp. 400, 444-445. Valade-Gabel (1801-1879) was a teacher at the INSMP from 1825 to 1838 before being appointed principal of the Bordeaux institution (he returned to Paris later, in 1850, to finish his career).
8. Session of the board of governors on March 16, 1822, cited in Buton, *L'administration des faveurs*, pp. 123-124. During another session, four months later, on August 10, the same board moved to increase the wages of all INSMP employees, with the sole exception of Massieu.

The situation of the Deaf Desongnis,[9] from Arras, admitted to the INSMP in 1827 as a trainee teacher, for board and (unfurnished) lodging alone – no wages – and that of another Deaf man, Gazan, who was never promoted beyond assistant *répétiteur*,[10] reveal a distinct lack of recognition, given that "[…] *in 1825-1826, the operation of the Institution essentially depended on the deaf-mute tutors who, trained by Bébian and Massieu, dispensed lessons in four out of six of the boys' classes.*"[11] One could also cite the dashed hopes of Bébian's former pupil Foussier, from Savoie,[12] forced to give up his ambition of founding a "new school", as a result of the *Third Circular*.[13] The INSMP's self-proclaimed superiority over the other institutions and their methods was not limited to judging or "*evaluating the work of others, either in situ or at the rue Saint-Jacques; they also sought, on occasion, to harm them, as the case of Auguste Bébian demonstrates.*"[14]

These daily slights were without doubt hard to stomach for someone not originally destined for teaching. His motivation grew out of a realization that the existing teaching system was not fit for purpose. As early as 1817, at the very point where he was taking up a teaching role, he published his *Essay on the Deaf and Natural Language, or Introduction to a Natural Classification of Ideas with Their Proper Signs,* in many ways a defining work, in which he explains his arguments, his reasoning in favor of the use of sign language, and sets out all of his future actions. Ferdinand Berthier, Bébian's pupil, friend, and only biographer, whom we have already seen and frequently quoted, published a vibrant eulogy a few months after

9. Desongnis, who joined the INSMP from March 7, 1827 to September 1829, went on to become the principal of the Arras Institution until 1855. *Le Messager de Abbé de l'Épée*, Oct. 1897, p. 299 and Bernard, *Approche de la gestualité*, p. 564.
10. Yves Delaporte, *Les sourds c'est comme ça*, Paris: MSH, 2002, p. 273.
11. François Buton, *L'administration des faveurs. L'État, les sourds et les aveugles (1789-1885)*, Rennes: Presses universitaires de Rennes, 2009, p. 201.
12. *Le Constitutionnel*, n° 253, issue of September 10, 1833 (letter dated September 8, p. 2).
13. See note 33, p. 177.
14. Buton, *L'administration des faveurs*, p. 142.

Bébian's death.[15] He paints the portrait of a man and of a peerless teacher and, through him, denounces the oppression inflicted upon deaf people. We have also seen Berthier's political acumen, his tactical sense: the choice of the Abbé de l'Épée as a figurehead was both consensual and strategic in inaugurating the tradition of the banquets in 1834, an important date in Deaf history, as the reader may recall.[16] Likewise, Berthier is doubtless at the origin of the Bébian myth. With a view to resisting the return to the primacy of speech, a reversal consecrated by the Milan Congress of 1880, Bébian – hearing, bilingual, bicultural, and the author of several renowned works – served as a perfect counter-example.[17]

---

15. Berthier, *Notice*.
    The relations between the two men continued, in a sense, after Bébian's death, as we see from the letter addressed ten years later, in 1849, by Berthier to Bébian's brother-in-law, the "man of letters" Félix Lemaistre (1807-18…), inviting him to the annual banquet of the Deaf (we also learn that there were previous invitations, and that Berthier had kept in touch with Bébian's widow): " *My dear Félix,"* he writes, *"the deaf-mutes will meet together on Sunday 25th inst. at five p.m. at Chapard's restaurant, 26 Place d'Angoulême, to celebrate, as is their custom, the memory of Abbé de l'Épée. I am writing to entreat you more strongly than ever to attend this ceremony in person, and indeed, I would hesitate to be so insistent, having sadly seen my efforts to persuade you fail at each of these anniversaries, if I did not know that your friendship is the equal of my own feelings towards you. Yours, etc., etc. My compliments and best wishes to Madame Bébian; I am ashamed to say that I have not yet seen her since returning from vacation."*
    Banquets des sourds muets réunis pour fêter les anniversaires de l'abbé de l'Épée, vol. II, Paris: Hachette, 1864, p. 3.
    We do not know whether Félix Lemaistre attended the dinner, but a letter addressed to Berthier in 1858 shows that they had not lost contact and even seemed quite close: *"My dear Berthier,"* he writes, *"I shall endeavor to be there. Write to me with the time and place. I believe you mentioned Chapard. Is that not the restaurant in the Place d'Angoulême? Do tell me more! Friendly compliments… " ibid.*, p. 146.
16. See in particular p. 103.
17. The intervention of Édouard Fournié (p. 64), deputy chief physician at the INSMP, shows that there was no consensus, and accredits the idea of an *"ambush"* and a *"set-up"* (Christian Cuxac, *Le langage des sourds*, Paris: Payot, p. 128). *"De l'instruction physiologique du sourd-muet"* (On the physiological instruction of the deaf-mute), taken from session minutes, and papers read or deposited at the International Otology Congress, September 6-9, 1880, cited by François

Auguste Bébian invites us to rethink the "golden century" of Deaf historiography, which runs from the founding initiative of Abbé de l'Épée in 1760 to the Milan Congress of 1880, the symbol of repression against sign language. That gathering was no mere epiphenomenon: its consequences were brutal, violent and very real, and can be still felt today, but *"the historiographic literature attributes at the same time too great and too little importance to the Milan Congress."*[18] As we have seen throughout this book, hostility to sign language had been building up since the beginning of the 19th century, a decade after the death of Abbé de l'Épée, in a variety of forms, which were all ultimately the expression of the same attitude. From a viewpoint of resistance, Bébian's role can therefore be seen as that of a bulwark against an "oralist" wave that reached its high-tide mark in Milan.[19] And beyond this histo-

---

Legent, "Approche de la pédagogie institutionnelle des sourds-muets jusqu'en 1900", Medic@, 2005 and Fabrice Bertin, *Les Sourds. Une minorité invisible,* Paris: Autrement, 2010, pp. 166-169.

Sign language was decried as synonymous with obscurantism, and its prohibition was hailed as a considerable "step forward". For Félix Deltour, the total adoption of articulation symbolized the transformation of the INSMP into *"a true house of intellectual, professional, and moral education, from which emerge every year young people restored to the role and dignity of man, capable of exchanging and relating with their fellows and making a useful place for themselves in this society, from which their double infirmity seemed forever to have excluded them."* F. Deltour, "L'Institution nationale des sourds-muets de Paris ", *Revue des Deux Mondes*, vol. 111, 1892, pp. 175-207.

18. *"The place of this congress in the history of Deaf education is comparable to that of the battle of Waterloo in the political and military history of 19th century France: it symbolizes the defeat of sign language, and is generally seen as the decisive moment in the reform of teaching methods in France, leading to the prohibition of sign language. And yet, while it is hard to dispute that the Milan Congress was an important step on the path leading to the prohibition of sign language, the idea of it being a 'decisive' congress has more to do with legend than with historical accuracy. "*
François Buton, "Le congrès de Milan, entre mythe et réalités", *Surdités* n° 4, 2001, p. 46.

19. "Oralism " tends to be thought of as a monolithic bloc, in opposition to "gesturalism". The reality, however, is far more complex, as Jean-René Presneau explains perfectly by distinguishing between a moderate oralism and a more radical (institutional and "pedagogical" oralism) and reminding us that "the

riographic timeline, it is the binary opposition between oralist and gesturalist that he asks us to rethink.[20] This dichotomy took hold especially from the end of the 19th century onward, under the cover of a contested argument: that sign language is incompatible with the oral modality of the French language, and to make use of the former is to jeopardize the acquisition of the latter – an absurdity that has been constantly critiqued and which represents a fault line between different approaches.[21] And yet this man, like the issues he raised, remains largely, if not totally, unknown outside the Deaf world. Here, he belongs to the pantheon of the great; outside, he is just another anonymous figure: Auguste Bébian, among all others, is the most revealing example – perhaps the most emblematic by the symbolism he has come to embody – of the gulf that separates Deaf people from the society in which they live. An entire portion of human history is denied, as though it never existed, as though a whole community did not exist. An invisibility reminiscent of that encountered in 1802 by the young

partisans of the oral method were not united" (Jean-René Presneau, *Signes et institution des sourds, XVIIIe-XIXe siècles*, Champ-Vallon, 1998, pp. 176, 177 and 178). This first form of oralism could be described as pragmatic, and was looked upon favorably by some Deaf people, such as Ernest Dusuzeau: he balances out *"the need, for social and pedagogical reasons, to learn spoken French, and the obligation, for psychical and cultural reasons, to maintain the language of gestural signs"* (*ibid.*, p. 177). Bébian would no doubt have been comfortable with this current of thought: *"instruction must therefore begin by the study of language. Speech cannot be its principle, nor its basis; but it can and must be made the most ready and convenient complement for the deaf-mute, when he finds himself in the company of somebody who does not understand his signs and* [...] *the particular aim of the education of the deaf-mute is to teach him the language of his country."* (Bébian, *Journal de l'instruction*, n° 3, p. 107 and n° 4, p. 60).

20. See previous note.

21. The Deaf American James L. Smith wrote in 1900: *"Deaf-mutes are not opposed to the teaching of speech. Quite the contrary. Most deaf-mutes would consider it a great privilege to learn to speak intelligibly. They are convinced that all deaf-mute children must learn to speak. But they oppose the teaching of speech to the detriment of the other methods. They protest against those who make speech the only purpose of education and the only method to be used."* James L. Smith, *Congrès international pour l'étude des questions d'éducation et d'assistance des sourds-muets*, Paris, 1900.

Guadeloupean arriving in Paris, whose journey we have traced. But what may have been understandable two centuries ago is far harder to comprehend today. It is doubtless because Deaf people and their unique visio-gestural, three-dimensional language raise questions that challenge the "*ordinary categories of thought*,"[22] as our society cannot conceive of there being a culture where it sees only a "*disability*". In France, in Paris, a small meeting room at the INJS, where he held office for four years, was named for him in 1981; a meager monument to one who was a precursor in many fields. Although a greater homage is paid to him on his native island, his name no longer evokes any memories there, and seems bound up only with the mutual school that he managed for little over a year.[23]

The vicissitudes of history prevent us from gaining closer knowledge of Auguste Bébian, but his work and his thinking opened up a path that cannot be ignored, at a time where, at last, *le langage d'action* or, as we now call it, French Sign Language (*LSF*), is recognized by French law.[24] Auguste Bebian led the way in recognizing deaf identity and culture. His approach to deafness, as a singular way of being in the world rather than as a physiological deficit or sign of infirmity, is totally unprecedented and foreshadows a form of

22. Delaporte, *Les Sourds, c'est comme ça*, p. 11.
23. One of the oldest streets in Pointe-à-Pitre, originally Rue Saint-Louis, then Rue de la Loi, was renamed Rue Bébian in 1884, following a submission to the local council by a Dr. Isaac; Similarly, in Basse-Terre in 1912 where the Rue de la Nouvelle-Cité and the Place du Clocher were renamed (for reasons that remain unknown). Minutes of the municipal council of Basse-Terre, Nov. 28, 1912. Rodolphe Enoff, *Guide historique des noms de rues à Basse-Terre et à Pointe-à-Pitre,* E. Enoff, 1993. An informational brochure published by the Mutuelle Générale de l'Éducation Nationale (MGEN), from 1991, gives a few details (some of them erroneous) about Bébian in connection with the street that bears his name in Pointe-à-Pitre.
24. Law n° 2005-102 of 11 February 2005, Article 75.
It has to be said, however, that this is a very timid recognition, a long way from illustrating Bébian's maxim "*the sign is the shadow of the idea*": LSF is given lip-service as an object of teaching… and as a second language, but not as a first language! As for teaching in LSF… that remains almost non-existent!

"deafhood" or "surditude", previously overlooked. A deafhood that puts a name to a collective lived experience which is worthwhile, "*a space of exploration and expression, by the Deaf themselves, of what they are, their resources, and what binds them to the fate of other people, Deaf and non-Deaf, across differences of culture and social context.*"[25] But "[…] *neither surditude nor negritude belong to the discourse of scientific analysis. And that is no doubt one of the pitfalls we must avoid: making these movements out to be what they are not* […]."[26] The driving force behind all our future struggles and demands is enshrined in the guiding principle of Auguste Bébian's thinking: the sign is the shadow of the idea.[27]

25. Sophie Dalle-Nazébi, Fabrice Bertin, "De la négritude à la surditude : penser l'hétérogénéité des Sourds" / "From Negritude to Surditude: towards an Analytic for thinking about Deaf Diversity", forthcoming.
26. *Ibid.*
27. "*The sign follows the idea as the shadow follows the body*" (*Journal de l'instruction*, 1826, n° 1 p. 28); "*the sign follows the idea as its shadow; it is its faithful representation*" (*Essai sur les sourds-muets*, p. 55).

Sources and Methods

Tracking an elusive figure, in Guadeloupe…

To approach Auguste Bébian as closely as possible, to better understand how he came to be the man he was, how he changed throughout his life, it is essential to try to reconstitute his environment, to seek to retrace his journey as accurately as we can. In so doing, we can uncover insightful cross-references and attempt to analyze them in the light of all the evidence we have unearthed.

But the archives that record his life are hard to find: due to their dispersal (between the island of Guadeloupe, where he was born and where he died, Paris, where he arrived as a young adolescent, and Rouen, where he briefly worked); due to the twists and turns of his personal and professional life, for which few documents were preserved; and also due to the lack of regard afforded to this historical resource. Additionally, the many inconsistencies and approximations make the task even more complex: dates and places sometimes differ.

Christian Schnakenbourg has drawn up an inventory of archives concerning Guadeloupe:[1]

> *"With the exception of a small number of rare – and also very incomplete – collections (the civil registry and the Conseil Supérieur in Martinique and Guadeloupe, the notaries in Guadeloupe, and various odds and ends), the departmental archives contain precious few original sources from before 1815. Wars, hurricanes, earthquakes, fires, woodlice, the deplorable conditions in which the archives were stored (or, more accurately, piled up), not to forget (alas!) acts of indifference and sometimes even stupidity (Guy Lasserre for example tells us that in 1941, 'a governor' had the archives of the former immigration ser-*

1. Christian Schnakenbourg, "Histoire économique" in Danielle Bégot (ed.), *Guide de la recherche en histoire antillaise et guyanaise: Guadeloupe, Martinique, Guyane, Saint-Domingue, XVIIe-XXe siècles*, Paris: CTHS, 2011, p. 93.

vice in the sub-prefecture building in Pointe-à-Pitre burned because 'deemed to be of no utility'),[2] *all contributed to the disappearance of the oldest documents."*

The only biographies of Auguste Bébian were written by Ferdinand Berthier,[3] as we noted earlier, and to a lesser degree by Louis-Émile Vauchelet.[4] Vauchelet went to France for four years, probably between 1880 and 1891,[5] during which time he visited the INSMP, where he admired *"his full-length portrait, religiously preserved at the Deaf-Mute establishment In Paris."*[6] He also attests that more than fifty years after Bébian's dismissal from that establishment at the beginning of 1821,[7] his memory was still very

2. Guy Lasserre, *La Guadeloupe, étude géographique*, Bordeaux, doctoral thesis, 1961, p. 308.
3. Ferdinand Berthier, *Notice sur la vie et les ouvrages d'Auguste Bébian, ancien censeur de l'Institut royal des Sourds-Muets,* Paris: Ledoyen, 1839.
   By that time, Ferdinand Berthier had been a full teacher at the INSMP for ten years. He was, with Alphonse Lenoir, the only Deaf teacher (making two Deaf Teachers out of a total of nine teachers in 1836).
4. Vauchelet worked on the Guadeloupean newspaper *Le Colonial*, and wrote a short biography in 1910, which was published in the newspaper from May 19 to June 14, 1911.
5. i.e. between the painting of Bébian's portrait and the opening of Théophile Denis' museum.
6. See p. 10.
7. A folder kept at the *Institution nationale des jeunes sourds* (INJS) in Paris holds all the items relating, directly or indirectly, to Bébian's presence in these premises from 1817 to 1821. It includes writings by Baron de Gérando, chairman of the INSMP's board of governors, and by Ferdinand Berthier, the Institution's first Deaf professor and a friend of Bébian. It contains:
   - A 20-page register (certified copies of the originals, made in March 1840) concerning the Bébian affair, amounting to a list of charges against him. The register consists of:
     - Ten pages organized into two columns, providing an annotated commentary on Berthier's biographical work *Notice sur la vie et les ouvrages de Bébian*, published the previous year. The left-hand column contains quotations from this work, while in the right-hand column all the quotations in praise of Bébian are refuted point by point. The author is anonymous;
     - A letter from Louis-Pierre Paulmier to the board of governors, dated January 4, 1821, recounting the altercation with Bébian;

much alive: "*You would scarcely believe how his memory is venerated at the Paris Establishment*", he writes in a letter to the chief editor.[8] Vauchelet's biography draws very largely on Berthier's account,

---

- A letter from Abbé Sicard to Baron Keppler (January 3, 1821) about Bébian's assault on Paulmier, and asking the board of governors to suggest how best to avoid a scandal;
- A letter from Abbé Sicard (January 4, 1821) thanking the governors of the institution for sacking Bébian;
- A letter from Abbé Sicard to de Gérando (October 20, 1820), in which he asks for Bébian to be appointed first deputy;
- Finally, a second letter from Abbé Sicard to De Gérando, rescinding the previous one;

- A 9-page memo addressed by Berthier to Duchatel, the Interior Minister (January 22, 1840), accompanied by a letter for the cabinet secretary of the Interior Ministry. Berthier is proactive in defending his book on Bébian from the anticipated attacks by De Gérando;
- A letter from De Gérando to the Interior Minister (August 11, 1832) requesting assistance and encouragement for Abbé Chazotte, who "*obtains the most remarkable success, and owes it to methods that are his and his alone*";
- A letter from De Gérando to a State Councilor, announcing his desire to publish the results of a survey, conducted by the Ministry of Foreign Affairs, on the methods used in the various schools for the Deaf in Europe and America, and requesting assistance in drawing up a equivalent table of the French schools.

Most of these records are therefore letters, written for administrative purposes. As for the dismissal of Auguste Bébian, the facts of the case are known to us through a letter addressed by Louis-Pierre Paulmier to the board of governors on January 4, 1821, relating the events of the previous day: "*At 11 a.m., he went to Monsieur Sicard, his respected master, to ask him to kindly divide the pupils up into 4 equal classes as he had previously resolved to do…*" Bébian also went to see Sicard, and it was this allocation of students which triggered a dispute that culminated in Bébian hitting Paulmier and injuring his head. The institution's physician, Jean-Marc Itard, issued the following medical certificate: "*Monsieur Paulmier came to me to have a wound dressed that he had just received on his head; on examining this part carefully, I found on the top of the cranium, near the sagittal suture, two small and perfectly round bruises representing a circular incision such as might have been made by a pastry-cutter and which seemed to me to be the result of two blows delivered to that part by a hand armed with a heavy door-key…*"

8. *Ibid.*

and to a lesser degree on those of Alphonse Esquiros[9] or Jules Ballet.[10] The journalist Vauchelet recalls:[11]

> *"[...] I was a child when I met Bébian on Basse-Terre. He had been entrusted to the guidance of my father, who at that time was a notary..."*

Louis' father Antoine Vauchelet, the Basse-Terre notary, probably knew Auguste's father Joseph Bébian. The Bébian family tree contains several notaries or other legal practitioners; his mother, Félicité, was godmother to his nephew Jean-Jacques, also a notary.[12]

Most of my research was conducted at the National Institute for Deaf Children in Paris, the city where Auguste Bébian arrived in 1802 and where he was baptized by Abbé Sicard, who had by then been the principal of the establishment for 12 years (a late baptism, at the age of eleven or thirteen, depending on which date of birth is correct).[13] Ferdinand Berthier relates Bébian's arrival In Paris:[14]

> *"...sent to Abbé Sicard two years after (1800), he was presented at the font by the famous teacher."*

---

9. Alphonse Esquiros (1812-1878) politician and writer, author of *Paris, ou Les sciences, les institutions, et les mœurs au XIXe siècle* in two volumes (1847), in which he outlines the state of affairs in the capital at that time.
10. The Guadeloupean Jules Ballet (1825-1904) was employed as registrar of mortgages in Pointe-à-Pitre and as board member of the Banque de Guadeloupe. His hand-written notes bear witness to social and cultural change in 19th-century Guadeloupe (19 volumes and 10 binders kept at the Archives nationales d'Outre-Mer, (France's Overseas Territories National Archives) (ANOM).
11. Antoine Vauchelet's records are kept at ANOM (DPCC, GUA 2800 and following). Examination of these records did not reveal any recorded exchange between Bébian and Vauchelet *père*.
12. Jean-Jacques Cicéron (1772-1838) was the son of Bébian's elder sister Marguerite, and her third child (she had 10 with her first husband, 3 with the second) (genealogy established by his descendant Paul Michaux: *http://gw.geneanet.org/pmchx* (branch 24).
13. Annex 2.
14. Berthier, *Notice*, p. 5.

Having been born in 1789 or 1791, one can only wonder why Auguste was baptized so late, when he was almost no longer a child.[15] And why was Abbé Sicard chosen as his godfather? In an attempt to answer these questions and reconstitute the environment in which the young Auguste grew up, I traced the genealogy of his parents, Joseph Bébian (1749-1836) and Marie-Félicité Michaux (1754-1813?).

The genealogy support group *Entraide généalogique du midi toulousain* (EGMT), as well as a personal file kept at the National Archives,[16] confirm that his father came from Toulouse. When, how, and why exactly did he set sail for Guadeloupe? The manifest of passengers from Comminge[17] heading for the French West Indies lists three different names:[18]

---

15. Contrary to standard Catholic practice – transl.
16. File on Joseph Bébian (ANOM ref. EE/137/13).
17. Comminges was a former region of the province of Gascony, lying astride the current départements of Haute-Garonne, Hautes-Pyrenées, Gers and Ariège.
18. The passenger manifests, conserved in the departmental archives of Haute-Garonne (ref. BR082605) record: in 1768, the embarkation of one "Jean Joseph de Bébian", and another "Bébian de Pachen, aged 19 years, born in Toulouse, bound for Guadeloupe." In 1777 there is a "Joseph de Bébian, 25, equerry, bound for Saint Domengue (sic)" and five years later, in 1780, another "Joseph de Bébian, 27, equerry, bound for Martinique." This fits, give or take a few details, with another source: "Pierre André (?) Joseph (de) Bébian sails for Guadeloupe on September 20, 1768; Jean Joseph Bébian de Pachen, 19, from Toulouse; sails for Bordeaux on July 16, 1778 and reembarks at Bordeaux on April 24, 1780 for Martinique; Joseph de Bébian, 27 (*Généalogie et histoire de la Caraïbe*, n° 240, October 2010, p. 6496). With the exception of Pierre-André, the entry, written by Gustave Chaix d'Est-Ange, in the *Dictionnaire des familles françaises anciennes ou notables à la fin du XIXe siècle,* (Évreux, imprimerie Hérissey, vol. 13, p. 116) also provides some information: "*Pierre-André de Bébian, born in 176-, died in Pointe-à-Pitre in 1836, had an only daughter, Mme de Sonis, mother of General de Sonis*" (in fact, he did not have an only daughter; he had two sons and two daughters, by two different wives, see Annex 2). Are Jean Joseph Bébian de Pachen and Pierre André Joseph de Bébian the same person? Auguste's father is commonly referred to by the first name Joseph (affidavit or death certificate); the "de Pachin" alongside the name "de Bébian" appears only once thereafter, following "the death in 1853 of the Baronne de Vernou, born Marie-Françoise de Bébian de Pachin" (Auguste's sister), at the age of de 60, in Angers; or so we are told by *the Annuaire de la Noblesse de France* (according to the GHC (Généalogie et Histoire de la Caraïbe), she died on April 8, 1852, at the age of

- Jean Joseph Bébian de Pachen
- Joseph de Bébian
- Pierre André Joseph (de) Bébian

Are they in fact one and the same person? Judging by his age when he died (at 87, in 1836), Joseph Bébian must have been born in 1749. His forebears, it seems, were of noble – or at least bourgeois – stock,[19] as his own father, Raimond, was a Capitoul of the city of Toulouse.[20]

In 1775, Joseph Bébian married Marie-Félicité Michaux, who was born on the island (in a place called "Mancenilliers", municipality of

---

61). Meanwhile, the noble particle "de" in "de Bébian" crops up sporadically: on several much later civil registry deeds, in 1828 (the opening of an account by Joseph Bébian for his son Auguste on February 7, 1828, or the deed of sale of a building by Joseph Bébian to his other son Louis, on October 14). According to the "Pierfit" database made available online on the website *Généanet* in order to retrace the genealogy of Gaston de Sonis, Pierre-André Joseph (de) Bébian, presumably Auguste's father, left for the Antilles with his brother, Jean-Joseph (or Joseph). Chaix d'Est-Ange (*op. cit.*) does indeed mention two brothers.

19. The attribution of the pews in the church of Notre-Dame de la Dalbabe in Toulouse (Carmes district) dated April 12, 1708, ascribes a place in the 15th row (out of 24; along with the footboard in front of the baluster and the stone steps leading to the sacristy) to a "Monsieur Bébian, silk manufacturer and merchant", next to a number of parliamentary dignitaries (records of Blaise Boyer, notary at Toulouse, Departmental Archives of Haute-Garonne, ref. 3E1817).

20. The role of Capitoul dates back to Alphonse Jourdain (1103-1148), son of Raymond IV of Toulouse (1042-1105). The Capitouls formed a "municipal council" with administrative – and to a lesser degree, following the creation of the parliament of Toulouse in the 14th century, legal – powers. To be a Capitoul was a sign of social class; one had to exercise an "honorable" profession such as lawyer, magistrate, or notary. The memoirs of General de Sonis, grandson of Joseph Bébian, published in 1890, recall: "*As for grandfather, who hailed from Toulouse, he was fulsome* (in his praise? The words are missing in the original text) *for his city of origin, where a Bébian, he used to tell us, had been a Capitoul.*" Monseigneur L. Baunard, *Le général de Sonis, d'après ses papiers et sa correspondance*, Paris: Poussielgue frères, 1890 (10th edition). Gaston de Sonis was Sylphide's third child, resulting from her second marriage to Louis-Gaston de Sonis (Sylphide's first marriage was to Charles de Lestortière, with whom she had a daughter, Charlotte; Charles-Joseph Lanvre de Lestortière was probably poisoned by one of the enslaved people from the "La Grippière" plantation, which he owned (Ary Brousillon, *L'exécution de l'esclave Gertrude : l'empoisonneuse de Petit-Bourg*, Les Abymes: Créapub', 1999, p. 3).

Petit-Canal, in the western part of Grande-Terre, in 1754). Marie-Félicité came from a large family, originally from Gourbeyre, in the south of Guadeloupe proper (or Basse Terre),[21] which subsequently spread out to the Saintes islands and Grande-Terre through marriage. Her father was a goldsmith in the village of Le Moule, not far from Petit-Canal, which would seem to indicate a certain social standing.

It was not until the fourteenth or sixteenth year of their marriage that their first children were born. We have no birth certificates for them; only an "*acte de notoriété*",[22] an official document established in 1828 at the behest of Joseph Bébian to correct an "oversight", specifying the place of birth of Auguste and his sister Marie-Honorine, the couple's only two children (Joseph and Marie-Félicité would divorce in December 1795, after twenty years of marriage): the Bergopzoom *habitation*[23] at Morne-à-l'Eau, in the west of Grande-Terre island (possibly in the Grands Fonds region,[24]

21. See Annex 1 for a simplified genealogy.
    Personal communication from the historian Gérard Lafleur, whose written works include a study of Gourbeyre.
    It seems the Michaux family was made up of people of mixed European and African ancestry.
    Gérard Lafleur, *Gourbeyre: une commune de Guadeloupe*, Paris: Karthala, 1997.
22. Document reproduced in Annex 4.
    An acte de notoriété is a "*document by which a government official gathers testimonies in order to establish a circumstance or material fact that has been observed by a large number of people, or which has come to their attention, or which seemed to them to be attested. It records 'hearsay evidence'. The* acte de notoriété *is consequently used in matters of filiation.*"
    Serge Braudo, honorary counsel at the Versailles Court of Appeal and Alexis Baumann, lawyer at the Paris bar, *Dictionnaire du droit privé français de Serge Braudo* (*www.dictionnaire-juridique.com*).
23. The *habitation*, as an agricultural concern, is a highly structured system. Frédéric Régent, *Esclavage, métissage, liberté. La Révolution française en Guadeloupe*, Paris: Grasset, 2004, p. 93) offers a typical example, which is not always generalizable. Two characteristics suggest that *Bergopzoom* was small: its hard-to-reach location, and the fact that coffee crops are much less labor-intensive than sugarcane crops.
24. *L'encyclopédie Désormeaux* states that Bébian was born in the "Grippon" district of Morne-à-l'Eau, which was at that time an isolated town with an insalubrious coastline. *Dictionnaire encyclopédique Désormeaux: dictionnaire encyclopédique*

which sits astride three municipalities: Morne-à-l'Eau, Le Moule and Saint-Anne). This plantation does not feature on any map, and is not listed by the royal surveyor engineers in the second third of the 18th century, several decades before the birth of Auguste;[25] it is mentioned only in the affidavit.[26] Berg-op-Zoom is the name of a town in the Netherlands, the site of a victorious siege by the French Army in September 1747, during the Austrian War of Succession (1740-1748).[27] Was this most un-French of names chosen to mark that event? Bergopzoom is unknown to the departmental archives and to local historians alike:[28] was it perhaps too small,[29] or too short-lived? Or perhaps it changed its name?[30]

---

des Antilles et de la Guyane, Jack Corzani (ed.), Fort de France: Désormeaux, 1992-1993, vol. 2, p. 330.

25. *Carte générale des îles de Grande Terre et Guadeloupe, réduite* [...], *levée par les ingénieurs géographes pendant les années 1764 à 1768, et mémoire contenant la légende de la carte, 1768* (ANOM ref.: DPCC Port X A 260).
Also consulted: *Plan de diverses habitations des bourgs du quartier du Norroy dans la paroisse du Moulle en l'isle Grande-Terre, avec chacune leur nom,* Mercier fils arpenteur, Bourgeois notaire royal, July 4, 1746. (ANOM ref.: $F^3$288 n°48); the Moreau de Saint-Méry atlas (ANOM ref. F^3); and the manuscripts of Ballet (1825-1904) (19 vols. and 10 dossiers, 8 of which are dedicated to economic changes; ANOM ref. 2J).

26. The name was given by Auguste Bébian's father himself, Joseph, in the affidavit drawn up at his request in 1828 by Maître Ruttre, notary of Pointe-à-Pitre.

27. The siege of Berg-op-Zoom, which ended on September 11, 1747, was, along with the siege of Maastricht (May 14, 1747), a turning point of the war, definitively tipping the balance of forces in favor of the French.

28. Gérard Lafleur (*Gourbeyre, op. cit.*), Raymond Boutin (*La population en Guadeloupe de l'émancipation à l'assimilation, 1848 à 1946,* Cayenne: Ibis rouge, 2006) and Danielle Bégot (ed.), (*Guide de la recherche, op. cit.*).

29. A coffee crop requires a smaller labor force than for sugarcane, for example, and a smaller area: some five or six squares or *carrés* (*a carré* being about 2.3 acres). However, one must be wary of hasty generalizations: one coffee plantation in Gosier, in 1833, measured 138 *carrés*). Moreover, the nature of the plantation is sometimes not indicated.

30. In 1813, Félicité Michaux' younger brother Jean-Jacques (born 1769, and thus fifteen years younger than his sister Félicité, Auguste's mother, who – we learn from her daughter's marriage certificate – was no longer alive in 1813) died at the Saintrac, plantation, four years before his wife Flore Élisabeth Classe. Auguste's aunt Flore is recorded as having died at the "Beagopsoom"

While his place of birth is uncertain, the exact date is a mystery.[31] As we saw above, Joseph Bébian omitted to officially register the birth of his first child, Auguste: the affidavit established later, at his request, on October 6, 1828, by a notary in Pointe-à-Pitre, Maître Ruttre, is the sole authoritative document.[32] It lists only the month, August, and the year, 1789, without mentioning the date, which other sources give as either the 4th or the 14th. These birth details are mentioned sixteen times in various sources (Annex 2).

The date of birth is most often given as August 4, 1789 in Pointe-à-Pitre or, more generally, in Guadeloupe. Only one legal document, from 1828 – a ruling following an "*enquête de notoriété*" (verification of affidavit) – pins down the date and place with any degree of certainty. The various sources disagree, influenced, perhaps, not only by the concomitance with a key event of the Revolution, the abolition of the feudal system, but also with the year of the death of Abbé de l'Épée,[33] seen as the spiritual father of "Deaf-Mutes". Coincidental or symbolic? This simultaneity does not escape Timothée Oriol:[34]

---

plantation (perhaps the creolization of a hard-to-remember name?). Were Saintrac and Bergopzoom joined together in the same place? Only through painstaking scrutiny of land registers would it be possible to confirm this, but mortgage records for Guadeloupe do not start until 1830. Bégot (ed.), *Guide de la recherche*.

31. Most of the sources (eleven out of sixteen consulted: see the summary table in Annex 2) indicate this date. It is debatable, however, to what extent they are independent of each other: Fernand Buisson's *Dictionnaire de pédagogie et d'instruction primaire, for example,* draws extensively on the writings of Ferdinand Berthier. He describes Auguste Bébian's arrival in Paris, for instance, in the exact same terms. But where did Berthier get his information? He fails to cite his sources, gives the wrong place of birth (Pointe-à-Pitre instead of Morne-à-l'Eau) and, as we have seen elsewhere, his objectivity is sometimes questionable.
32. This affidavit, reproduced in Annex 4, was copied into the civil register of Morne-à-l'Eau on November 2, 1828 (n° 23).
33. Abbé de l'Épée died on December 23, 1789. Maryse Bezagu-Deluy, *L'abbé de l'Épée. Instituteur gratuit des sourds et muets 1712-1789*, Paris: Seghers, 1990, p. 28.
34. T. Oriol, *Les hommes célèbres de la Guadeloupe*, Basse-Terre, Imprimerie catholique, 1935, p. 61.

"A fine talking-point for lovers of astrology or those who ascribe symbolic meaning to dates of birth."

Not only does the exact day fluctuate, even the year oscillates between 1789 and 1791: a confusion we can put down to Auguste Bébian himself. Six years after arriving in Paris, in 1808, he enrolled in a class taught by the naturalist Lamarck[35] and wrote his age on the register, in line 25:

25 Roch Ambroise Bébian de la Guadeloupe agé de 16 ans, &c.

At the following year's *Concours général* competitive examinations, where he ranked third in the "*Accessit des nouveaux*" (Commended Newcomers) category for translation from Ancient Greek, his name is similarly followed by an inscription meaning "born August 4, 1791 in Guadeloupe".

This confirms the written declaration made by the Mayor of Rouen a quarter-century later:[36]

"Mr. Bébian was born in Guadeloupe, in the canton of Morne-à-l'Eau, on August 14, 1791."

According to the aforementioned affidavit, however, 1791 was the year his sister Marie-Honorine was born. An error on his part? Deliberate or otherwise? The mystery remains unsolved.[37]

35. From the spring of 1795 through to 1823, Jean-Baptiste Lamarck gave lessons at the Museum of Natural History in Paris (founded by decree on June 10, 1793), where he was "Professor of Insects and Worms" and in charge of the library. Bébian enrolled for these courses in 1808 (one of 35 enrollees that year; the details and signatures are kept in the Museum's central library (ref. AM 569)).
36. Letter from the Mayor of Rouen to the Prefect of Seine Inférieure, December 26, 1832. (ADSM, Series 2T1).
37. Affidavit of October 6, 1828, Annex 5.
    On May 14, 1991, in a lecture delivered at Bébian Mixed School in Basse-Terre, the lawyer and historian Félix Rodes established Auguste Bébian's birthplace as being Morne-à-l'Eau (*Le Progrès social*, 15 June, 1991, n° 1788).

Whatever his date of birth, Auguste was born in the heart of a slave plantation. Managing this *habitation* does not seem to have been the main activity of his father Joseph Bébian, ever on the lookout for new opportunities:[38] in October 1790, he was part of the deputation sent to Saint-Pierre-de-la-Martinique.[39] The documents kept in the National Archives[40] seem to suggest that Joseph Bébian played an active role in the government of Guadeloupe from the outset of the administration of Captain General Jean-Baptiste Lacrosse.[41] As from the summer of 1801 (from 6 Messidor, Year IX, to be precise) "Citizen Bébian"[42] was assigned the mission of collecting

---

To do so, he used Joseph Bébian's affidavit of October 6, 1828, which he also published in his journal (*Le Progrès social*) with the aim of settling the controversies around Auguste's Bébian birth: a sign of how historians can struggle to pin facts down.

38. A certain "Bébian" is mentioned as being a "slave-owner", not at Morne-à-l'Eau but in a neighboring municipality, Le Moule (Oruno D. Lara, *Les propriétaires d'esclaves en 1848*, Paris: L'Harmattan, 2010, p. 152). Is this Joseph Bébian? Various official documents attest to this status of slave-owner, but in reference to Pointe-à-Pitre: the 1796 census, the affidavit, the marriage certificate of his daughter Sylphide in 1818, the deed of sale of a property on January 14, 1828, and his death certificate all mention Joseph Bébian as a landowner domiciled in Pointe-à-Pitre (the noble particle 'de' is attached to his name on the deed of sale). Was there some confusion over administrative boundaries? The Grands Fonds region, as mentioned earlier, stretches across three municipalities.
39. Pierre-François-Regis Dessalles mentions him in *Historique des troubles survenus à la Martinique pendant la Révolution,* (foreword by Henri de Frémont), Société d'histoire de la Martinique, 1982, p. 421). The precise role played by Joseph Bébian remains to be elucidated.
40. ANOM C7A55F°54.
41. Jean-Baptiste Raymond de Lacrosse (1761-1829), a naval officer, was appointed Captain General of Guadeloupe in 1801 by First Consul Bonaparte. His aide-de-camp was Louis Delgrès (1766-1802), who renounced this role and played a key part in the 1802 revolt. Oruno Lara, *La Guadeloupe dans l'histoire : la Guadeloupe physique, économique, agricole, commerciale, financière, politique et sociale, 1492-1900*, Paris: L'Harmattan, 1921; Jacques Adélaïde-Merlande, *Histoire générale des Antilles et des Guyanes, Des Précolombiens à nos jours*, Paris: L'Harmattan, 1994.
42. The first name is not mentioned, but the family name is not a common one in Guadeloupe.

funds held by the "Prize Commissioner of Havana", and then three days later was sent to Jamaica, which was then a Spanish island but holding French prisoners. His functions in government seem to have accrued, as between the summer of 1801 and the winter of 1802 he was appointed "Commissioner of the Government of Guadeloupe Assigned to the Spanish Islands."[43] In 1822, he occupied the post of "Commissioner for Trade Relations and Authorized Representative to the Captaincy General for the Government of Guadeloupe in Havana."[44] By his death in 1836, in Pointe-à-Pitre, aged 87, he had acquired a certain renown, and a relatively substantial fortune.[45]

Was Auguste's departure in 1802 linked to the political upheavals in Guadeloupe that year?[46] Or to his father's second marriage two years earlier?[47] Or was it perhaps motivated by the recent creation of those new secondary education establishments, the "*lycées*"?[48] How did a young adolescent cope with an Atlantic crossing lasting some five weeks at the time? Alone or accompanied? At which port did he embark in Guadeloupe, and where did he disembark in Europe? The passenger lists are unfortunately silent on these questions.[49]

… and in France

There are almost no traces of young Auguste in Paris:

43. On 9 Nivôse, Year X, he wrote to the minister, using this title (ANOM C7A55 F°242).
44. ANOM EE137/13.
45. Post-mortem inventory of the possessions of Joseph Bébian, established on September 6, 1836 by Maître Anothe (ANOM ref.: NOT GUA 12).
46. A letter from the mayor of Rouen to the prefect of Seine Inférieure, dated December 26, 1832, alludes to a revolt: "*The civil records of that parish having been destroyed in the fire that swept the town during the revolt of the Negroes, he was unable to produce his birth certificate…* " (ADSM, Series 2T1).
47. On December 21, 1798 at Goyave, and not in 1800, as Ferdinand Berthier suggests.
48. The Act of 11 Floréal, Year X (May 1st, 1802) organized public secondary education: the "écoles centrales" were replaced by lycées, which differed in that they accepted boarders.
49. ANOM, Series E and EE, Table F5b 62, civilian personnel registration numbers dispersed throughout Series D2c.

An inscription on the registers of the lectures given by the naturalist Jean-Baptiste de Lamarck in 1808,[50] and a mention as an award-winner of the *Concours général* in 1809, confirm Ferdinand Berthier's description of him as a scholar:[51]

> *"From the outset of his career in the letters and the sciences, the young Bébian stood out by dint of two qualities that are rarely found together: a brilliant imagination and an inexhaustible patience. In 1806 or 1807, as a student at the Lycée Charlemagne, he achieved remarkable success in the Concours général."*

His appointment as répétiteur on August 20, 1817, following a report by the "Head of the second division" to "His Excellency the Minister, State Secretary at the Department of the Interior":[52]

> *"A post of répétiteur is currently vacant, subsequent to the resignation of Mr. Pissin, appointed by the decision of Your Excellency on July 28, 1816* [...] *The abbot, Mr. Sicard, principal of the Institution of Deaf-Mutes, presents, as a replacement for Mr. Pissin, one Mr. Bébian (Roch, Ambroise, Auguste). Mr. Sicard provides a most flattering account of this young man, and declares that he is perfectly suited to the position for which he might be considered."*
>
> *A letter from the principal of the Royal Institute of Deaf-Mutes in Paris, Abbé Sicard, to Baron de Gérando dated October 20, 1820, proposing the appointment of his godson as first deputy:*[53]
>
> [Bébian is] *perhaps the only one of my disciples to have perfected the spirit of my method. Last Saturday I inspected his class and was truly astonished to see young pupils (one of whom is just 9 years of age, and has been at the Institution for only a year) correct themselves and*

50. See p. 259.
51. Berthier, *Notice*, p. 6.
52. AMHCS, Bébian bundle, Pinart collection.
53. *Ibid.*
This letter was subsequently retracted, however, by a second – undated – letter from Sicard to de Gérando: *"The letter you received was copied from a draft written by this ambitious young man himself; I had to copy it out for the sake of peace."*

solve grammatical difficulties which, under any other master, would trouble the most advanced students."

Later, the mystery thickens: between 1821, when Auguste Bébian was dismissed from the INSMP, and 1832, when he was selected to head the Deaf-Mute Institute in Rouen (discussed *below*), what exactly did he do? According to Berthier, it was a period of intense reflection, entirely dedicated to France's Deaf community:[54]

"The envy aroused by his shining merit pursued him to the depth of his modest retreat. Bébian was not a man to be daunted by obstacles; he wanted the good for its own sake, he was aware of his strength, he had complete faith in his perseverance... He devoted every moment of his time to meditating on ways to perfect an education that was taking up his every waking moment. Aside from his works lauded in the most flattering manner by our administration and by the development committee established in 1826, he worked on other books which would later fill the bookcases of deaf-mutes..."
"Young women teachers had been recommended to him by the same governors who would have found it wrong for him to take charge of the Royal School in Paris. Among these ladies, we might mention Miss Morel, Mr. de Gérando's niece, who went to Bébian's house for five or six hours a day over a periodw of several months.
Bébian received some persuasive offers; he was approached to become principal of the Imperial Institution in Saint-Petersburg or the school in New York, but the love of France burned brightly in his Creole soul.... In 1826, at the insistence of a great many students' fathers, he founded a special school for deaf-mutes in the Boulevard du Mont-Parnasse."
"In 1826, he again submitted to Count Alexis de Noailles[55] a short paper on a system of industrial education."

54. Berthier, *Notice*, pp. 24, 27 and 37.
55. Louis Joseph Alexis, Comte de Noailles (1783-1835) was at that time the parliamentary representative for Corrèze (from 1824 to 1831), after previously representing the *département* of Seine (1815-1816); *Dictionnaire des parlementaires français, www.assemblee-nationale.fr*

Auguste Bébian himself attests to the creation of this "special school" and signs his books as "Principal of the Special Institution for Deaf-Mutes".[56] He gives its address as n° 24*bis* Boulevard Montparnasse, which now corresponds to n°s 58-60.[57] To date, no trace of this school has been found, whether in the National archives, the Paris Departmental Archives or the Paris History Library.[58] At the time, he was married to Honorine (or Adrienne) Lemaistre[59], by whom he had a son, Honoré.[60]

His speech at the National Assembly session of March 8, 1826, during a debate on a draft law regarding compensation for the colonialists in Saint-Domingue, suggests that he was aware of the realities on the ground in the French West Indies (speech reproduced in Le *Moniteur,* March 10, 1826).

56. From the very first issue of his *Journal des sourds-muets et des aveugles* in August 1826.
57. N° 24*bis* Boulevard Montparnasse became n°s 58 and 60 in 1851 (*Almanach-Bottin du commerce de Paris*, 1851, p. 37 reproduced in Jeanne Pronteau, *Les numérotages des maisons de Paris du XVe siècle à nos jours*, Paris: Imprimerie municipale, 1966).
58. Perhaps all traces were lost in the Paris town hall fire of 1871?
59. Her death certificate tells us that Honorine, Adrienne, Marie-Christine Lemaistre, born in Grenoble, 1801, died in Paris, 1884, married Auguste Bébian at the church of Sainte-Élisabeth du Temple in Paris, on December 9, 1822. She was descended from the revolutionary representative for Isère, Antoine Barnave. (Auguste's death " […] *left his widow, the granddaughter of Constituent Assembly member Barnave, in a precarious position,"* writes canon Ballivet in 1916 (Ballivet, "D'un vicaire et d'un instituteur", p. 287). It seems that she was not in fact his granddaughter but his grandniece (her grandmother, Françoise-Adelaïde Barnave, was the representative's sister).
   Did this marriage involve moving home? In 1828, on the first page of his *Nouvelle méthode pour apprendre à lire sans épeler,* he gives his address as n° 15, Rue des Beaux-Arts, Paris; two years earlier, in 1826, at the foot of the publishing prospectus for his *Éducation des sourds-muets mis à la portée des institutions primaires et de tous les parents,* he lists the address as n° 13, Rue des Cannettes.
60. The certificate of his death, on August 20, 1836, at the age of six, reveals that he was born in Paris in 1830. A former Deaf pupil of Bébian's, who became a renowned painter, Frederic Peyson, was chosen as a witness to register the birth at the town hall of the 11th arrondissement in Paris (now in the 6th) as Ferdinand Berthier recounts in the journal *L'ami des sourds-muets*, June 29, 1840.

In 1832, following the death of Abbé Huby,[61] a disciple of Abbé de l'Épée, and the Rouen municipal council's vote on May 22, 1832 in favor of "the establishment of a free course of instruction,"[62] Bébian applied, and won out over Paulmier – the same Paulmier with whom he had had an altercation nine years earlier, and who had retired from the INSMP in 1829.[63] On September 5, 1832, he took up his post for fourteen months (until March 1834; the exact date of, and reasons for, his leaving remain unknown). Was Bébian in a hurry to leave France for Guadeloupe on November 10, 1834?[64] He mentions his illness and alludes to the wet climate in Rouen.[65]

Just as it was with the ship that took him to Europe in 1802, thirty-two years earlier, his name does not appear in the passenger lists. Where did he embark and disembark? Given the length of the voyage, the Bébian family – Auguste, his wife Adrienne[66] and their young son Honoré, aged three – must have landed at the end of 1834 or beginning of 1835.[67] The main press organ, the *Gazette of-*

61. Georges Dubois, *L'abbé Huby, instituteur des sourds-muets de Rouen*, Rouen, imprimerie Albert Lainé, 1935.
62. ADSM: Series X (Assistance et prévoyance sociale (1800-1940)), in particular 3XP (Assistance sociale, 3XP12 : Affaires diverses de 1801 à 1896 and 3XP702 : Affaires générales, correspondance et instruction, 1813-1878; Series 2T (Imprimerie, Librairie, Presse), 2T1 (Brevets d'imprimeurs – Lithographes : Autorisation, Rejet, Mutation, Transfert. Individual folder, with one on Bébian).
63. François Buton, *L'administration des faveurs. L'État, les sourds et les aveugles (1789-1885)*, Rennes: Presses universitaires de Rennes, 2009, p. 200.
64. It would seem so, to judge by the letter from the minister to the prefect of Seine Inférieure, dated March 19, 1834 ("*Mr. Bébian has abandoned his pupils*") and from the mayor of Rouen to the prefect, dated May 31, 1834 (evoking the "*disappearance of Sieur Bébian…*" who had only three students at the time).
65. Berthier speaks of "*the damp and unpredictable climate of Rouen* becoming *deleterious to Bébian*'s *health*." Berthier, *Notice*, 1839, p. 38.
66. On Auguste Bébian's own death certificate it is written that he married Adrienne, Marie-Christine Lemaistre, from Grenoble, on December 9, 1822 at the church of Sainte-Élisabeth de Hongrie (aka "du Temple", now in the 3rd arrondissement of Paris). Her first name, Honorine, is not mentioned.
67. He still had family in Guadeloupe: his father, two siblings, and the latter's children (Auguste had a total of seventeen nephews and nieces); his mother however, Félicité Michaux, had died, exactly when we do not know, but before 1813, so at least twenty-one years earlier). Joseph Bébian was

ficielle de la Guadeloupe, says nothing of their return. According to Antoine Abou, author of a doctoral thesis on school enrolment in Guadeloupe in the 19th and 20th centuries,[68] Auguste Bébian was appointed principal of the mutual school in 1837:

> *"On the beginnings of the mutual school on Basse-Terre in 1831 at the initiative of the government, the data is lacking. We know only that A. Bébian became principal in February 1837, after Jeanson and Asseline, and that it was supposed to close when the Ploërmel Brothers came to Guadeloupe.[69] They arrived in 1838 and set up on Basse-Terre. While they waited for other Brothers to be sent out, to open new schools, the mutual school was moved to Pointe-à-Pitre. Bébian's school at this time had three hundred pupils; people of color and even whites sent their children there."*

---

living in Pointe-à-Pitre with his daughter Sylphide, her husband, and her two youngest children (two of Auguste's nephew/nieces) in a three-story house at the corner of Quai Lardenoy and Rue de la Martinique (now Rue Delgrès). The second floor was occupied by Sylphide's family, while Joseph lived on the third with his second wife Marie-Louise Latran Lagrange, the grandmother and godmother of Gaston de Sonis. Auguste's half-brother Louis-Valentin was, at that time, living at Anse Bertrand in the north of Grande-Terre island, where he had purchased a sugar plantation, after fathering seven children in Pointe-à-Pitre up until 1829 (where he probably lived). His last daughter was born in 1833 on the Durieux *habitation* at Anse Bertrand. Finally, Auguste's sister Marie-Honorine was then in Guadeloupe. She had been married since 1813 to Jean-Marie Maximilien de Vernou de Bonneuil (a widower 15 years her senior). They seem, from correspondence with Cardinal de Cheverus, to have spent several years in Boston, though they both eventually died in France: they had to leave Guadeloupe after the abolition of slavery. By the end of 1835, just a few months after Auguste's return, both his sister and his half-sister would be dead. The following year, he lost his son and his father.

68. Antoine Abou, *Un siècle de scolarisation à la Guadeloupe 1848-1948*, Université René Descartes Paris V, 1983.
69. The order of the Brothers of Christian Instruction of Ploërmel was founded by abbots Jean Marie de la Mennais and Gabriel Deshayes in 1819, with the specific goal of opening schools. Deshayes in particular set up schools for Deaf children at Auray and elsewhere in western France.

Chanoine Ballivet[70] confirms this appointment, as does Oruno Lara.[71] Did Bébian reside in Pointe-à-Pitre on his return from Paris? Did the town, in 1912, give his name to the Rue de la Nouvelle-Cité and the Place du Clocher,[72] now Rue Bébian and Place Bébian respectively, to commemorate his presence there? Strangely, the sources on this matter are contradictory and, in part, silent.[73]

A number of inconsistencies make it difficult to establish a precise chronology, starting with the account of Antoine Abou[74], who dates the beginnings of the mutual school on Basse-Terre to 1831; it would seem that the school was not created until the following year.[75] *L'Annuaire de la Guadeloupe* is also imprecise about founding of the school,[76] but says nothing of any position being taken up by

---

70. *"It was at this point that he returned to Guadeloupe, where for some time he ran the mutual school on Basse-Terre, until it passed from his hands to those of the Brothers of Ploërmel. He was then appointed to run the school in Pointe-à-Pitre. "* Chanoine Ballivet, "D'un vicaire et d'un instituteur", *L'Écho de la Reine*, n° 45, September 1916, p. 285.
71. *"On February 9, 1837, Bébian was appointed principal of* Basse-Terre Mutual School, *replacing the late Mr. Anselme. On February 16, he had the school relocated from Basse-Terre to Pointe-à-Pitre, to n°s 58 and 60 of the Rue de la Loi, which now bears his name."* Oruno Lara, *La Guadeloupe dans l'histoire*, p. 214.
   In fact, the governor's order transferring the school to Pointe-à-Pitre is dated February 16, 1838.
72. Minutes of the Basse-Terre municipal council, November 28, 1912. Rodolphe Enoff, *Guide historique des noms de rues à Basse-Terre et à Pointe-à-Pitre,* E. Enoff, 1993.
73. Issue n° 240 (October 2010) of *Généalogie et Histoire de la Caraïbe* (GHC) reports that Bébian *"set up a boarding school for young people in Pointe-à-Pitre, then directed the Mutual School for children of color in Pointe-à-Pitre"* (p. 6496) or Berthier again: *"finally, our fine friend left Paris, with wife and son, on November 10, 1834, to set up home in Pointe-à-Pitre.* [...] *He informed me* [...] *that, yielding to the insistence of several families, he had just opened a new school* [...]." Berthier, *Notice*, p. 44.
   There is no mention of him settling on Basse-Terre.
74. Abou, *Un siècle de scolarisation.*
75. The newspaper *Le Semeur, journal religieux, politique, philosophique et littéraire,* vol. VIII, n° 36, Sep. 4, 1839, p. 288.
76. *L'Annuaire de la Guadeloupe* of 1833 names one Madame Ballin as principal of the mutual schools for the instruction of young girls, but without specifying where. The following year, 1834, Mr. Janson is indicated as principal of the mutual school on Basse-Terre, succeeded by Mr. Asseline in 1835 and 1836.

Bébian in February 1837. Did he initially set up a school in Pointe-à-Pitre,[77] later to be joined by the school from Basse-Terre, in 1838?[78] Close scrutiny of the available archives[79] has shed no light on this point. Whatever the circumstances surrounding his appointment, Auguste Bébian did indeed run a mutual school in Pointe-à-Pitre, as Oruno Lara reports:[80]

> *"It was a real success, this school opened in Pointe-à-Pitre for the free population, and the curious flocked to the Bébian School, to see these young blacks and mulattos, with sparkling eyes and quick minds, spelling out the alphabet. Old Black men – former slaves – and goodly grandmothers with trembling heads, accompanying children, watched this spectacle with a heavy heart and eyes laden with regret for lost time, and with hope for the future."*

According to Chanoine Ballivet,[81] Auguste Bébian was not behind the creation of this school, but he did later set up another:

The registers for 1837 mention the existence of a successor (unnamed) – again as principal of the mutual school on Basse-Terre – and this latter person is succeeded in 1838 by "Mr. Bébian, director of mutual education in Pointe-à-Pitre ".

77. The municipal council of Pointe-à-Pitre, meeting on February 11, 1884, renamed the Rue de la Loi to Rue Bébian.
    Louis Belmont writes in the newspaper *La République* of April 3, 1903: *"Until the day when his name was given to the Rue de la Loi, nothing in Guadeloupe recalled the memory of this good man, who sleeps his last sleep in some forgotten corner of our town cemetery."*
78. The order of the governor of Guadeloupe, dated February 16, 1838, commands the transfer of the mutual school from Basse-Terre to Pointe-à-Pitre. *Bulletin officiel de la Guadeloupe*, 1838 (ref. ADG 3 K 1/11).
79. In the ANOM, decisions relating to public education and the opening of schools from 1816 to 1868 (SG/GUA/539) and archives relating to public education: inspection reports on the department (1818-1901), (SG/GUA//316). In the ADG, documents relating to the mutual school (3 K 1/11) and decisions relating to public education and the opening of schools from 1816 to 1868 (1 Mi 687/1).
80. Oruno Lara, *La Guadeloupe dans l'histoire*, p. 214.
81. Ballivet, "D'un vicaire et d'un instituteur", p. 283.

"Toward the end of his days, he opened a private school in the Rue de the Loi, now Rue Bébian, in Pointe-à-Pitre, in the house that today bears the numbers 58 and 60."

Is this the school listed by Abbé Darras – chaplain to the deaf-mute institute at Saint-Médard-lès-Soissons in France, and editor of the journal *Le Bienfaiteur des sourds-muets et des aveugles* in 1853 and 1854 – in his table of Deaf schools?[82]

Auguste Bébian died in Pointe-à-Pitre at the age of fifty, and his death was recorded on February 24, 1839.[83] The exact location of his grave is undetermined: where was Auguste Bébian buried? In the town where he died?[84] Just one hypothesis… perhaps the

82. *Le Bienfaiteur des sourds-muets et des aveugles*, 1853, n° 4, p. 100.
The existence such a school, if indeed it did exist, seems to have left no trace, which is both surprising and intriguing.
Ferdinand Berthier does, however, imply that Bébian was in contact with the Deaf ("*… we heard no more news from him; we learned only that, during a long illness that afflicted him, he had the misfortune to lose his son…*" He specifies in a footnote that "*the first news came to us through the parent of a deaf-mute child, who was a neighbor of our unfortunate friend.*" Berthier, *Notice*, pp. 44-45.
L'Almanach des sourds-muets de 1900 by Benjamin Dubois and E. Endrès (Paris: Imprimerie d'ouvriers sourds-muets, 1900, reprinted by Fox), shows that the Deaf community in Paris was fairly well-informed about news from Guadeloupe: on January 8, 1811 and on March 27, 1843 it made a collective donation for the victims of the Guadeloupe earthquake (see Note 85). (However, in this almanac, the creation by Bébian of the "first journal for the deaf-mute and the blind" is dated to 1820 (in fact it was in 1826) and it is also announced on June 1, 1839 that "*the deaf-mutes learn of the death of Bébian in Guadeloupe*," i.e. a little over three months after he died).

83. Death certificate dated February 24, 1839. He probably died as the result of a long-standing condition: in 1832, while he was in Rouen, "[…] *he was constantly unwell, and had suffered more than one attack serious enough to alarm his family, as well as his adopted family* [of pupils] […] *One day, lying utterly incapacitated in his bed, unable to sit up, having a little movement only in his right hand, he made use of it to assuage the concerns of his friends by writing us a note that read* […] *'I have not yet accomplished my mission. God will not call me to him until my task is done'* " Berthier, *Notice*, p. 31.

84. In the early 20th century, the Guadeloupean writer Gilbert de Chambertrand (1890-1984) commented, as had Louis Belmont (Note 77), on this absence of a burial-place: "*In the cemetery of Pointe-à-Pitre, under the plaintive melody of the*

grave disappeared in the earthquake that devastated Guadeloupe in 1843?[85]

In the 20th century, the writer Gilbert de Chambertrand laments:[86]

> *"Of all the noblest figures of Guadeloupe, the one that best expresses, in my view, the special character of the race – a mixture of modesty and independence, of pride and devotion, of disdain for riches and dedication to service – is Auguste Bébian. He died as he had lived. All that remains are his ideas, in his books, and his example, in the hearts of a few people."*

His widow left Guadeloupe shortly after.[87] On her death certificate, dated March 6, 1884, the address given is 106 Avenue Kléber, Paris; the letters she sent to the minister of the Interior and Public Instruction in 1846 and 1852 give an earlier address, in the Rue Bréda, then in the 16th arrondissement (pre-Haussmann: subsequently in the 9th).

---

whistling pines, I searched in vain for his grave. Nobody now remembers where it stood. No material trace remains of Bébian." *Images guadeloupéennes*, (Paris: Ceux d'outre-mer, 1939) cited in the informational leaflet of the MGEN, 1991.

85. The earthquake of October 8, 1843 in the Lesser Antilles was the most violent ever recorded on the American continent until the one of May 22, 1960, which had its epicenter in Chile.
    Jacqueline Picard (ed.), *La Pointe-à-Pitre n'existe plus…! Relations du tremblement de terre de 1843 en Guadeloupe*, Gosier, Caret, 2003.
86. Gilbert de Chambertrand, *op. cit.*
87. The exact date is not known.

Sources: Archives and Bibliography

Archives

National Archives

Sites in Paris and Aix-en-Provence
(Archives for the French Overseas Territories: ANOM)

Carte générale des îles de Grande-Terre et Guadeloupe, réduite [...], *levée par les ingénieurs géographes pendant les années 1764 à 1768, et mémoire contenant la légende de la carte*, 1768 (ANOM ref. DPCC Port X A 260).

Plan de diverses habitations des bourgs du quartier du Norroy dans la paroisse du Moulle en l'isle Grande-Terre, avec chacune leur nom, Mercier fils arpenteur, Bourgeois notaire royal, July 4, 1746 (ANOM ref. $F^3$288 n°48).

Moreau Atlas of Saint-Méry (ANOM ref. F^3).

Ballet manuscripts (1825-1904)= 19 volumes and 10 bundles, including 8 on economic development (ANOM ref. 2J).

Passenger manifests: Series E and EE, table from F5b 62 (crossings from 1833 to 1838), registration numbers of civilian personnel dispersed throughout Series D2c.

Decisions relating to public education and the opening of schools (1816-1868) (ANOM ref. SG/GUA//539).

Public education: inspection reports (1818-1901) (ANOM ref. SG/GUA//316).

Folder on Joseph Bébian (ANOM ref. EE/137/13). *Gazette officielle de la Guadeloupe* (1834-1839).

Departmental Archives of Seine-Maritime

Series X: Social assistance and provision (1800-1940), in particular:

- 3XP: Social assistance
- 3XP12: Miscellaneous cases, 1801-1896
- 3XP702: General cases, correspondence and investigation, 1813-1878

Series 2T: Printing, Booksellers, Press.

Series 2T1: Printers' patents – Lithographs: Authorization, Rejection, Amendment, Transfer. Individual files, including one concerning Bébian.

Departmental Archives of Guadeloupe

3K1/11 (relating to the mutual school).

1Mi 687/1 (Decisions relating to public education and the opening of schools (1816-1868).

Archives of the INJS in Paris

In particular the Pinart collection.

Bibliography

History of Guadeloupe and the Antilles

ABOU Antoine, *Un siècle de scolarisation à la Guadeloupe 1848-1948*, Université René Descartes Paris V, 1983.

ADELAÏDE-MERLANDE Jacques, *Histoire générale des Antilles et des Guyanes, Des Précolombiens à nos jours*, Paris: L'Harmattan, 1994.

BEGOT Danielle (ed.), *La plantation coloniale esclavagiste XVIIe-XIXe siècles*, CTHS, 2008.

BEGOT Danielle (ed.), *Guide de la recherche en histoire antillaise et guyanaise Guadeloupe, Martinique, Saint-Domingue, Guyane, XVIIe-XXe siècles*, CTHS, 2011.

BOUTIN Raymond, *La population en Guadeloupe de l'émancipation à l'assimilation, 1848 à 1946*, Cayenne: Ibis rouge, 2006.

BROUSILLON Ary, *L'exécution de l'esclave Gertrude : l'empoisonneuse de Petit-Bourg*, Les Abymes: Créapub', 1999.

CORZANI Jack (ed.), *Dictionnaire encyclopédique Désormeaux : dictionnaire encyclopédique des Antilles et de la Guyane*, Fort de France: Désormeaux, 1992-1993.

COUSSEAU Vincent, *Prendre nom aux Antilles. Individu et appartenances (XVIIe-XIXe siècles)*, CTHS, 2012.

COUSSIN Joseph, *Paysages de la Guadeloupe*, with an introduction by Raymond Clermont, Basse-Terre: Société d'histoire de la Guadeloupe, Bibliothèque d'histoire antillaise, 1986.

DEBIEN Gabriel, "Plantations à la Guadeloupe. La caféière et la sucrerie Bologne au Baillif (1787)", *BSHG* n° 3-4, 1965, pp. 11-21.

DESSALLES Pierre-François-Regis, *Historique des troubles survenus à la Martinique pendant la Révolution*, (foreword by Henri de Frémont), Société d'histoire de la Martinique, 1982.

ENOFF Rodolphe, *Guide historique des noms de rues à Basse-Terre et à Pointe-à-Pitre*, E. Enoff, 1993.

LAFLEUR Gerard, *Gourbeyre : une commune de Guadeloupe*, Paris: Karthala, 1997.

LAFLEUR Gérard, "La culture du café en Guadeloupe, de son introduction à sa quasi-disparition", *BSHG*, n° 145, 2006, pp. 59-120.

LARA Oruno, *La Guadeloupe dans l'histoire : la Guadeloupe physique, économique, agricole, commerciale, financière, politique et sociale, 1492-1900*, Paris: L'Harmattan, 1921.

LARA Oruno Denis, *La Liberté assassinée, Guadeloupe, Martinique, Guyane et La Réunion, 1848-1856*, Paris: L'Harmattan, 2005.

LARA Oruno Denis, *Les propriétaires d'esclaves en 1848*, Paris: L'Harmattan, 2010.

LASSERRE Guy, *La Guadeloupe : étude géographique*, Bordeaux: Doctoral thesis in geography, 1961.

LONGIN Félix, *Voyage à la Guadeloupe*, Le Mans: Monnoyer, 1848; reprinted and enriched with an index and a critical version by the Société d'Histoire de Guadeloupe, 2013.

MAURO Frédéric, *Histoire du café*, Paris: Desjonquières, 1991.

ORIOL Timmy, *Les hommes célèbres de la Guadeloupe*, Basse-Terre: Imprimerie catholique, 1935.

PEROTIN-DUMON Anne, *La ville aux îles, la ville dans l'île, Basse-Terre et Pointe-à-Pitre, 1650-1820*, Paris: Karthala, 1999.

PETRE-GRENOUILLEAU Olivier, *La Traite négrière, essai d'histoire globale*, Gallimard, 2004.

PICARD Jacqueline (ed.), *La Pointe-à-Pitre n'existe plus…! Relations du tremblement de terre de 1843 en Guadeloupe*, Gosier: Caret, 2003.

REGENT Frédéric, *Esclavage, métissage, liberté. La Révolution française en Guadeloupe, 1789-1802*, Paris: Grasset, 2004.

SAINTON Jean-Pierre (ed.), *Histoire et Civilisation de la Caraïbe, le temps de genèse, des origines à 1685*, vol. I, Paris: Karthala, 2004.

SAINTON Jean-Pierre (ed.), *Le temps des matrices : économie et cadres sociaux du long XVIIIe siècle*, vol. II, Paris: Karthala, 2012.

Deaf history and the linguistics of sign language

ALARD J., *Controverse entre l'abbé de l'Épée et Samuel Heinicke au propos de la "Véritable manière d'instruire les sourds-muets"*, traduite du latin et état actuel de la question, Paris: Imprimerie G. Pelluard, 1881.

ALLIBERT Joseph-Eugène, *"Discours", Banquets des sourds-muets, réunis pour fêter les anniversaires de la naissance de l'abbé de l'Épée*, Paris: Ledoyen, 1849.

BÉBIAN Auguste, *Journal de l'instruction des sourds-muets et des aveugles*, Paris: IRSM, 1826.

BÉBIAN Auguste, *Manuel d'enseignement pratique des sourds-muets*, Paris: Méquignon l'Aîné père, 1827.

BÉBIAN Auguste, *Nouvelle méthode pour apprendre à lire sans épeler*, Paris: Imprimerie de Craquelet, 1828.

BÉBIAN Auguste, *Examen critique de la nouvelle organisation de l'enseignement dans l'Institution royale des sourds-muets de Paris*, Paris: Teuttel & Wurtz, 1834.

BENVENUTO Andrea, *Qu'est-ce qu'un sourd ? De la figure au sujet philosophique*, doctoral thesis, Université Paris VIII, 2009.

BERTHIER Ferdinand, *Notice sur la vie et les ouvrages de Auguste Bébian*, Paris: Ledoyen, 1839.

BERTHIER Ferdinand, *Les sourds-muets avant et depuis l'abbé de l'Épée*, Paris: Ledoyen, 1840.

BERTHIER Ferdinand, *L'Abbé de l'Épée. Sa vie, son apostolat, ses travaux. Sa lutte et ses succès* [...], Paris: M. Lévy frères, 1852.

BERTHIER Ferdinand, *L'abbé Sicard, célèbre instituteur des sourds-muets, successeur immédiat de l'abbé de l'Épée. Précis historique sur sa vie, ses travaux et ses succès. Suivi de détails biographiques sur ses élèves sourds-muets les plus remarquables, Jean Massieu et Laurent Clerc, et d'un appendice contenant des lettres de l'abbé Sicard au baron de Gérando*, Paris: Douniol, 1873.

BERNARD Yves, *Approche de la gestualité à l'institution des sourds-muets de Paris XVIIIe-XIXe siècles*, doctoral thesis, Université Paris V, 1999.

BERTIN Fabrice, *Les Sourds, une minorité invisible*, Paris: Autrement, 2010.

BEZAGU-DELUY Maryse, *L'abbé de l'Épée. Instituteur gratuit des sourds et muets 1712-1789*, Paris: Seghers, 1990.

BINET Alfred, SIMON Théodore, "Étude sur l'art d'enseigner la parole aux sourds-muets", *L'année psychologique*, Paris, 1909, pp. 373-396.

BOURGALAIS Patrick, *Les miroirs du silence*, Rennes: Presses universitaires de Rennes, 2008.

BOUVET Danielle, *La parole de l'enfant sourd*, Paris: PUF, collection "Le fil rouge", 1982.

BUTON François, "Le congrès de Milan, entre mythe et réalités", *Surdités* n° 4, 2001.

BUTON François, "L'éducation des sourds-muets au XIXe siècle. Description d'une activité sociale", *Le Mouvement social*, 2008/2, n° 223.

BUTON François, *L'administration des faveurs. L'État, les sourds et les aveugles (1789-1885)*, Rennes: Presses universitaires de Rennes, 2009.

CHAIX D'EST-ANGE Gustave, in *Dictionnaire des familles françaises anciennes ou notables à la fin du XIXe siècle*, Évreux: imprimerie Hérissey, vol. 13.

CUXAC Christian, *Le langage des sourds*, Paris: Payot, 1983.

CUXAC Christian, *Les voies de l'iconicité*, Paris: Ophrys, 2000.

CUXAC Christian, BERTIN Fabrice (coord.), "La LSF : enjeux culturels et pédagogiques", Suresnes, CNEFEI, *La nouvelle revue de l'adaptation et de la scolarisation*, n° 23, 2003.

CLAVEAU Octave, *De la parole comme objet et comme moyen d'enseignement dans les institutions de Sourds-Muets*, Paris: Imprimerie nationale, 1881.

DALLE-NAZEBI Sophie, *Chercheurs, Sourds et langues des signes. Le travail d'un objet et de repères linguistiques en France du XVIIe au XXIe siècle*, doctoral thesis, Université Toulouse II – Le Mirail, 2006.

DE GÉRANDO Jean-Marie, *De l'éducation des Sourds-Muets de naissance*, Paris: Méquignon l'Ainé père, 1827.

DELAPORTE Yves, *Les sourds c'est comme ça*, Paris: MSH, 2002.

DENIS Théophile, "Le premier instituteur des Sourds-Muets en France", *Revue française de l'éducation des sourds-muets*, Paris, n° 10, Jan. 1887, pp. 217-19 and n° 11, pp. 242-46.

DENIS Théophile, "Étienne de Fay. Nouveaux renseignements sur cet instituteur de sourds-muets", *Revue française de l'éducation des sourds-muets*, Paris, n°s 6-7, Dec. 1893-Jan. 1894, pp. 137-41.

DESCHAMPS Abbé, *Cours élémentaire d'éducation des Sourds-Muets*, followed by AMMAN Jean-Conrad, Dissertation sur la parole, translated from the Latin by M. Beauvais de Préau, doctor of medicine, Paris: Debure frères, 1779.

DESLOGES Pierre, *Observations d'un Sourd et Muet sur un cours élémentaire d'éducation des Sourds et Muets*, publié en 1779 par M. l'abbé Deschamps, chapelain de l'église d'Orléans, Amsterdam and Paris: B. Morin, 1779, reprinted in Coup d'œil n° 44.

DIDEROT Denis, *Lettre sur les Sourds et Muets à l'usage de ceux qui entendent et parlent*, Paris: Flammarion, 1749 (2000 edition).

DUBOIS M., *L'abbé Huby. Instituteur des sourds-muets à Rouen*, Rouen: Imprimerie Albert Lainé, 1935.

ENCREVÉ Florence, *Les Sourds dans la société française au XIXe siècle. Idée de progrès et langue des signes*, Paris: Créaphis, 2012.

ÉPÉE Charles-Michel (Abbé de l'), *La véritable manière d'instruire les sourds et muets, confirmée par une longue expérience*, Paris: Nyon, 1784.

FISCHER Renate, *Looking back: international studies on sign language and communication of the Deaf*, Hamburg: Sigmum Press, 1993.

FOURGON Fernand, "Historique de la pédagogie des sourds-muets", *Communiquer*, n° 37, 1978.

FUSELIER-SOUZA Ivani, *Sémiogenèse des langues des signes : Étude de Langues des signes primaires (LSP) pratiquées par des sourds brésiliens*, doctoral thesis in language sciences, Université de Paris VIII, 2004.

GARCIA Brigitte, *Sourds, surdité, langue(s) des signes et épistémologie des sciences du langage. Problématiques de la scripturisation et modélisation des bas niveaux en Langue des signes française (LSF)*, dissertation for the research supervision diploma (HDR), Université Paris VIII, 2010.

Groupe d'études et de recherches sur la surdité, *Être biculturel : le cas des sourds*, Actes des journées d'étude GERS du 25 novembre 2006, Paris: L'Harmattan.

INJS, *Exhibition catalogue: "Le pouvoir des signes"*, INJS, 1989.

International congress, *Pour l'amélioration du sort des sourds-muets, tenu à Milan, du 6 au 11 septembre 1880* (minutes), Rome: Héritiers Botta, 1881.

ITARD Jean-Marc Gaspard, *Traité des maladies de l'oreille et de l'audition*, Paris: Méquignon-Marvis, 1821.

KARACOSTAS Alexis, *L'institution nationale des sourds-muets de 1790 à 1800, histoire d'un corps à corps*, medical thesis, Université Paris V, Paris, 1981 (typed).

KILIAN C., *Historique de l'enseignement des sourds-muets en Allemagne*, Conférences recueillies par M. Dupont, Paris: Pelluard, 1855.

LABORIT Emmanuelle, *Le cri de la mouette*, Paris: Laffont, 1994.

LACHANCE Nathalie, *Territoires, transmission et culture sourde*, Laval: Presses Universitaires, 2007.

LANE Harlan, *When the Mind Hears*, New York: Random House, 1984

LANE Harlan, "A Chronology of the Oppression of Sign Language in France and the United States", in *Recent Perspectives on American Sign Language*, New York: Psychology Press, 1989.

LA ROCHELLE Ernest, *Jacob Rodriguès Pereire, premier instituteur des sourd-muets en France ; sa vie, ses travaux*, Paris: Paul Dupont, 1882.

MENIERE Prosper, *De la guérison de la surdi-mutité et de l'éducation des sourds-muets, report on the debate held at the Imperial Academy of Medicine*, Paris: Germer-Baillère, 1853.

MEYNARD André, *Quand les mains prennent la parole*, Toulouse: Érès, 1995.

MEYNARD André, *Surdité, l'urgence d'un autre regard*, Toulouse: Érès, 2001.

MOTTEZ Bernard, "Les banquets des sourds-muets et la naissance du mouvement Sourd", in *Le pouvoir des signes, INJS exhibition catalogue*, 1989.

MOTTEZ Bernard, *Les Sourds existent-ils ?*, texts collected and presented by Andrea Benvenuto, Paris: L'Harmattan, 2006.

Oraison funèbre de Charles-Michel de l'Épée [...]. *Funeral oration given in the parish church of Saint-Etienne-du-Mont on Tuesday February 23, 1790* by Abbé Fauchet, Paris: J.-R. Lottin de Saint Germain, 1790.

PADDEN Carol, HUMPHRIES Tom, *Deaf in America: Voices from a culture*, Cambridge: Harvard University Press, 1988.

PELLETIER Armand, DELAPORTE Yves, *Moi, Armand, né sourd et muet*, Paris: Plon Terre humaine, 2002.

Periodic International Congress of Otology, *Congrès de Milan de 1880*, Trieste: G. Caprin, 1882.

POIZAT Michel, *La voix sourde*, Paris: Metailié, 1996.

PRESNEAU Jean-René, *Signes et institution des sourds, XVIIIe-XIXe siècles*, Champ-Vallon, 1998.

QUARTARARO Anne T., *Deaf identity and social images in nineteenth-century France*, Washington: Gallaudet University Press, 2008.

SACKS Oliver, *Seeing Voices: A Journey Into the World of the Deaf*, University of California Press, 1989.

SAINT-LOUP Aude (de), "Les sourds-muets au Moyen Âge. Mille ans de signes oubliés", *Sourds et citoyens, exhibition catalogue*, INJS, 1989.

SAINT-LOUP Aude (de), "Histoires de malentendus, histoires de sourds", *Diogène*, 1996.

SAINT-LOUP Aude (de), DELAPORTE Yves, RENARD Marc, *Gestes des moines, regards des sourds*, Paris: Ophrys, 1998.

SALLANDRE Marie-Anne, *Compositionnalité des unités sémantiques en langues des signes. Perspectives typologique et développementale*, dissertation for the research supervision diploma (HDR), Univ. Paris VIII, 2014.

SEBAN-LEFEBVRE Dominique, TOFFIN Christine, *L'enfant qui n'entend pas. La surdité, un handicap invisible*, Paris: Belin, 2008.

SÉGUILLON Didier, *"Une histoire à corps et à cris", exhibition catalogue*, Paris: INJS, 1994.

SICARD Roch-Ambroise, *Cours d'instruction d'un sourd-muet de naissance, pour servir à l'éducation des sourds-muets, et qui peut être utile à ceux qui entendent et qui parlent*, Paris: Le Clere; London, Charles Prosper, 1803.

TRUFFAUT Bernard, *Cahiers de l'Histoire des sourds*, Orléans, Association Étienne de Fay, 1989-1991 (monthly booklets).

VIAL Monique, PLAISANCE Joëlle, & STIKER Henri-Jacques, *Enfants sourds, enfants aveugles au début du XXe siècle : Autour de Gustave Baguer*, CTNERHI/ CNEFEI, "Histoire du handicap et de l'inadaptation", 2000.

VIROLE Benoît, *Psychologie de la surdité*, Brussels: De Boeck Université, 1996.

General works

ARISTOTLE, *History of Animals.*

AUGUSTINE OF HIPPO (Saint Augustine), *De Magistro.*

BARTH Britt-Mari, *L'apprentissage de l'abstraction*, Paris: Retz, 1987 (reprinted 2001).

CALVET Jean, *Linguistique et colonialisme,* Paris: Payot, 2002.

CARON Jean-Claude, *La France de 1815 à 1848*, Paris: A. Colin, 2002.

CESAIRE Aimé, "What is negritude to me?" in C. Moore, *African Presence in the Americas,* Trenton: Africa World Press, 1995.

CHAPPEY Jean-Luc, *La Société des observateurs de l'homme (1799-1804). Des anthropologues au temps de Bonaparte*, foreword by Claude Blanckaert, Paris: Société des études robespierristes, 2002.

CHAPPEY Jean-Luc, CHRISTEN Carole and MOULLIER Igor (eds.), *Joseph-Marie de Gérando (1772-1842). Connaître et réformer la société,* Rennes: Presses Universitaires de Rennes, 2014.

CHARLE Christophe, *Histoire sociale de la France au XIX*e *siècle*, Paris: Seuil, 1991.

CHARLE Christophe, *Le siècle de la presse (1830-1939)*, Paris: Seuil, 2004.

CORBIN Alain, *The life of an unknown: The rediscovered world of a clog maker in nineteenth-century France*, trans. A . Goldhammer, Columbia University Press. [Le monde retrouvé de Louis-François Pinagot, sur les traces d'un inconnu 1798-1876, Paris: Flammarion, 1998].

COURTINE Jean-Jacques, CORBIN Alain, VIGARELLO Georges (eds.) (2005, 2006), *Histoire du corps*, 3 vols., Paris: Seuil.

DORIGUZZI Pascal, *L'histoire politique du handicap, de l'infirme au travailleur handicapé*, L'Harmattan, 1994.

DUPRAT Catherine, Usages et pratiques de la philanthropie. *Pauvreté, action sociale et lien social, à Paris, au cours du premier XIX*e *siècle*, Paris: Comité d'histoire de la Sécurité sociale, 2 vols., 1996 and 1997.

EBERSOLD Serge, *L'invention du handicap. La normalisation de l'infirme*, Paris: Centre technique national d'Études sur les Handicaps et les Inadaptations, 1997.

ESQUIROS Alphonse, *Paris, ou les sciences, les institutions et les mœurs au XIX*e *siècle*, 2 vols., Paris: Comptoir des imprimeurs unis, 1847.

FEYEL Gilles, *La presse en France des origines à 1944*, Paris: Ellipses, 1999.

FOUCAULT Michel, *Histoire de la folie à l'âge classique*, Paris: Gallimard, 1976 [Madness and Civilization].

FOUCAULT Michel, *Surveiller et punir*, Paris: Gallimard, 1984 [Discipline and Punish].

GOFFMAN Erving, *Stigma: Notes on the Management of Spoiled Identity*, NY: Touchstone, 1963.

GUMPERZ John, *Engager la conversation. Introduction à la sociolinguistique interactionnelle*, Paris: Éditions de Minuit, "Le sens commun", 1989.

HAGEGE Claude, *L'enfant aux deux langues*, Paris: O. Jacob, 2005.

HAGEGE Claude, "Les Français, trop fiers de leur langue ?", *Philosophie magazine*, n° 30, June 2009.

Handicap : identités, représentations, théories (Dossier), *Sciences sociales et Santé*, vol. XII, n° 1, March 1994.

HERACLITUS, *Fragments*.

JUANEDA-ALBAREDE Christiane, "Les méthodes de lecture au XIXe siècle", *Actes de lecture* n° 37, Association française pour la lecture, 1992.

JUANEDA-ALBAREDE Christiane, *Cent ans de méthodes de lectures*, Paris: Albin Michel, 1998.

LOUE Thomas, "Religion et culture au XIXe siècle en France", *Cahiers d'histoire. Revue d'histoire critique*, n° 87, 2002.

LUC Jean-Noël, *La petite enfance à l'école, XIXe-XXe siècles*, Paris: INRP, 1982.

MANGUEL Alberto, *Une histoire de la lecture*, Paris: Actes Sud, transl. 1998.

MOLLAT Michel, *Les pauvres au Moyen Âge*, Paris: Complexe, 1978.

MONTAIGNE Michel de, *Essais*, Paris: LGF, 2002.

NOIRIEL Gérard, *Penser avec, penser contre*, Paris: Belin, 2003.

PERNOUD Régine, *Pour en finir avec le Moyen Âge*, Paris: Folio, 1979.

PESSIN Alain, BERNARD-GRIFFITHS Simone, *Peuple, mythe et histoire*, Toulouse: Presses Universitaires du Mirail, 1997.

PLATO, *Cratylus*.

POULOT Dominique, *Une histoire des musées de France XVIIIe-XXe siècles*, Paris: La Découverte, 2005.

PRONTEAU Jeanne, *Les numérotages des maisons de Paris du XVe siècle à nos jours*, Paris: Imprimerie municipale, 1966.

RABELAIS François, *Le Tiers-livre*, Paris: Points, 1997 (1546).

RANCIERE Jacques, *Le maître ignorant. Cinq leçons sur l'émancipation intellectuelle*, Paris: Fayard "10/18", 1987.

RAYNAUD Philippe, "L'éducation spécialisée en France (1882-1982)", *Esprit*, n°s 5 and 7/8, 1982.

REYNAERT François, *Nos ancêtres les Gaulois et autres fadaises*, Fayard, 2010.

ROBERT Vincent, *Le temps des banquets. Politique et symbolique d'une génération (1818-1848)*, Paris: Publications de la Sorbonne, 2010.

SCHMITT Jean-Claude, *La raison des gestes dans l'Occident médiéval*, Paris: Gallimard, 1990.

STICKER Henri-Jacques, *Corps infirmes et sociétés*, Paris: Dunod, 1997.

STICKER Henri-Jacques, VIAL Monique, BARRAL Catherine, (eds.) *Fragments pour une histoire : notion et acteurs*, Paris: Alter, 1996.

TODD Emmanuel, *Le destin des immigrés. Assimilation et ségrégation dans les démocraties occidentales*, Paris: Seuil, 1994.

VIAL Monique, *Un fonds pour l'histoire de l'Éducation spécialisée, Inventaire des archives de l'enfance "anormale" conservées au Musée national de l'Éducation*, Paris: INRP, 1993.

VYGOTSKI Lev Semionovitch, *Pensée et langage*, Paris: Sociales, 1985 (original 1934).

VIGARELLO Georges, *Histoire des pratiques de santé. Le sain et le malsain depuis le Moyen Âge*, Paris: Seuil, 1993.

WATZLAWICK Paul, HELMINN-BEAVIN Janet, JACKSON Don D., *Une logique de la communication*, Paris: Seuil, 1972.

WEYGAND Zina, *Vivre sans voir. Les aveugles dans la société française, du Moyen Âge au siècle de Louis Braille*, Paris: Créaphis, 2003.

Books or articles on Auguste Bébian

BALLIVET (Chanoine), "D'un vicaire et d'un instituteur", *L'Écho de la Reine*, n° 45, September 1916.

BERNARD Yves, "La Mimographie de Bébian (1789-1839). Le signe est l'ombre de l'idée", *Liaisons, Bulletin du CNFEJS (Centre national de formation des enseignants intervenant auprès des jeunes sourds)*, n° 7, 1995, pp. 34-64.

BERNARD Yves, *Approche de la gestualité à l'institution des sourds-muets de Paris, au XVIIIe et au XIXe siècle*, doctoral thesis, Paris V, 1999. Published in 2014 as *L'esprit des Sourds* (Les-Essart-le-Roi: Éditions du Fox; Bébian is mentioned 307 times.

BERTHIER Ferdinand, *Notice sur la vie et les ouvrages de Auguste Bébian, ancien censeur des études de l'Institut royal des sourds-muets de Paris*. Paris: chez Ledoyen, 1839.

Le Colonial, issues from May 17, 24, 31 and June 14, 1911: biographical section.

CUXAC Christian, "La Mimographie de Bébian : finalité et destin d'une écriture de la LSF", *Surdités*, 2004, n°s 5-6, pp. 81-95.

DAVIAUD Jules [Montfort Brother of St. Gabriel], *Historique de l'enseignement des sourds-muets,* typewritten document, Poitiers: 1952; reprinted by Frères de Saint Gabriel, 2005.

RENARD Marc, *Écrire les signes. La Mimographie d'Auguste Bébian et les notations contemporaines*, Les Essarts-le-Roi: Fox, 2004, 2014.

La Sentinelle du peuple, *"Les sourds-muets vont réclamer au Roi Louis-Philippe leur ci-devant instituteur Bébian ; puis de Clerc, de Massieu, de Berthier et Lenoir"*, 1830, issue of November 14.

Annexes

Annex 1
Genealogy of Auguste Bébian

Simplified genealogy of Auguste's mother, Félicité Michaux

From this family tree, we can see that Auguste's maternal line included a large number of notaries, among her ancestors and descendants alike, as well as landowners. It was an extended family, with numerous cousins, inter-cousin marriages, and roots in the Saintes islands. The parents of Marie-Marguerite Classe, Auguste's grandmother, lived and died on the Saintes; among her descendants (not shown here) many were born on "Terre de Bas" or Basse-Terre and many at Le Moule (a municipality that borders Morne-à-l'Eau).

Auguste's grandfather and granduncle were goldsmiths: both died before he was born. Félicité, Auguste's mother, had only two children (while the second of her three sisters, Marguerite, had thirteen, of whom the first was born in 1769, twenty years before Auguste). She was also godmother to her sister's third child, a boy called Jean-Jacques born at Le Moule in 1772, who would later become a notary and legal advisor, and who died in 1838 (still at Le Moule). Auguste therefore had a large extended maternal family from Le Moule to Basse-Terre.

Sources: Civil register and généanet (research by Paul Michaux).

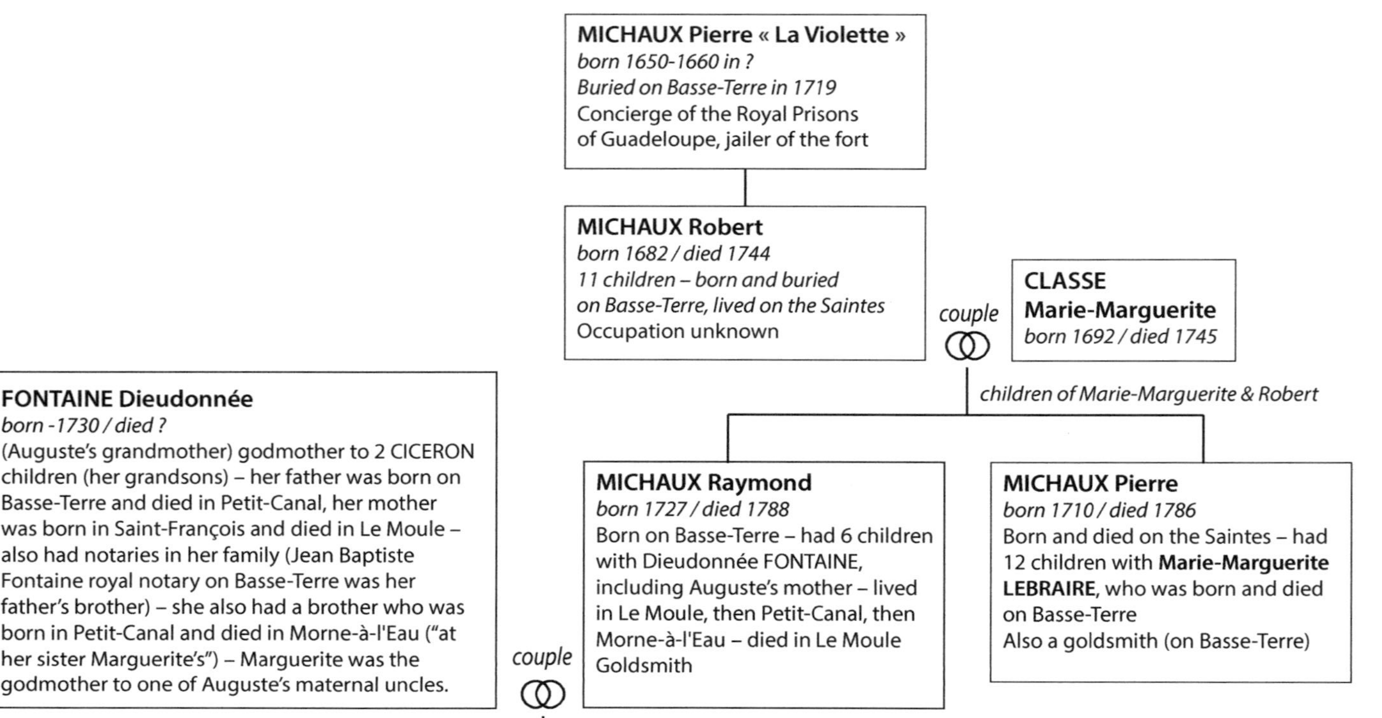
MICHAUX Pierre « La Violette »
born 1650-1660 in ?
Buried on Basse-Terre in 1719
Concierge of the Royal Prisons of Guadeloupe, jailer of the fort
MICHAUX Robert
born 1682 / died 1744
11 children – born and buried on Basse-Terre, lived on the Saintes
Occupation unknown
couple
CLASSE Marie-Marguerite
born 1692 / died 1745
children of Marie-Marguerite & Robert
FONTAINE Dieudonnée
born -1730 / died ?
(Auguste's grandmother) godmother to 2 CICERON children (her grandsons) – her father was born on Basse-Terre and died in Petit-Canal, her mother was born in Saint-François and died in Le Moule – also had notaries in her family (Jean Baptiste Fontaine royal notary on Basse-Terre was her father's brother) – she also had a brother who was born in Petit-Canal and died in Morne-à-l'Eau ("at her sister Marguerite's") – Marguerite was the godmother to one of Auguste's maternal uncles.
couple
MICHAUX Raymond
born 1727 / died 1788
Born on Basse-Terre – had 6 children with Dieudonnée FONTAINE, including Auguste's mother – lived in Le Moule, then Petit-Canal, then Morne-à-l'Eau – died in Le Moule
Goldsmith
MICHAUX Pierre
born 1710 / died 1786
Born and died on the Saintes – had 12 children with Marie-Marguerite LEBRAIRE, who was born and died on Basse-Terre
Also a goldsmith (on Basse-Terre)

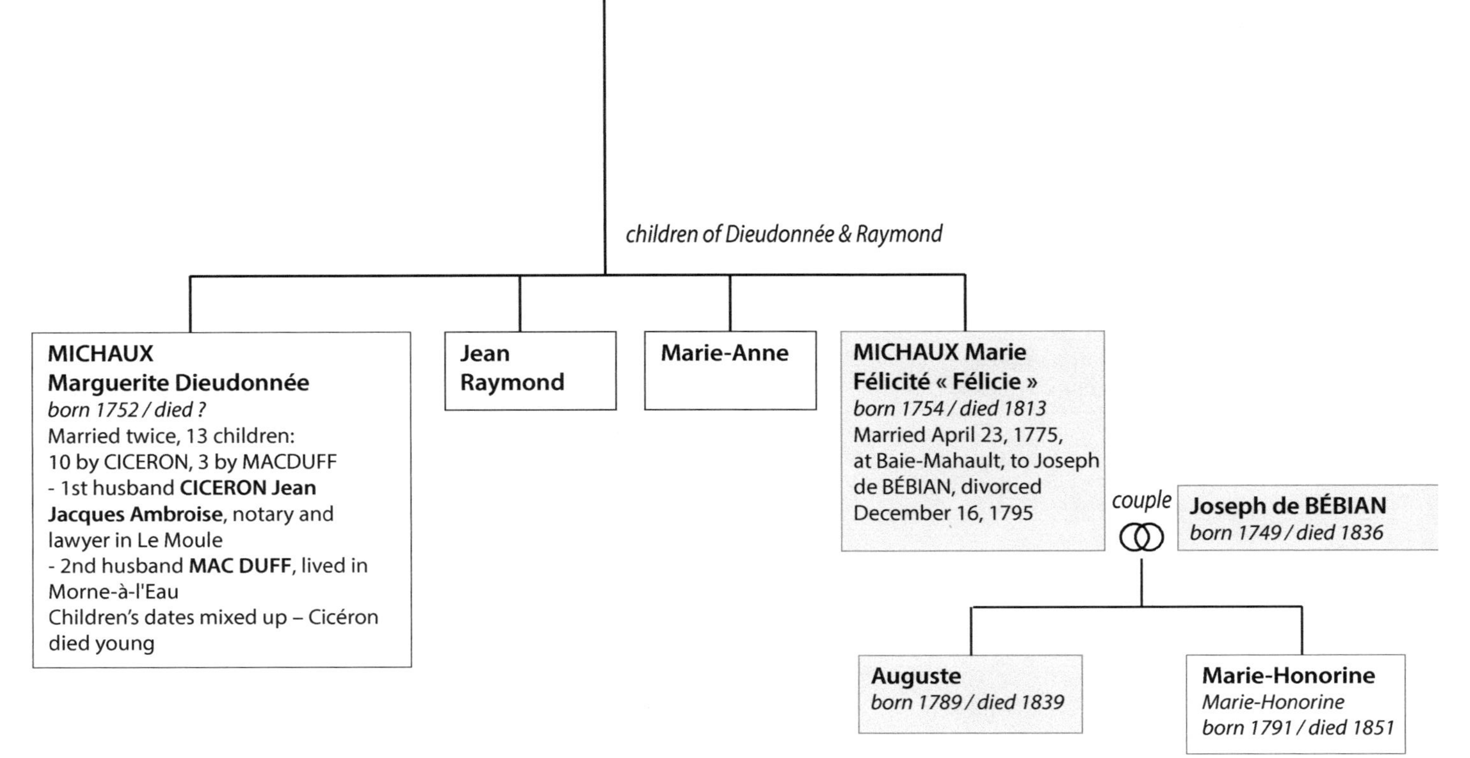
children of Dieudonnée & Raymond
MICHAUX
Marguerite Dieudonnée
born 1752 / died ?
Married twice, 13 children:
10 by CICERON, 3 by MACDUFF
- 1st husband CICERON Jean Jacques Ambroise, notary and lawyer in Le Moule
- 2nd husband MAC DUFF, lived in Morne-à-l'Eau
Children's dates mixed up – Cicéron died young
Jean Raymond
Marie-Anne
MICHAUX Marie Félicité « Félicie »
born 1754 / died 1813
Married April 23, 1775, at Baie-Mahault, to Joseph de BÉBIAN, divorced December 16, 1795
couple
Joseph de BÉBIAN
born 1749 / died 1836
Auguste
born 1789 / died 1839
Marie-Honorine
Marie-Honorine
born 1791 / died 1851

Simplified genealogy of Auguste's father, Joseph Bébian

A number of family trees on Généanet assign Joseph the branch name "Bébian de Pachin". Having found a trace of this name only in the Bordeaux embarkation records but not in any document from Guadeloupe, we indicate it for information only and consequently start the tree with Joseph Bébian.

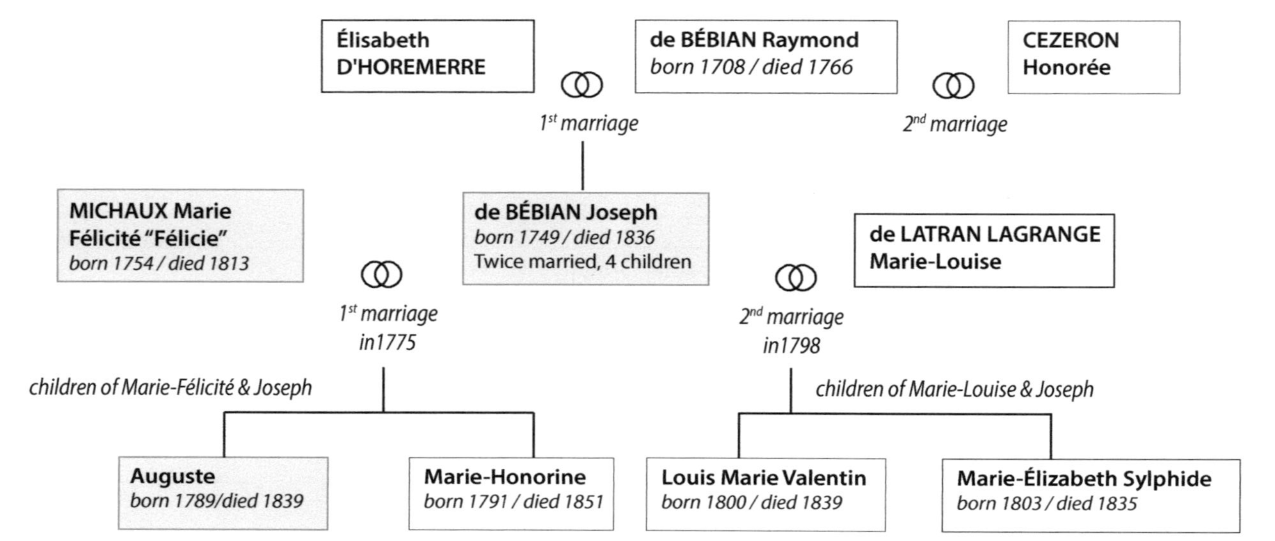

Annex 2
A disputed date and place of birth

N°	Sources	Author	Date	Date of birth	Place of birth
1	*Notice sur la vie et les ouvrages d'Auguste Bébian, ancien censeur de l'Institut royal des Sourds-muets*	Ferdinand Berthier	1839	August 4, 1789	Pointe-à-Pitre
2	*La Guadeloupe dans l'Histoire : La Guadeloupe physique, économique, agricole, commerciale, financière, politique et sociale de 1492 à 1900*	Oruno Lara	1922	August 4, 1789	Pointe-à-Pitre
3	*Les hommes célèbres de la Caraïbe*	Jacques Adelaïde Merlande	1998	August 4, 1789	Pointe-à-Pitre
4	Registres de la distribution générale des prix de l'université impériale		1809	August 4, 1791	Guadeloupe
5	*Dictionnaire encyclopédique Désormeaux, dictionnaire encyclopédique des Antilles et de la Guyane*		1992-1993	August 14, 1789	Morne-à-l'Eau
6	*Revue du monde colonial, asiatique et américain*		1865	1789 (only)	Pointe-à-Pitre
7	*Les hommes célèbres de la Guadeloupe*	T. Oriol	1935	August 4, 1789	Pointe-à-Pitre
8	*Dictionnaire de pédagogie et d'instruction primaire*	Fernand Buisson (ed.), Announcement written by Etcheverry	1887	August 4, 1789	Pointe-à-Pitre

N°	Sources	Author	Date	Date of birth	Place of birth
9	*Dictionnaire de la conversation et de la lecture, inventaire raisonné des notions générales les plus indispensables à tous par une société de savants et de gens de lettres*	M. W. Duckett (ed.) Announcement written by F. Berthier	1852	August 4, 1789	Guadeloupe
10	*Hommes et destins : le dictionnaire biographique d'outremer*	Robert Cornevin (ed.)	1977	August 4, 1789	No location specified
11	*La Guadeloupe, l'instruction à la Guadeloupe de 1635 à 1897*	Jules Ballet	1979	August 4, 1789	Pointe-à-Pitre
12	"D'un vicaire et d'un instituteur", *L'Écho de la reine*	Chanoine Ballivet	1916	August 4, 1789	Morne-à-l'Eau
13	Self-enrolment for Lamarck's lectures	?	1808	August 14, 1791	Guadeloupe
14	Letter from the mayor of Rouen to the prefect of Seine Inférieure, December 26, 1832	Mayor of Rouen	1832	August 14, 1791	Morne-à-l'Eau
15	Lecture given at Bébian Mixed School on Basse-Terre	Félix Rodes	1991	August 4, 1789	Morne-à-l'Eau
16	Verification of the affidavit of Joseph Bébian	Joseph Dupuy Désislets Mondésir	1828	August 4, 1789	Morne-à-l'Eau

Annex 3
Chronology of French and Guadeloupean history, Deaf history, and the life of Auguste Bébian (key events)

Date	History of France and Guadeloupe	Deaf history	Life of Auguste Bébian
1789	**July 14:** Taking of the Bastille, the prison that symbolize royal power **August 4:** Abolition of feudal privileges **August 26:** Ratification of the Declaration of the Rights of Man and of the Citizen	**December 23:** Death of Abbé de l'Épée	**August 4**: Birth in Morne-à-l'Eau on the Bergopzoom plantation (affidavit by Joseph Bébian)
1790	**February 13:** Suppression of the monastic orders **June 19:** Suppression of the nobility **July 22:** Civil constitution of the clergy (subordination to the state)	The municipality of Paris attributes the Convent of the Célestins to the school of Abbé de l'Épée **April 4:** Abbé Sicard is appointed principal (confirmed by the National Convention January 7, 1795)	

Date	History of France and Guadeloupe	Deaf history	Life of Auguste Bébian
1791	**January 3:** Priests are obliged to swear loyalty to the civil constitution of the clergy		
		April 3: Jean Massieu becomes the first Deaf teacher at the INSMP (appointed by Louis XVI)	
		April 20: Order by the *département* of Paris assigning the former Convent of the Céles-tins to the "deaf-mute and blind"	
		July 21: The Consti-tuent Assembly adopts a decree in favor of the teachers at the INSMP	
		July 29: A decree by the Constituent As-sembly awards official status to the INSMP	
			August 14: Birth of his sister Marie-Honorine Félicité in Morne-à-l'Eau on the Bergopzoom plantation (affidavit by Joseph Bébian)
	September 13: Promulgation of the Constitution of the Constitutional Monarchy, accepted by the king, Louis XVI		

Date	History of France and Guadeloupe	Deaf history	Life of Auguste Bébian
1792	**September 21:** Abolition of the monarchy; proclamation of the 1st Republic by the Convention	**August 26:** As a priest who refused to swear loyalty, Abbé Sicard is arrested and imprisoned; then freed and again arrested the following year (he was not restored to his functions until 1796)	
1793	**January 21:** Execution of Louis XVI		
1794	**February 2:** The Convention votes to abolish slavery	**April 4:** The INSMP moves to the Rue Saint-Jacques, to the premises of the former Saint-Magloire seminary	
1795	**August 22:** Constitution of Year III, establishing the Directory		**July:** His parents Félicité Michaux and Joseph Bébian (married since 1775) divorce
1796			
1797			

Date	History of France and Guadeloupe	Deaf history	Life of Auguste Bébian
1798			His father remarries, to Marie-Louise Sophie Latran Lagrange (two children are born to this union: Louis and Sylphide)
1799	**December 25:** Constitution of Year VIII, establishing the Consulate	**November 9:** Abbé Sicard is pardoned	
1800		Laurent Clerc becomes a student at the INSMP **October 3:** Jean-Marc Gaspard Itard applies to the governors of the INSMP for the position of in-house physician (previously, the institute relied on *officiers de santé* healthcare officials)	
1801	**May 29:** Jean-Baptiste Raymond de Lacrosse, appointed Captain General, lands in Guadeloupe **July 12:** Toussaint Louverture proclaims himself governor of the island of Saint-Domingue; turmoil in the French West Indies		

Date	History of France and Guadeloupe	Deaf history	Life of Auguste Bébian
1802	**January 7:** General Richepance is sent by First Consul Bonaparte to put down the revolt in Guadeloupe. Bloody repression follows **May 20:** Bonaparte reinstates slavery by decree **May 25/28:** Ignace and Louis Délgrès, symbols of the Guadeloupean uprising, commit suicide		Sails for Paris, where he is taken in by Jean-Baptiste Clair Jauffret
1803		**September 28:** Birth of Ferdinand Berthier in Louhans (Saône-et-Loire)	
1804	**May 18:** Constitution of Year XII (1st Empire: Bonaparte becomes Emperor Napoleon I)		
1805			
1806			
1807		**March 21:** Birth of Frédéric Peyson in Montpellier (Hérault)	
1808			Attends lectures given by Lamarck

Date	History of France and Guadeloupe	Deaf history	Life of Auguste Bébian
1809			Award-winner in the *Concours général* of the Imperial University (as 'commended newcomer' (*accessit des nouveaux*) in Greek translation)
1810			
1811		**June 11:** Ferdinand Berthier enters the INSMP as a student	
1812			
1813		**August 20:** Jean Massieu is appointed principal of the Lille Institute	Marriage of his sister Marie Honorine Félicité. On the certificate, their mother is recorded as deceased
1814	**May 3:** 1st Restoration: the king of France Louis XVIII enters Paris	**January 14:** "Deaf-mutes shall not be disbarred by reason of their infirmity" (court of Lyon)	
1815	**March 20:** Napoleon enters Paris (abdicates in June, after the 100 Days) **July 8:** 2nd Restoration: return of Louis XVIII		
1816		**May 27:** Abbé Sicard authorizes Gallaudet to take Laurent Clerc with him to the USA **June 12:** Laurent Clerc sails for America	

Date	History of France and Guadeloupe	Deaf history	Life of Auguste Bébian
1817		**May 23:** Frédéric Peyson enters the INSMP	**August 20:** Appointed as *répétiteur* at the INSMP. Publication of his first book, the *Essai…* (Essay on the Deaf and Natural Language, or Introduction to a Natural Classification of Ideas with Their Proper Signs)
1818			
1819		Claudius Forestier becomes a student at the INSMP (until 1826; he is an aspiring teacher at the INSMP in 1837)	**April 30:** Appointed deputy principal of the INSMP
1820			
1821			**January 14:** Resignation from the INSMP
1822		**May 10:** Death of Abbé Sicard; Abbé Goncelin is appointed principal of the INSMP (resigns in September)	**December 9:** Marriage to Adrienne Marie-Christine Lemaistre (at Sainte-Élisabeth du Temple, Paris)
1823		**July 18:** Abbé Périer (head of the Rodez establishment) takes the helm of the INSMP	
1824	**September 16:** Death of King Louis XVIII, succeeded by his brother Charles X		

Date	History of France and Guadeloupe	Deaf history	Life of Auguste Bébian
1825			Publication of *Mimographie…* (Mimography: An Essay on the Writing of Sign in order to Standardize the Language of the Deaf)
1826		Claudius Forestier is *répétiteur* at the INSMP **August:** publication of the first Deaf newspaper: the *Journal d'instruction des sourds-muets et des aveugles*	**August:** Founder-editor of the *Journal*
1827		**June 30:** Abbé Borel becomes principal **September 18:** First circular of the INSMP Publication by Baron de Gérando of his work *De l'éducation des Sourds-Muets* Creation of teacher conferences	Publication of the *Manuel…* (Manual for the Practical Instruction of Deaf Mutes)
1828			Publication of *Lecture instantanée…* (Instant Reading: A New Method for Learning to Read Without Spelling)
1829		**February 3:** The board of governors instates Ferdinand Berthier and Alphonse Lenoir as full teachers at the INSMP Second circular of the INSMP	

Date	History of France and Guadeloupe	Deaf history	Life of Auguste Bébian
1830	**July 27, 28, 29:** The *Trois Glorieuses*: the arrival of Louis-Philippe I (the July Monarchy)		Birth of his son Honoré
1831		**November 15:** Désiré Ordinaire (rector of the Strasbourg educational administration) becomes the first non-cleric to be made principal of the INSMP	
1832		Third circular of the INSMP	**September 5:** Takes up a position in Rouen
1833			
1834		**November 30:** First Deaf-Mute Banquet in memory of Abbé de l'Épée, at the restaurant *Le veau qui tète*, Place du Châtelet, Paris	**November 10:** Returns to Guadeloupe with his wife and son
1835			
1836			**July 20:** Death of his father Joseph, aged 87 **August 21:** Death of his son Honoré, aged 4
1837		**June 22:** Protests against a refusal to authorize the marriage of two deaf people	

Date	History of France and Guadeloupe	Deaf history	Life of Auguste Bébian
1838		**May 8:** Foundation of the *Société centrale des sourds-muets.* **August 18:** Désiré Ordinaire is revoked by the central administration **October 19:** Alphonse de Lanneau (principal of Sainte-Barbe college and mayor of the 12th arrondissement of Paris) takes over as principal of the INSMP until 1858	**February 16:** The governor of Guadeloupe issues a decree transferring the mutual school from Basse-Terre to Pointe-à-Pitre Appointed principal of the mutual school
1839		**June 1:** "The deaf-mute learn of the death of Bébian in Guadeloupe" (*Almanach des sourds-muets de 1900*, Paris, Imprimerie des S.-M., 1900) Ferdinand Berthier publishes a Notice… (*Notice on the Life and Work of Auguste Bébian, Former Deputy Principal of the Royal Institute of Deaf-Mutes in Paris*)	**February 24:** Death in Pointe-à-Pitre

Date	History of France and Guadeloupe	Deaf history	Life of Auguste Bébian
1840		**March 2:** The board of governors of the INS-MP refutes Berthier's claims point by point **April 24:** Claudius Forestier becomes teacher, then principal of the Lyon Institution (appointed October 1, 1842)	

Sources

ADELAÏDE-MERLANDE Jacques, *Delgrès ou la Guadeloupe en 1802*, Paris: Karthala, 1986.

BOUREL Guillaume, CHEVALLIER Marielle, JOUBERT Guillaume, GUILLAUSSEAU Axelle, *Bescherelle, Chronologie de l'histoire de France. Le récit illustré des événements fondateurs de notre histoire, des origines à nos jours*, Paris: Hatier, 2013.

Bulletin officiel de la Guadeloupe, civil register documents (death certificates of Honoré Bébian and Joseph Bébian, marriage certificate of Marie-Honorine Bébian) and other legal documents (verification of the affidavit of Joseph Bébian)

BUTON François, *L'administration des faveurs*, Rennes: PUR, 2009.

DUBOIS Benjamin & Estrées E., *Almanach 1900*, Paris: Imprimerie de Sourds-muets, 1900.

LANE Harlan, *When the Mind Hears*, New York: Random House, 1984.

RÉGENT Frédéric, *Esclavage, métissage, liberté*, Paris: Grasset, 2004.

Annex 4
Judgment on the Affidavit of Joseph Bébian – October 6, 1828

Departmental Archives of Guadeloupe

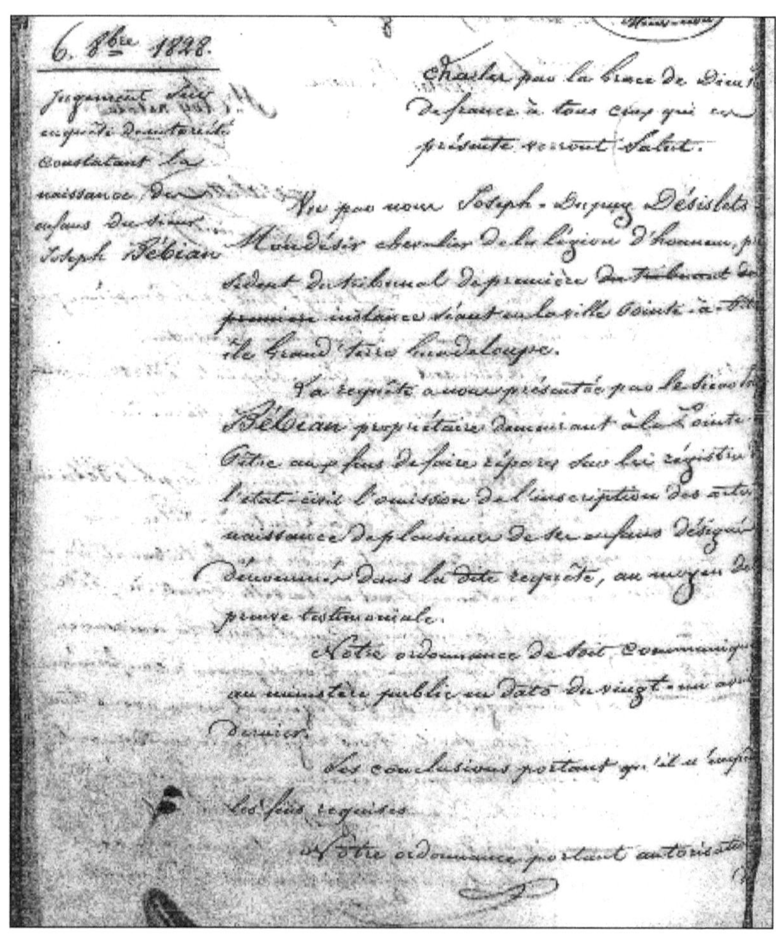

6. 8bre 1828.

Jugement sur enquête d'autorité constatant la naissance des enfans du sieur Joseph Bébian

Charles par la grâce de Dieu [illegible] de France à tous ceux qui ces présentes verront Salut.

Vu par nous Joseph-Dupuy Désislets Mondésir chevalier de la légion d'honneur, président du tribunal de première ~~du tribunal de~~ première instance séant en la ville Pointe-à-Pitre île Grande terre Guadeloupe.

La requête à nous présentée par le sieur [illegible] Bébian propriétaire demeurant à la Pointe-à-Pitre aux fins de faire réparer sur les registres de l'état-civil l'omission de l'inscription des actes de naissance de plusieurs de ses enfans désignés dénommés dans la dite requête, au moyen de preuve testimoniale.

Notre ordonnance de soit communiqué au ministère public en date du vingt-un [illegible] dernier.

Ses conclusions portant qu'il a [illegible] les fins requises.

Notre ordonnance portant autorisation

de faire l'enquête devant Mr Hutter, notaire, que nous avons commis à cet effet.

Le procès-verbal d'enquête à la date du seize juillet dernier.

Notre ordonnance portant qu'il sera communiqué à la suite des conclusions du ministère public tendant à l'homologation

Tout vu et examiné

Attendu que l'enquête est régulière et concluante.

Nous avons homologué et homologuons la dite enquête pour sortir son plein et entier effet, en conséquence reconnaissons pour fait constant et avérés que du premier mariage du sieur Joseph Bélian avec Dame Félicitée Michau sont nés sur l'habitation dite Bergopzoom située en cette colonie, quartier du Morne-à-l'eau, en août mil sept cent quatre vingt neuf Floch-ambroise Auguste Bélian et dans le même mois de mil sept cent quatre vingt onze Demoiselle Marie Honorine Félicité, aujourd'hui épouse du sieur Venda de Bouvail et que de son second mariage avec Dame Sophie Lagrange, est également né sur la même habitation Louis-Marie-Valentin Bélian le douze Pluviose an huit correspondant au premier février mil huit cent ; qu'expédition du présent jugement sera délivrée pour être présentée à de l'officier de l'état-civil du Morne-à-l'eau pour y être transcrit sur les registres courans; qu'à la requête du ministère public mention sera faite du jugement en marge des registres de 1789, 1791, & 18.. qui peuvent se trouver au greffe & dans les archives de l'officier de l'état-civil aux dates correspondantes; que pareille mention sera faite sur les registres des mêmes années déposés aux archives dites de ...

Pointe-à-Pitre ce six octobre mil huit cent vingt-huit.

Mandons & ordonnons à tous huissiers sur ce requis de mettre le présent jugement à exécution, à nos procureurs généraux & aux procureurs près les tribunaux de première instance d'y tenir la main, à tous commandans & officiers de la force publique d'y prêter main forte lorsqu'ils en seront légalement requis.

En foi de quoi la minute a été signée par Monsieur le président. — ainsi signé Desislets Mondésir. /

Collationné

Scellé le d. jour &c. signé Dupont, g.ffier /

signé — Dupont, g.ffier /

Pour copie conforme

... du tribunal de première ... rayés nul

Attes...

officier civil

October 6, 1828

Judgment
on the affidavit
concerning the birth
of the children
of Joseph Bébian esq.

Charles by the Grace of God
King of France; salutations to
all who receive this letter

Seen by myself, Joseph Dupuy Désislets Mondésir, Knight of the Légion d'Honneur, president of the Court of First Instance at Pointe à Pitre , Grande Terre Island, Guadeloupe:

The request submitted to us by Joseph Bébian esq., landowner, domiciled in Pointe-à- Pitre, to remedy the absence on the civil register of the registration of the birth of several of his children as named or designated in said request, by means of affidavit;

Our notification order to the public ministry[1] dated April twenty-first last;

The conclusions to the effect that the latter does not object to the requested purposes;

Our order authorizing the investigation to be carried out by Maître Ruttre, notary, who we commissioned to that effect;

The report of the investigation, dated July sixteenth last;

Our order that it be communicated, followed by the conclusions of the public ministry recommending approval of the request.

Seen and examined

Whereas the investigation is regular and conclusive,

We have authorized, and do authorize, said investigation to take full force and effect. Consequently, we recognize as a constant and proven fact that, from the first marriage of Monsieur Joseph Bébian to Madame Félicitée Michaux were born, on the habitation known as Bergopzom in this colony, in the district of Morne-à-l'Eau, in August seventeen hundred eighty-

1. The *ministère public* was (and indeed still is) a civil and legal authority with many similarities to an Attorney General's office in the USA – transl.

nine, Roch-Ambroise Auguste Bébian and in the same month, in seventeen hundred ninety-one, Miss Marie-Honorine Félicité, today the wife of Vernou de Bonneuil esq., and that from his second marriage, to Madame Sophie Lagrange, was also born, at the same habitation, Louis-Marie-Valentin Bébian on the twelfth day of Pluviose, year eight, corresponding to the first day of February, eighteen hundred; that this judgment shall be delivered for presentation to the civil registrar of Morne-à-l'Eau, there to be transcribed onto the current registers; that at the request of the public ministry the judgment shall be entered in the margin of the registers for 1789, 1791 and 1800 which may be found in the court clerk's office and in the archives of the civil registrar at the corresponding dates; that the same entry be made in the registers of the same year deposited in the archives of Versailles. Pointe à Pitre, this sixth day of October, eighteen hundred twenty-eight.

I order and empower all bailiffs so required to put this judgment into application, our general prosecutors and a Prosecutor of the courts of first instance to uphold it, and all commanders and officers of the forces of law and order to enforce it when legally required.

In witness whereof, this judgment is signed by the Court President, the undersigned Desislets Mondésir

Compared and collated
Sealed on said day and year — Signed – Dupont, Jr.,
Clerk of Court
Certified a true copy
= Salettes, Registrar

Annex 5
Plates from the *Manual for the Practical Instruction of Deaf Mutes* (T. II) *and Education brought within reach of all*

INJS Paris.

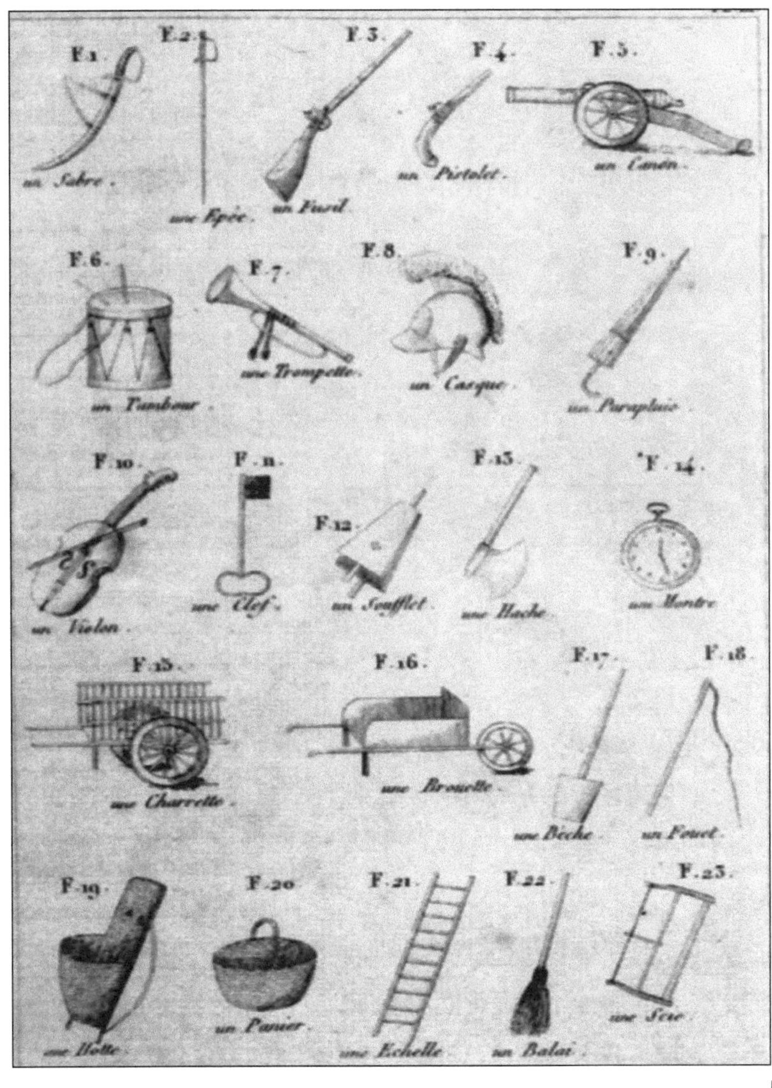

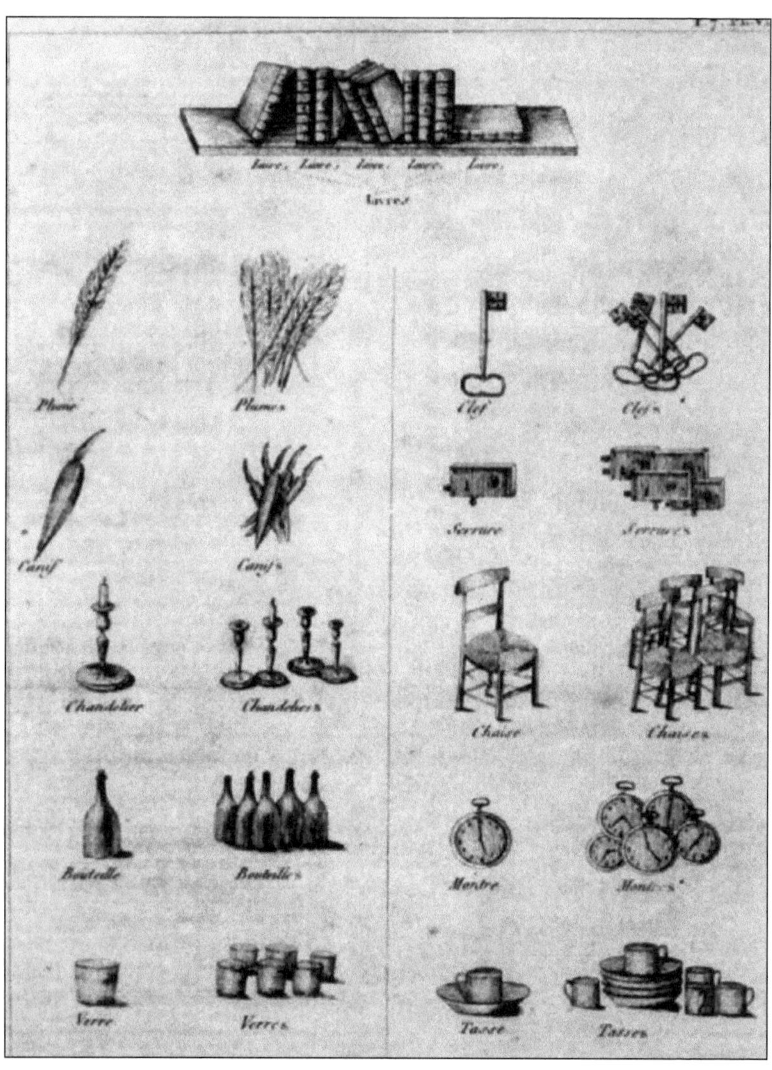
Livres
Plume
Plumes
Clef
Clefs
Canif
Canifs
Serrure
Serrures
Chandelier
Chandeliers
Chaise
Chaises
Bouteille
Bouteilles
Montre
Verre
Verres
Tasse
Tasses

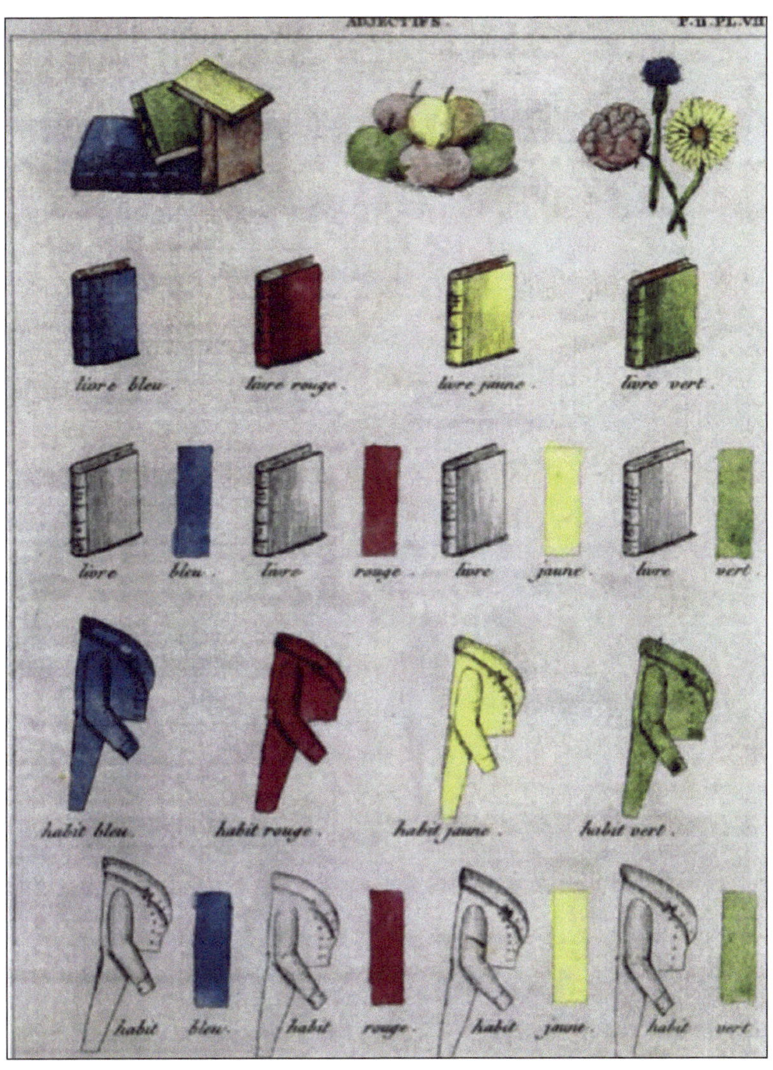
ADJECTIFS.
P. II. PL. VII
livre bleu.
livre rouge.
livre jaune.
livre vert.
livre
bleu.
livre
rouge.
livre
jaune.
livre
vert.
habit bleu.
habit rouge.
habit jaune.
habit vert.
habit
bleu.
habit
rouge.
habit
jaune.
habit
vert.

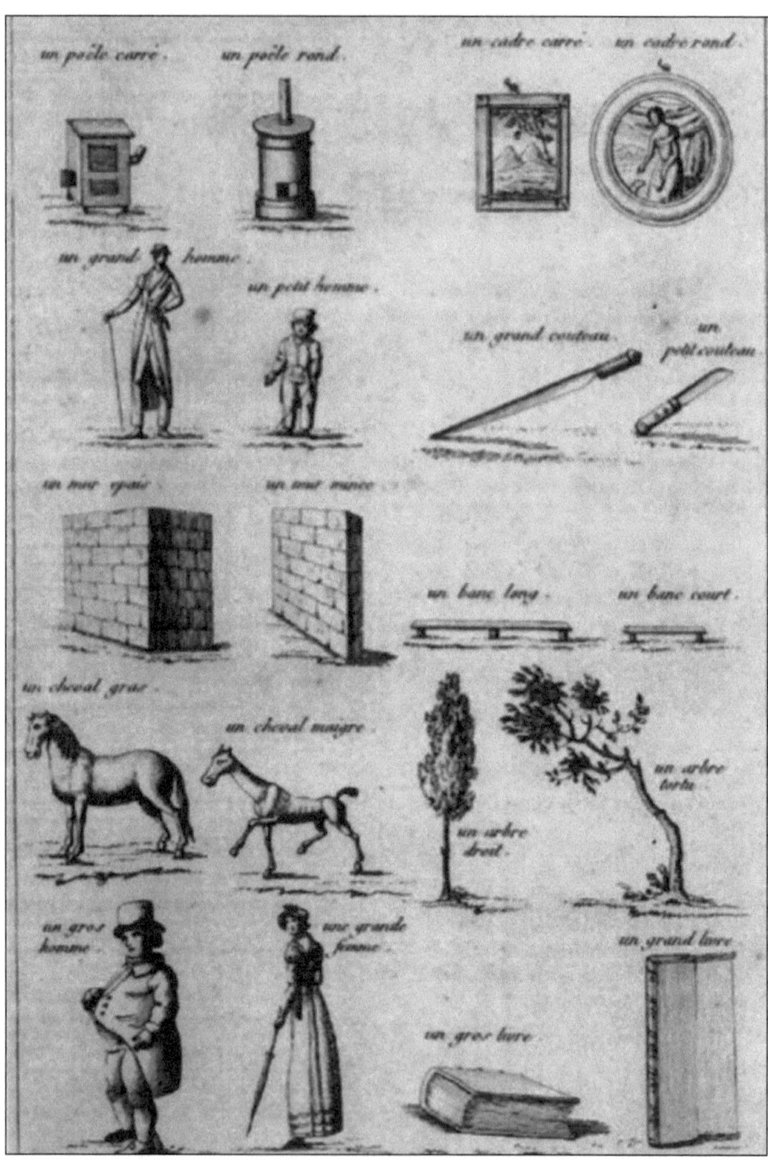
un poêle carré.
un poêle rond.
un cadre carré.
un cadre rond.
un grand homme.
un petit homme.
un grand couteau.
un petit couteau.
un mur épais.
un mur mince.
un banc long.
un banc court.
un cheval gras.
un cheval maigre.
un arbre droit.
un arbre tortu.
un gros homme.
une grande femme.
un gros livre.
un grand livre.

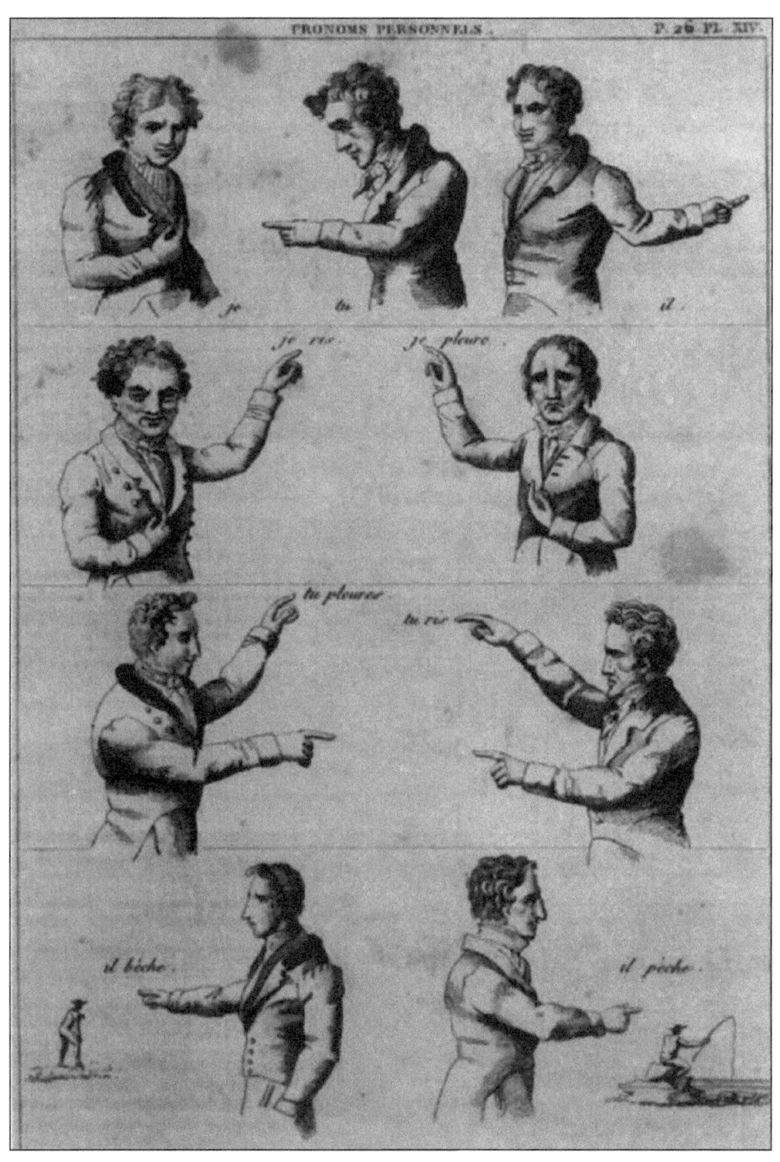
PRONOMS PERSONNELS.
P. 26 PL. XIV.
je
tu
il.
je ris.
je pleure.
tu pleures
tu ris
il bêche.
il pêche.

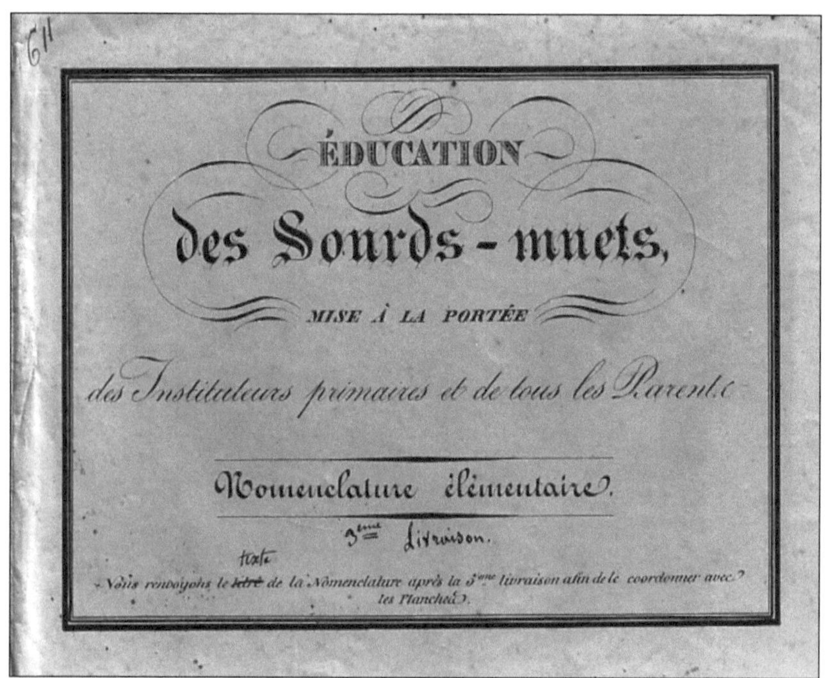

ÉDUCATION

des Sourds-muets,

MISE À LA PORTÉE

des Instituteurs primaires et de tous les Parents

Nomenclature élémentaire.

3ème Livraison.

Nous renvoyons le ~~titre~~ texte de la Nomenclature après la 3ème livraison afin de le coordonner avec les Planches.

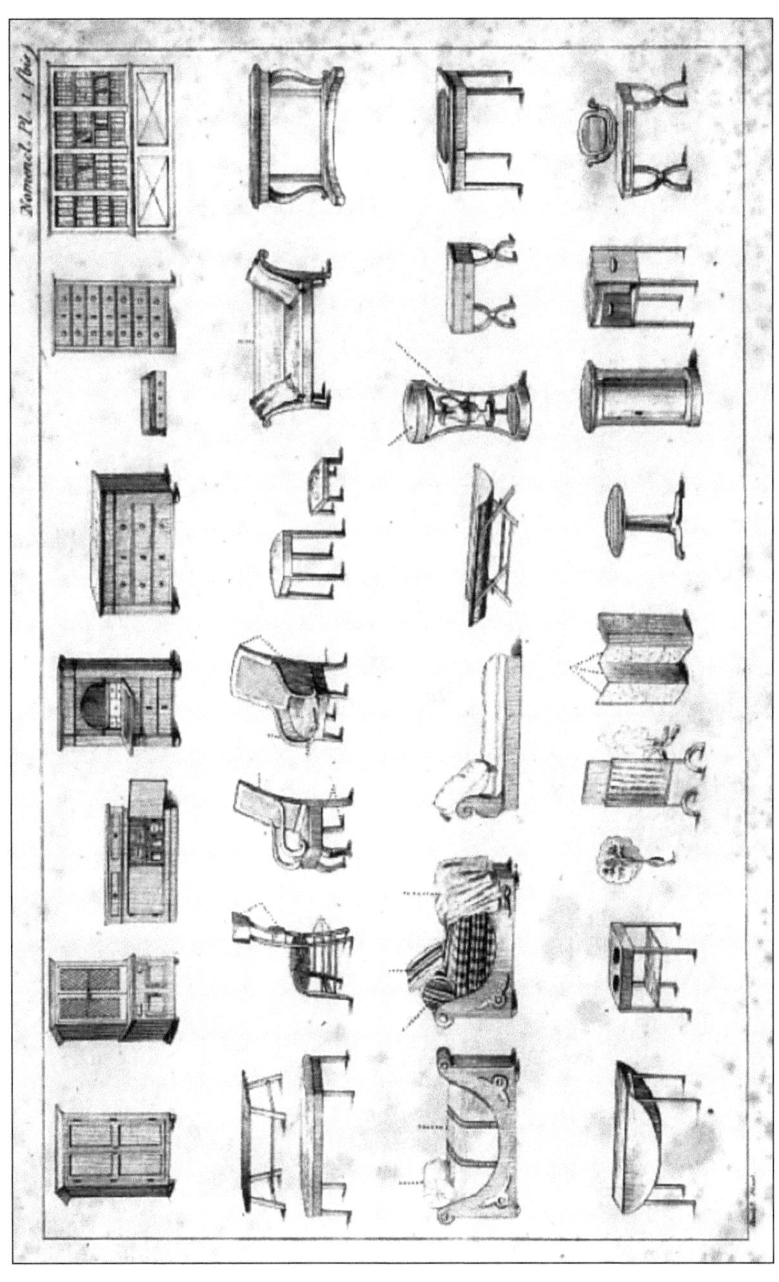
Nomencl. Pl. 1 (bis)

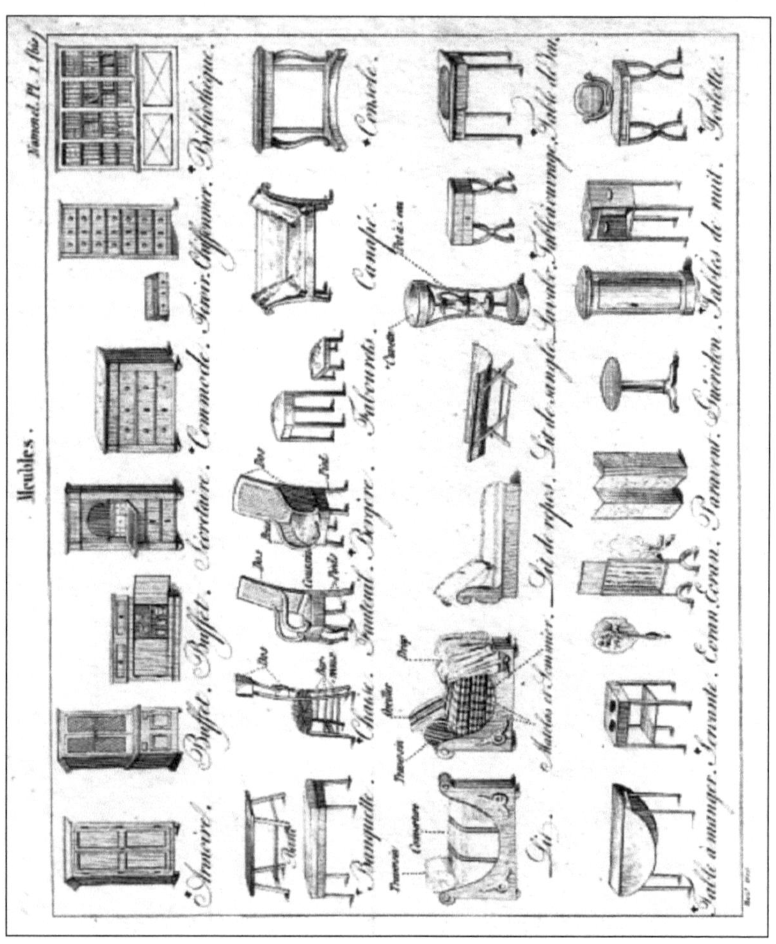
Meubles.
Armoire. Buffet. Buffet. Secrétaire. Commode. Tiroir. Chiffonnier. Bibliothèque.
Banquette. Chaise. Fauteuil. Bergère. Tabourets. Canapé. Console.
Lit. Matelas et Sommier. Lit de repos. Lit de sangle. Lavabo. Table à ouvrage. Table de Jeu.
Table à manger. Servante. Ecran. Ecran. Paravent. Guéridon. Tables de nuit. Toilette.

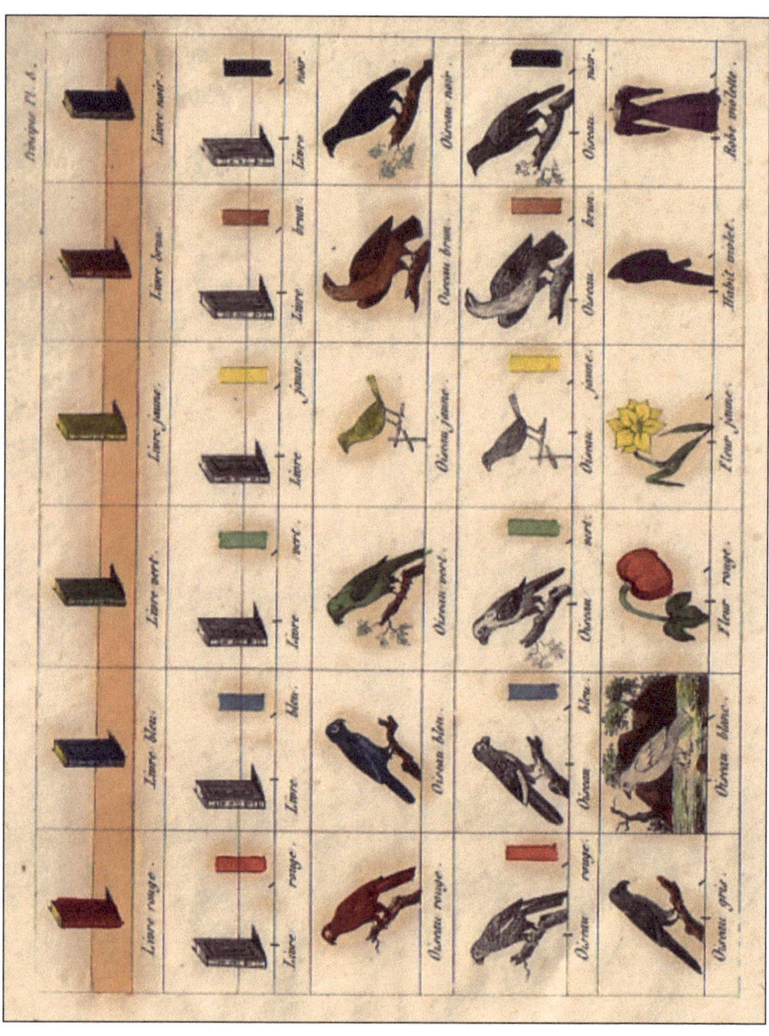
Principes Pl. 8.
Livre rouge.
Livre bleu.
Livre vert.
Livre jaune.
Livre brun.
Livre noir.
Livre rouge.
Livre bleu.
Livre vert.
Livre jaune.
Livre brun.
Livre noir.
Oiseau rouge.
Oiseau bleu.
Oiseau vert.
Oiseau jaune.
Oiseau brun.
Oiseau noir.
Oiseau rouge.
Oiseau bleu.
Oiseau vert.
Oiseau jaune.
Oiseau brun.
Oiseau noir.
Oiseau gris.
Oiseau blanc.
Fleur rouge.
Fleur jaune.
Habit violet.
Robe violette.

Annex 6
Statistics on the silent press in the 19th century

In the last quarter of the 19th century, there was a blossoming of newspapers published by the Deaf in France. The first of the 15 titles of this "silent press" came out in 1870, the second in 1884, and so on as shown below.

	Title	Published	Place of publication	Editor
1	*Le bulletin de la société universelle*	1870- ?	Paris	B. Dubois
2	*La défense des sourds-muets*	1884-1886	Aix-en-Provence	J. Turcan
3	*Le courrier français des sourds-muets*	1887-1888	Aix-en-Provence	J. Turcan
4	*La sincérité*	1887- ?	Paris	L. Rémond
5	*L'abbé de l'Épée*	1888-1889	Bourges	B. Dubois
6	*L'écho de la société d'appui fraternel des sourds-muets de France*	1889-1890	Paris	J. Cochefer
7	*La gazette des sourds-muets*	1890-1895	Nancy	H. Rémy
8	*La France silencieuse*	1894	Paris	R. Desperriers
9	*Le journal des sourds-muets*	1894-1906	Paris	H. Gaillard
10	*L'avenir des sourds-muets*	1894-1895	Paris	P. Villanova
11	*Le sourd-muet illustré*	1897- ?	Paris	J. Berthet
12	*La silencieuse*	1898	Paris	H. Gaillard
13	*La république de demain*	1899-1900	Paris	H. Gaillard
14	*Le pilori silencieux*	?	Paris ?	?
15	*La revue pédagogique de l'enseignement des sourds-muets*	1899-1900	Paris	H. Gaillard

The striking statistic in this table is the short lifespan of these publications (the number of dots in each row corresponds to the number of years in print).

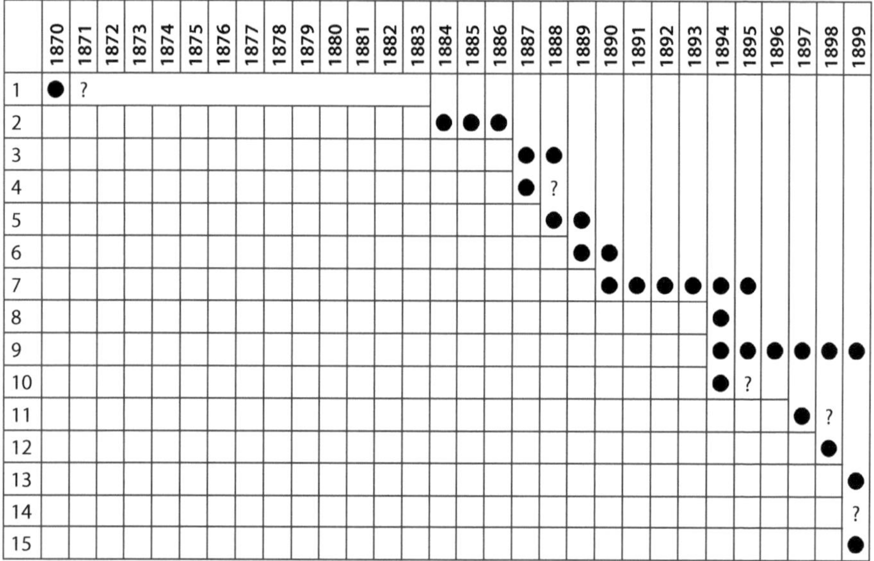

	1870	1871	1872	1873	1874	1875	1876	1877	1878	1879	1880	1881	1882	1883	1884	1885	1886	1887	1888	1889	1890	1891	1892	1893	1894	1895	1896	1897	1898	1899
1	●	?																												
2															●	●	●													
3																		●	●											
4																		●	?											
5																			●	●										
6																				●	●									
7																					●	●	●	●	●	●				
8																									●					
9																									●	●	●	●	●	●
10																									●	?				
11																												●	?	
12																													●	
13																														●
14																														?
15																														●

Source: *Cahiers de l'histoire des sourds*, Orléans, n°3, 1990.

Annex 7
Report by the Board of Governors of the INSMP, dated March 2, 1840

Refutation of the *Notice sur la vie et les ouvrages de Auguste Bébian* [Notice on the Life and Work of Auguste Bébian] published the year before by Ferdinand Berthier. INJS Paris.

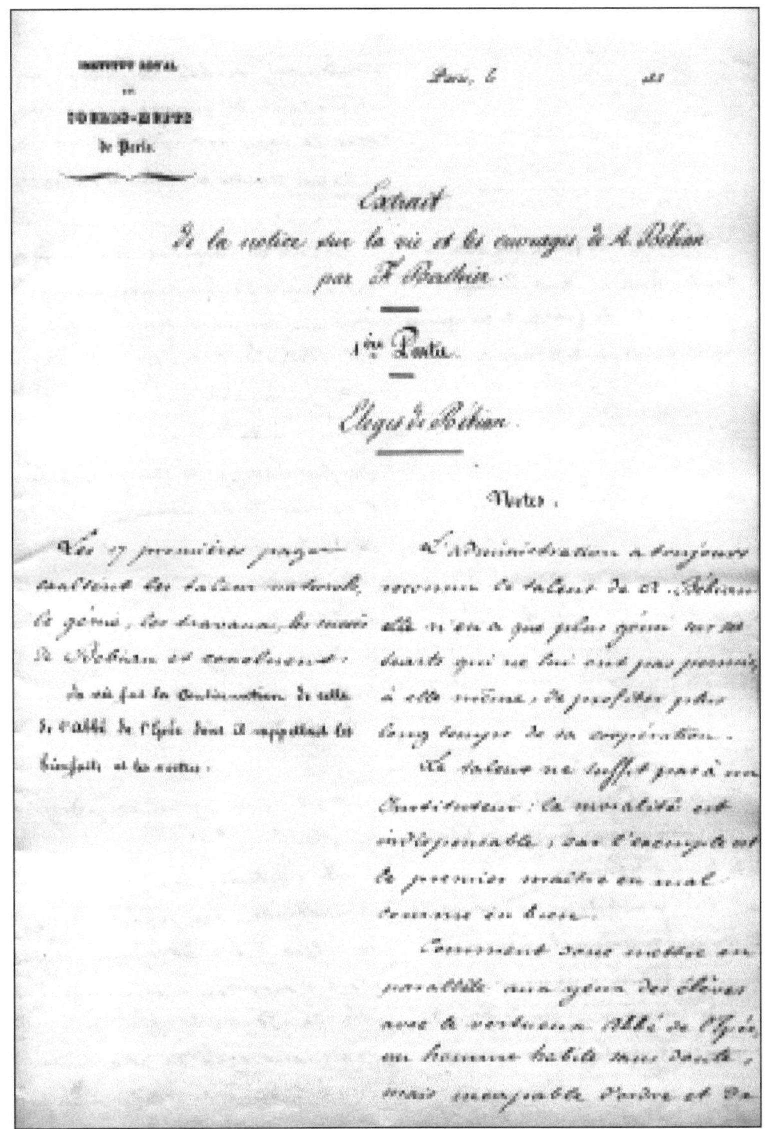

Institut Royal des Sourds-Muets de Paris.

Paris, le 18

Extrait
de la notice sur la vie et les ouvrages de A. Bébian
par F. Berthier.

1re Partie.

Eloge de Bébian.

Notes.

Les 17 premières pages renferment les talens naturels, le génie, les travaux, les succès de Bébian et consolent.

Sa vie fut la continuation de celle de l'Abbé de l'Epée dont il rappelait les bienfaits et les vertus.

L'Administration a toujours reconnu le talent de M. Bébian; elle n'en a que plus gémi sur ses écarts qui ne lui ont pas permis à cette institution de profiter plus long temps de sa coopération.

Le talent ne suffit pas à un instituteur: la moralité est indispensable, car l'exemple est le premier moteur en mal comme en bien.

Comment donc mettre en parallèle aux yeux des élèves avec le vertueux Abbé de l'Epée, un homme habile sans doute, mais incapable d'ordre et de conduite, criblé de dettes, et méritant de graves reproches sous le rapport moral !

On peut consulter les archives de l'Institution.

Page 17. Il fonde une école de Sourds-Muets au Mont-Parnasse.

Page 18. La faiblesse de ses ressources ne lui permet pas de la soutenir.

Ce fut de [illegible] qui [illegible] est vrai ; ce fut l'intrigue de Bébian toujours occupé à débaucher les élèves de l'Institution Royale et les jeunes professeurs qu'il détournait de leurs devoirs. On fut obligé de lui interdire l'entrée de la maison, et de défendre tout rapport avec lui. M. Berthier est cité pour avoir oublié les reproches qu'il a reçus [illegible] à cette occasion.

Voir les délibérations du Conseil.

Page 20 — Discours au Roi

Ses ouvrages servent de guide aux Institutions de France et de l'étranger.

C'est sa méthode qu'on suit partout. Il n'a cessé de [illegible] son zèle et sa [illegible] fortune à cet enseignement.

Ses travaux n'ont jamais obtenu du pouvoir le plus léger encouragement.

C'est ainsi qu'on [illegible] au Roi.

M. Bébian n'a pas fondé de méthode ; on n'a pas suivi ses idées à l'Institution Royale. C'est l'excellent ouvrage de M. de Gérando qui a [illegible] la méthode...

La fortune de Bébian a été

INSTITUT ROYAL
des
SOURDS-MUETS
de Paris.

Paris, le 18

[illegible] et non employé.

N'est-ce donc rien qu'un ouvrage incomplet payé 1500f par le Ministre sur la demande du Conseil ?

Page 36. Le maire de Rouen s'adresse au Ministre qui désigne Bébian, [illegible] empressement répondit à une si honorable proposition.

Toujours des faits altérés.

Voici la vérité :

Le Maire de Rouen avait annoncé l'ouverture d'une école de Sourds-muets. Bébian se proposa pour Chef. Le maire prit des informations auprès du Ministre. Le Ministre en demanda au Conseil qui rendit témoignage au talent et se tut sur la moralité.

Bébian fut admis.

Page 37. Aussi bien servi au 2 jour du temps [illegible] . . . . . . Malheureusement Bébian ne fut pas plus heureux à Rouen qu'à Paris.

L'auteur sait bien qu'à Rouen comme à Paris Bébian, homme d'esprit, mais incapable de conduite, n'avait jamais d'argent, commençant à dissiper les pensions et les abonnements ; il sait bien qu'il fut contraint de faire de

Rouen et ne laissa pas un morceau de pain aux élèves pour la journée.

Le Maire en fournit.

On peut savoir des autorités de Rouen et de M. l'abbé Lefèvre qui y établit une école peu après, la réputation laissée par Bébian et les obstacles qu'elle présenta aux efforts de M. Lefèvre pour son propre établissement.

2ème Partie.

Blâme sur l'Administration.

Page 18. L'Adm. aime mieux juger le travail sur simple lecture que sur une expérience qui eut été décisive.

L'auteur appelle simple lecture un examen fait dans le Cabinet par MM. Cuvier et de Gérando qui en ont fait rapport au Conseil.

Si l'expérience devait être décisive pourquoi M. Bébian ne l'a-t-il pas faite à Rouen où il était chef?

Page 22. Bébian venait sans prévenir et malgré les Membres du

L'auteur veut faire à Bébian un mérite de ce qui était un

INSTITUT ROYAL
DES
SOURDS-MUETS
de Paris.

Paris, le 18

[illegible] grandes places au milieu d'eux et [illegible] à leurs oreilles des [illegible] [illegible] : c'était peu qu'il [illegible] [illegible] [illegible] [illegible] et [illegible] [illegible].

grave inconvenance, on [illegible] blâmer la faiblesse du Conseil qui la souffrirait.

Des deux côtés il a tort, le fait est inventé.

Le Conseil a puni les fautes [illegible] du [illegible] par [illegible] en regrettant l'inutilité d'un [illegible] [illegible] par sa conduite.

Les Directeurs sont obligés de prier l'agent de présenter leurs propositions et d'adresser une demande d'audience qui leur est souvent refusée.

Ceci est absolument faux ; les Directeurs ont toujours été admis et même appelés au Conseil pour y présenter leurs réflexions et leurs propositions.

Jamais aucun fonctionnaire n'a demandé à y être reçu sans l'être de suite.

Pages 12 et 13. Une visite [illegible] [illegible], mais [illegible] [illegible] [illegible] [illegible] [illegible] [illegible] [illegible] [illegible] [illegible] [illegible] [illegible]. Un jour il [illegible] un employé [illegible] La Duchesse de Berry était venue visiter [illegible] [illegible] en 1820 [illegible]

Voici la vérité :

Mme la Duchesse de Berry était venue à l'Institution le 17 Décembre 1820. Elle avait vu les élèves à l'examen fait à son occasion.

Le propos tenu par [illegible]

qu'on avait éloigné à dessein arrivent tout à coup . . . Madame demande à voir ses élèves... impossible! répond l'honorable Censeur, ils sont nus et même dans l'impossibilité depuis quatre mois d'aller à la promenade faute de vêtement.

Deux jours après on lui suscita une vive explication à la suite de laquelle il se vit obligé de quitter.

Qu'on se figure le désespoir des élèves, [illegible]

Ainsi parle l'auteur.

est dans une circonstance. Mais on voulait donner le change sur la cause de son expulsion. Voici le fait.

Le 3 janvier 1821 M. Paulmier Doyen des professeurs était chez M. Sicard au moment du déjeuner. Ils parlaient de la séparation des élèves. Bébian survint et dit au [illegible] avoir envoyé [illegible] M. Paulmier. Celui-ci lui dit qu'il ne les avait pas [illegible] était un mensonge.

Sur cette réponse Bébian s'élance sur Paulmier, renverse la table, saisit Paulmier à la gorge et le frappe à la tête de trois coups d'une clef forée qui fait jaillir le sang. Le Directeur se trouve mal, et Bébian est mis à la porte par la servante.

Procès-verbal est dressé, plainte au Conseil, et Bébian est renvoyé le 5 janvier.

(voir la lettre de Paulmier, les lettres de l'abbé Sicard.)

Cette scène avait bien ...

INSTITUT ROYAL
DES
SOURDS-MUETS
de Paris.

Paris, le 18

avait agréé que Bébian, qui voulait avancer à tout prix, avait contraint l'abbé Sicard à demander pour lui la place d'Instituteur adjoint. (Voir la lettre de M. Sicard à M. de Gérando dans laquelle il explique une première lettre et demande qu'on n'ait aucun égard à cette lettre dictée par un jeune ambitieux et [illegible] pour le [illegible] la [illegible].

Voilà l'homme que notre M. Berthier faisant revivre les bienfaits et les vertus de l'abbé de l'Epée !

Page 83. Le Conseil de perfectionnement qui ne s'entendait pas mieux que le Conseil d'administration à la méthode et insistant sur la nécessité de s'adjoindre comme auxiliaire... M.

Dans une réunion des deux Conseils il fut décidé à l'unanimité que Bébian serait proposé au Ministre.

Il attendit en vain ; une force occulte a écarté dans l'ombre tout ce qui pouvait le [illegible] etc...

Nous relevons pour le [illegible] de ce passage, beaucoup [illegible] à démontrer le faux.

Et le nom de Bébian a été prononcé dans cette réunion [illegible] a été pour être de toute éternité malgré le talent et l'esprit, à cause de sa [illegible].

C'est là la véritable force occulte qui repoussait toujours Bébian.

Ma

Page 46. Se présenter à l'Institution, l'intrigue [illegible] et [illegible] les chemins à l'homme d'honneur et de talent.

Un professeur qui fait payer son ouvrage à ses élèves appelle intrigue la juste sévérité du Conseil.

Il en appelle l'homme d'honneur celui dont l'exemple est dangereux, dont le désordre est à son comble, et qui fugitif [illegible] d'un établissement confié à ses soins, est réduit à s'expatrier après être sorti de prison grâce à quelques personnes généreuses qui ont satisfait pour lui.

Page 46. Dans une lutte engagée en 1832 entre les professeurs sourds-muets et le Comité d'après Bébian touchant constamment le courage de ces jeunes professeurs, [illegible] leur protection.

Il s'agissait de la [illegible] de la rotation, système [illegible], condamné par toutes les [illegible] du monde.....

Changement absurde ......

Le but caché d'une si étrange innovation paraissait être de laisser

On conserve l'opposition de M. Berthier pour la rotation quand on saura que les élèves dont on avait confié l'instruction ont été chaque année trouvés fort inférieurs à ceux des professeurs parlants.

Rien ne s'est été de ceux de M. Lenoir (voir les procès verbaux)

C'est bien ce qu'on [illegible]

INSTITUT ROYAL
des
SOURDS-MUETS
de Paris.

Paris, le 18

prévu et ce qui justifie les craintes de quelques membres du Conseil et des dispositions arrêtées par le Ministre pour y pourvoir.

les professeurs sourds-muets et de faciliter ainsi les voies au parvenu d'un professeur administrateur &c...

C'est un malheur, jamais il paraît tenir à l'état même des professeurs sourds-muets. M. Berthier voudrait-il qu'on sacrifiât les élèves aux professeurs? (voir à la page 21 de l'écrit).

Page 43. Les destinées d'une si belle institution se trouvent compromises par l'ignorance d'hommes haut placés, &c...

M. Berthier oublie que c'est de cette ignorance qu'est sorti l'ouvrage de M. De Gérando, le plus estimé, le plus répandu sur l'instruction des sourds-muets, un ouvrage que les étrangers ont adopté comme classique et qui fait aujourd'hui la gloire de l'Institution et lui donne l'avantage de former des chefs pour les autres écoles.

... l'injuste oubli dans lequel

L'auteur veut rejeter sur

Annex 8

Petition of 1830, signed by the student Charles Ryan

Student awarded a "3rd-class commendation" on August 11, 1826 (class of Mr. Rivière) ("Distribution of awards by the Royal Institution in Paris, 11 August, 1826", Auguste Bébian, *Journal de l'instruction des sourds-muets et des aveugles*, 1826, t. 1, p. 50). INJS Paris.

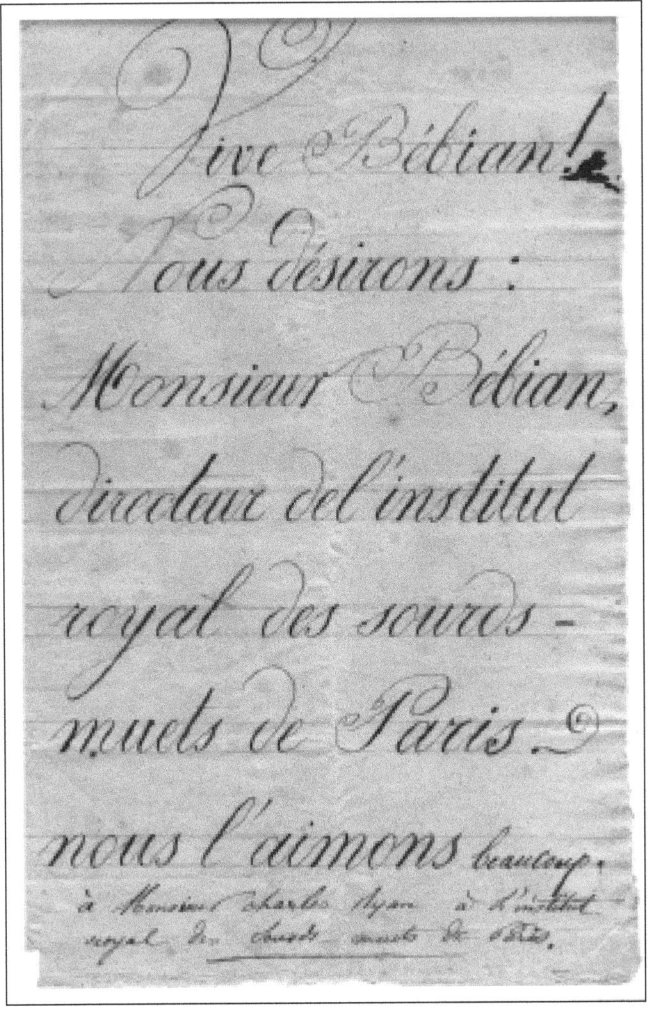

Vive Bébian!

Nous désirons :

Monsieur Bébian,
directeur de l'institut
royal des sourds-
muets de Paris.

nous l'aimons beaucoup.

à Monsieur Charles Ryan à l'institut

Annex 9

Journal de l'instruction des sourds-muets et des aveugles

Prospectus, and contents of the eight issues

INJS Paris.

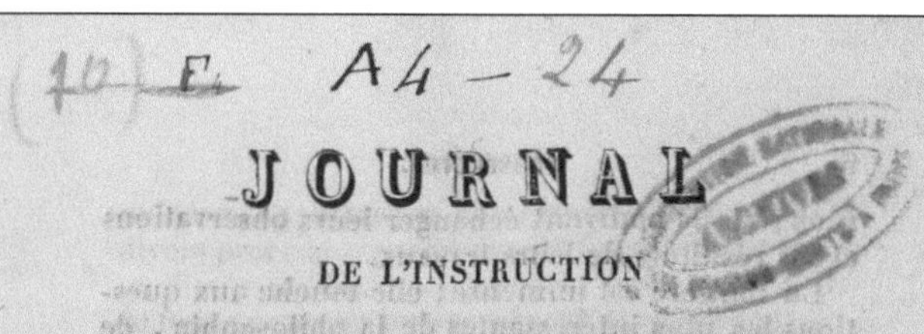

JOURNAL

DE L'INSTRUCTION

DES SOURDS-MUETS

Et des Aveugles,

Rédigé par M. BÉBIAN, *ancien Censeur des études de l'Institut royal des Sourds-Muets, Directeur de l'Institution spéciale des Sourds-Muets.*

PROSPECTUS.

Depuis que l'exemple et les succès de l'abbé de l'Épée ont éveillé l'intérêt public en faveur des Sourds-Muets, un grand nombre d'établissemens se sont élevés sur le modèle de l'institution dont il fut le fondateur. Mais l'art créé par son génie est loin d'avoir reçu les perfectionnemens que l'on était en droit d'attendre des efforts de tant d'habiles instituteurs. On n'est pas même encore aujourd'hui d'accord sur les vrais principes de cet enseignement. Chaque école a sa méthode, et souvent, dans la même école, chaque professeur adopte et suit un système différent.

Il manquait un foyer commun où vinssent se concentrer tous les rayons épars de la doctrine, pour réfléchir une lumière plus vive sur chaque branche de l'enseignement.

Le *Journal de l'instruction des Sourds-Muets* est destiné à offrir aux instituteurs ce point de réunion, où ils pourront échanger leurs observations et les résultats de leurs travaux.

La matière est immense; elle touche aux questions les plus intéressantes de la philosophie, de la morale, et même de la législation (1). Le rédacteur aurait craint de se charger d'une tâche si difficile, s'il n'avait l'assurance d'être secondé, dans cette entreprise, par plusieurs instituteurs français ou étrangers, avec qui ses travaux l'ont mis en relation depuis long-temps.

Ce Journal, dont il paraîtra tous les mois un cahier de 60 à 70 pages, renfermera :

1°. Les observations que nous avons recueillies dans une longue pratique, ou qui nous seront communiquées par les parens ou les instituteurs, sur l'état moral et intellectuel des Sourds-Muets avant leur instruction, sur le développement de leurs facultés, sur leurs idées et sur leur langage;

2°. Un examen comparatif des diverses méthodes employées jusqu'à ce jour pour l'instruction des Sourds-Muets, et l'analyse des ouvrages français et étrangers qui traitent de cette matière;

3°. Une notice historique sur toutes les écoles de Sourds-Muets que nous connaissons, et sur les instituteurs les plus célèbres.

Nous accueillerons toutes les questions qui nous seront adressées sur ce sujet. Les plus intéressantes seront proposées aux instituteurs, et nous leur soumettrons ensuite la solution qui en aura été donnée. Nous exposerons avec impartialité les

(1) Il y a dans notre seule Europe plus de 80,000 sourds-muets La plupart, privés de toute instruction, ignorant leurs droits et leurs devoirs, sont chaque jour exposés à enfreindre les lois, qu'ils ne connaissent pas; et le magistrat balance entre une dangereuse impunité ou un injuste châtiment.

opinions opposées ; et une libre discussion sur les divers procédés, permettra de fixer le choix sur la meilleure méthode, qui pourra encore s'enrichir de tout ce que les autres offrent d'avantageux.

Nous rendrons compte des tentatives de la médecine pour rendre l'ouïe aux Sourds-Muets. Nous parlerons particulièrement des travaux de M. *Itard*, médecin de l'institution royale des Sourds-Muets, et de ceux de M. *Deleau*, médecin attaché à l'hospice des Orphelins, dont les heureux essais ont mérité de partager le grand prix fondé par M. de Montyon.

Il a été souvent question, en Allemagne, de réunir dans une même institution les Sourds-Muets et les Aveugles, et cette réunion a même été opérée à Paris pendant un certain temps. L'idée en a été inspirée sans doute par une prévoyance charitable, qui voulait préparer, d'avance, une consolation et des moyens de communication aux Sourds-Muets, qui viendraient à perdre la vue ; malheur affreux dont nous avons plusieurs exemples. L'on ne sera donc pas étonné de trouver dans notre Journal des articles sur l'instruction des aveugles et sur les principaux établissemens consacrés à ces infortunés. C'est M. *Dufau*, *instituteur des jeunes aveugles*, qui veut bien se charger de cette partie de notre travail. De ce rapprochement de deux genres d'enseignement, destinés à soulager de si cruelles infirmités, il sortira, peut-être, quelques heureuses indications pour le perfectionnement de l'un ou de l'autre.

Enfin, grâce aux concours des hommes éclairés qui veulent bien nous aider dans notre entreprise, nous espérons que ce Journal fera disparaître les obstacles qui ont trop long-temps entravé les progrès de l'enseignement des Sourd-Muets ; et qu'il contribuera à perfectionner et à propager la pratique d'un art qui doit rendre tant de milliers d'infortunés à la vie sociale et aux consolations religieuses.

Peut-être serons-nous assez heureux pour avancer l'époque où, par des procédés plus simples et plus rapides, tous les Sourds-Muets pourront être admis au bienfait de l'instruction.

Le premier numéro paraîtra dans le mois d'août.

PRIX { De chaque numéro. . . . . . . 2 fr. 50 c.
Abonnement pour six mois (*Paris*). 12 »
Idem, pour les Départemens. . 15 »

AU BUREAU DU JOURNAL, à l'institution spéciale des Sourds-Muets, boulevart Mont-Parnasse, n. 24 *bis*.

CHEZ { MÉQUIGNON aîné, Libraire-Editeur du Cours d'enseignement pratique des Sourds-Muets, rue de l'Ecole de Médecine, n°. 9.
COLAS, Libraire, rue Dauphine, n°. 34.
TREUTTEL et WURTZ, rue Bourbon, n°. 17.
BOSSANGE, rue de Richelieu.
GALIGNANI, rue Vivienne, n°. 18.
Les Marchands de Nouveautés.

IMPRIMERIE DE SÉTIER,
Cour des Fontaines, n° 7, à Paris.

Contents of Tome I

Volume 1 (August 1826, pp. 5 to 60)

Volume 2 (September 1826, pp. 61 to 120)

Royal Institution for Blind Children in Paris

- Award ceremony of August 31, 1826 (118)

Volume 3 (October 1826, pp. 121 to 180)

Examination of the divers methods in use for the instruction of deaf-mutes

- P. de Ponce = instruction by articulation (98)
- J. Wallis = articulation, mimic signs (100)
- Conrad Amman (101)
- Teaching by dactylology (109)
- Syllabic dactylology (111)

Announcements

- Manual of Practical Education p. 162
- Extract from a report by the administrators of the Royal Institution of Deaf-Mutes in Paris, dated June 21, 1823, to His Excellency the Minister of the Interior, on the Manual for the Practical Instruction of Deaf Mutes by Mr. Bébian

Auricular medicine

- Report on a paper by Mr. Deleau when younger (131)

Volume 4 (October 1826, pp. 181 to 240)

Examination of the divers methods in use for the instruction of deaf-mutes

- Methodical signs, school of Abbé de l'Épée
- Methodical signs institutions (188)
- Erroneous principles of methodical signs (190)
- Two classes of methodical sign (196)
- Nomenclature signs
  Grammatical methodical signs (201)

Various

- Letters to the editor of the Globe on Deaf-Mutes who hear and speak (156)
- First letter (signed by Itard) – Second (ditto)
- Letter from Dr. Deleau to the editor of the *Journal des Sourds-Muets* (164)
- On the education of those who are born deaf-mute, by Baron de Gérando (170)

Volume 5 (December 1826, pp. 241 to 304)

Contents of Tome II

Volume 6 (March 1827, pp. 305 to 370)

- The Danville Institution, Kentucky (263)
- The Virginia Institution (263)

Documents on the divers institutions of deaf-mutes, gathered by the administration of the Royal Institute of Deaf-Mutes in Paris

- Nomenclature
- Practical teaching of deaf-mutes

Volume 7 (September 1827, pp.1 to 56)

The trial concerning the deaf-mute-blind woman

- Court of 1st Instance, August 8
- Victorine Morisseau (story in issues 1 and 2) (1)

Successors to Abbé de l'Épée

Royal Institute of Deaf-Mutes in Paris

- Award ceremony of August 14, 1827 (3)

Examination of the divers methods in use for the instruction of deaf-mutes (ctd.)

- Work of Abbé Sicard
- From the numerous excerpts from the course of instruction that we compared in our previous article, it was noticeable that the author had not formed a correct or indeed accurate opinion on faculties of deaf-mutes. His procedures must have suffered from the vagueness of his ideas […] (40)

Sicard's course of instruction, second article

- Critical discussion of Sicard's writings

Affair of the deaf-mute Filleron

- Court of Assizes of the Seine, August 1827

Volume 8 (October 1827, pp. 57 to 107)

Affair of the deaf-mute Filleron, ctd.

- Affair of the deaf-mute Sauron

Remark on the natural and conventional language of deaf-mutes

- Nomenclature of perceptible objects
- On grammatical gender

Practical teaching

Royal School of Fine Arts – medal-winners

- A prize for Peyson (107)

Various

Annex 10
Bibliography of Auguste Bébian

Works by Auguste Bébian

Essai sur les sourds-muets et sur le langage naturel ou introduction à une classification naturelle des idées avec leurs signes propres. [Essay on the Deaf and Natural Language, or Introduction to a natural classification of ideas with their proper signs]. Paris: J.-G. Dentu, 1817, XVI + 150 pages.

Éloge de l'abbé de l'Épée, ou essai sur les avantages du système des signes. Discours qui a obtenu le prix proposé par la Société royale académique des sciences. [Eulogy for Abbé de l'Épée, or Essay on the advantages of the system of signs. Speech obtaining the prize awarded by the Royal Academic Society of the Sciences]. Paris: J.-G. Dentu, 1819, 56 pages.

L'art d'enseigner à parler aux sourds-muets de naissance, par M. l'abbé de L'Épée, augmenté de notes explicatives et d'un avant-propos, par M. l'abbé Sicard,... précédé de l'éloge historique de M. l'abbé de L'Épée, par M. Bébian. [On the art of speaking to the Deaf-Mute from birth, by Abbé de l'Épée, with additional annotations and a foreword by Abbé Sicard... preceded by the historical eulogy for Abbé de l'Épée by Mr. Bébian]. De l'Épée (Abbé), Sicard (R.-A.), Bébian (A.). Paris, J.-G. Dentu, 1820, XII + 115 pages.

Mimographie ou Essai d'écriture mimique, propre à régulariser le langage des sourds-muets. [Mimography: An essay on the writing of sign in order to standardize the language of the Deaf]. Paris: Louis Colas, 1825, 42 pages. [Reprinted in full in: Marc Renard, *Écrire les signes*, Les-Essarts-le-Roi: Éditions du Fox, 2004, 2014].

Journal de l'instruction des sourds-muets et des aveugles, rédigé par M. Bébian. [Journal for the instruction of the Deaf-Mute and the Blind]. 1826 (180 pages) - 1827 (374 pages).

Manuel d'enseignement pratique des sourds-muets. [Manual for the practical instruction of Deaf-Mutes]. Vol. I: *Modèles d'exercices* (204 pages); Vol. II: *Explications* (371 pages). Paris: Méquignon l'Aîné, 1827.

Lecture instantanée. Nouvelle méthode pour apprendre à lire sans épeler. [Instant reading: A new method for learning to read without spelling]. Paris: Crapelet, 1828, XX + 28 pages.

Éducation mise à the portée de tous. [Education brought within the reach of all]. Unpublished. An advertising prospectus for this work (8 pages) can be viewed online at *www.bmlisieux.com*

Examen critique de la nouvelle organisation de l'enseignement dans l'Institution royale des sourds-muets de Paris. [Critical appraisal of the new organization of teaching at the Royal Institution for Deaf-Mutes]. Paris: Treuttel & Wurtz, 1834, IV + 67 pages.

Articles by Auguste Bébian

Journal *Le Constitutionnel*, December 7, 1828, July 16, 1833 (n° 197) and August 24, 1833 (n° 238).

Journal de l'instruction publique, "De l'enseignement des sourds-muets" [On the teaching of Deaf-Mutes], 1828, pp. 70-79 and "Opérations intellectuelles du sourd-muet", [Intellectual operations of the Deaf-Mute]. 1828, pp. 242-253.

Index of Names

A

B

F

G

H

I

J

K

L

M

N

O

W

Y

Auguste Bébian: Paving the Way for Deaf Emancipation

A partial version, in French Sign Language (LSF), and Internationals Signs (IS) of this book will soon be available on the Eyes éditions application.

Eyes éditions

Download the Eyes éditions application (free) to view future videos associated with this book and use this flashcode: